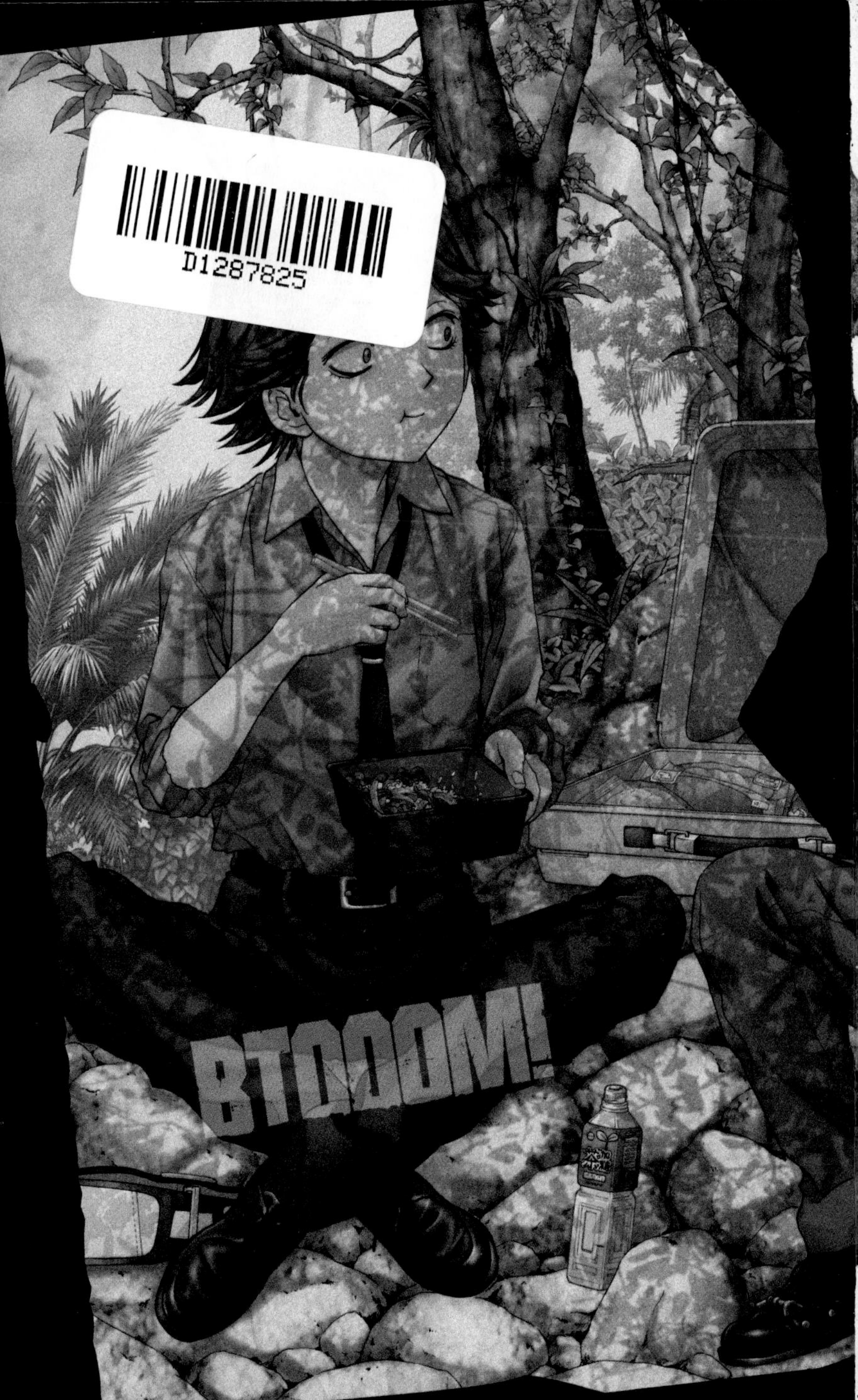
BTOOOM!

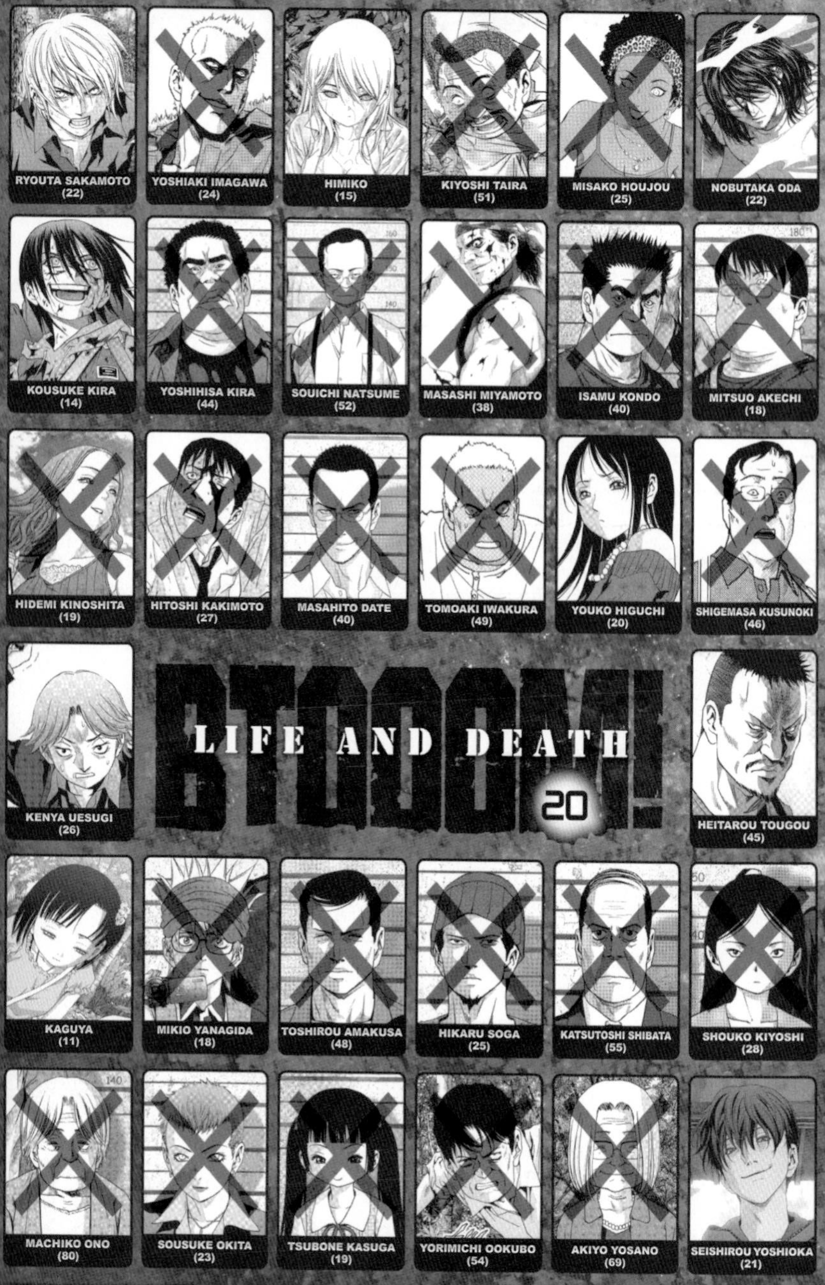
RYOUTA SAKAMOTO (22)
YOSHIAKI IMAGAWA (24)
HIMIKO (15)
KIYOSHI TAIRA (51)
MISAKO HOUJOU (25)
NOBUTAKA ODA (22)
KOUSUKE KIRA (14)
YOSHIHISA KIRA (44)
SOUICHI NATSUME (52)
MASASHI MIYAMOTO (38)
ISAMU KONDO (40)
MITSUO AKECHI (18)
HIDEMI KINOSHITA (19)
HITOSHI KAKIMOTO (27)
MASAHITO DATE (40)
TOMOAKI IWAKURA (49)
YOUKO HIGUCHI (20)
SHIGEMASA KUSUNOKI (46)
KENYA UESUGI (26)
BTOOOM!
LIFE AND DEATH
20
HEITAROU TOUGOU (45)
KAGUYA (11)
MIKIO YANAGIDA (18)
TOSHIROU AMAKUSA (48)
HIKARU SOGA (25)
KATSUTOSHI SHIBATA (55)
SHOUKO KIYOSHI (28)
MACHIKO ONO (80)
SOUSUKE OKITA (23)
TSUBONE KASUGA (19)
YORIMICHI OOKUBO (54)
AKIYO YOSANO (69)
SEISHIROU YOSHIOKA (21)

BTOOOM!

JUNYA INOUE

CHARACTER & DIGEST

YOUKO HIGUCHI

GENDER: Female
AGE: 20
BLOOD TYPE: A
JOB: Actress
HOME: Kanagawa

Before she was taken to the island, she was active as a popular porn star who went by the name of "Ichiyo." She has the uncanny ability to tell when someone's lying. She's a member of Tougou's team and likes strong men. When she made advances toward Tougou, he turned her down due to his impotence.

KOUSUKE KIRA

GENDER: Male
AGE: 14
BLOOD TYPE: AB
JOB: Junior high student
HOME: Tokyo

This junior high student harbors a sinister past of brutal murder. On the island, he blew up his own father and genuinely is enjoying this murderous game of "BTOOOM!" He's always been a big fan of the online version of the game, and his dream is to defeat the top world ranker, Sakamoto. However, he keeps failing at it. He joins Tougou's team and has matured as a result.

RYOUTA SAKAMOTO

GENDER: Male
AGE: 22
BLOOD TYPE: B
JOB: Unemployed
HOME: Tokyo

After spending every day cooped up in his home gaming online, he suddenly finds himself forced to participate in "BTOOOM! GAMERS," a killing game taking place on a mysterious uninhabited island. As a world ranker in the online third-person shooter "BTOOOM!", he uses his experience and natural instincts to survive and concoct a plan to get off the island along with his comrades, only for it to end in failure. While wallowing in despair, he arrives at the Sanctuary alone, where he teams up with Kaguya and Soga to beat Torio.

KENYA UESUGI

GENDER: Male
AGE: 26
BLOOD TYPE: AB
JOB: Office worker
HOME: Tokyo

A cowardly and easily flattered young man who used to dream of becoming an actor. He was almost killed by Kira, but thanks to Higuchi's ability to tell when someone's lying, he got away. He's currently accompanying Sakamoto.

HEITAROU TOUGOU

GENDER: Male
AGE: 45
BLOOD TYPE: A
JOB: Unemployed
HOME: Kagoshima

A former police officer, his superior leadership skills and knack for assessing a situation helped him form a team consisting of Uesugi, Higuchi, and later, Kira, with whom he plans to escape the island. However, the change in the rules shattered the team's cohesiveness. With his plentiful real-life experience and tolerance, he treats Kira like a son.

HIMIKO

GENDER: Female
AGE: 15
BLOOD TYPE: B
JOB: High school student
HOME: Tokyo

A foreign high school girl who has teamed up with Sakamoto. She harbors a deep resentment against men after a sordid experience in her past, but after surviving some battles thanks to Sakamoto, she begins to trust him. Her character in the online version of "BTOOOM!" is actually married to Sakamoto's character, and she has fallen in love with the real Sakamoto too.

BTOOOM! 20

TAKANOHASHI

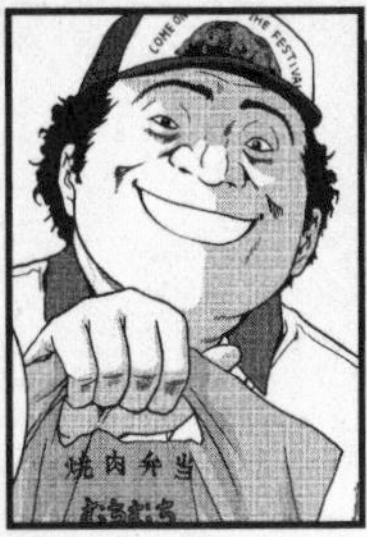

GENDER: Male
AGE: 45
BLOOD TYPE: AB
JOB: Game planner
HOME: Hokkaido

An executive staff member at Tyrannos Japan, he is the leader behind all the development of the online and real-life version of "BTOOOM! GAMERS." He considers Sakamoto a valuable player and debugger. As a result of Sakamoto's plan to hijack the helicopter, Takanohashi's precious game was almost forced to come to a premature end.

KAGUYA

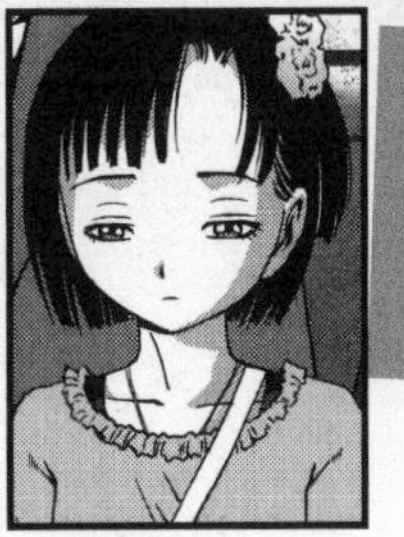

GENDER: Female
AGE: 11
BLOOD TYPE: AB
JOB: Elementary school student
HOME: Tokyo

A mysterious little girl who came across Sakamoto when he was washed ashore. She doesn't speak and uses a tablet to communicate. She's the figurehead of a cult called the Order of Moonlight. She can see dead people. In the Sanctuary, she worked with Sakamoto and Soga to defeat the real villain behind the tragedies, Torio.

SEISHIROU YOSHIOKA

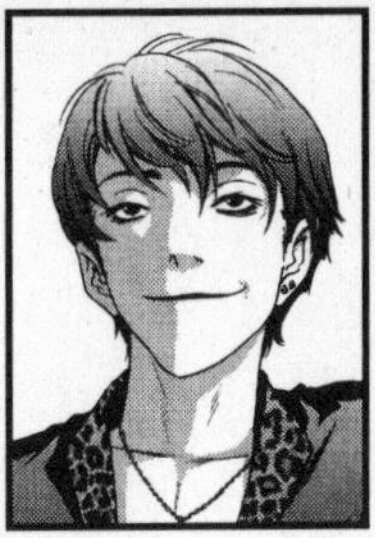

GENDER: Male
AGE: 21
BLOOD TYPE: B
JOB: Musician
HOME: Tokyo

Himiko's childhood friend and the lead vocalist of a popular band. He lured his band's fans—Himiko's classmates—into his room, where he raped them. He was arrested later on and is the reason why Himiko doesn't trust men and was sent to the island.

IN THE LAST VOLUME:

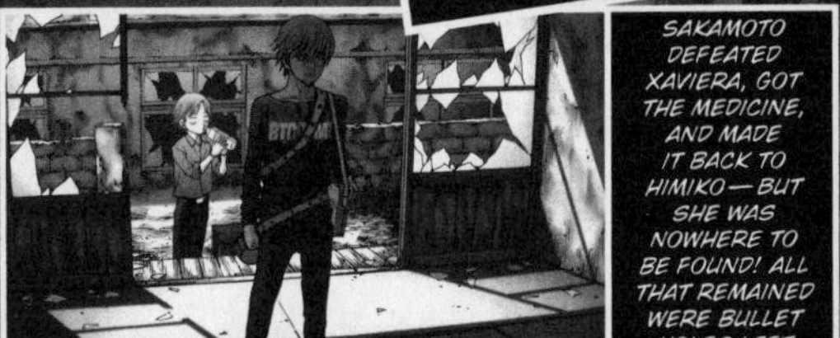
SAKAMOTO DEFEATED XAVIERA, GOT THE MEDICINE, AND MADE IT BACK TO HIMIKO—BUT SHE WAS NOWHERE TO BE FOUND! ALL THAT REMAINED WERE BULLET HOLES LEFT BY A SPRAY OF GUNFIRE...

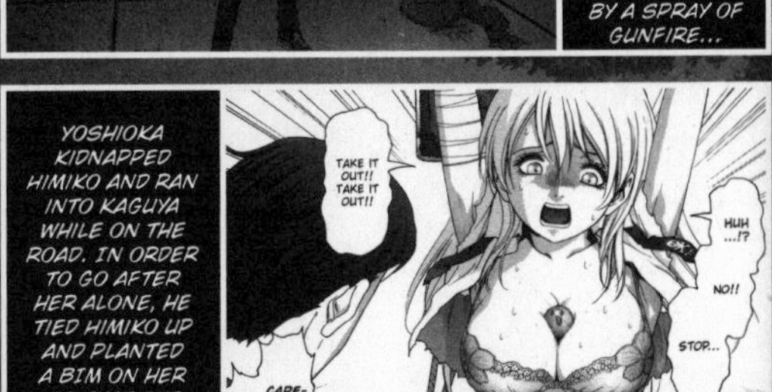
YOSHIOKA KIDNAPPED HIMIKO AND RAN INTO KAGUYA WHILE ON THE ROAD. IN ORDER TO GO AFTER HER ALONE, HE TIED HIMIKO UP AND PLANTED A BIM ON HER SO THAT SHE CAN'T MOVE FROM THAT SPOT.
HUH ...!?
NO!!
STOP...
TAKE IT OUT!! TAKE IT OUT!!
CAREFUL! YOU'LL MAKE IT GO OFF!!

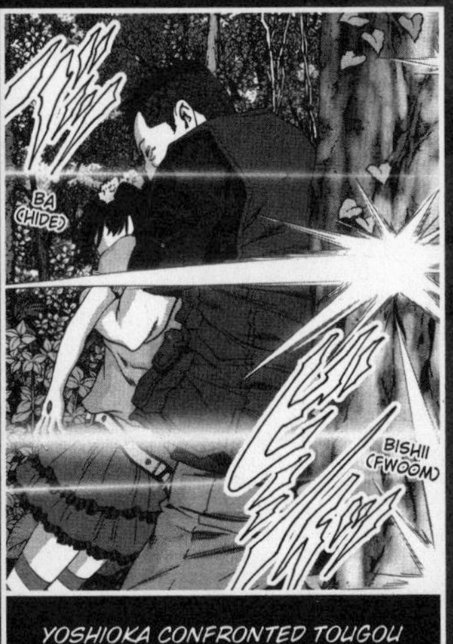
BA (HIDE)
BISHII (FWOOM)
YOSHIOKA CONFRONTED TOUGOU AND KAGUYA, TRYING TO SHOOT THEM DOWN WITH HIS MACHINE GUN IN ORDER TO GET THEIR CHIPS.

CONTENTS

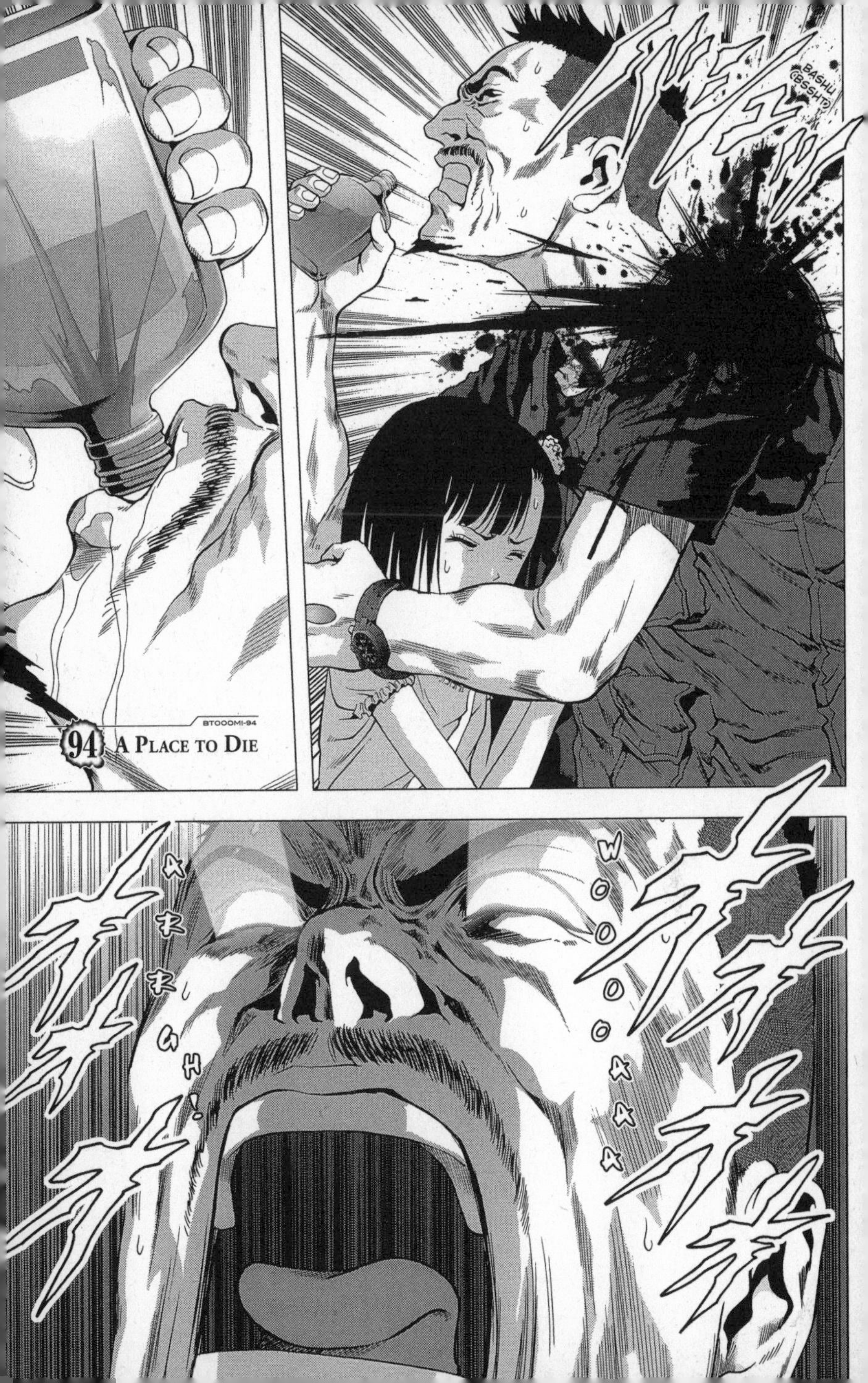
BASHU (BSSHT)
BTOOOM!-94
94 A PLACE TO DIE
WOOOOAAA
ARRGH!

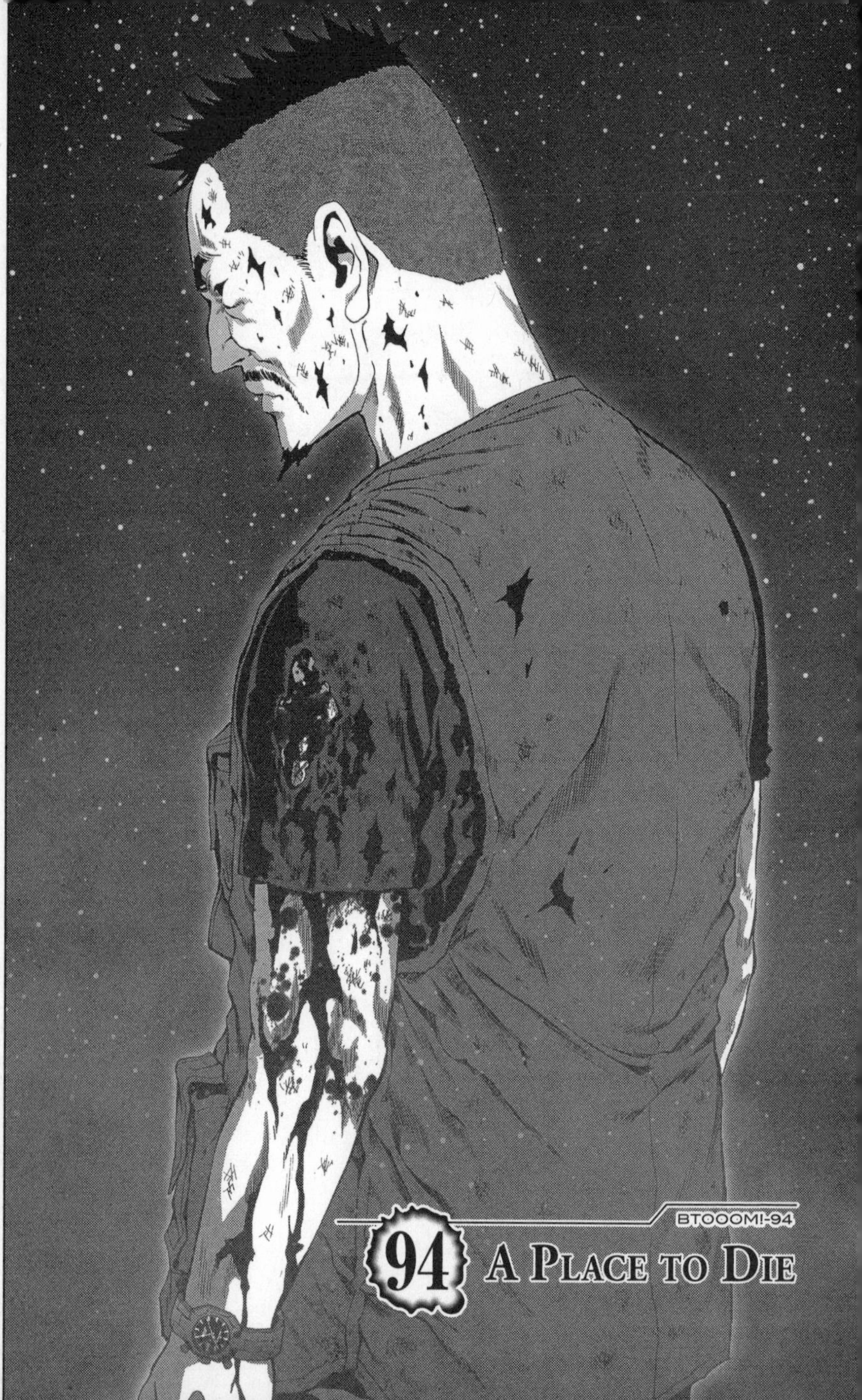
BTOOOM!-94
94
A PLACE TO DIE

KARAN (CLANG)

I KNEW IT...

KOOO (PANT)

CHUUU (WHEEZE)

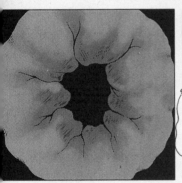

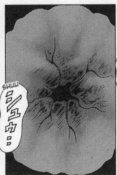

SHUU

KOOOO

HAAH!

THE ALCOHOL'S MAKING THE INFLAMMATION IN MY AIRWAYS RECEDE!!

MY BREATHING'S RETURNED A LITTLE!!

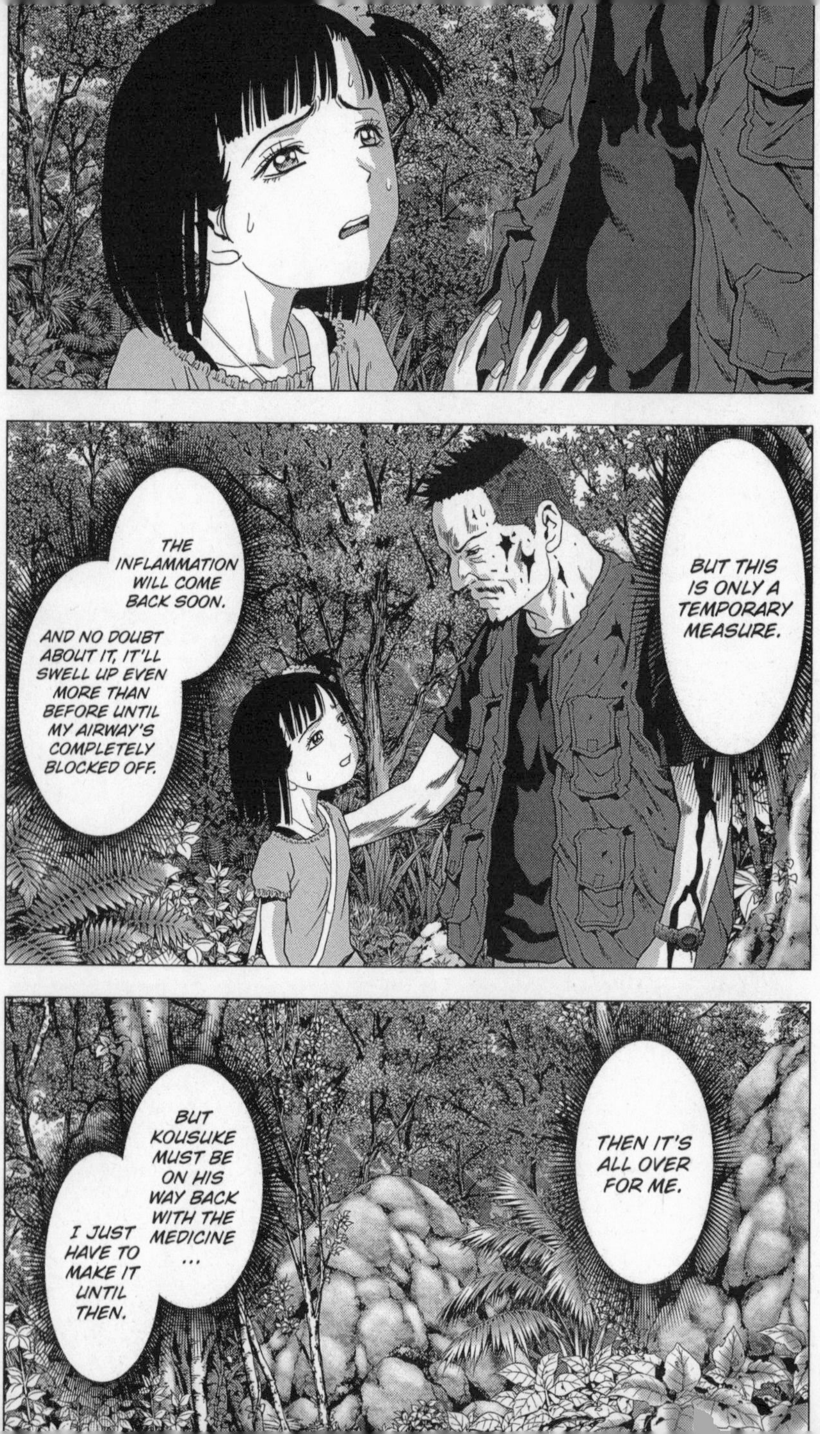
BUT THIS IS ONLY A TEMPORARY MEASURE.
THE INFLAMMATION WILL COME BACK SOON.
AND NO DOUBT ABOUT IT, IT'LL SWELL UP EVEN MORE THAN BEFORE UNTIL MY AIRWAY'S COMPLETELY BLOCKED OFF.
THEN IT'S ALL OVER FOR ME.
BUT KOUSUKE MUST BE ON HIS WAY BACK WITH THE MEDICINE ...
I JUST HAVE TO MAKE IT UNTIL THEN.

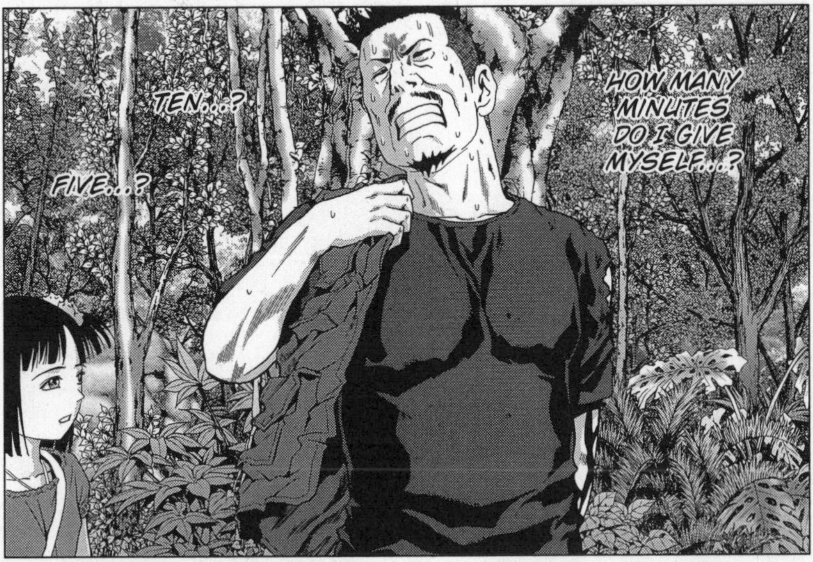
HOW MANY MINUTES DO I GIVE MYSELF...?
TEN...?
FIVE...?
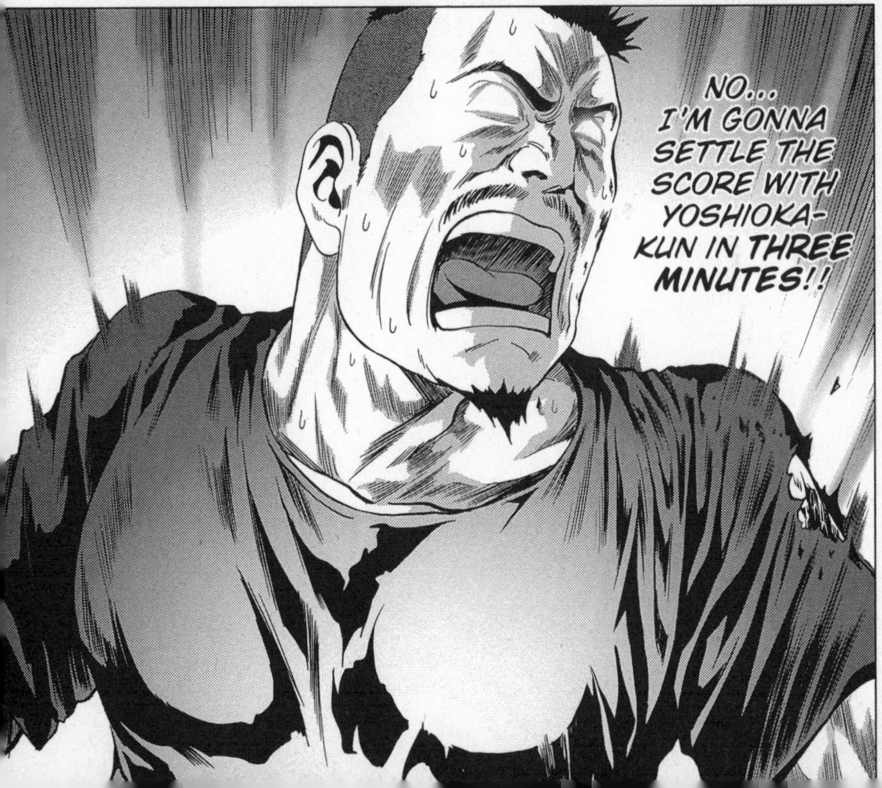
NO... I'M GONNA SETTLE THE SCORE WITH YOSHIOKA-KUN IN THREE MINUTES!!

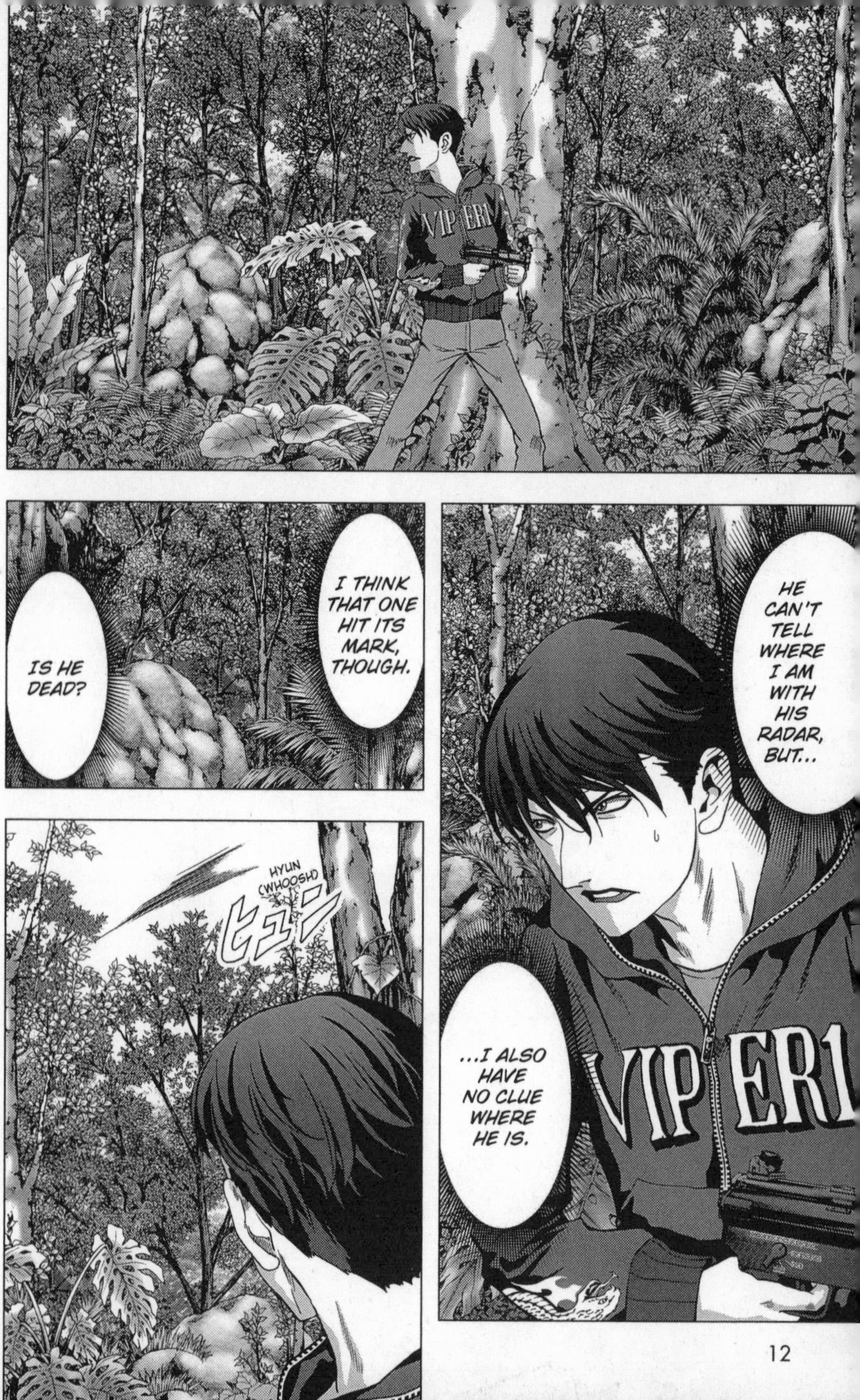
HE CAN'T TELL WHERE I AM WITH HIS RADAR, BUT...
...I ALSO HAVE NO CLUE WHERE HE IS.
VIP ER1
I THINK THAT ONE HIT ITS MARK, THOUGH.
IS HE DEAD?
HYUN (WHOOSH)
ヒュン

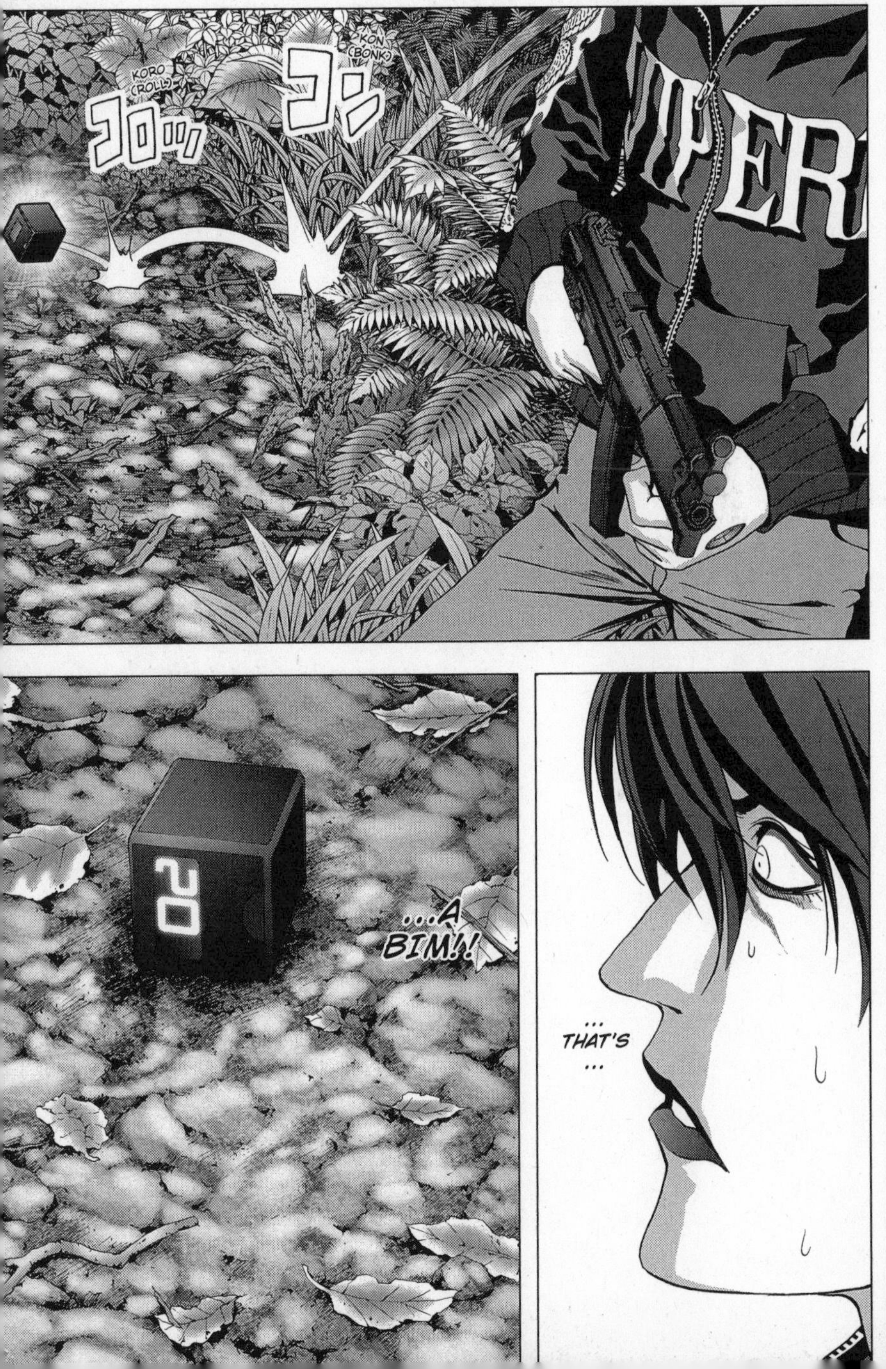
コン
KON
(BONK)
コロ
KORO
(ROLL)
... THAT'S ...
...A BIM!!

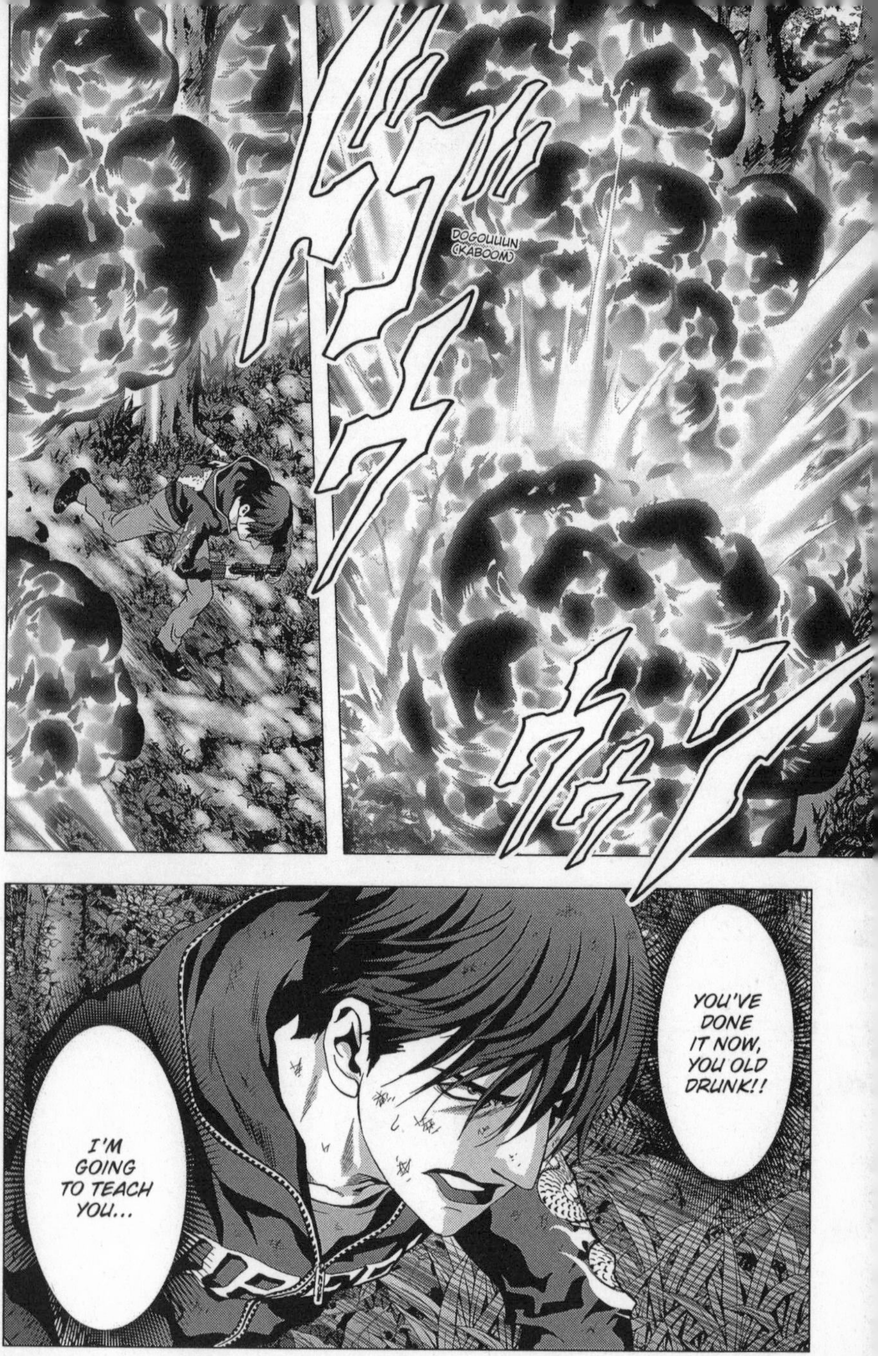
DOGOUUUN
(KABOOM)
YOU'VE DONE IT NOW, YOU OLD DRUNK!!
I'M GOING TO TEACH YOU...

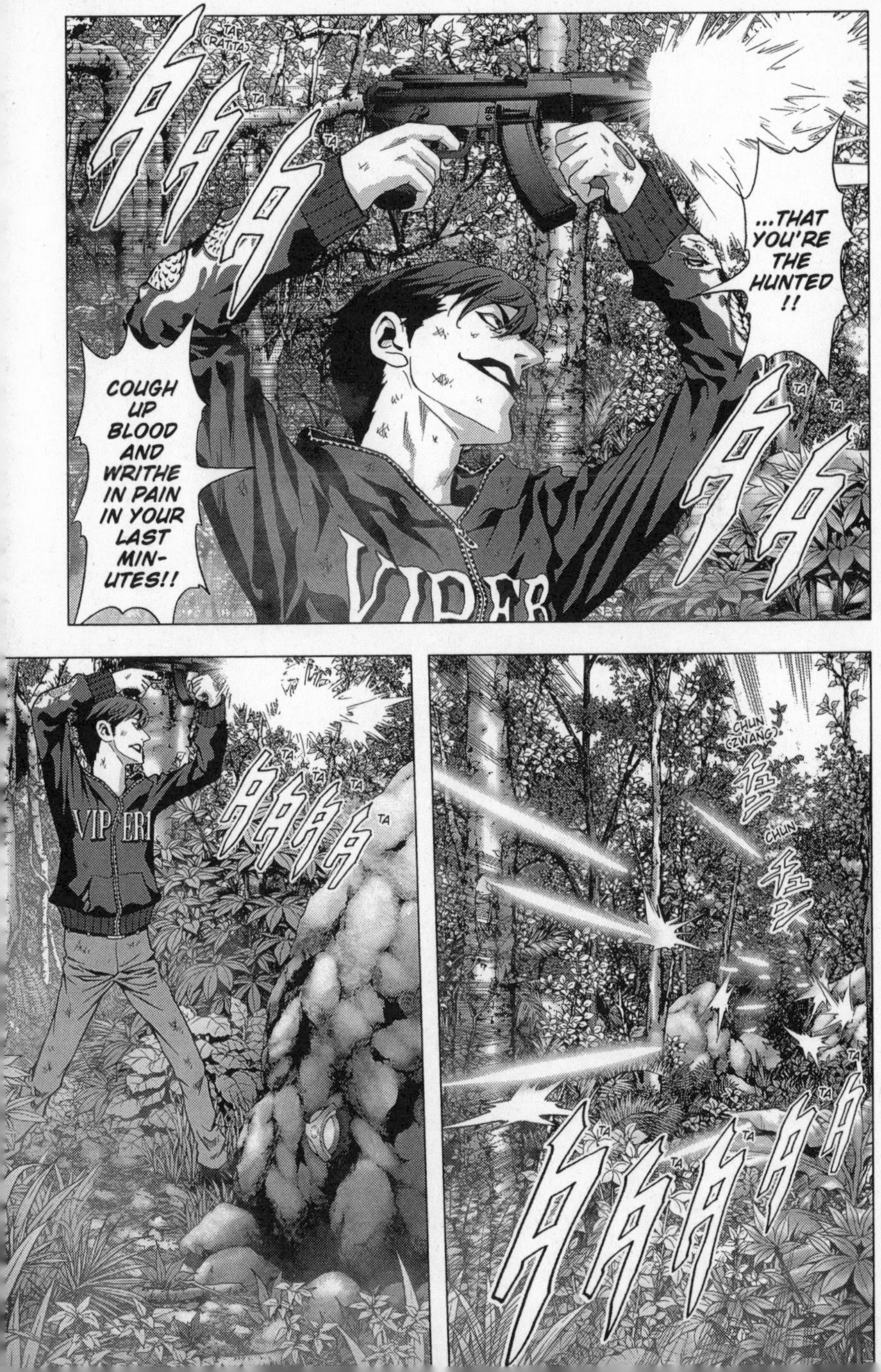
TA (RATTA)
TA
TA
...THAT YOU'RE THE HUNTED !!
COUGH UP BLOOD AND WRITHE IN PAIN IN YOUR LAST MIN-UTES!!
TA
TA
VIPER
CHUN (ZWANG)
CHUN
TA
TA
TA
TA
TA
TA
TA
TA
TA
VIP ER1

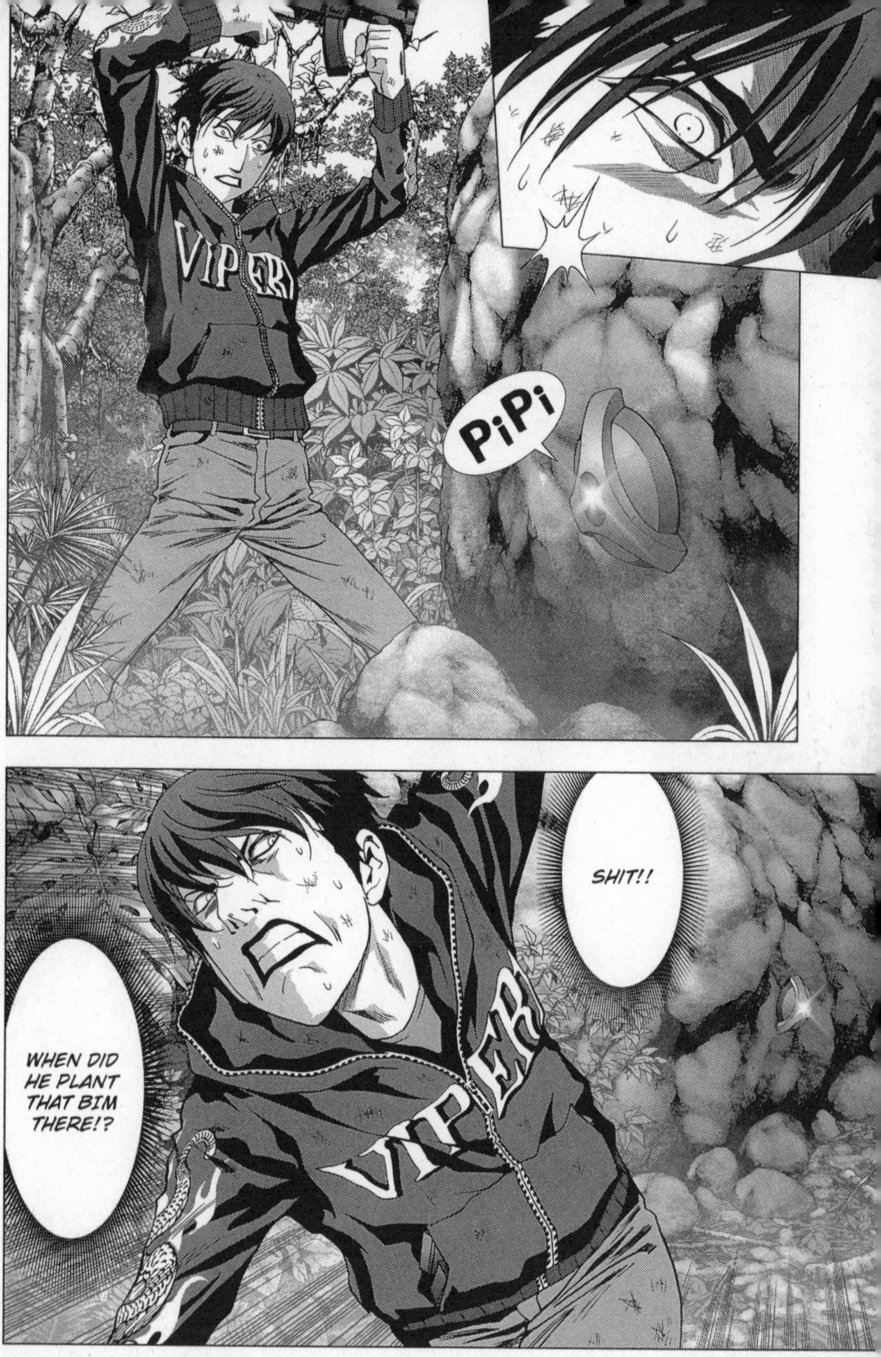
PiPi
SHIT!!
WHEN DID HE PLANT THAT BIM THERE!?

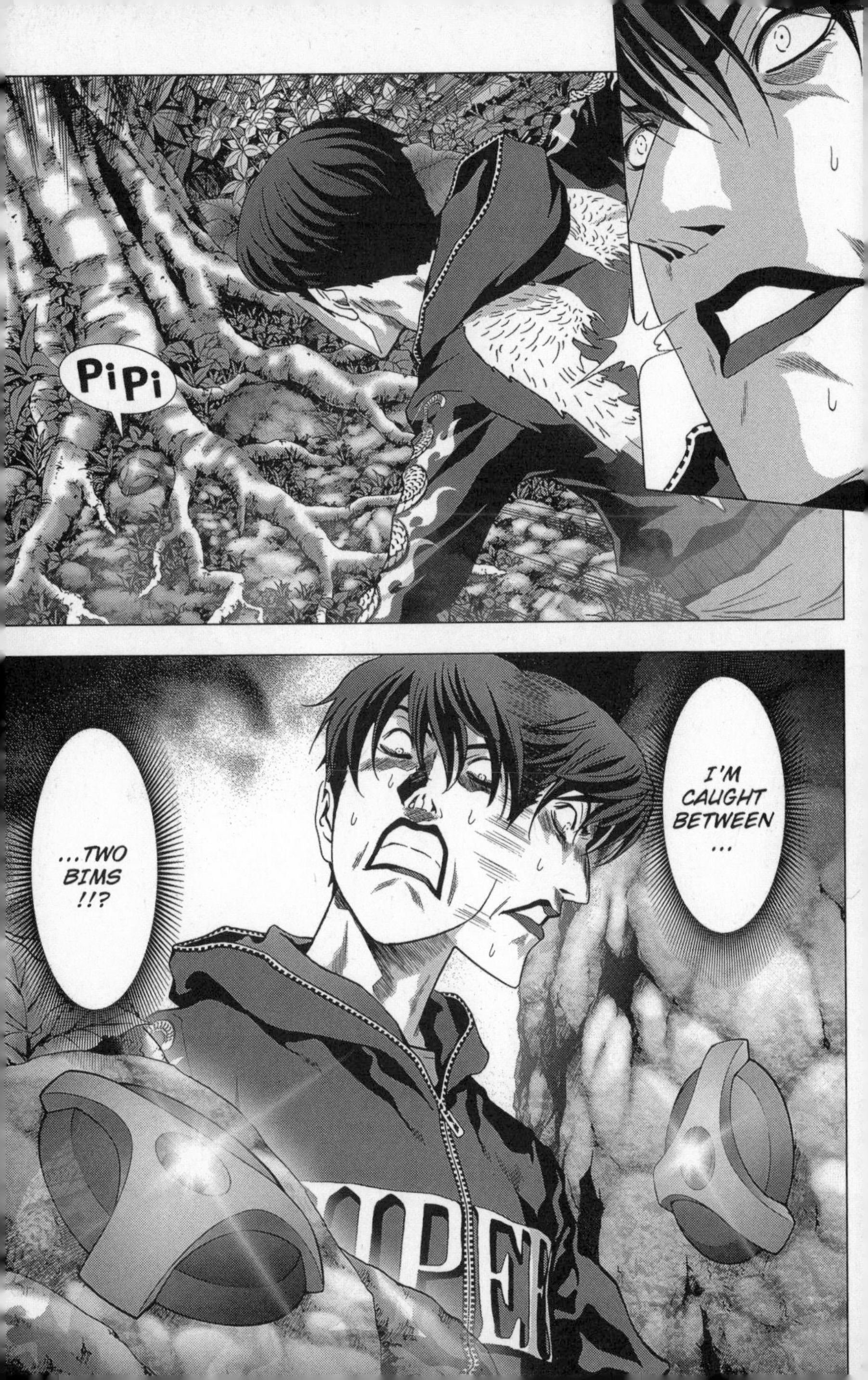
PiPi
I'M CAUGHT BETWEEN ...
...TWO BIMS !!?

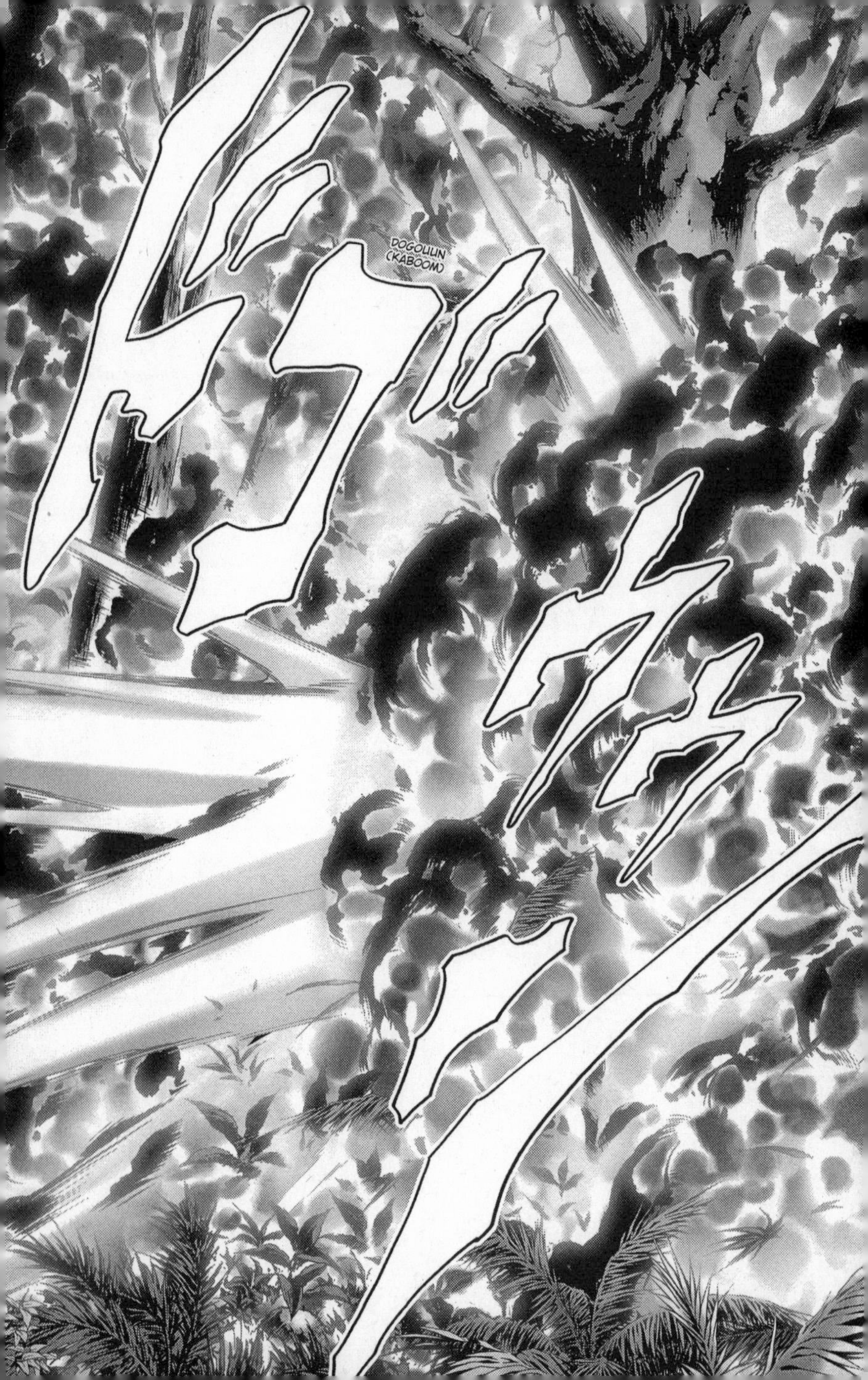
DOGOUUN
(KABOOM)

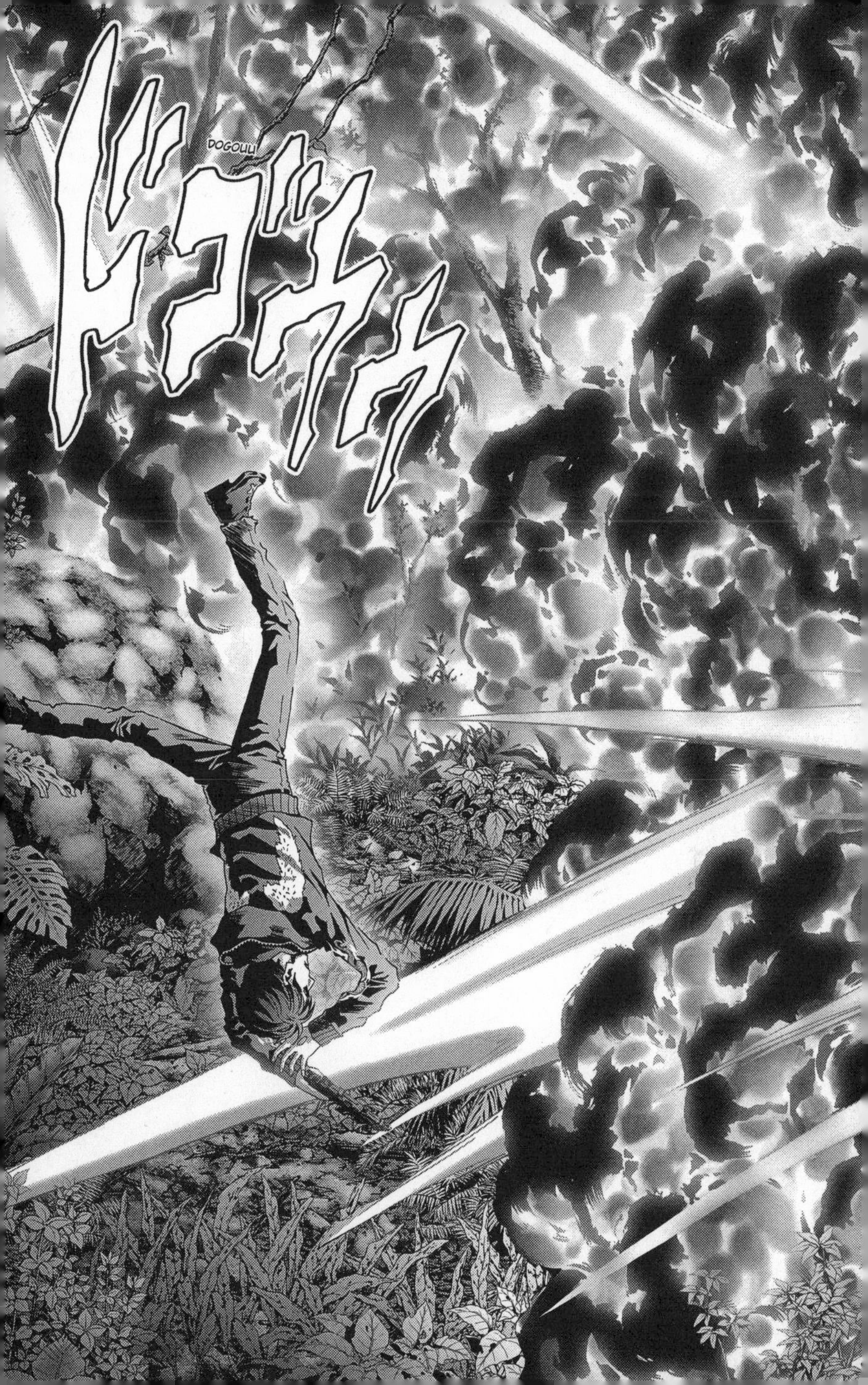
DOGOUU
ドゴウゥ

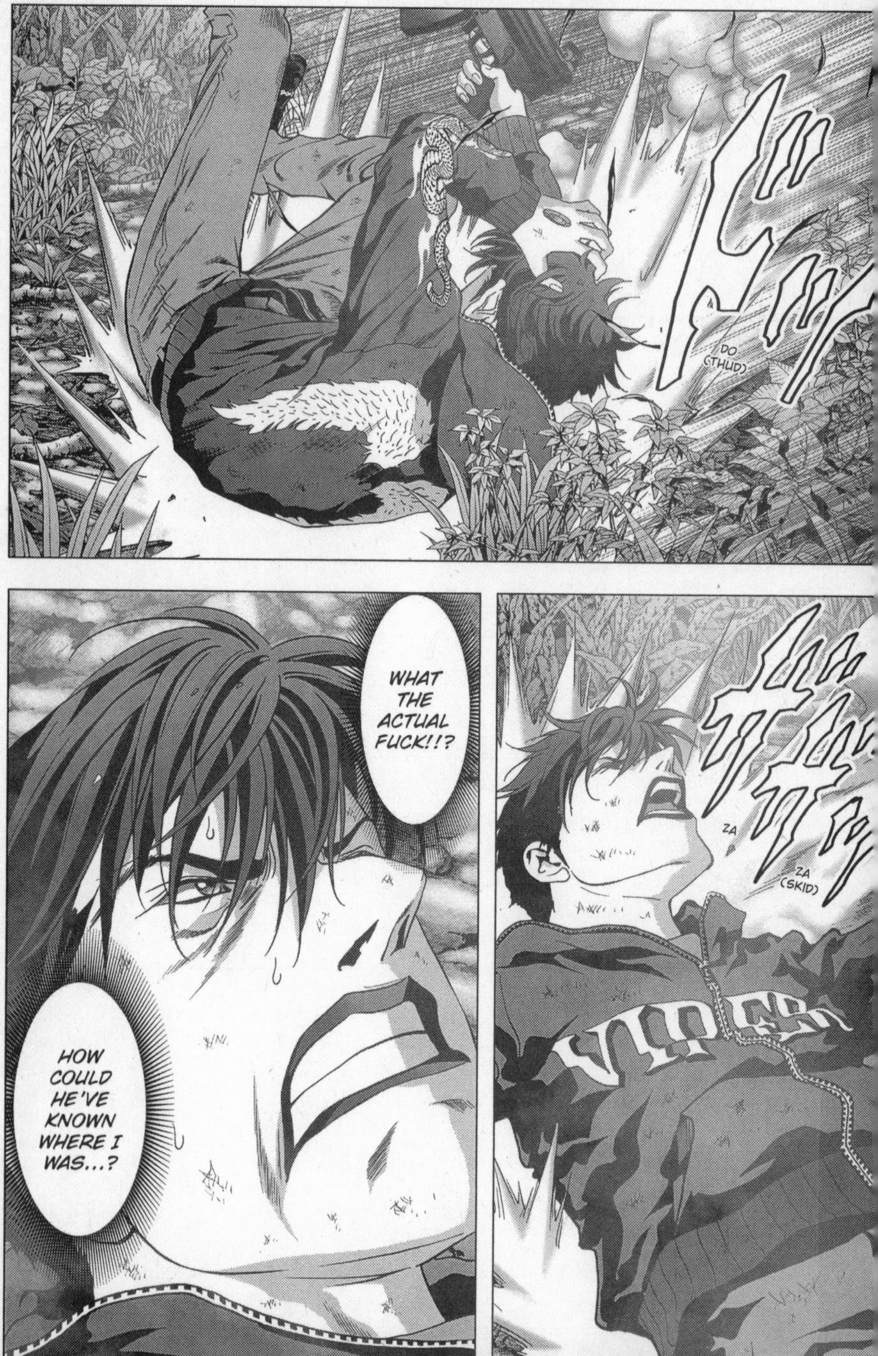
DO (THUD)
ZA
ZA (SKID)
WHAT THE ACTUAL FUCK!!?
HOW COULD HE'VE KNOWN WHERE I WAS...?

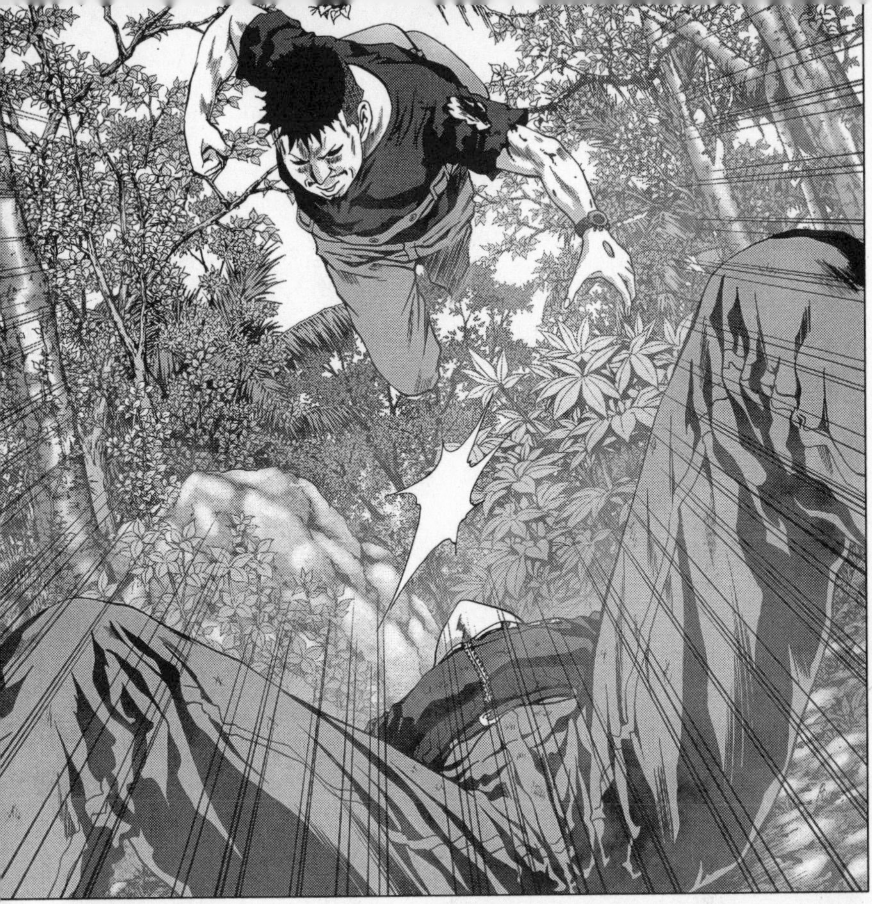

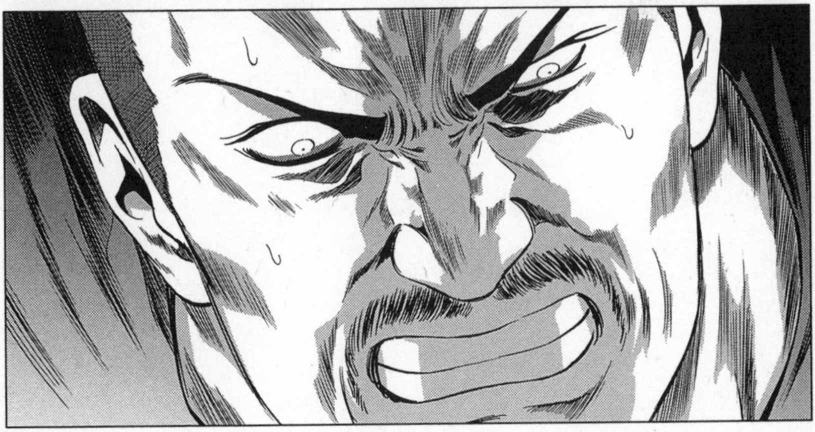

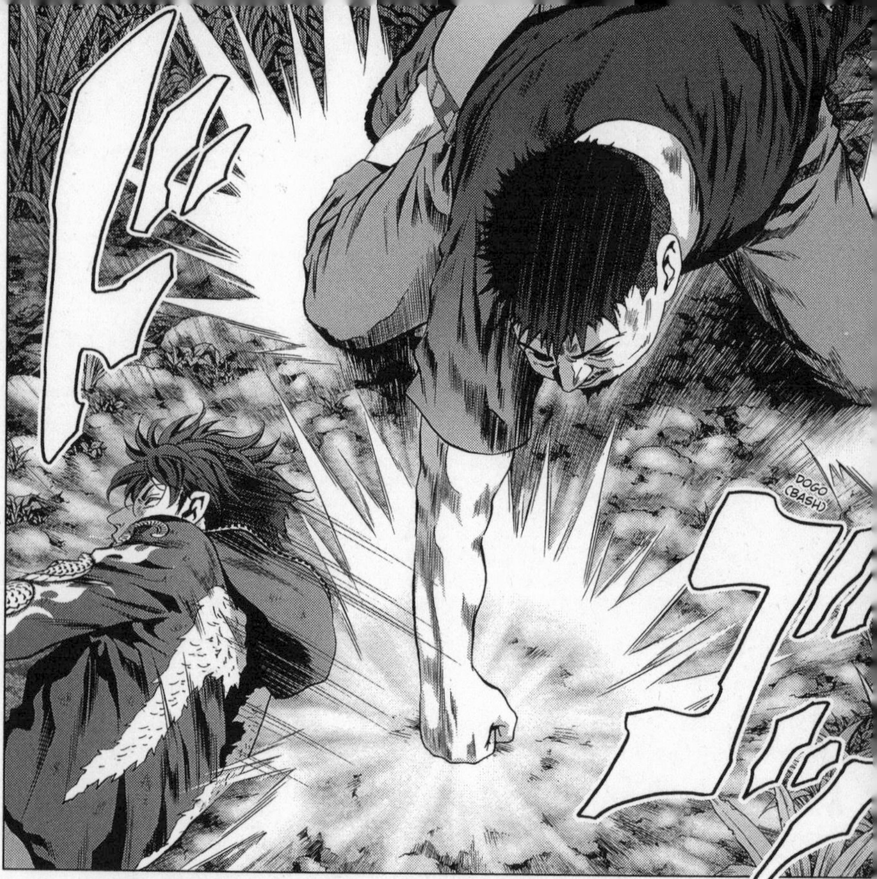
DOGO
(BASH)
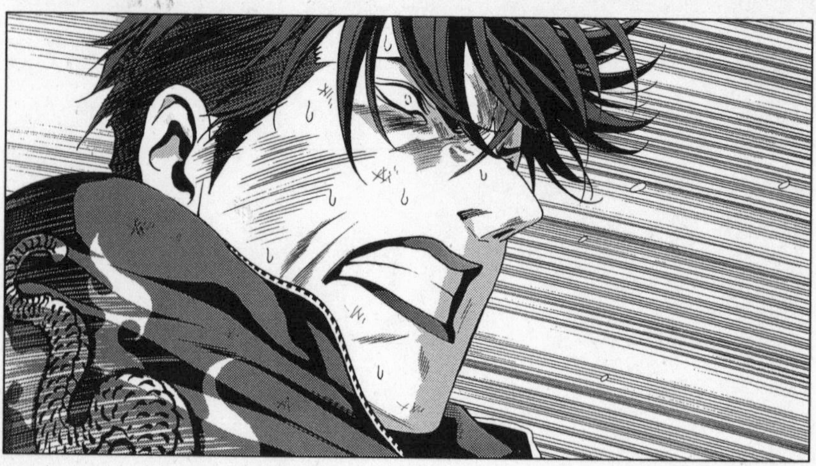

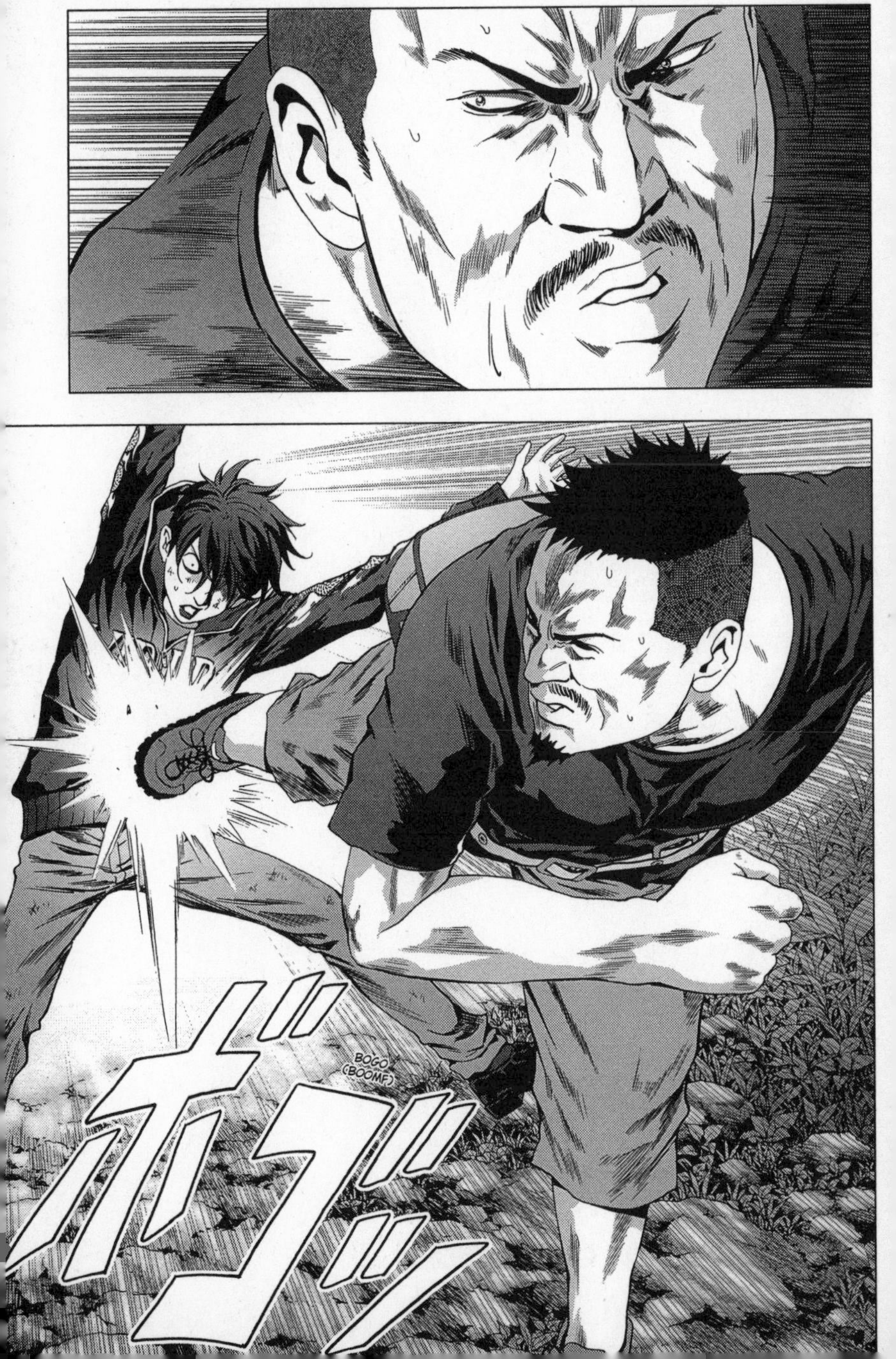
BOGO
(BOOMF)

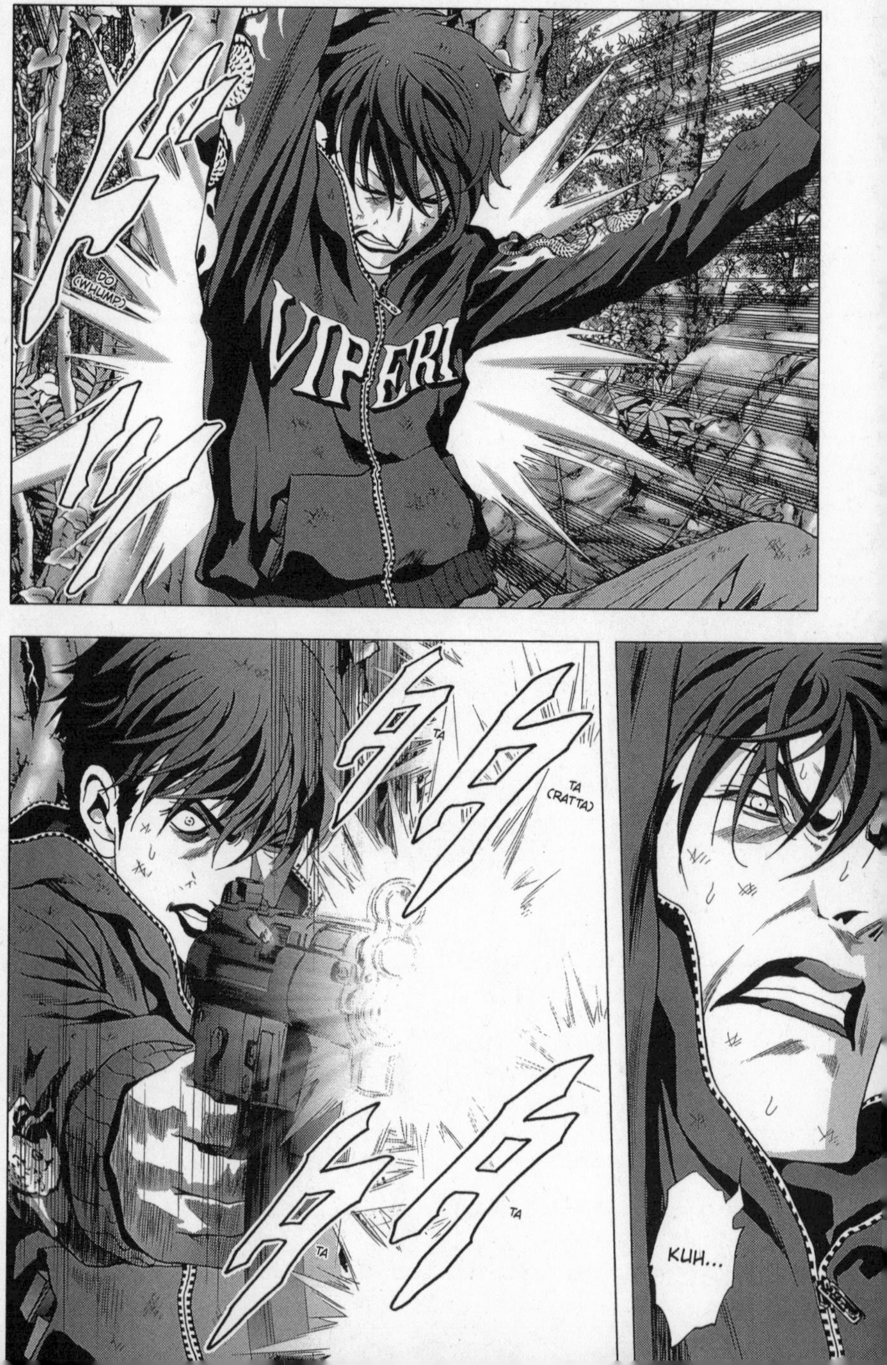
DO (WHUMP)
KUH...
TA
TA (RATTA)
TA
TA

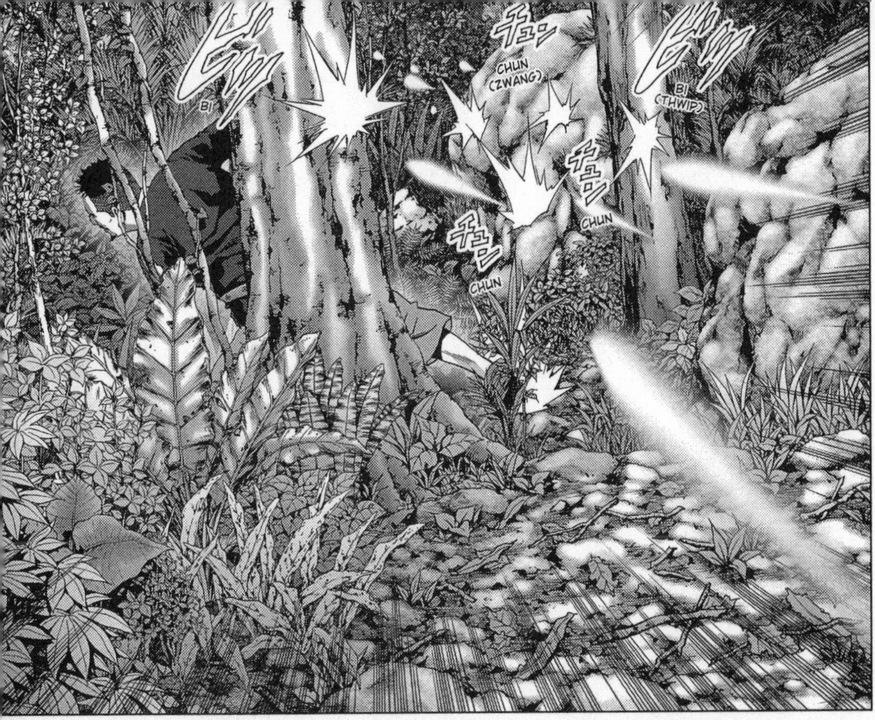
BI
(THWIP)
CHUN
(ZWANG)
CHUN
CHUN
BI
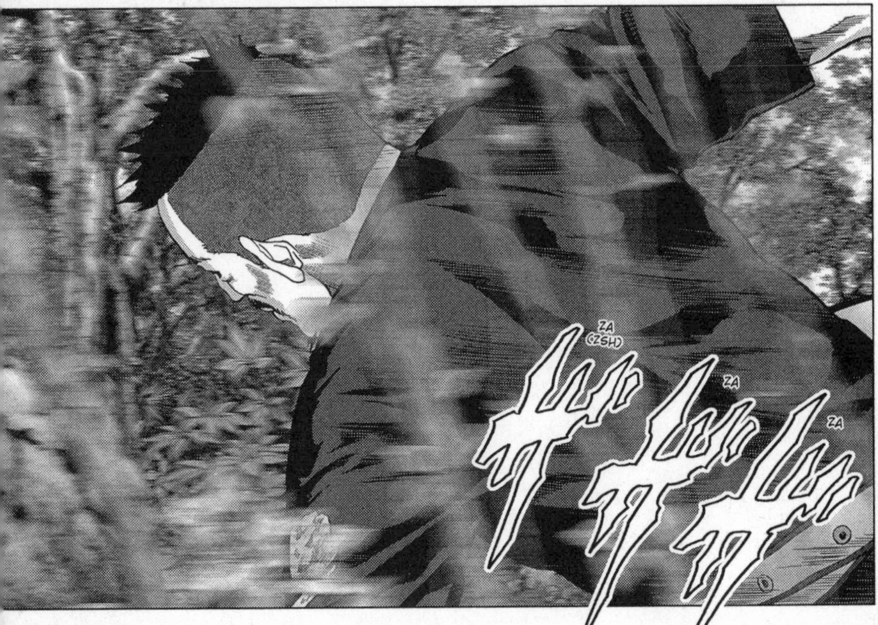
ZA
(ZSH)
ZA
ZA

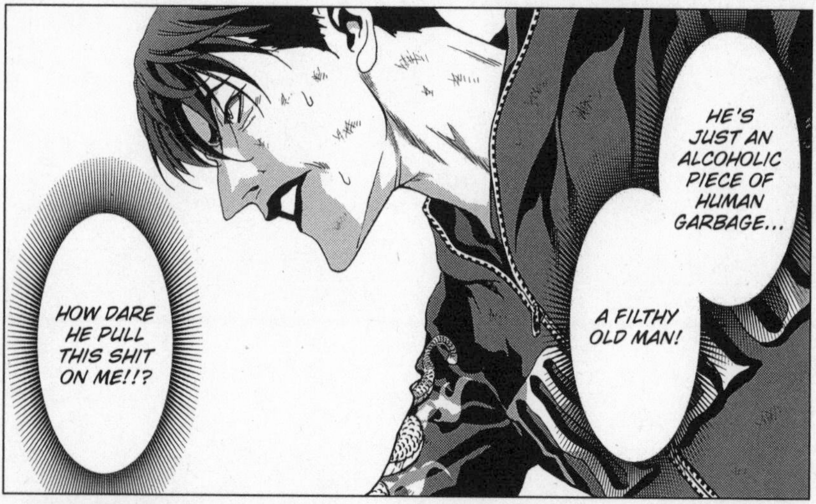
HE'S JUST AN ALCOHOLIC PIECE OF HUMAN GARBAGE...
A FILTHY OLD MAN!
HOW DARE HE PULL THIS SHIT ON ME!!?

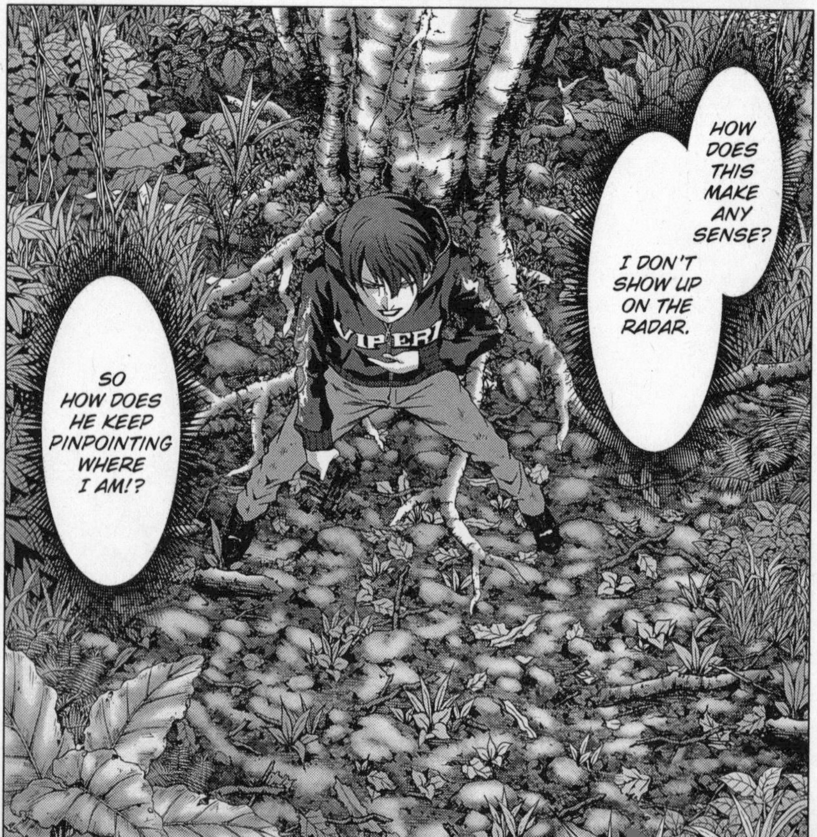
HOW DOES THIS MAKE ANY SENSE?
I DON'T SHOW UP ON THE RADAR.
SO HOW DOES HE KEEP PINPOINTING WHERE I AM!?

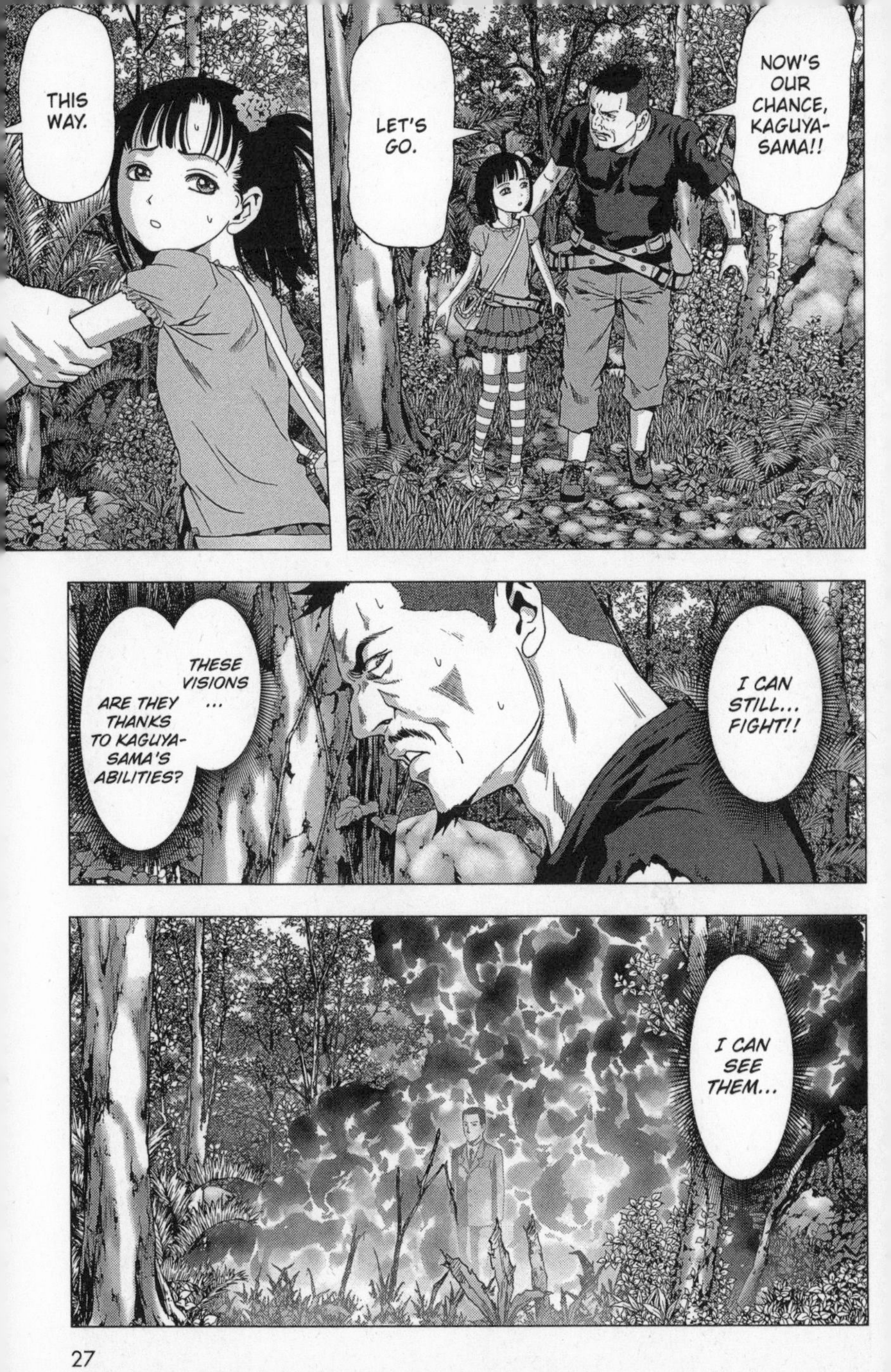
NOW'S OUR CHANCE, KAGUYA-SAMA!!
LET'S GO.
THIS WAY.
I CAN STILL... FIGHT!!
THESE VISIONS... ARE THEY THANKS TO KAGUYA-SAMA'S ABILITIES?
I CAN SEE THEM...

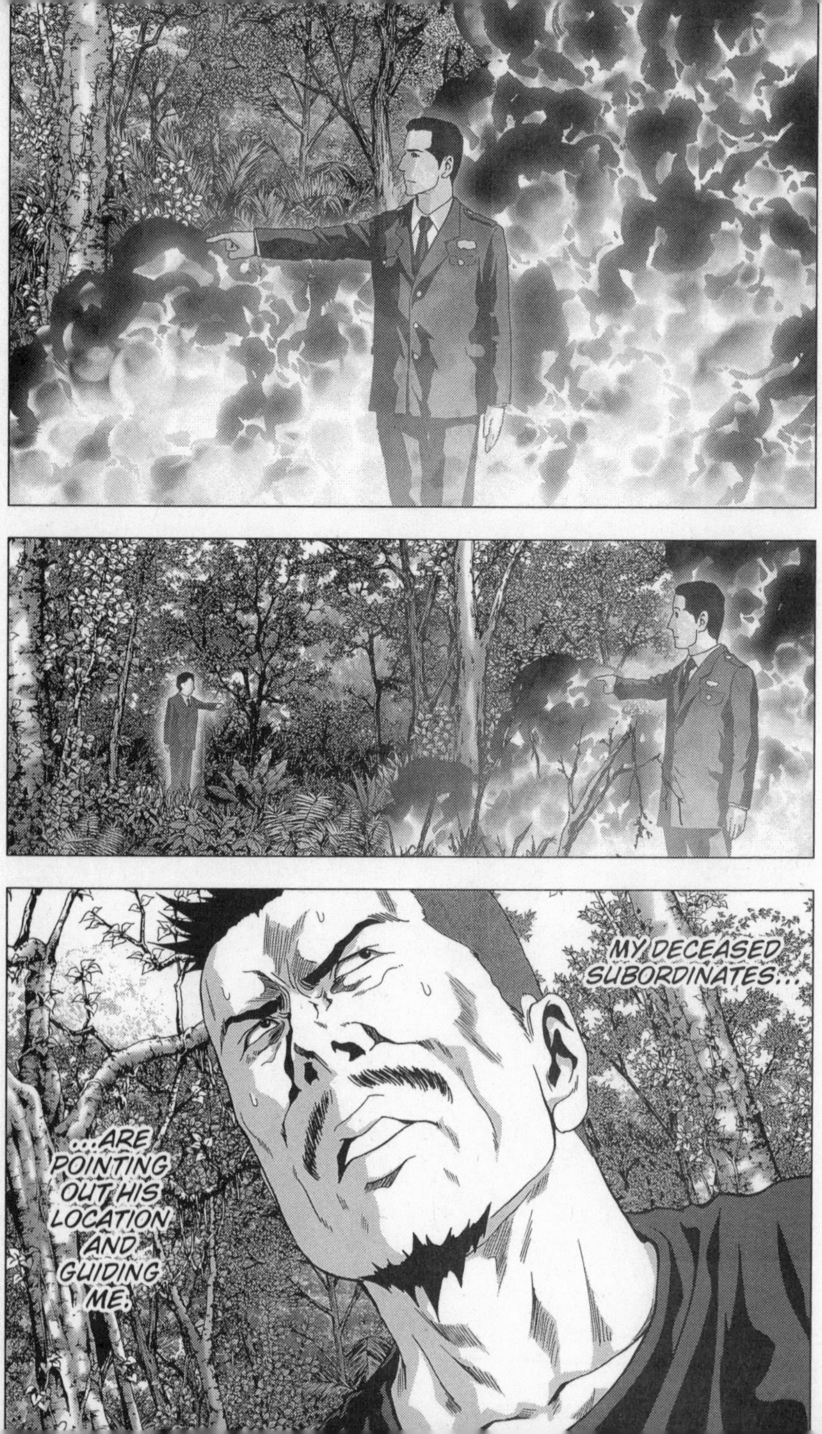
MY DECEASED SUBORDINATES...
...ARE POINTING OUT HIS LOCATION AND GUIDING ME.

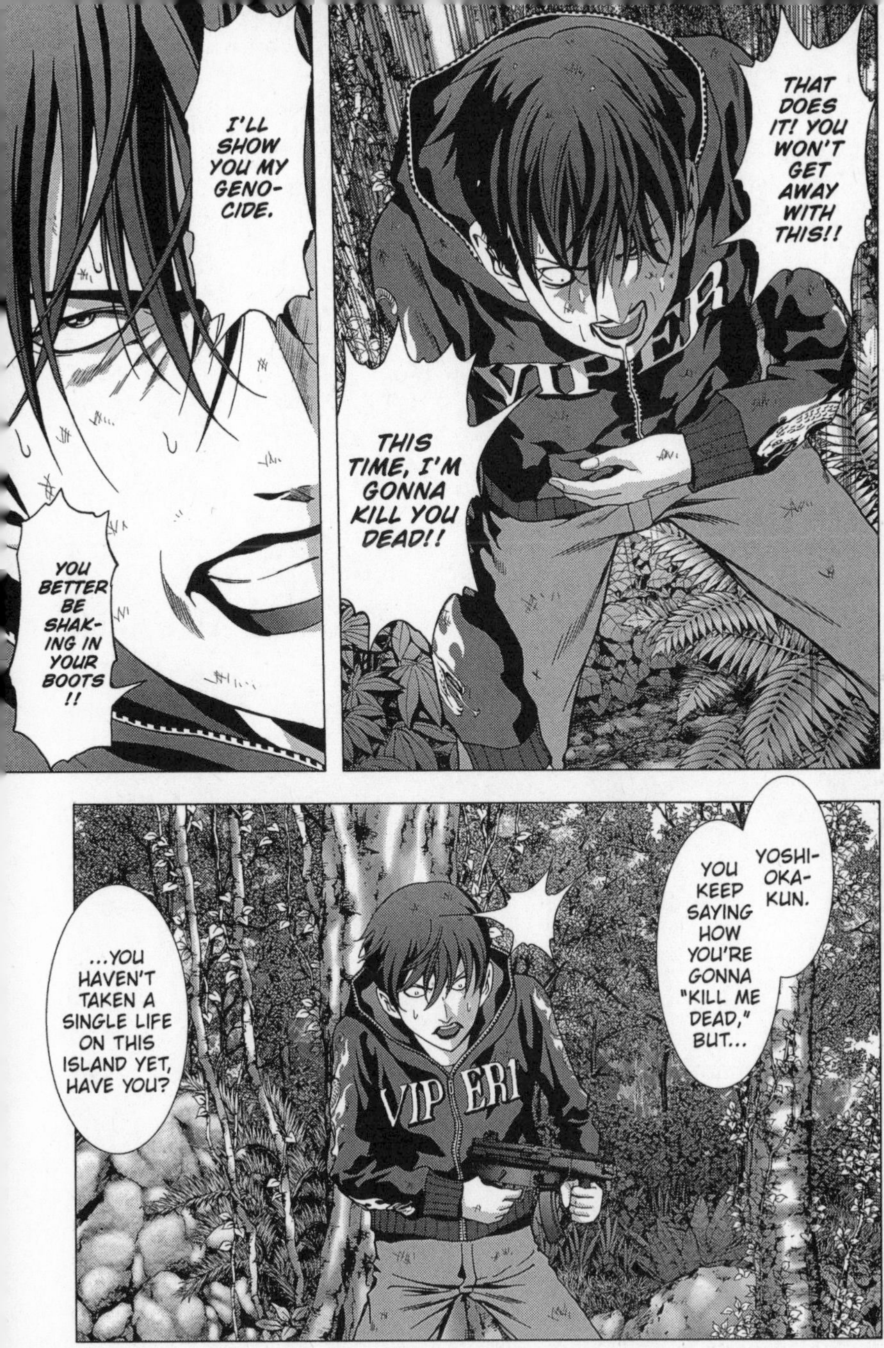
THAT DOES IT! YOU WON'T GET AWAY WITH THIS!!
THIS TIME, I'M GONNA KILL YOU DEAD!!
I'LL SHOW YOU MY GENO-CIDE.
YOU BETTER BE SHAK-ING IN YOUR BOOTS !!
YOSHI-OKA-KUN.
YOU KEEP SAYING HOW YOU'RE GONNA "KILL ME DEAD," BUT...
...YOU HAVEN'T TAKEN A SINGLE LIFE ON THIS ISLAND YET, HAVE YOU?
VIPER
VIP ER1

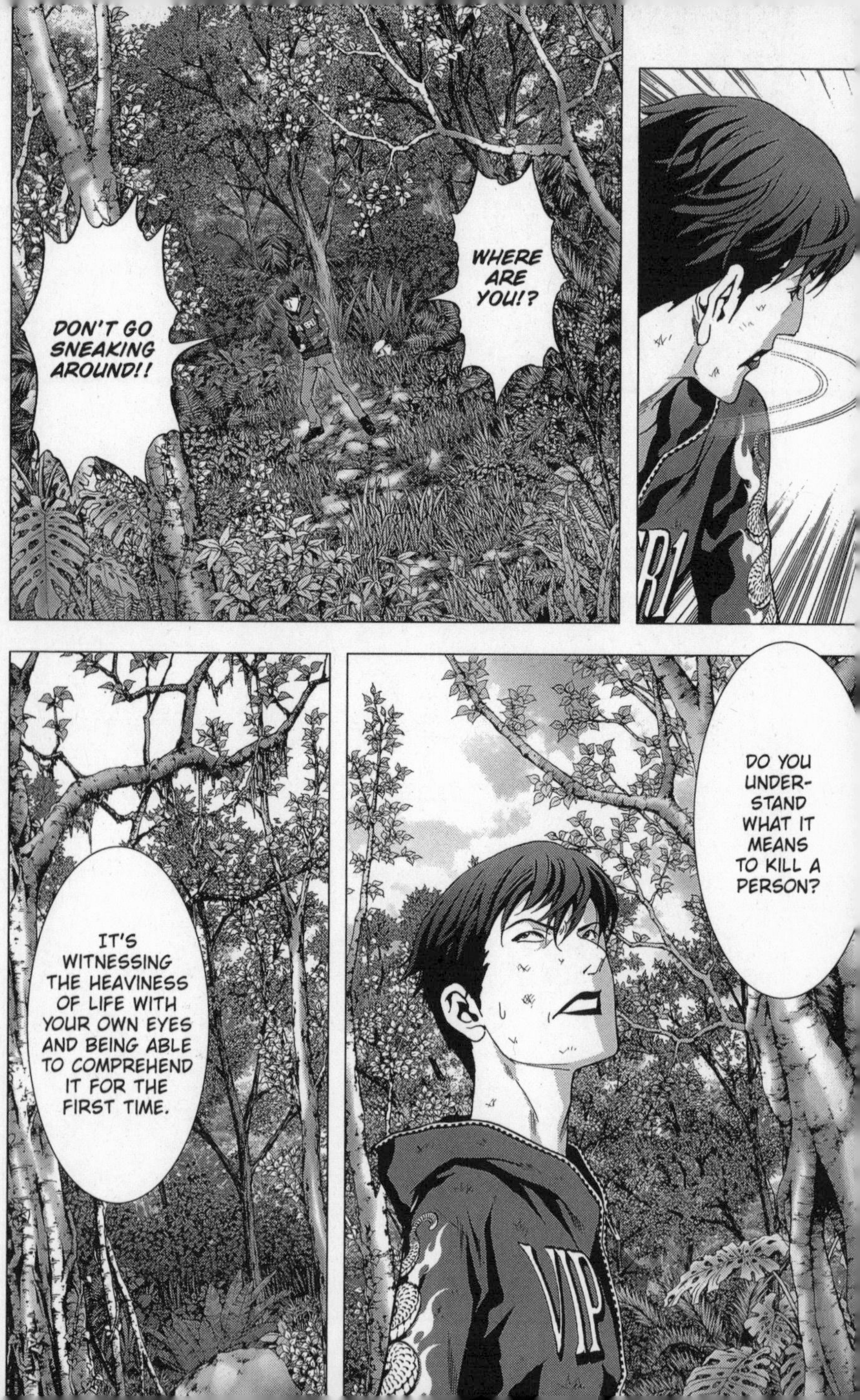
WHERE ARE YOU!?
DON'T GO SNEAKING AROUND!!
DO YOU UNDER-STAND WHAT IT MEANS TO KILL A PERSON?
IT'S WITNESSING THE HEAVINESS OF LIFE WITH YOUR OWN EYES AND BEING ABLE TO COMPREHEND IT FOR THE FIRST TIME.

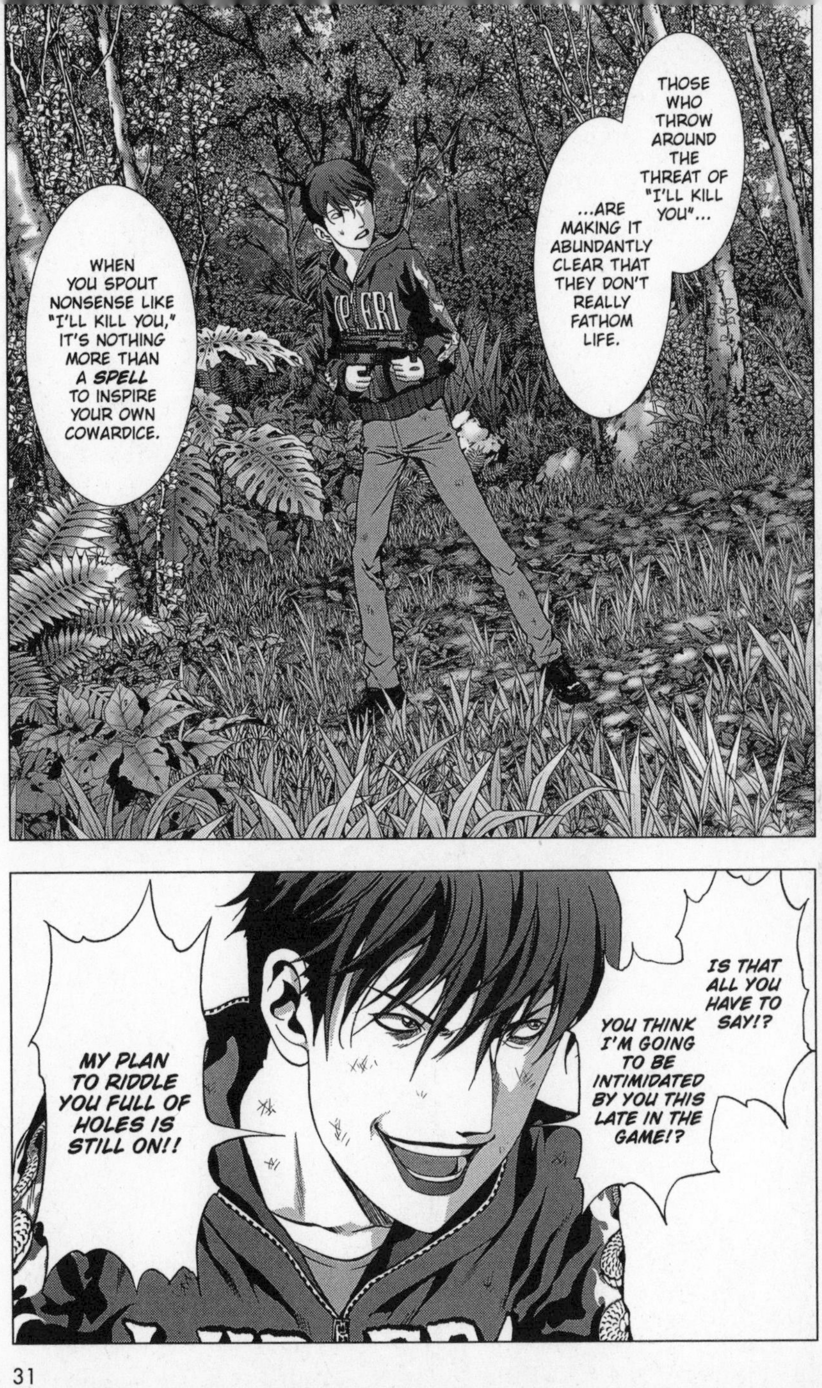
THOSE WHO THROW AROUND THE THREAT OF "I'LL KILL YOU"...
...ARE MAKING IT ABUNDANTLY CLEAR THAT THEY DON'T REALLY FATHOM LIFE.
WHEN YOU SPOUT NONSENSE LIKE "I'LL KILL YOU," IT'S NOTHING MORE THAN A ***SPELL*** TO INSPIRE YOUR OWN COWARDICE.
IS THAT ALL YOU HAVE TO SAY!?
YOU THINK I'M GOING TO BE INTIMIDATED BY YOU THIS LATE IN THE GAME!?
MY PLAN TO RIDDLE YOU FULL OF HOLES IS STILL ON!!

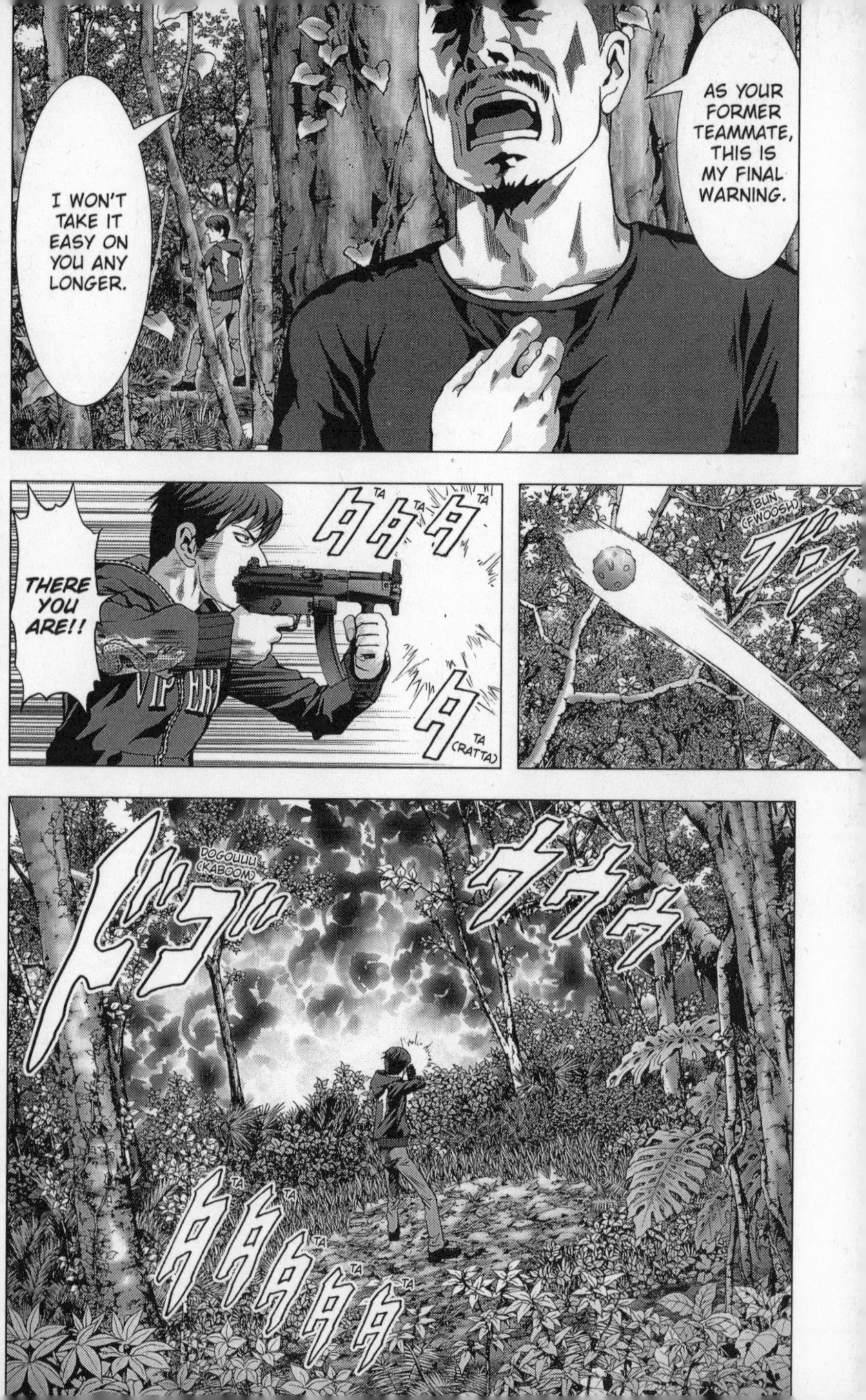
AS YOUR FORMER TEAMMATE, THIS IS MY FINAL WARNING.
I WON'T TAKE IT EASY ON YOU ANY LONGER.
BUN (FWOOSH)
THERE YOU ARE!!
TA TA TA
TA (RATTA)
DOGOUUU (KABOOM)
TA TA TA TA TA

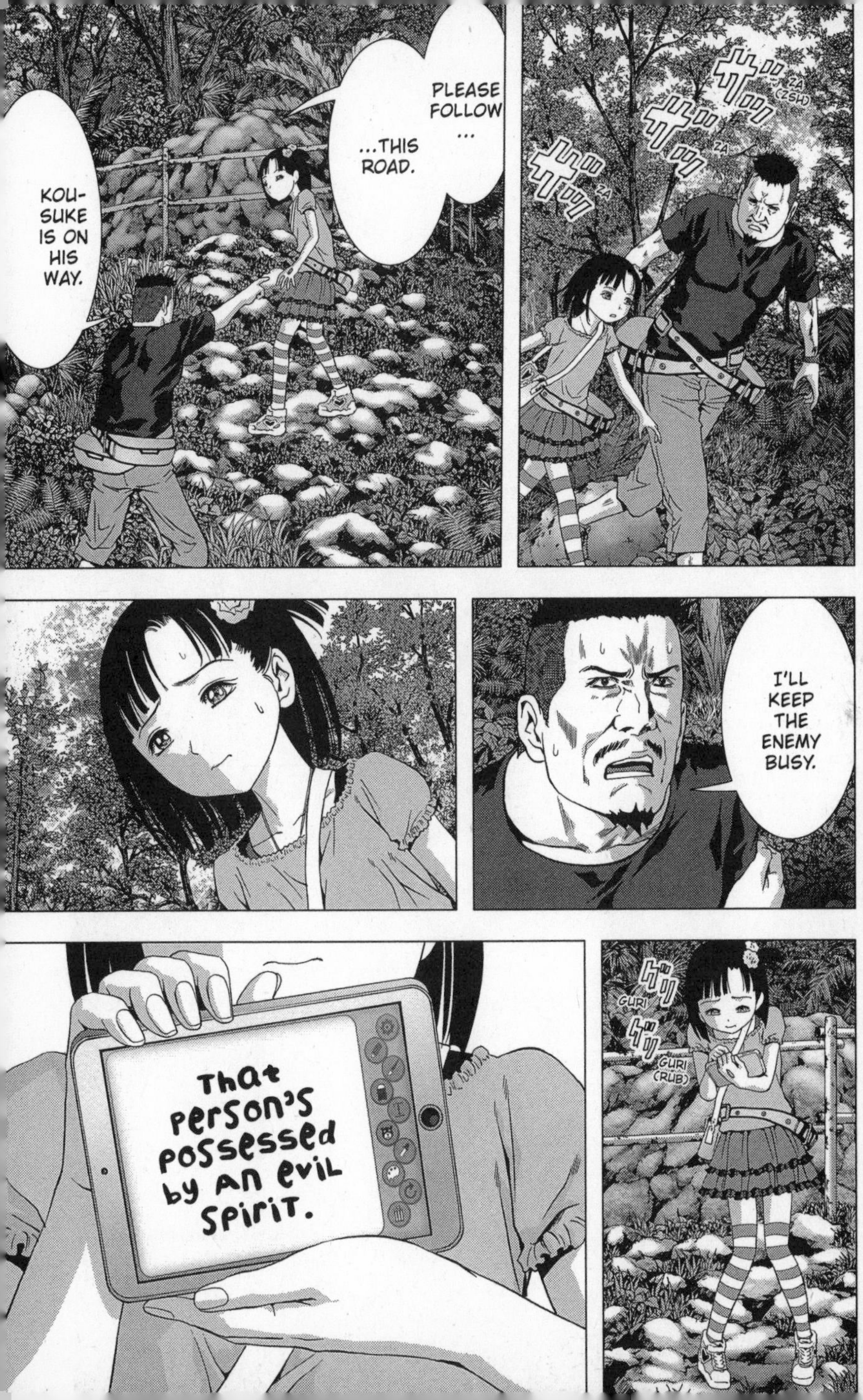
ZA (ZSH)
ZA
ZA
PLEASE FOLLOW ...
...THIS ROAD.
KOU-SUKE IS ON HIS WAY.
I'LL KEEP THE ENEMY BUSY.
GURI
GURI (RUB)
That person's possessed by an evil spirit.

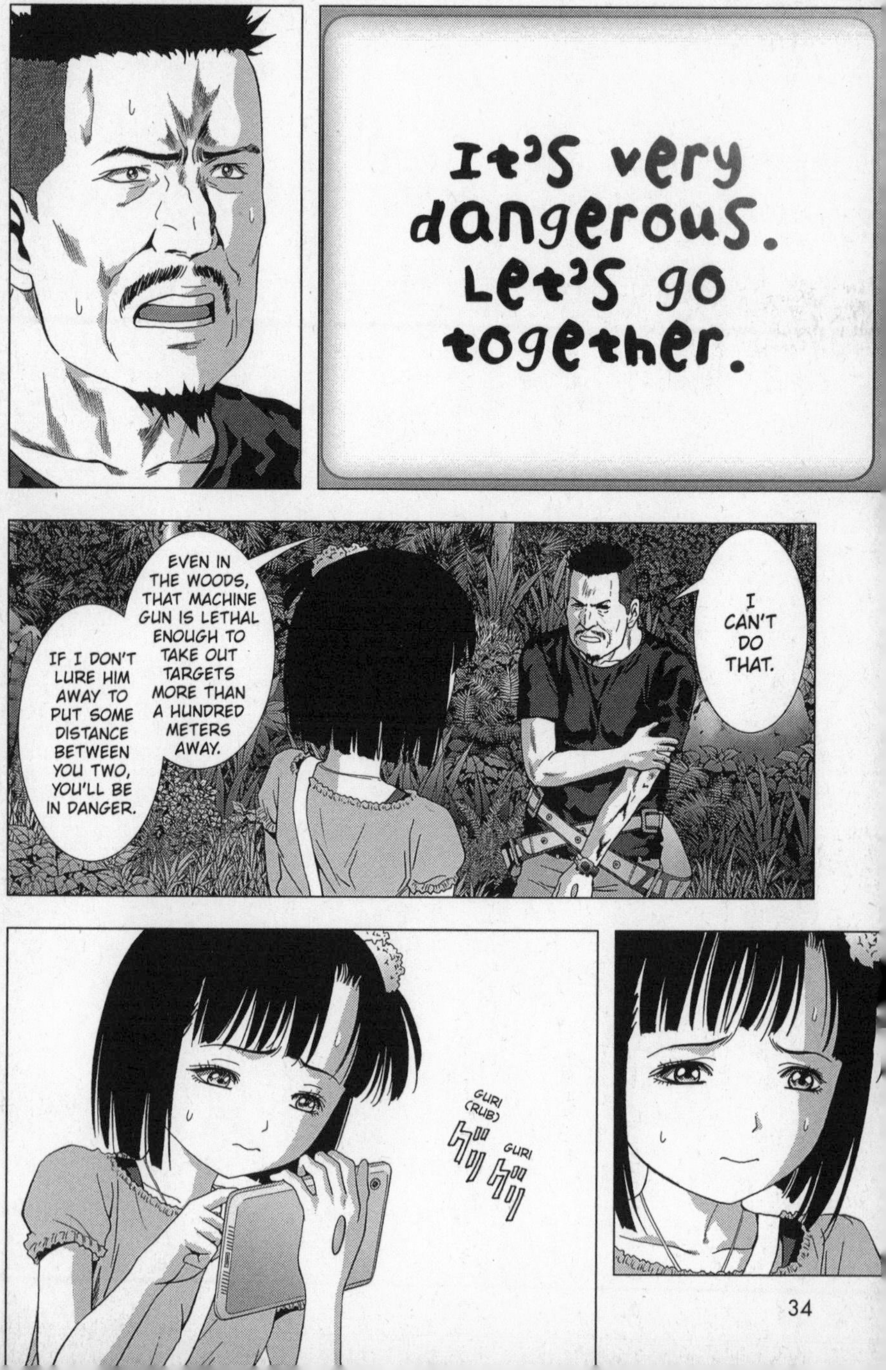
It's very dangerous. Let's go together.
I CAN'T DO THAT.
EVEN IN THE WOODS, THAT MACHINE GUN IS LETHAL ENOUGH TO TAKE OUT TARGETS MORE THAN A HUNDRED METERS AWAY.
IF I DON'T LURE HIM AWAY TO PUT SOME DISTANCE BETWEEN YOU TWO, YOU'LL BE IN DANGER.
GURI (RUB)
GURI

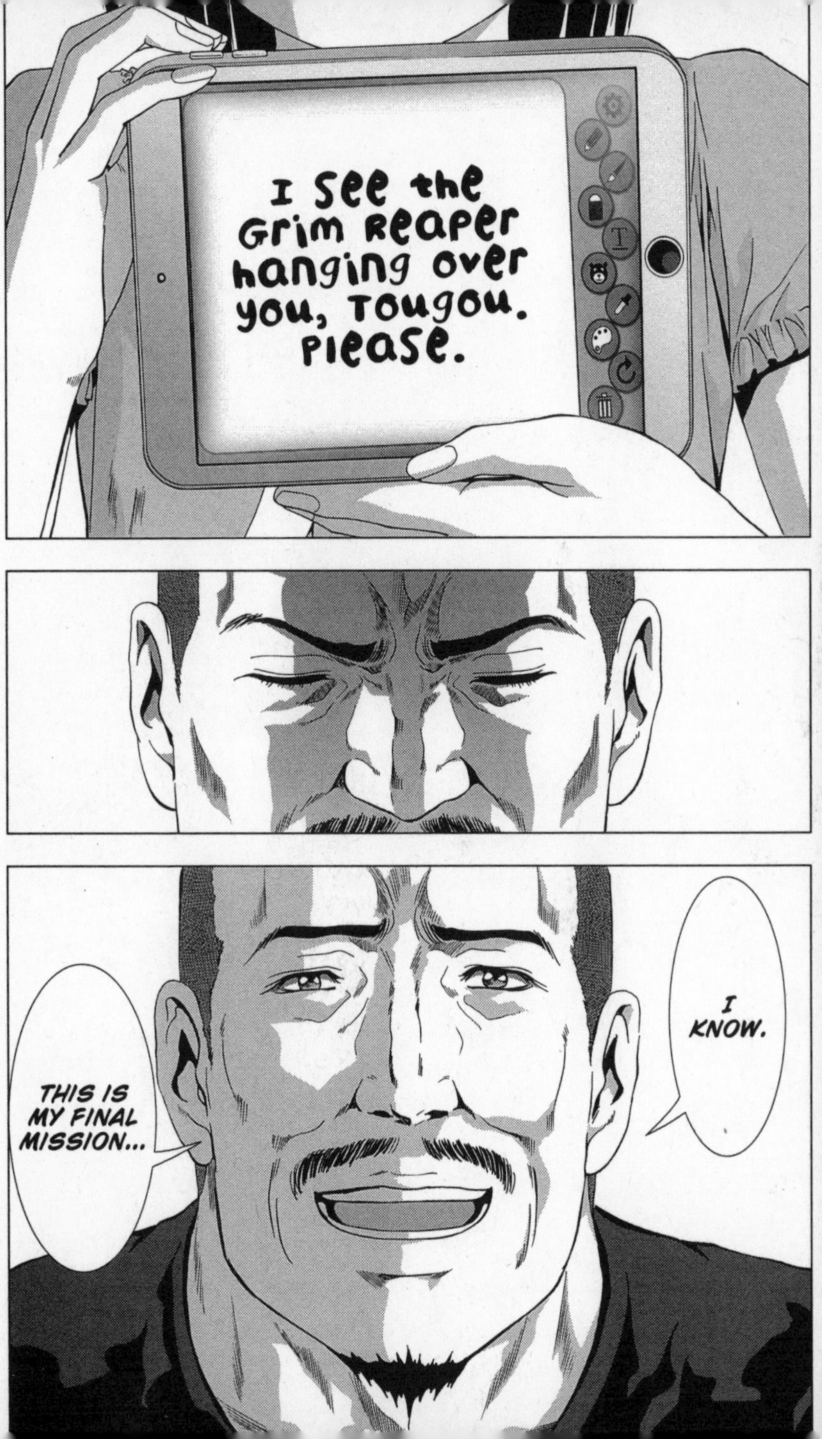
I see the Grim Reaper hanging over you, Tougou. Please.
I KNOW.
THIS IS MY FINAL MISSION...

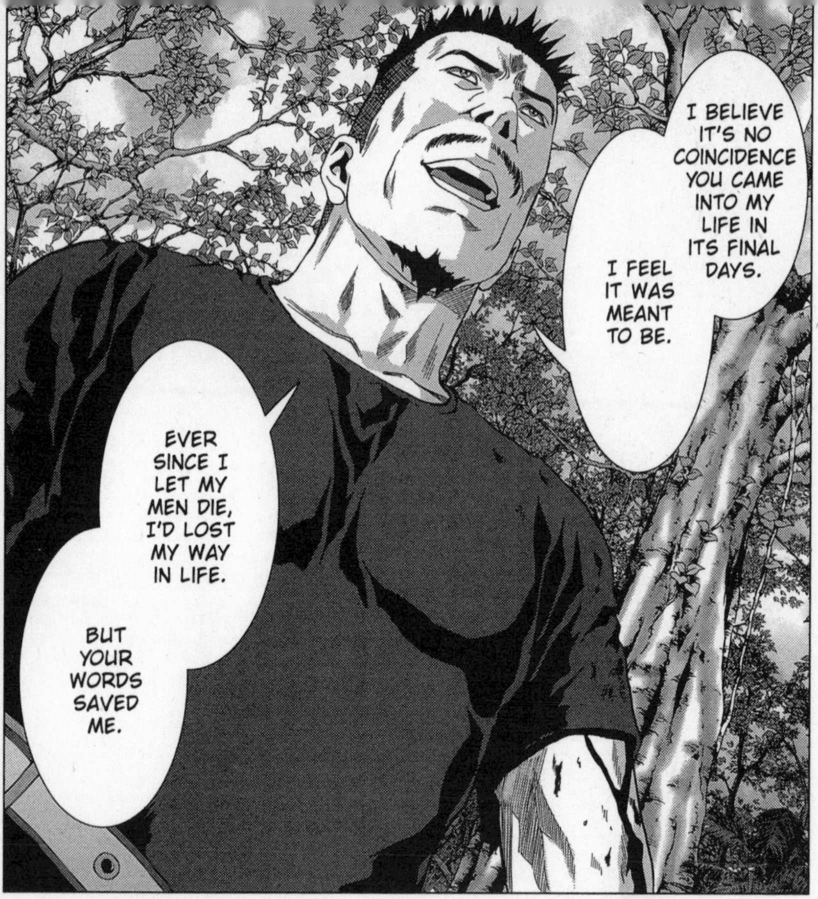
I BELIEVE IT'S NO COINCIDENCE YOU CAME INTO MY LIFE IN ITS FINAL DAYS.
I FEEL IT WAS MEANT TO BE.
EVER SINCE I LET MY MEN DIE, I'D LOST MY WAY IN LIFE.
BUT YOUR WORDS SAVED ME.

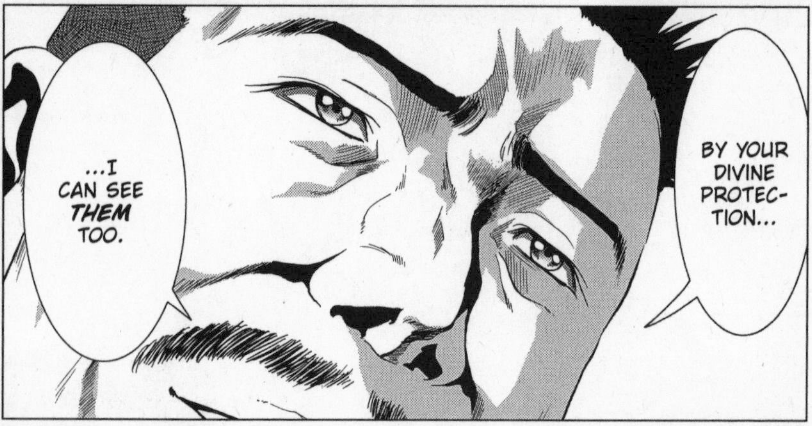
BY YOUR DIVINE PROTECTION...
...I CAN SEE *THEM* TOO.

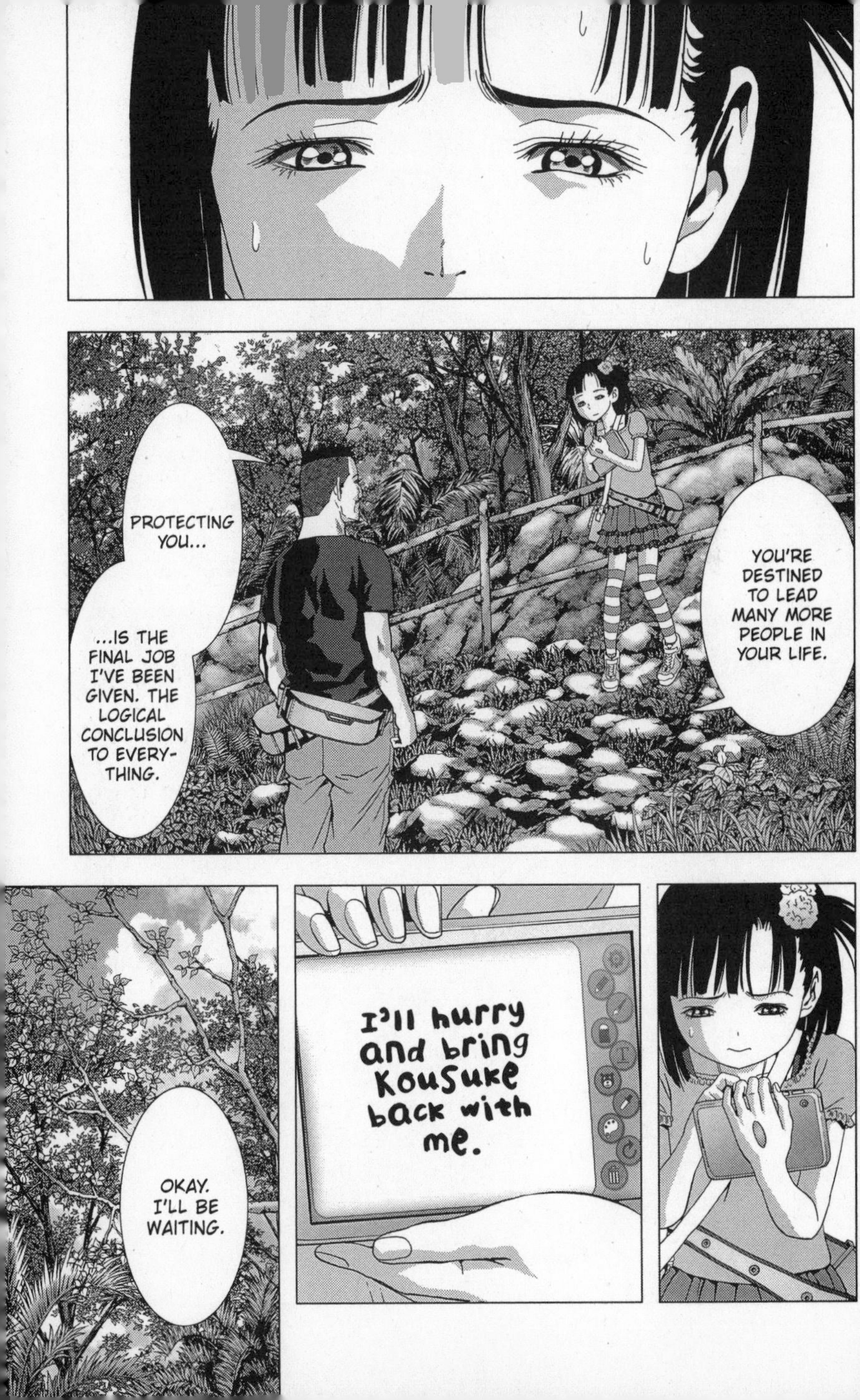
YOU'RE DESTINED TO LEAD MANY MORE PEOPLE IN YOUR LIFE.
PROTECTING YOU...
...IS THE FINAL JOB I'VE BEEN GIVEN. THE LOGICAL CONCLUSION TO EVERY-THING.
I'll hurry and bring Kousuke back with me.
OKAY. I'LL BE WAITING.

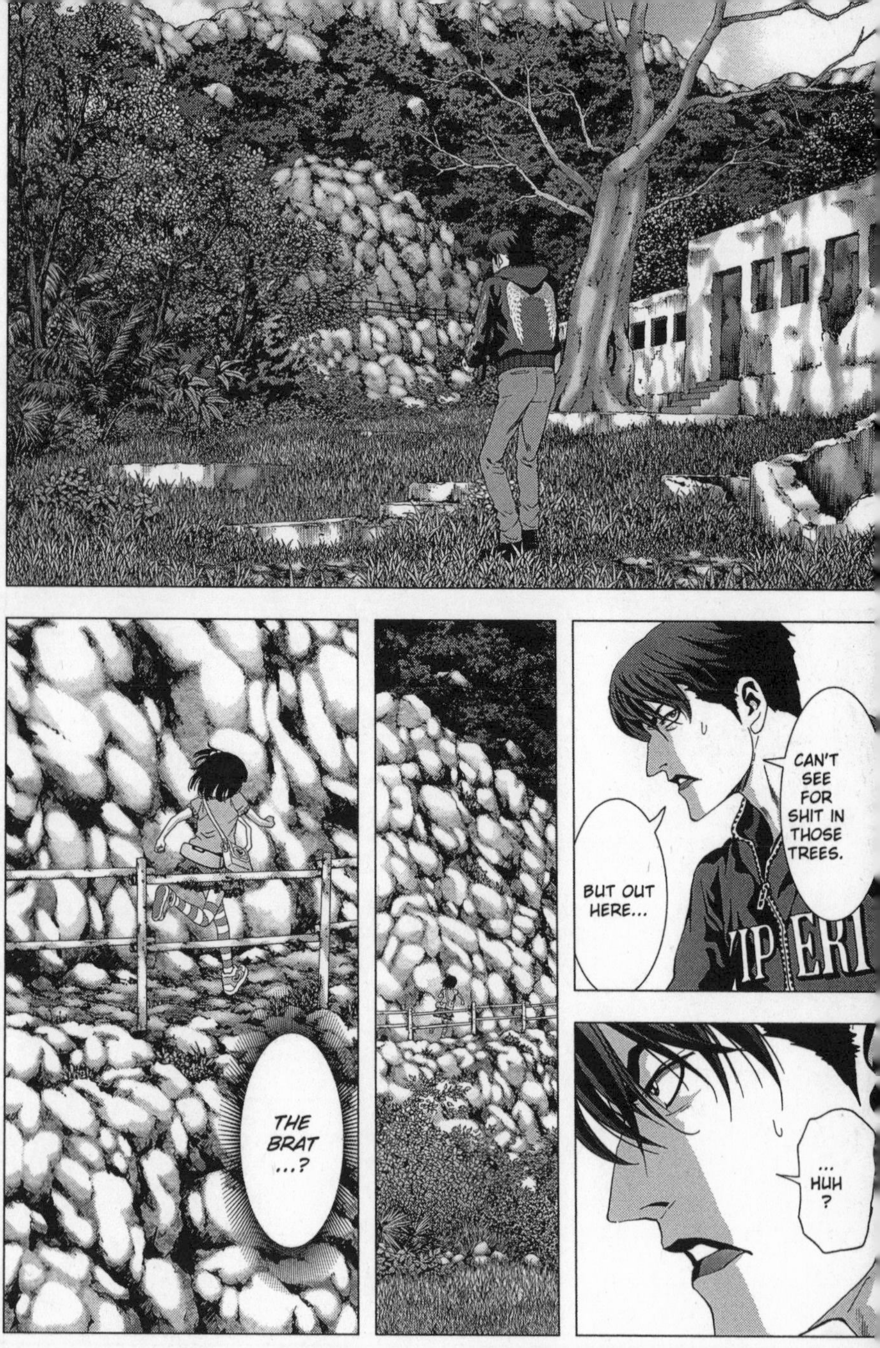
CAN'T SEE FOR SHIT IN THOSE TREES.
BUT OUT HERE...
...HUH?
THE BRAT...?

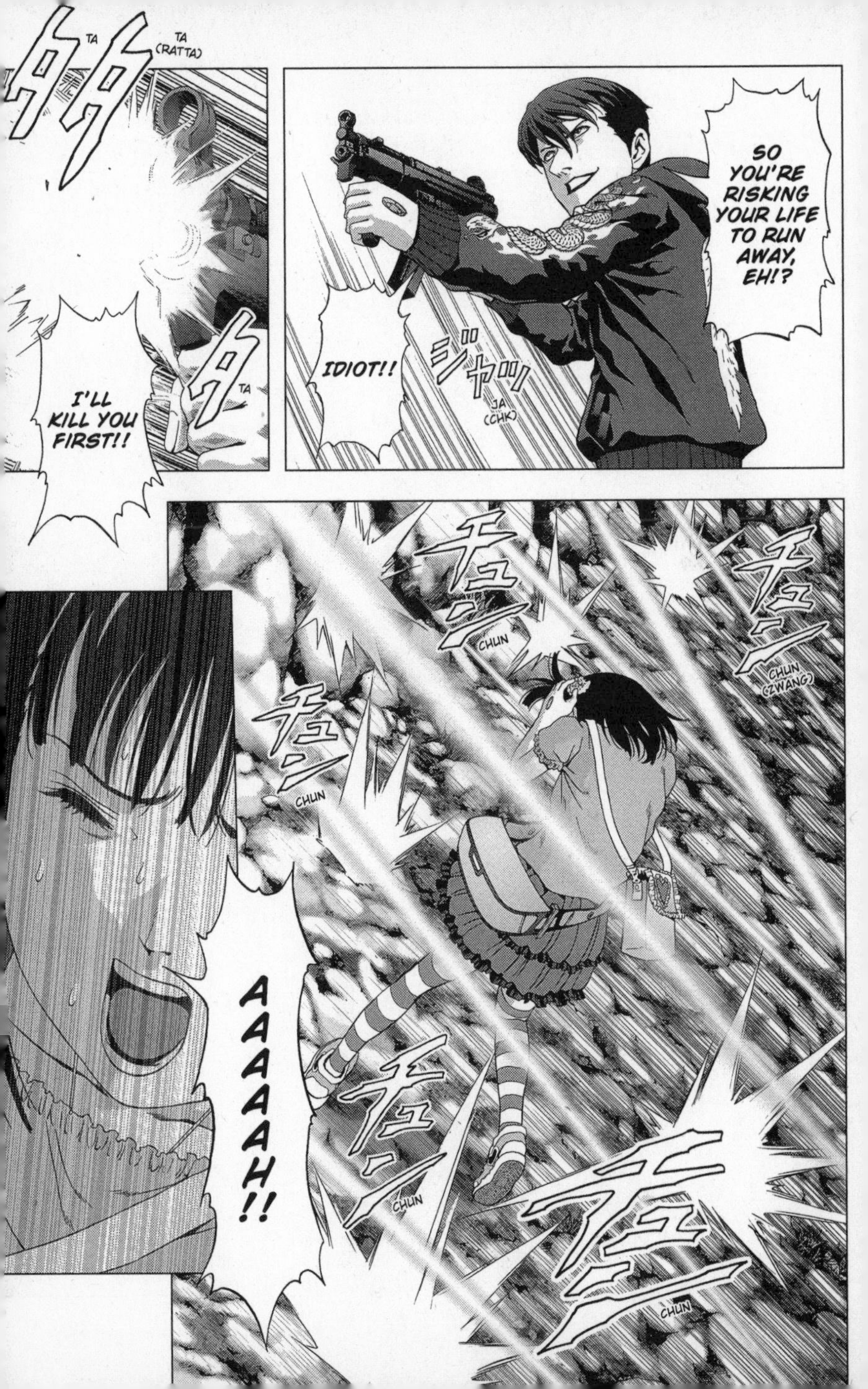

SO YOU'RE RISKING YOUR LIFE TO RUN AWAY, EH!?
ジャッ
JA (CHK)
IDIOT!!
タタ
TA TA (RATTA)
タ
TA
I'LL KILL YOU FIRST!!
チュン
CHUN (ZWANG)
チュン
CHUN
チュン
CHUN
AAAAAAH!!
チュン
CHUN
チュン
CHUN

DOGOUU
(KABOOM)

DOGO
(BOOM)

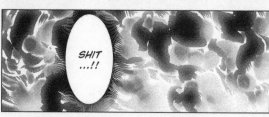

SHIT
...!!

YOU GOT ME GOOD, OLD MAN!!

I'M GONNA SNIPE YOU BOTH DOWN FROM HERE...

WITH ALL THIS SMOKE... I CAN'T SEE A THING!!

40

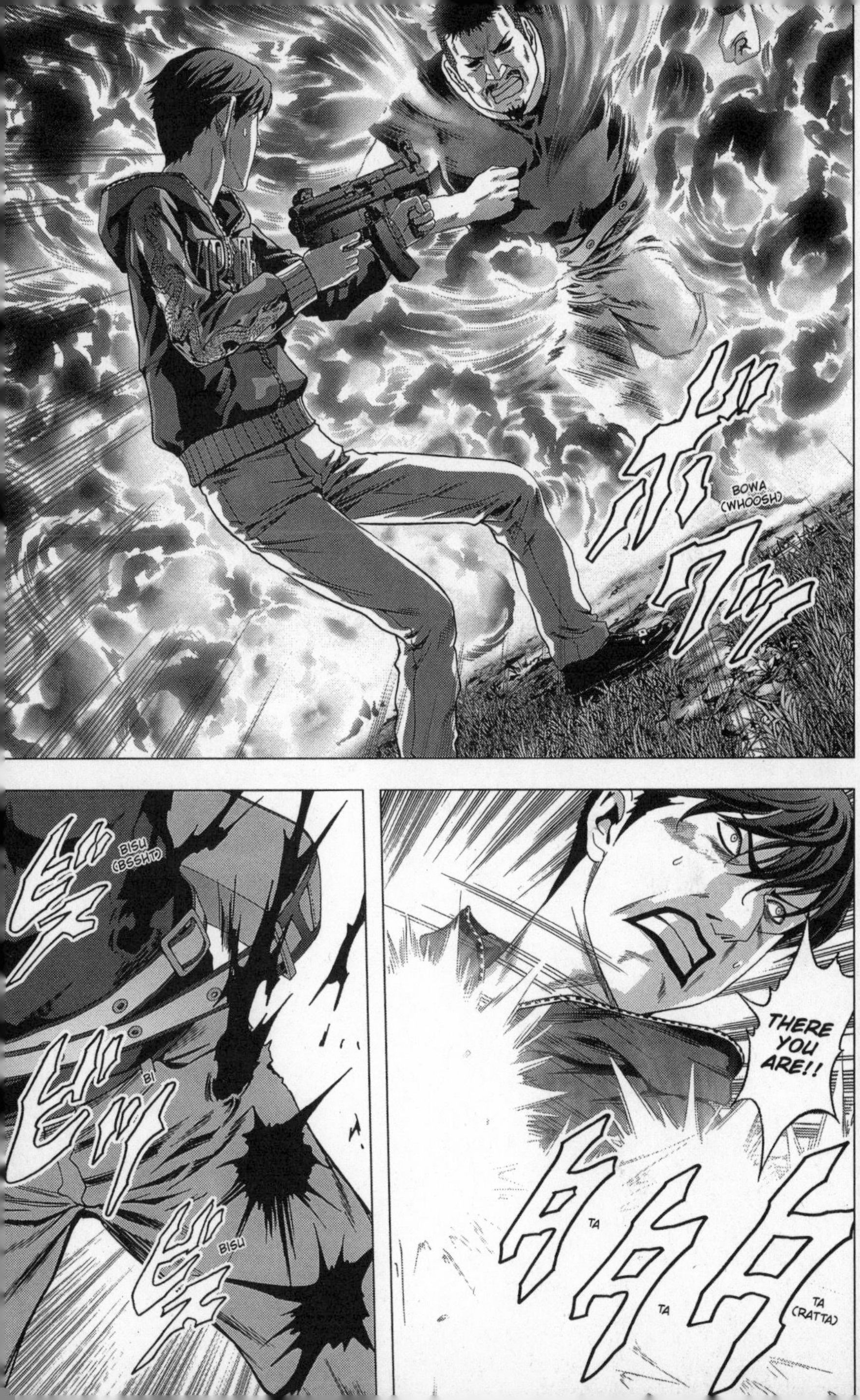
BOWA (WHOOSH)
THERE YOU ARE!!
TA
TA
TA (RATTA)
BISU (BSSHT)
BI
BISU

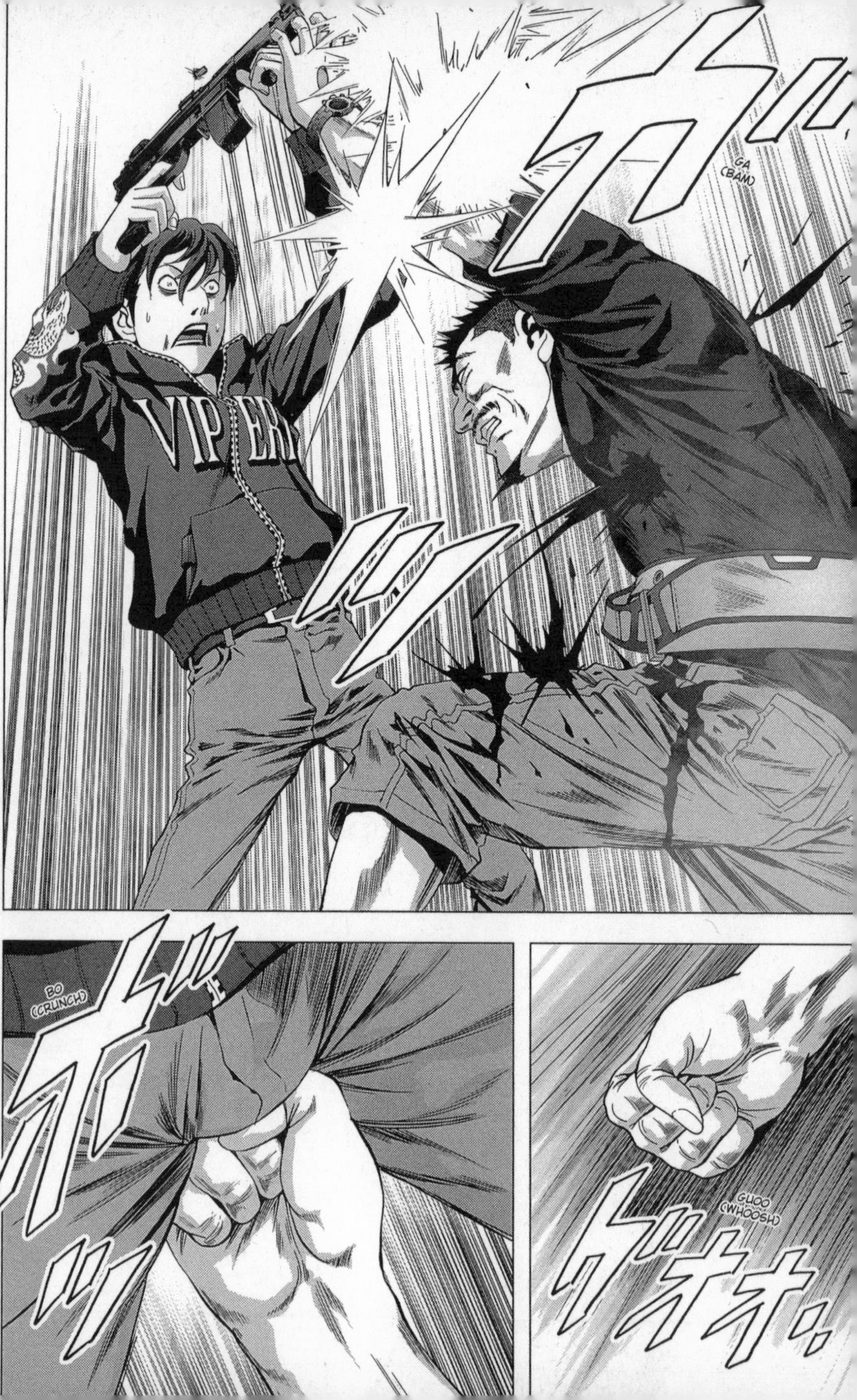
GA
(BAM)
GUOO
(WHOOSH)
BO
(CRUNCH)

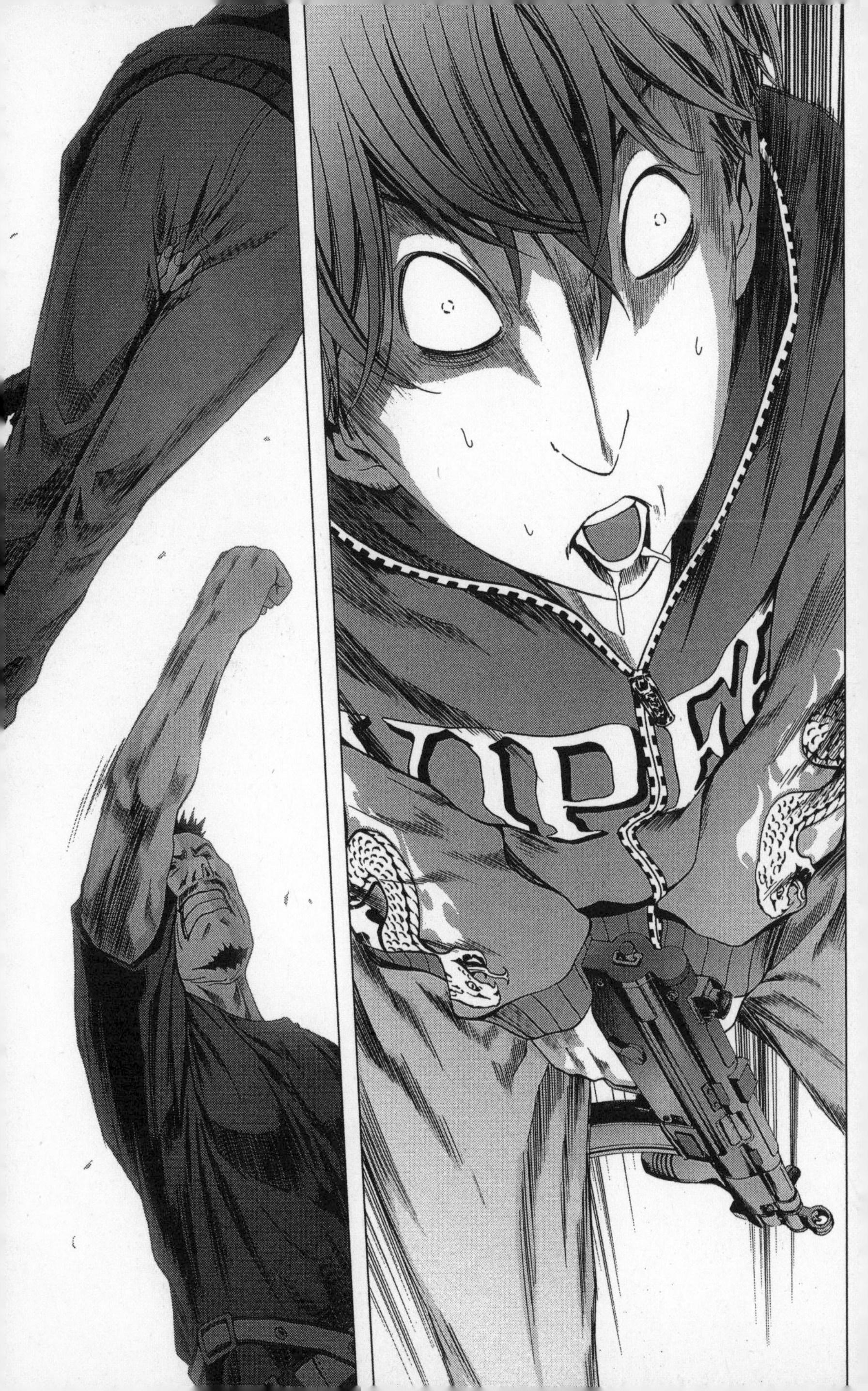

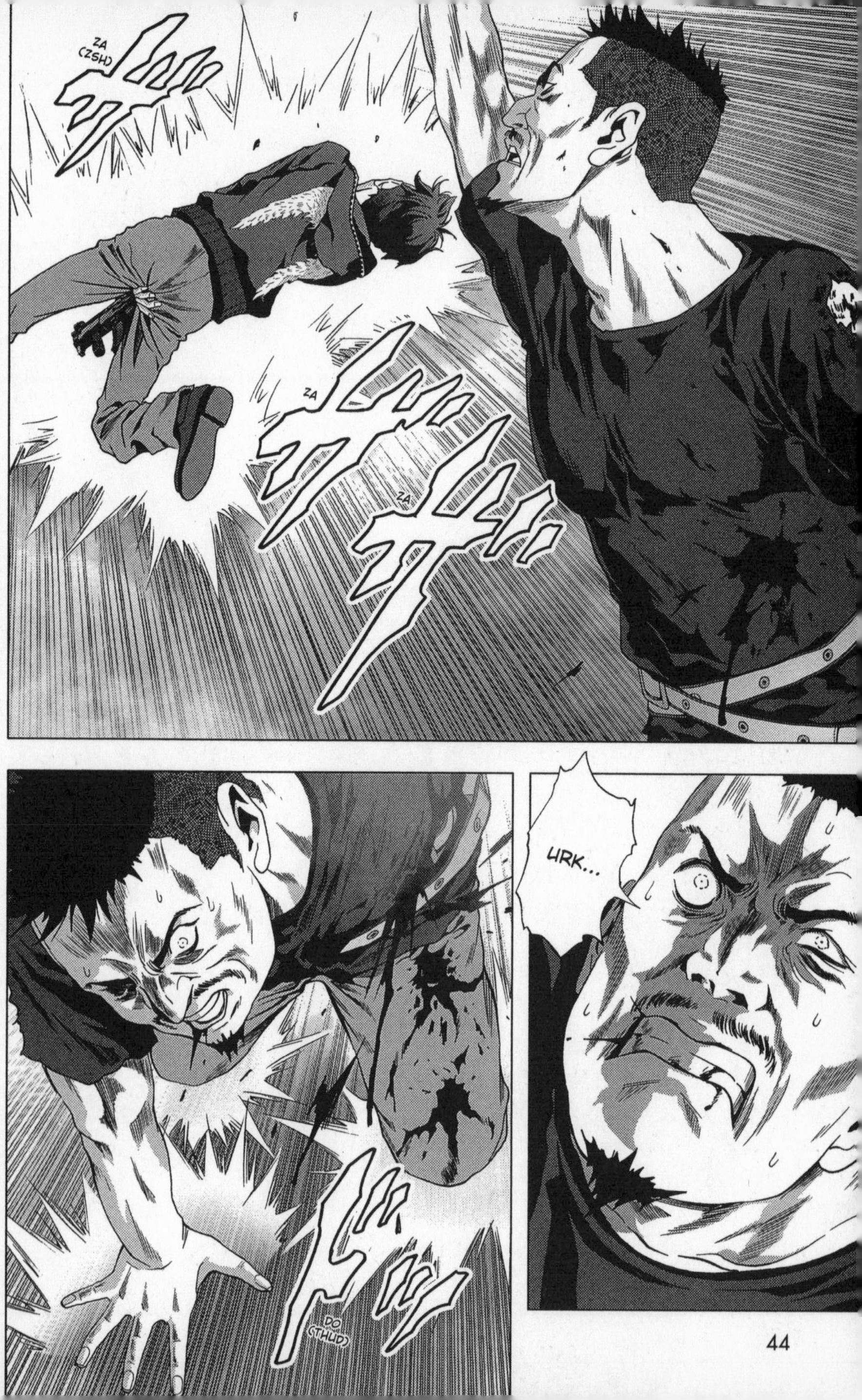
ZA
(ZSH)
ZA
ZA
URK...
DO
(THUD)

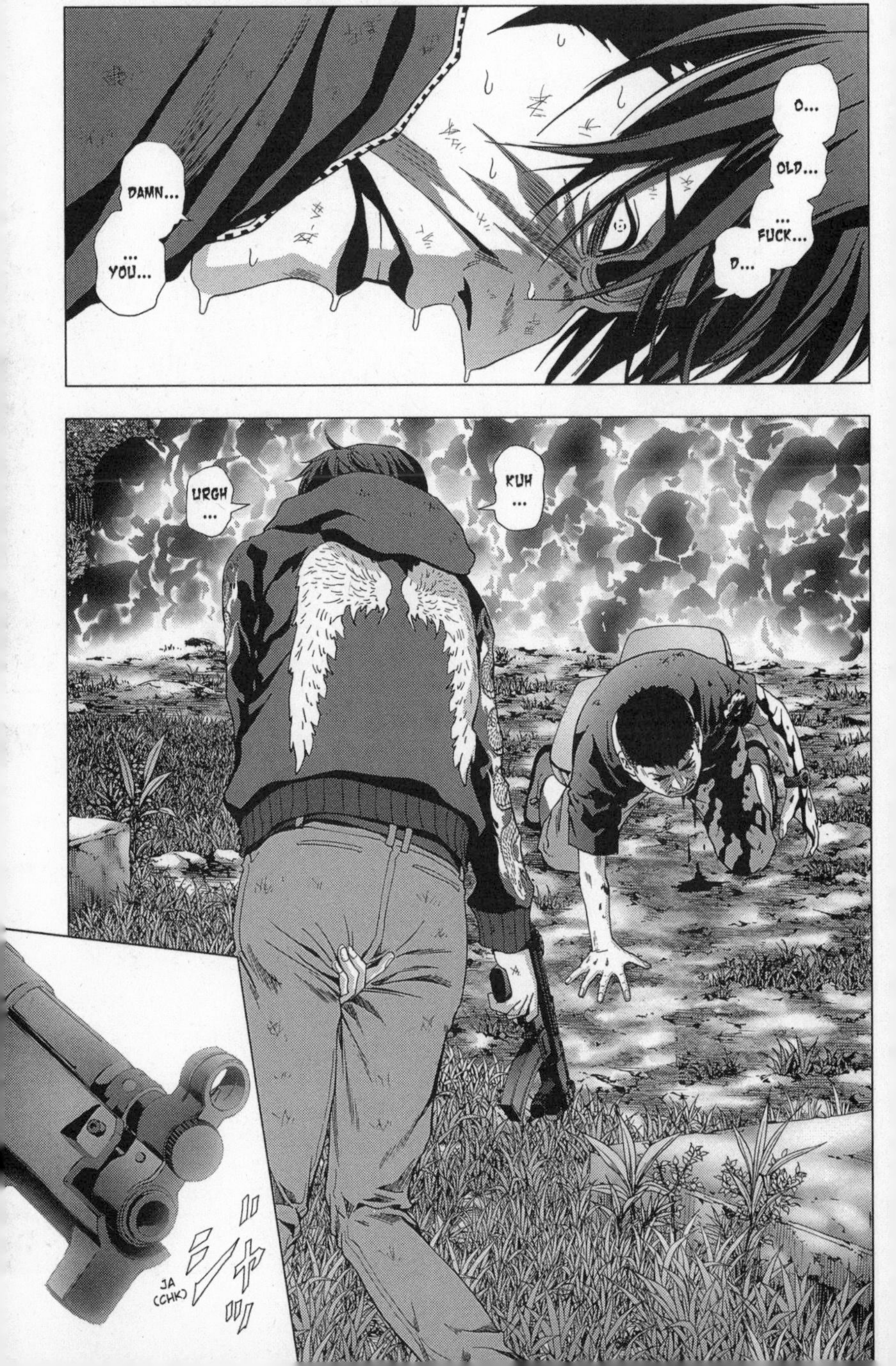
O...
OLD...
...FUCK...
D...
DAMN...
...YOU...
KUH
...
URGH
...
JA
(CHK)

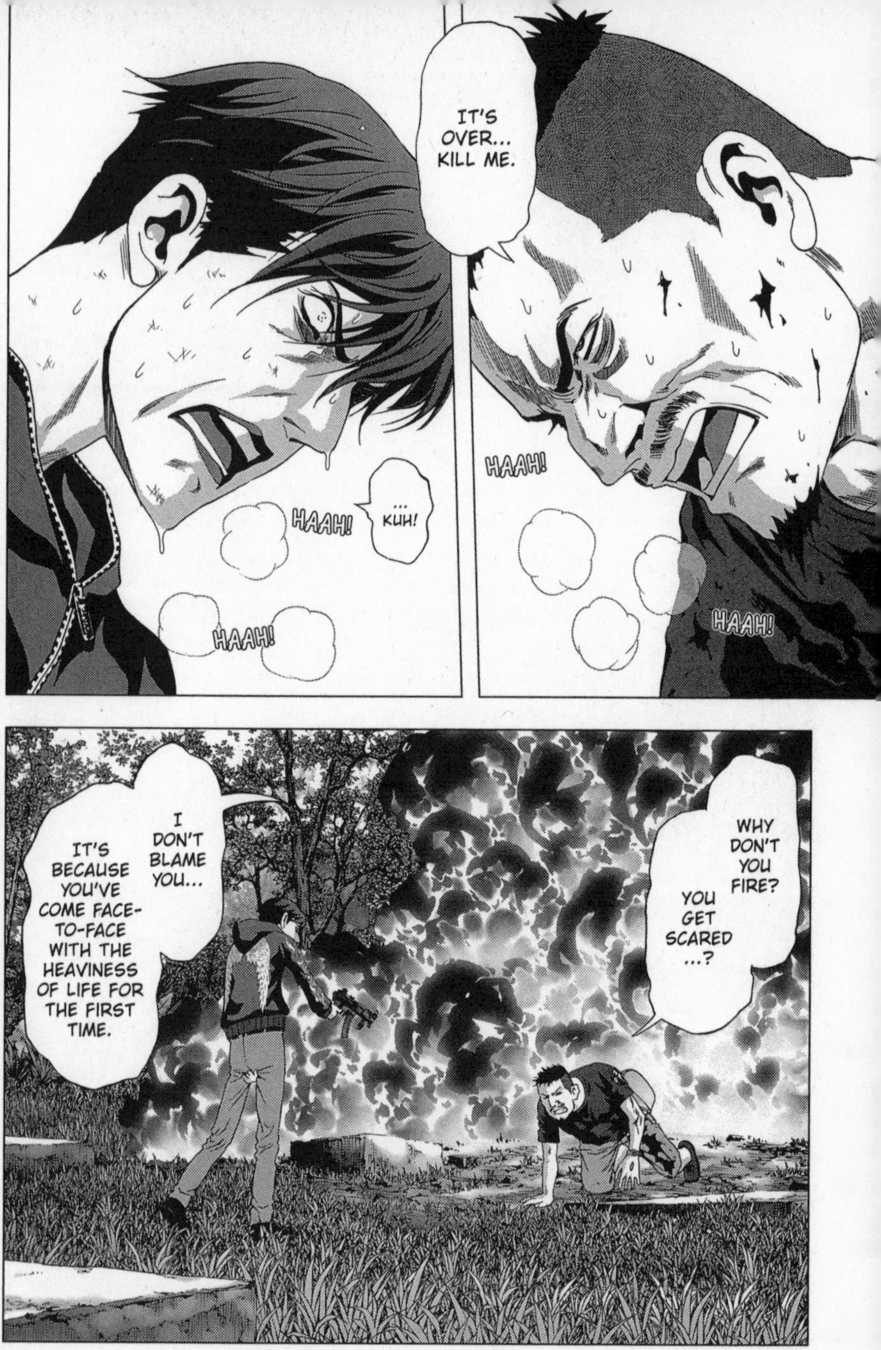
IT'S OVER... KILL ME.
HAAH!
HAAH!
... KUH!
HAAH!
HAAH!
WHY DON'T YOU FIRE?
YOU GET SCARED ...?
I DON'T BLAME YOU...
IT'S BECAUSE YOU'VE COME FACE-TO-FACE WITH THE HEAVINESS OF LIFE FOR THE FIRST TIME.

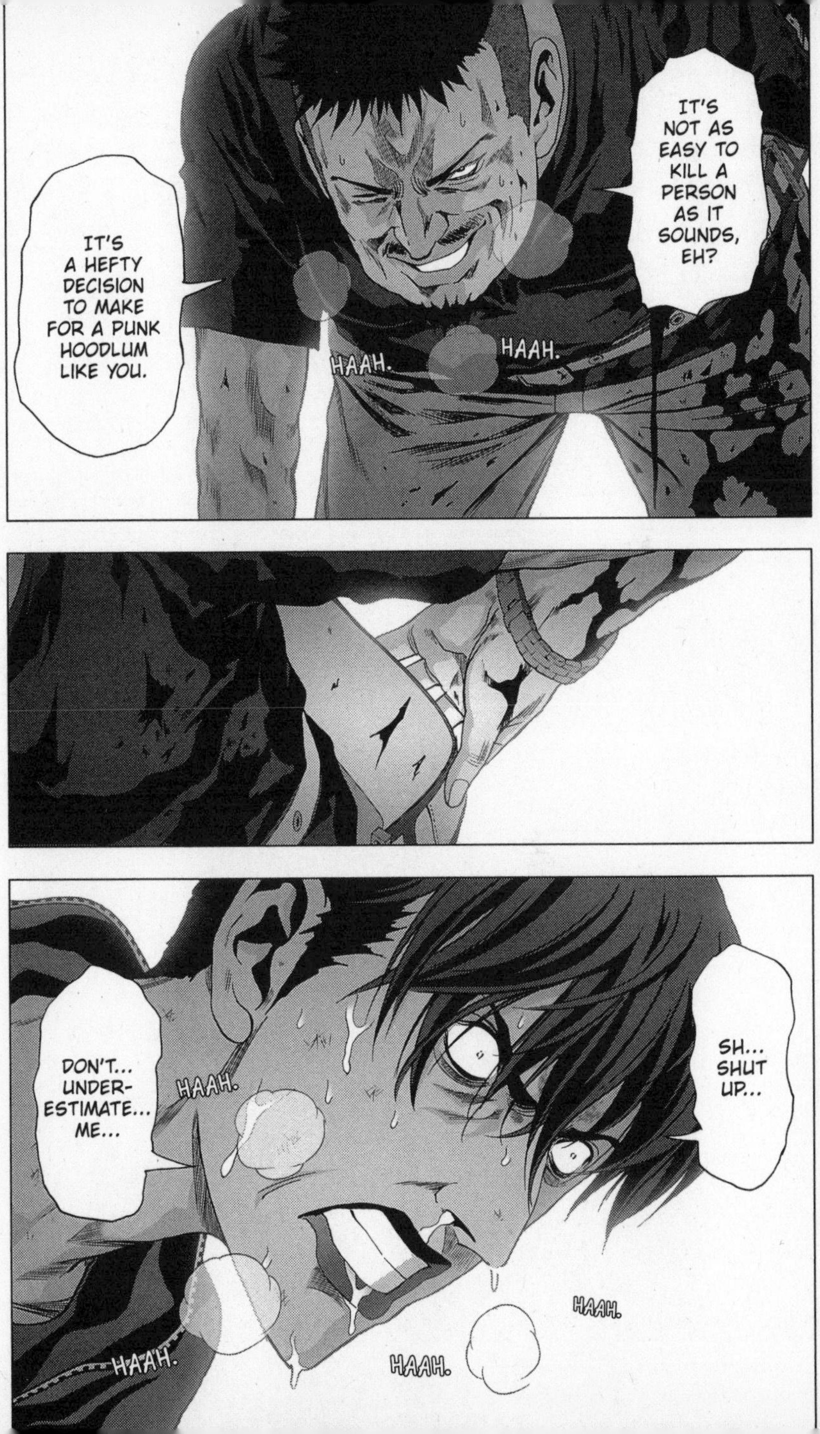
IT'S NOT AS EASY TO KILL A PERSON AS IT SOUNDS, EH?
HAAH.
HAAH.
IT'S A HEFTY DECISION TO MAKE FOR A PUNK HOODLUM LIKE YOU.
SH... SHUT UP...
HAAH.
DON'T... UNDER-ESTIMATE... ME...
HAAH.
HAAH.
HAAH.

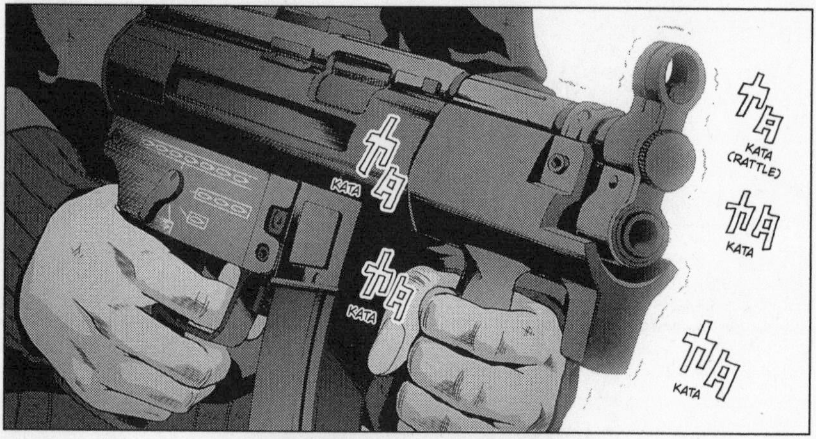
カタ
KATA (RATTLE)
カタ
KATA
カタ
KATA
カタ
KATA
カタ
KATA
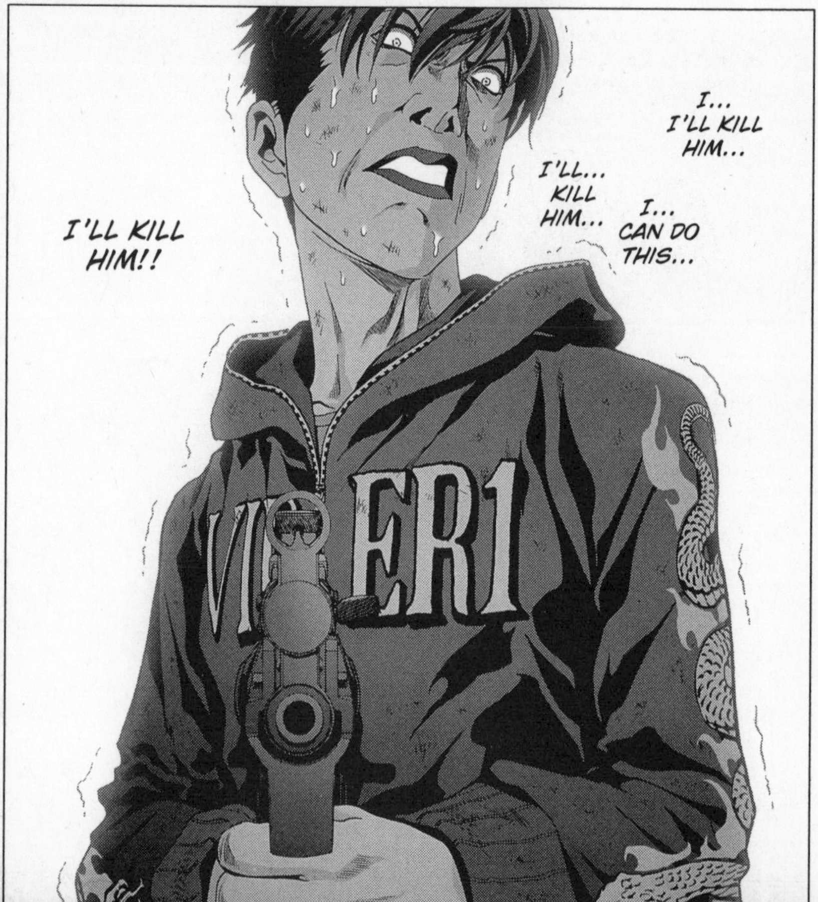
I... I'LL KILL HIM...
I'LL... KILL HIM...
I... CAN DO THIS...
I'LL KILL HIM!!

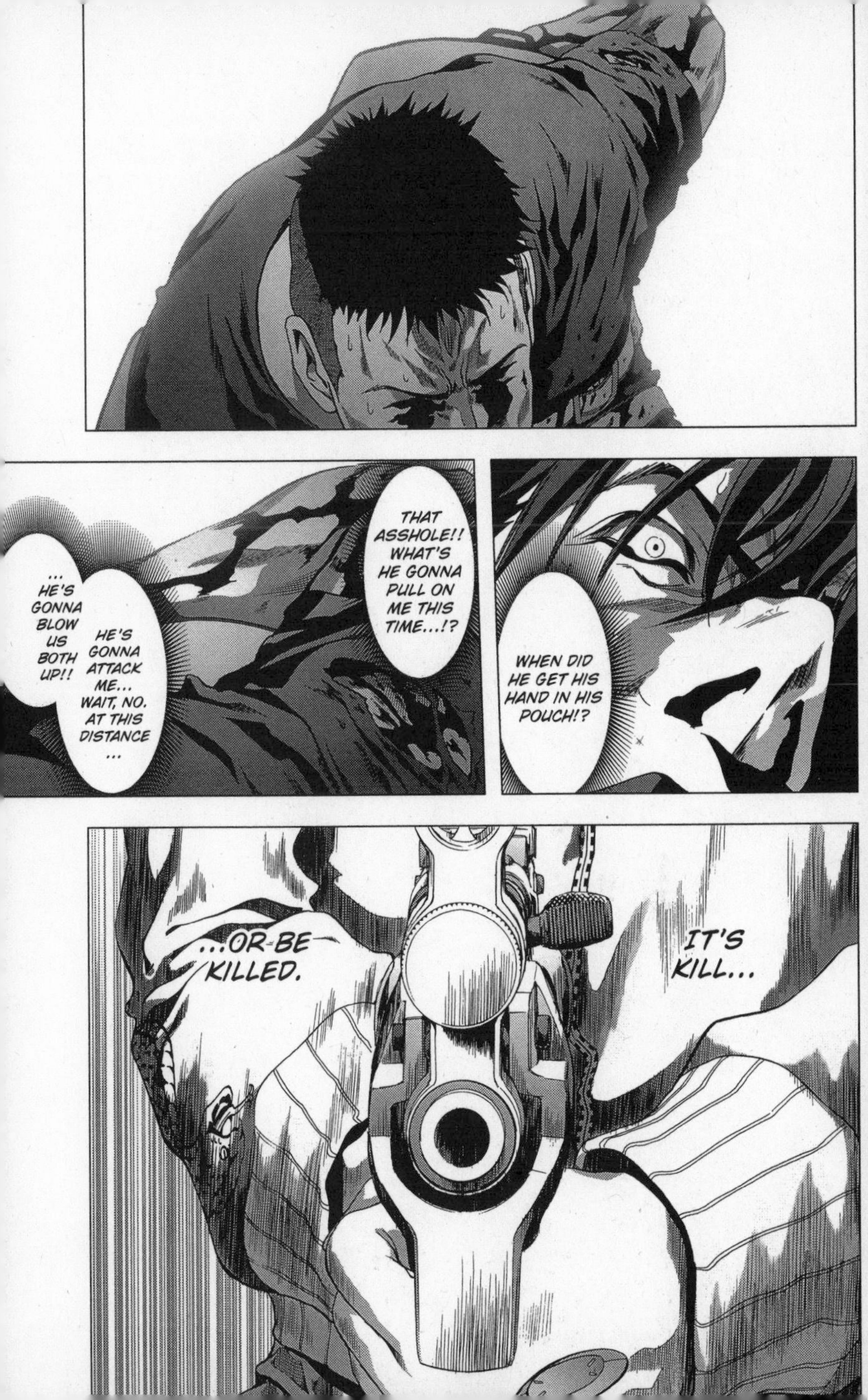
WHEN DID HE GET HIS HAND IN HIS POUCH!?
THAT ASSHOLE!! WHAT'S HE GONNA PULL ON ME THIS TIME...!?
HE'S GONNA ATTACK ME... WAIT, NO. AT THIS DISTANCE ...
... HE'S GONNA BLOW US BOTH UP!!
IT'S KILL...
...OR BE KILLED.

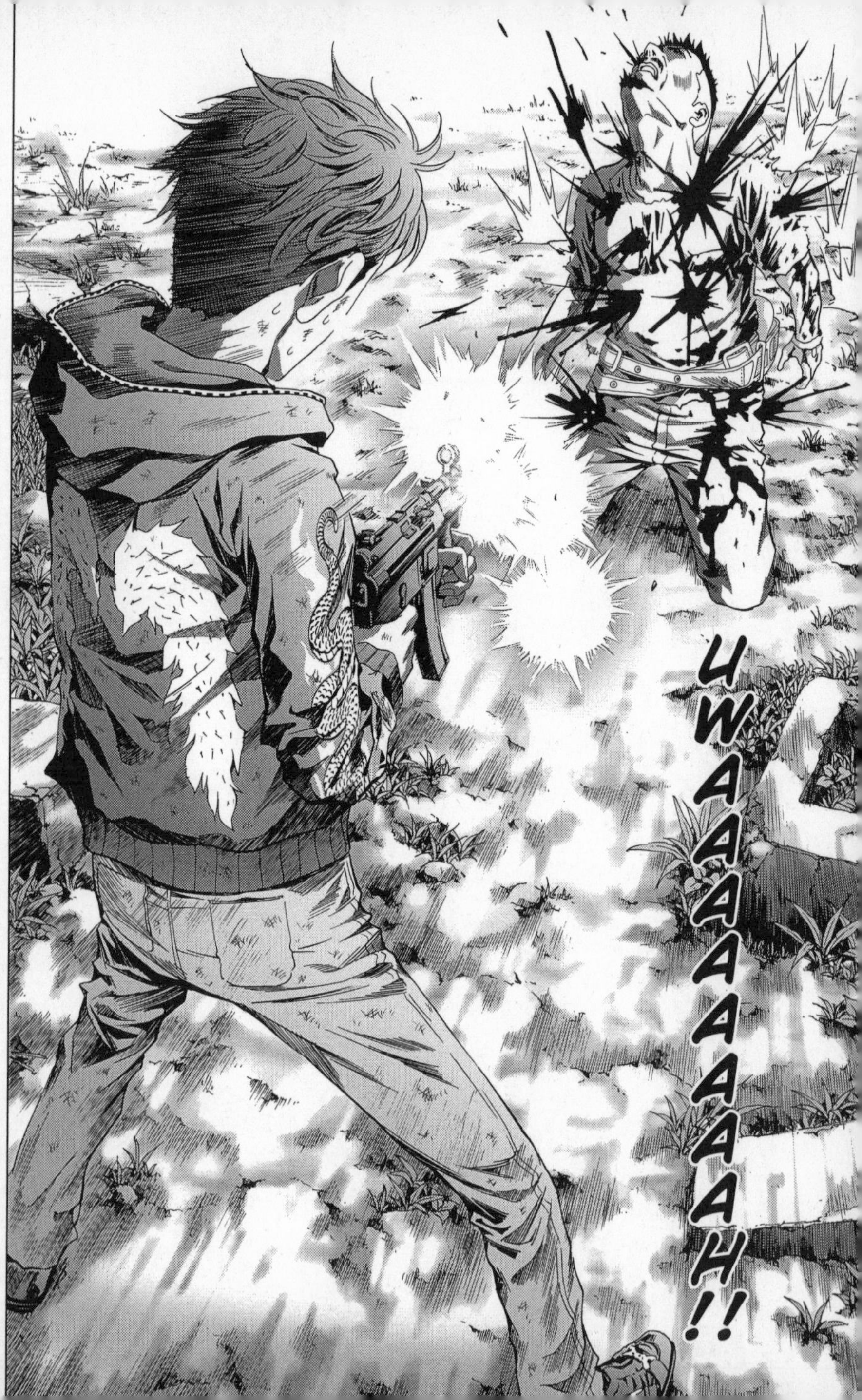
UWAAAAAAAAAH!!

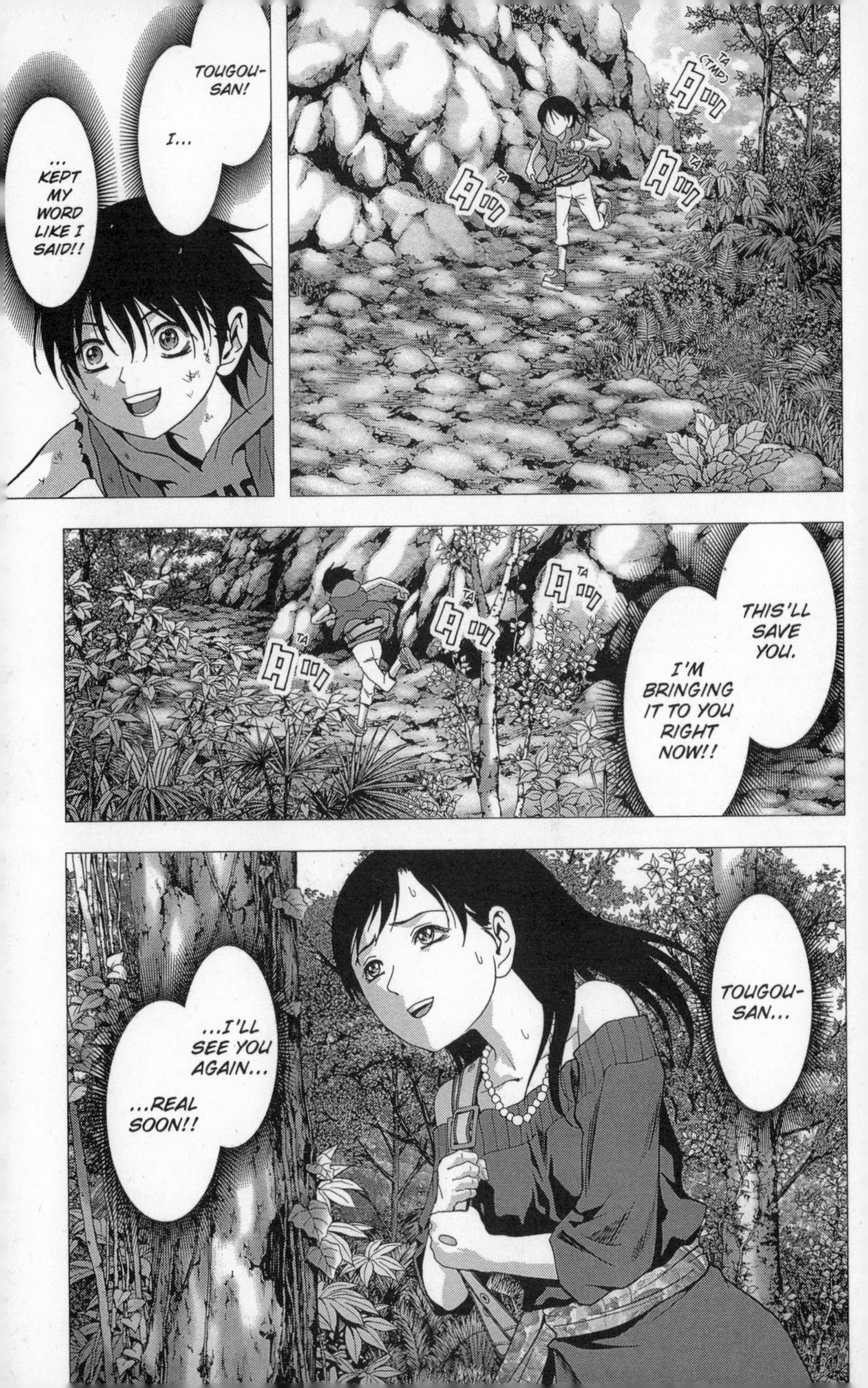
TA (TMP)
TA
TA
TOUGOU-SAN!
I...
...KEPT MY WORD LIKE I SAID!!
TA
TA
TA
THIS'LL SAVE YOU.
I'M BRINGING IT TO YOU RIGHT NOW!!
TOUGOU-SAN...
...I'LL SEE YOU AGAIN...
...REAL SOON!!

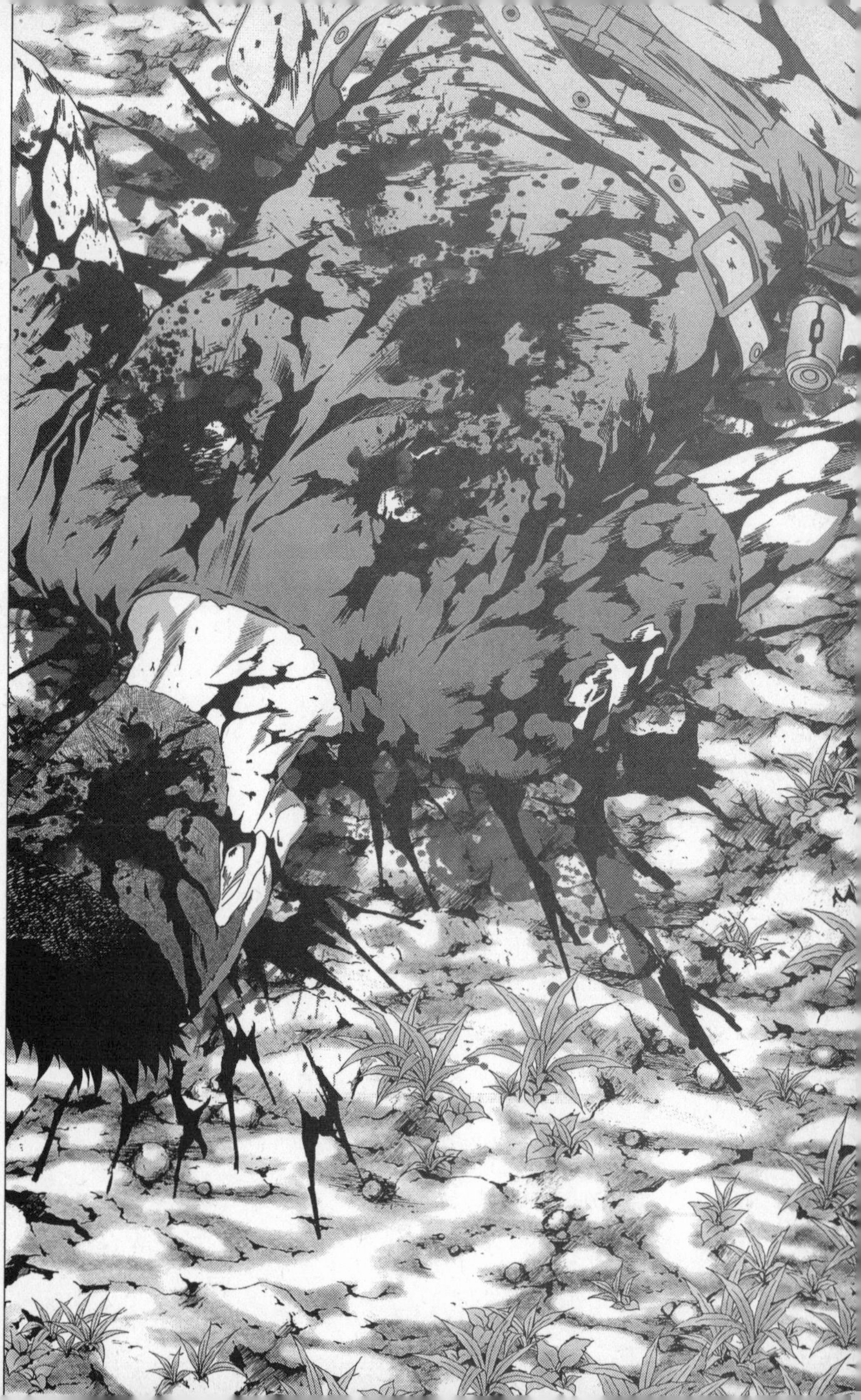

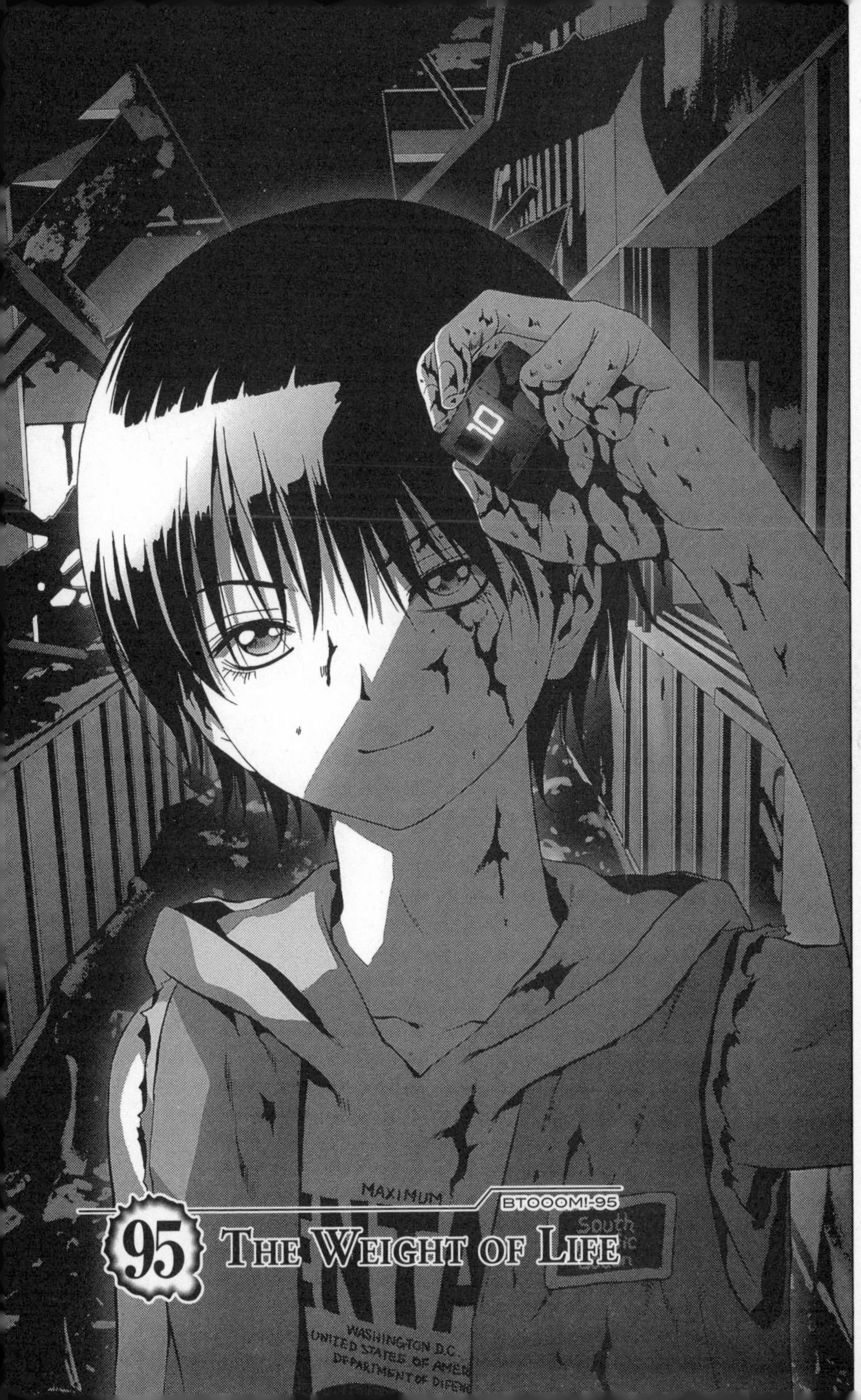
BTOOOM!-95
95
THE WEIGHT OF LIFE
MAXIMUM
WASHINGTON D.C.

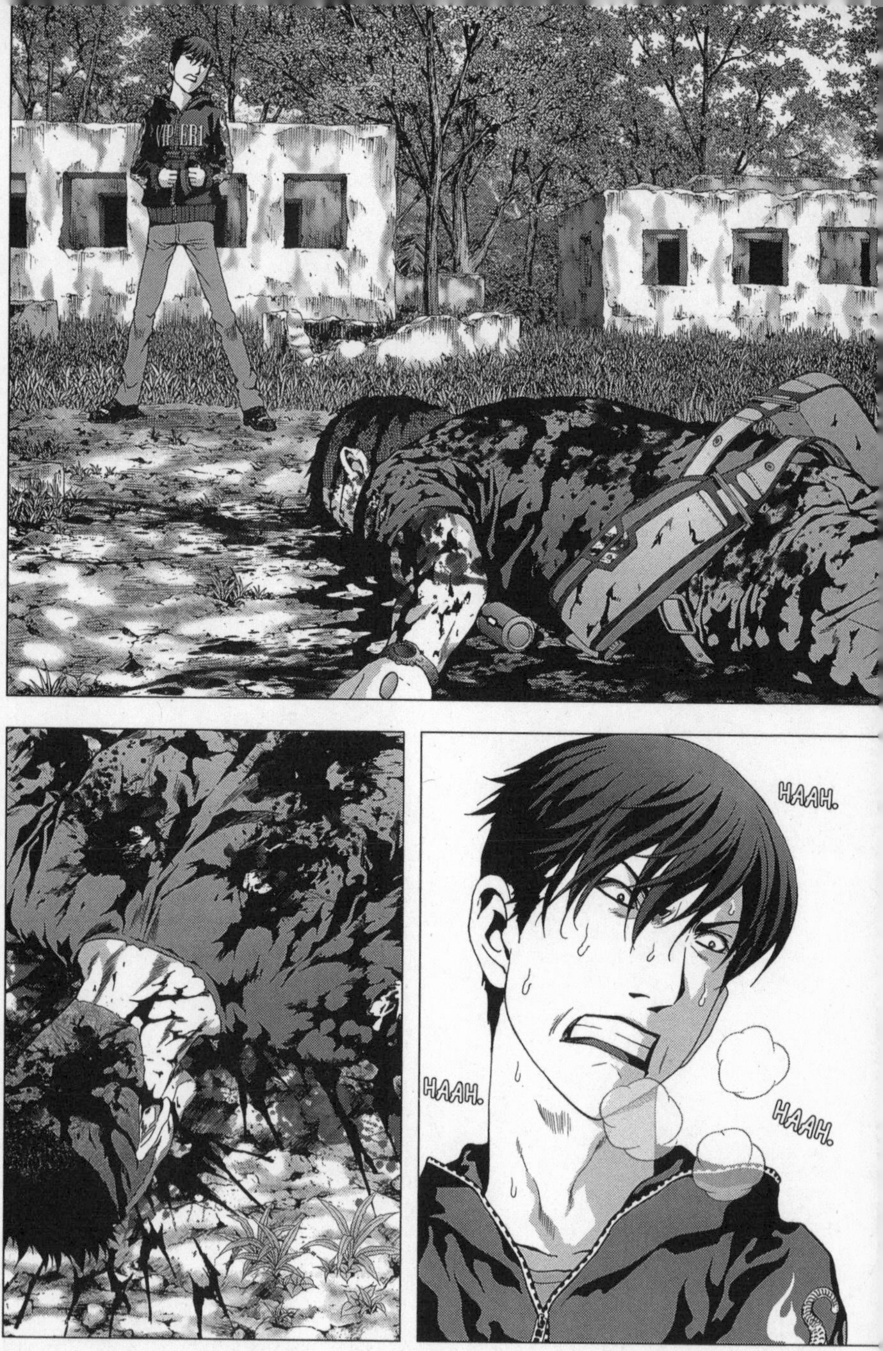
HAAH.
HAAH.
HAAH.

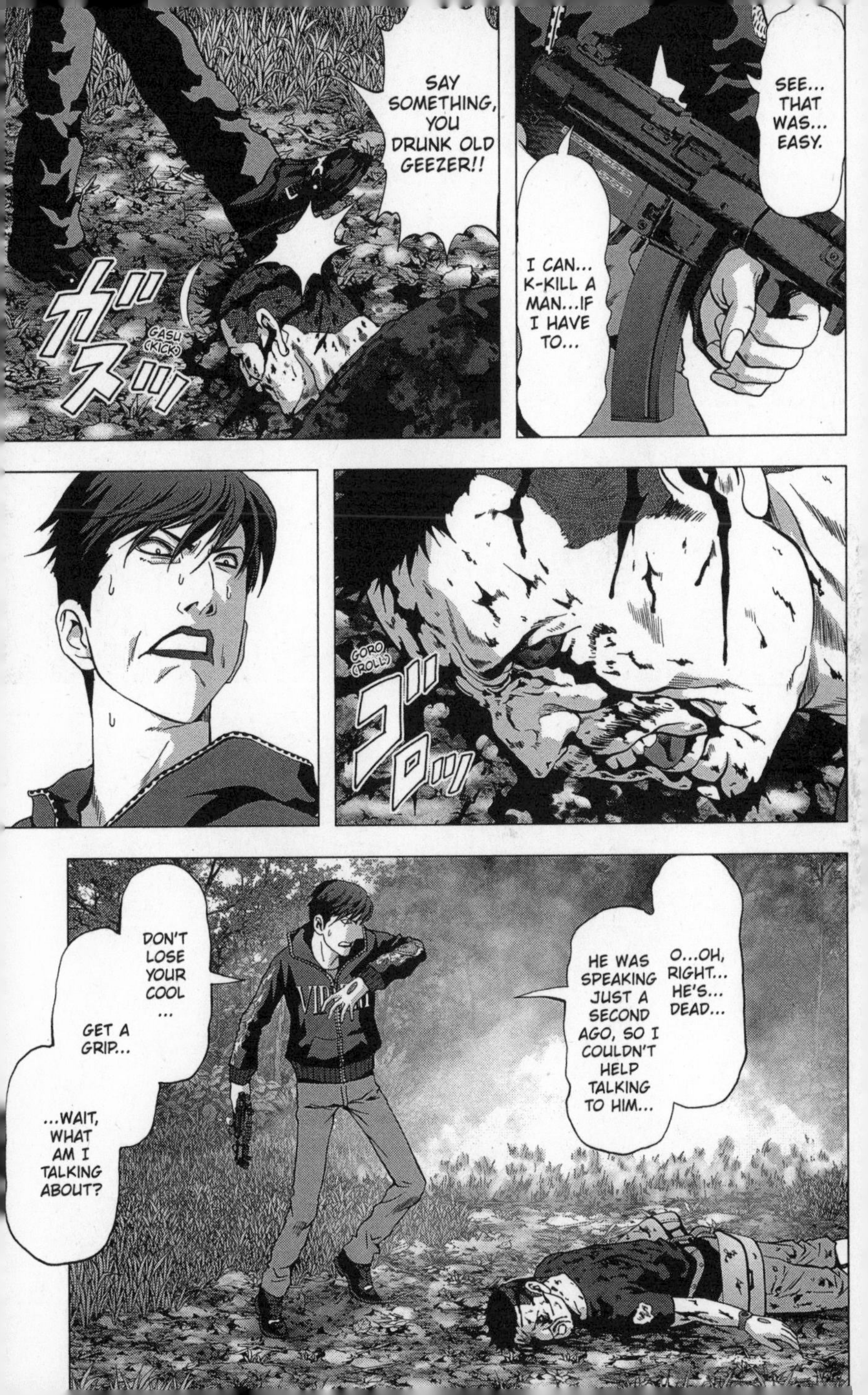
SEE... THAT WAS... EASY.
I CAN... K-KILL A MAN...IF I HAVE TO...
SAY SOMETHING, YOU DRUNK OLD GEEZER!!
ガスッ
GASU (KICK)
ゴロッ
GORO (ROLL)
O...OH, RIGHT... HE'S... DEAD...
HE WAS SPEAKING JUST A SECOND AGO, SO I COULDN'T HELP TALKING TO HIM...
DON'T LOSE YOUR COOL ...
GET A GRIP...
...WAIT, WHAT AM I TALKING ABOUT?

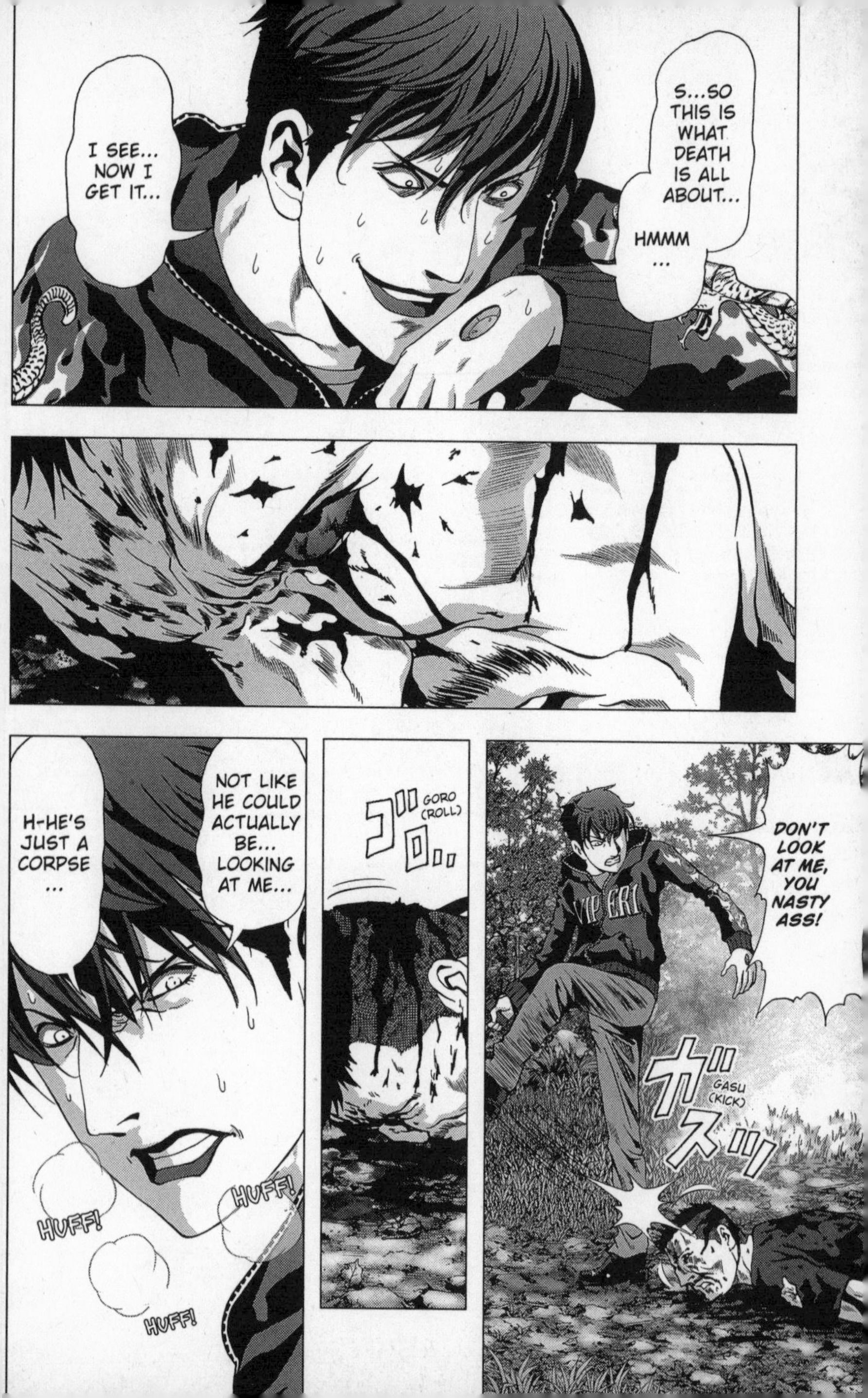
S...SO THIS IS WHAT DEATH IS ALL ABOUT...
HMMM ...
I SEE... NOW I GET IT...
DON'T LOOK AT ME, YOU NASTY ASS!
GASU (KICK)
GORO (ROLL)
NOT LIKE HE COULD ACTUALLY BE... LOOKING AT ME...
H-HE'S JUST A CORPSE ...
HUFF!
HUFF!
HUFF!

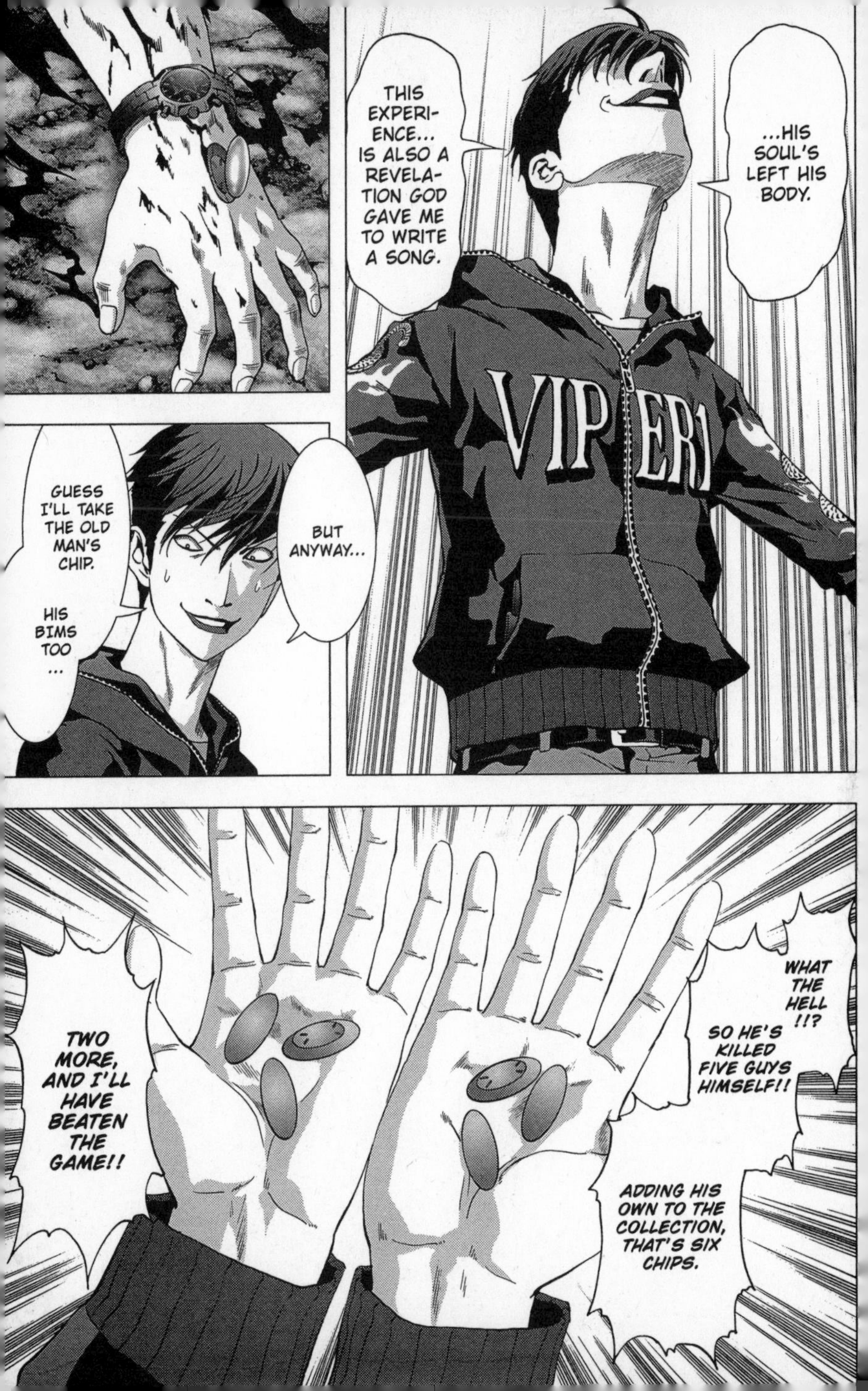
...HIS SOUL'S LEFT HIS BODY.
THIS EXPERIENCE... IS ALSO A REVELATION GOD GAVE ME TO WRITE A SONG.
VIPER1
BUT ANYWAY...
GUESS I'LL TAKE THE OLD MAN'S CHIP.
HIS BIMS TOO ...
WHAT THE HELL!!?
SO HE'S KILLED FIVE GUYS HIMSELF!!
ADDING HIS OWN TO THE COLLECTION, THAT'S SIX CHIPS.
TWO MORE, AND I'LL HAVE BEATEN THE GAME!!

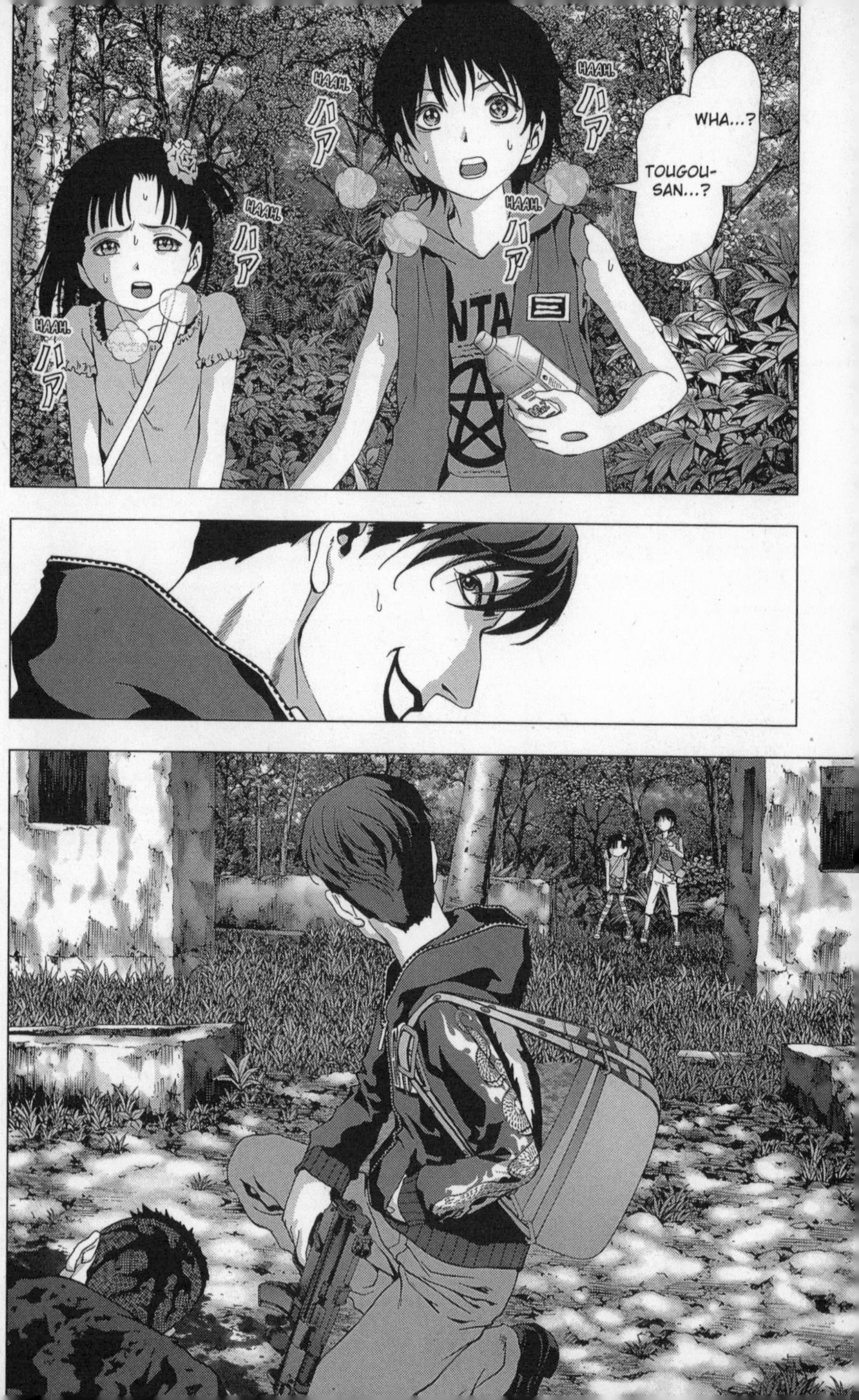
WHA...?
TOUGOU-SAN...?
HAAH. ハア
HAAH. ハア
HAAH. ハア
HAAH. ハア
HAAH. ハア

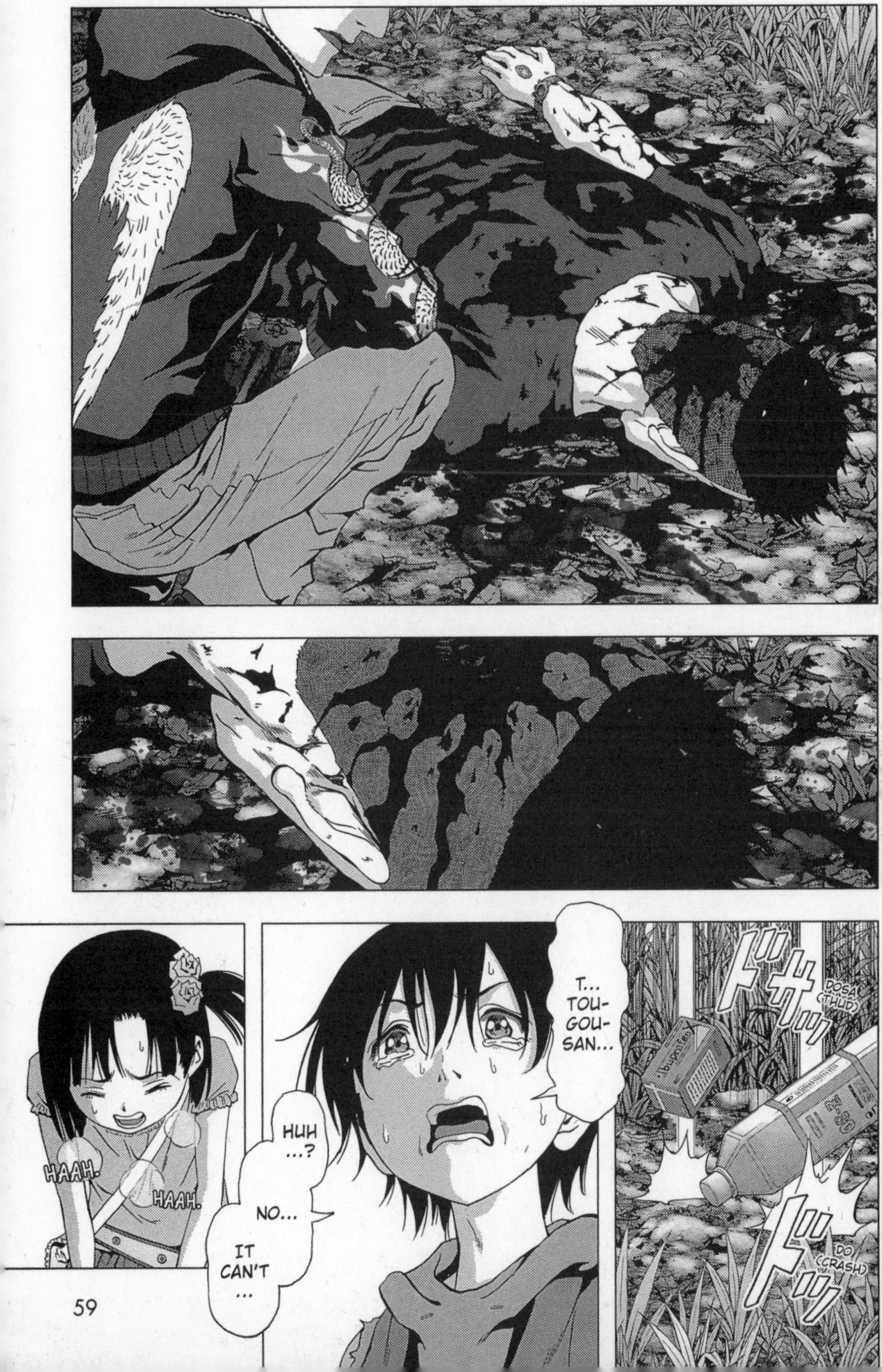
DOSA (THUD)
DO (CRASH)
T... TOUGOU-SAN...
HUH ...?
NO...
IT CAN'T ...
HAAH.
HAAH.

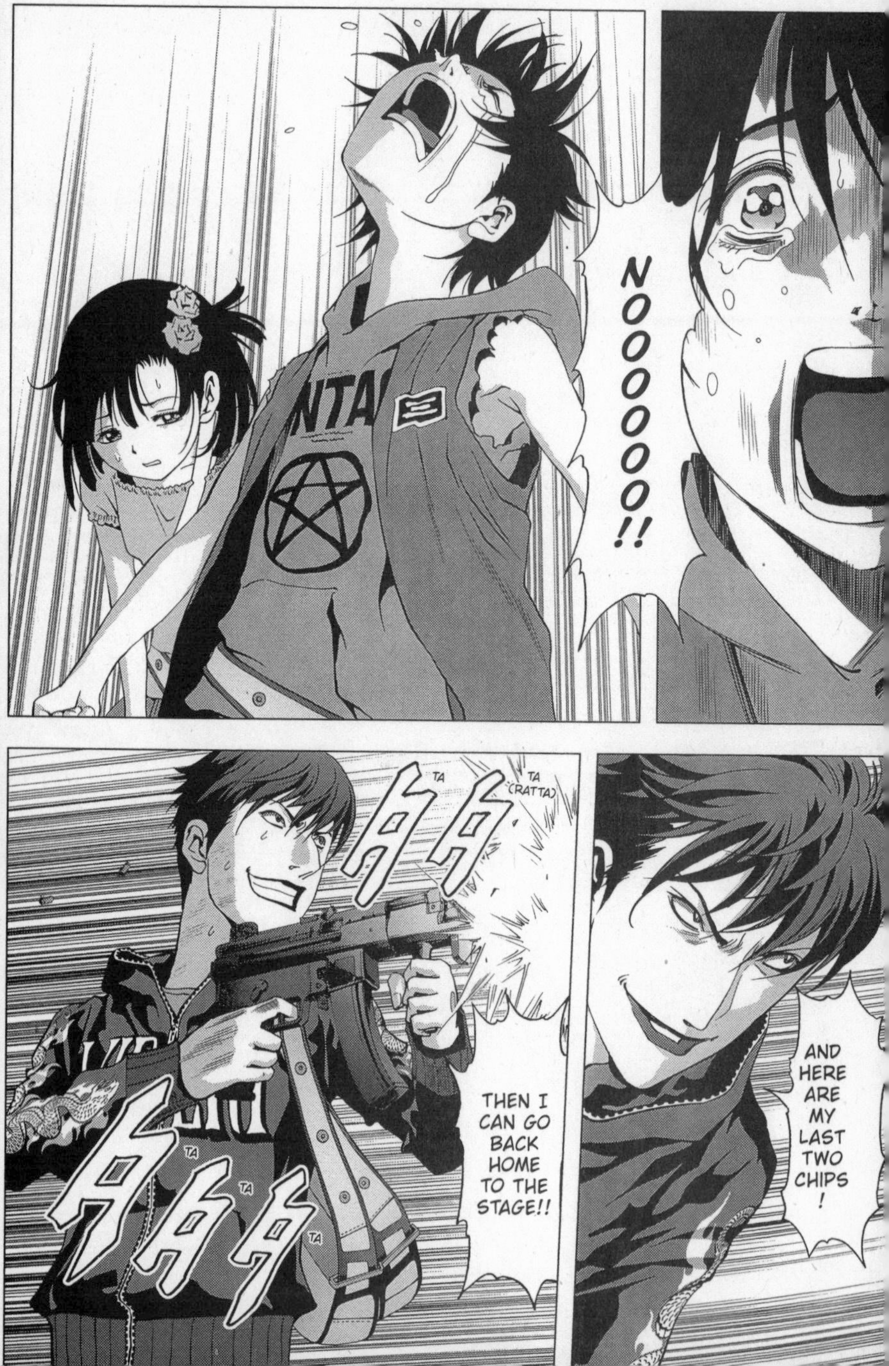
NOOOOOOOO!!
AND HERE ARE MY LAST TWO CHIPS!
TA
TA (RATTA)
THEN I CAN GO BACK HOME TO THE STAGE!!
TA
TA
TA

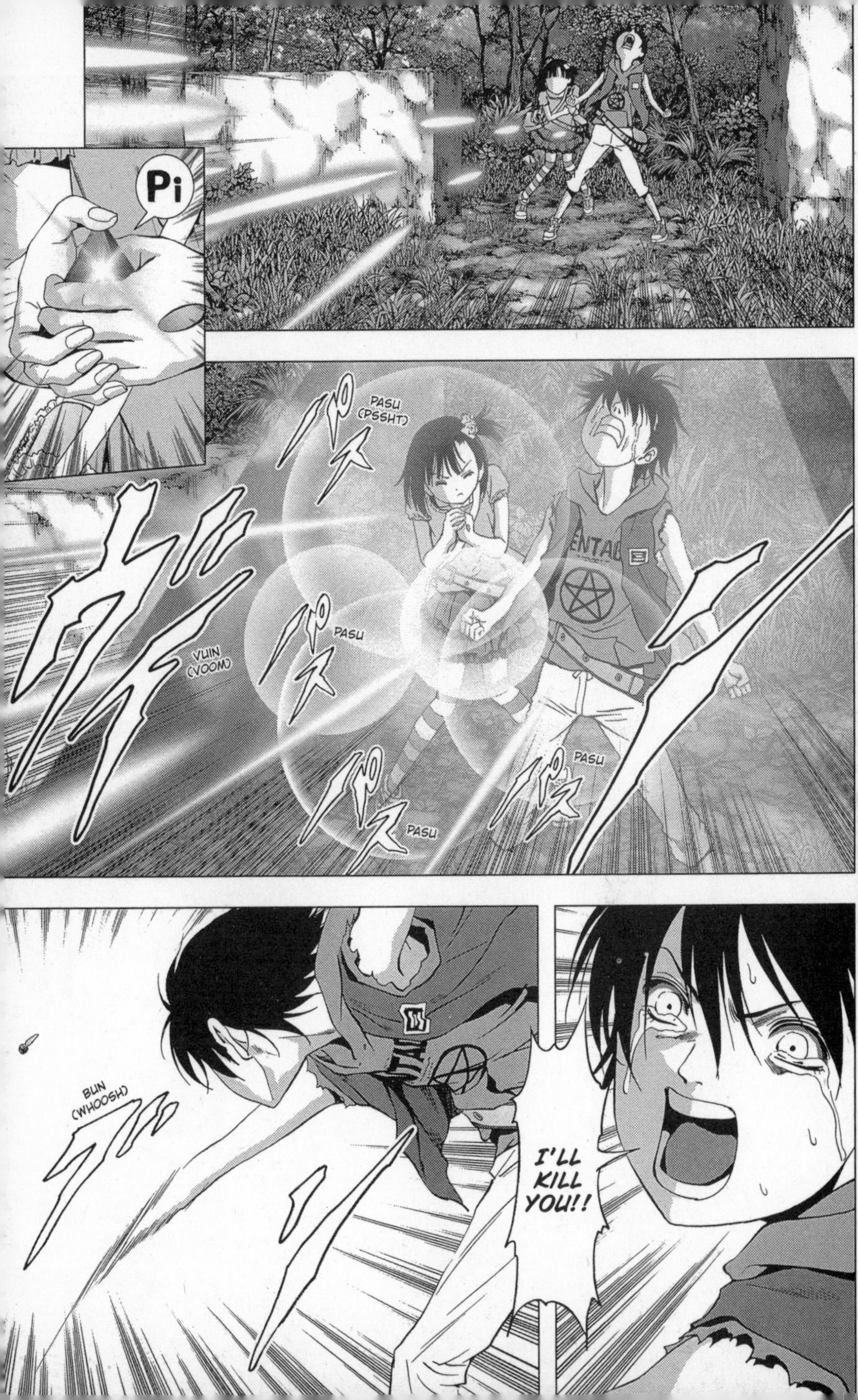
Pi
PASU (PSSHT)
PASU
VUIN (VOOM)
PASU
PASU
I'LL KILL YOU!!
BUN (WHOOSH)

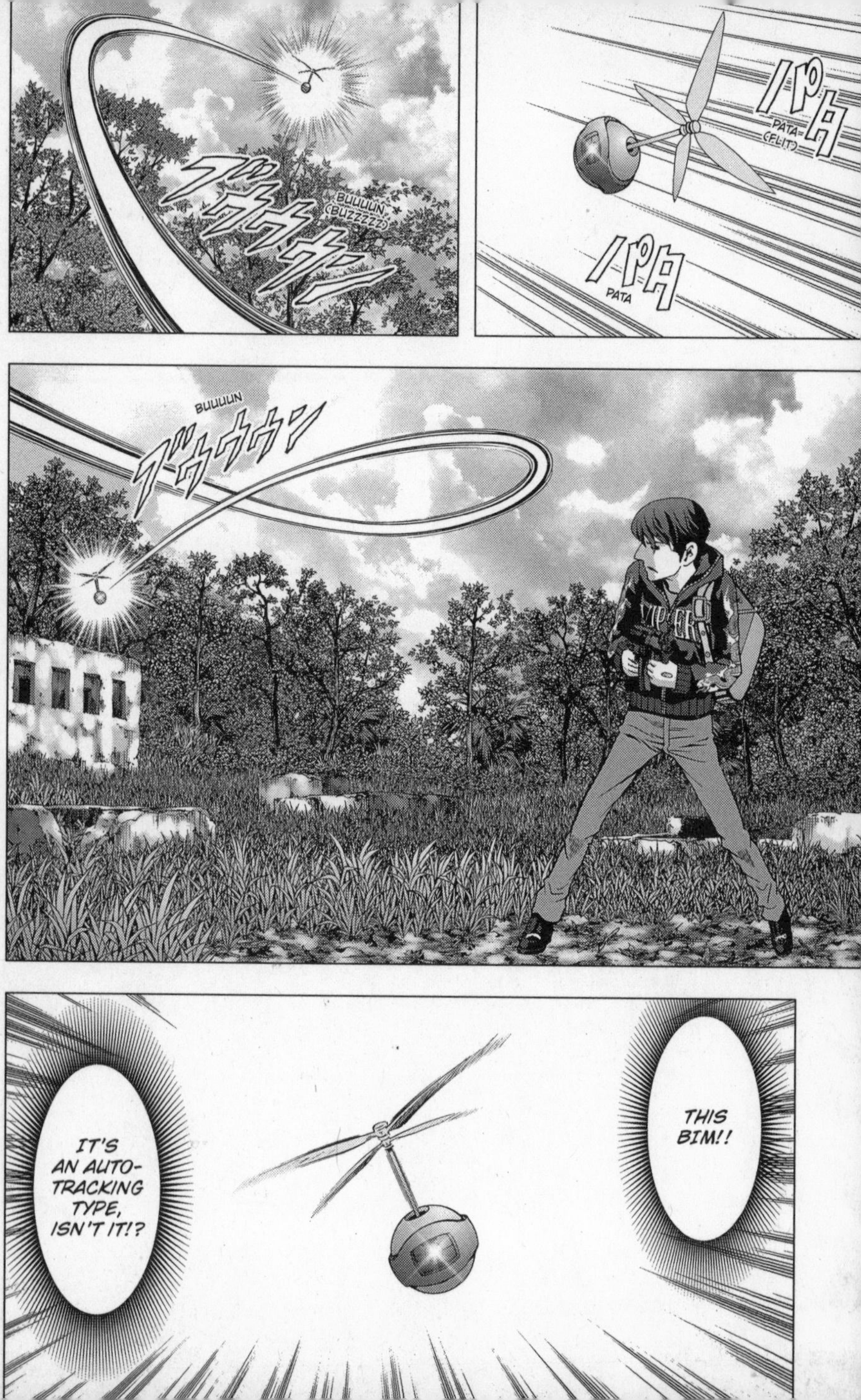

パタ
PATA (FLIT)
パタ
PATA
BUUUUN (BUZZZZZ)
BUUUUN
THIS BIM!!
IT'S AN AUTO-TRACKING TYPE, ISN'T IT!?

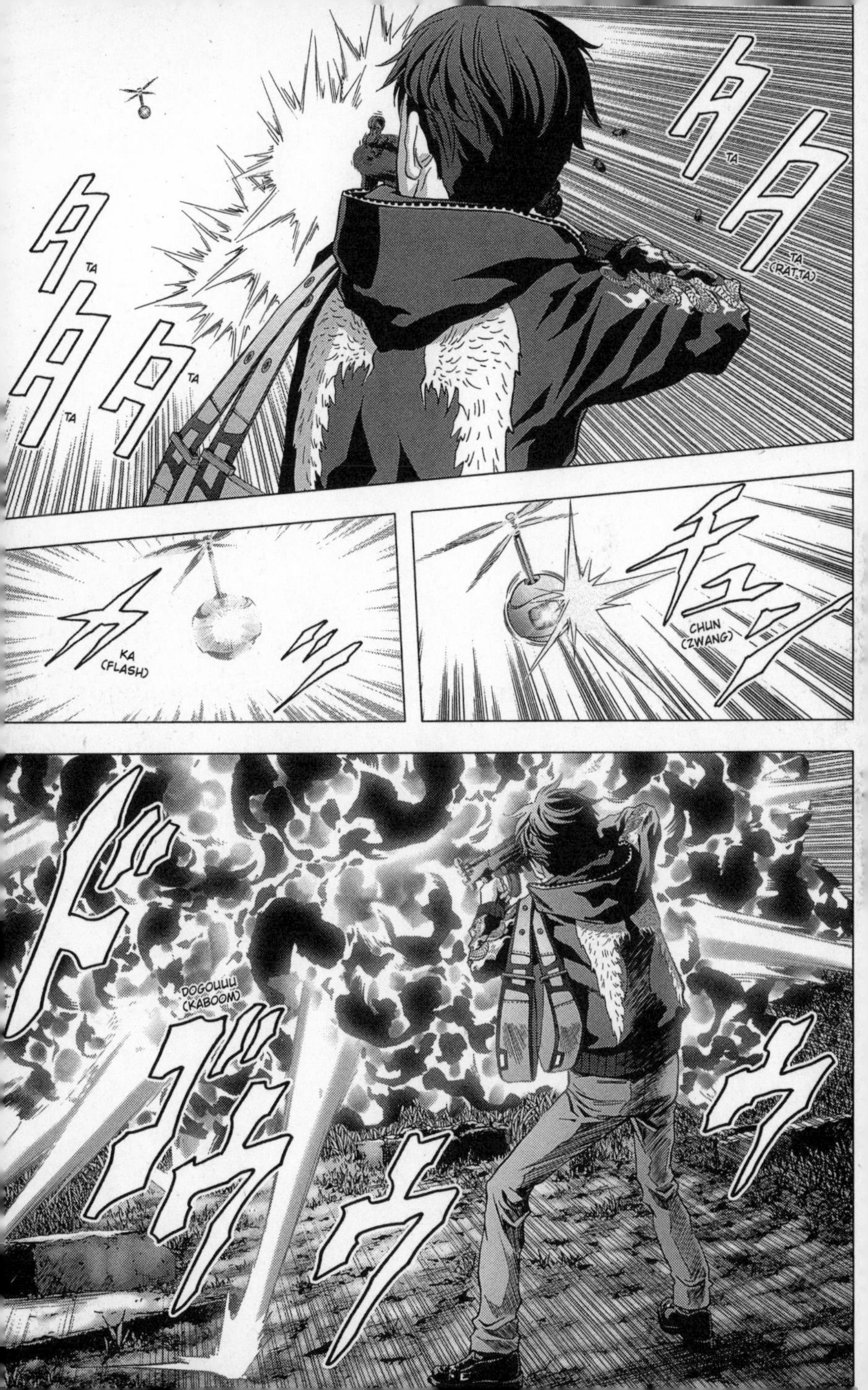
TA
TA
(RAT-TA)
TA
TA
TA
CHUN
(ZWANG)
KA
(FLASH)
DOGOUUU
(KABOOM)

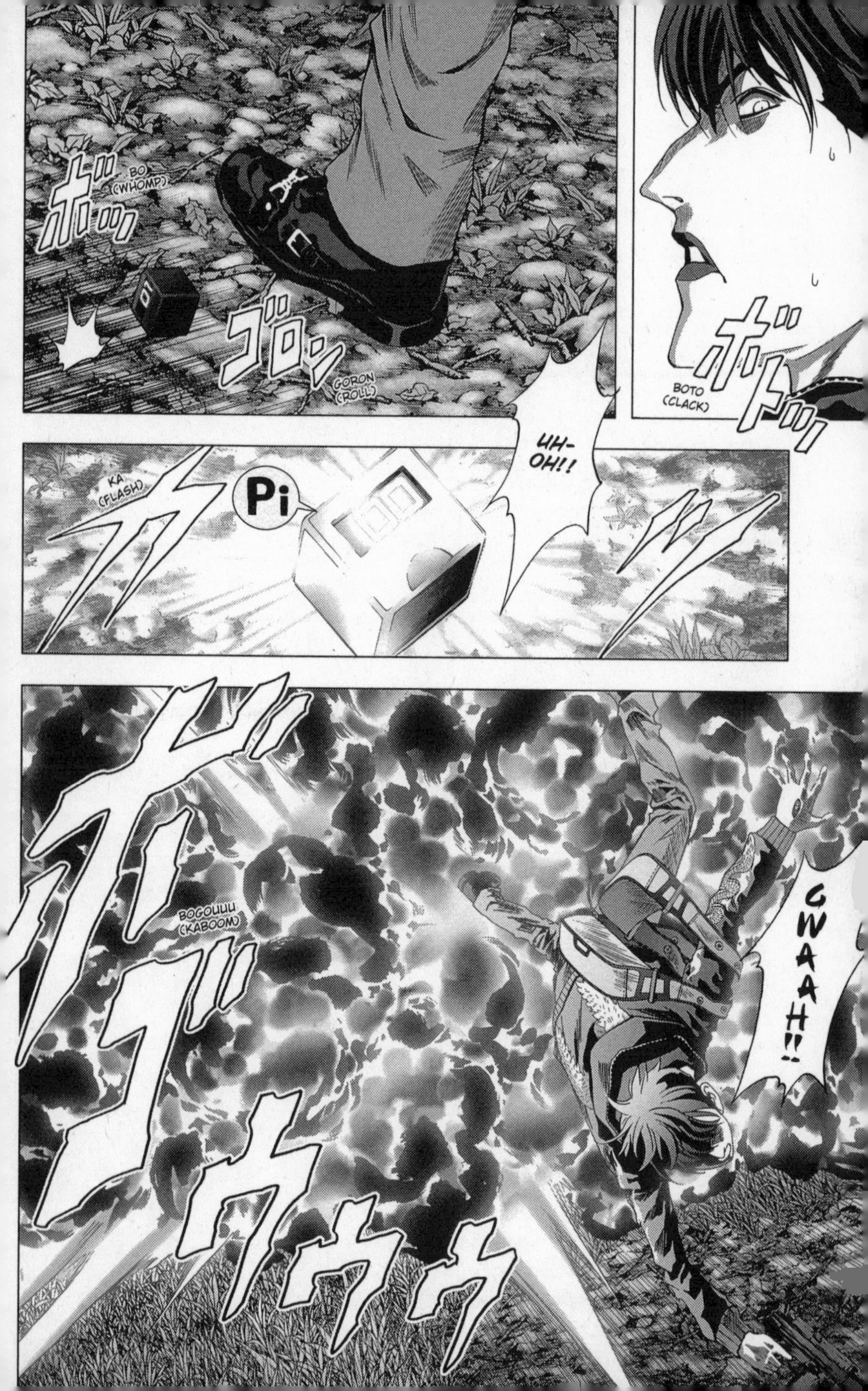
BOTO (CLACK)
BO (WHOMP)
GORON (ROLL)
UH-OH!!
KA (FLASH)
Pi
GWAAAH!!
BOGOUUU (KABOOM)

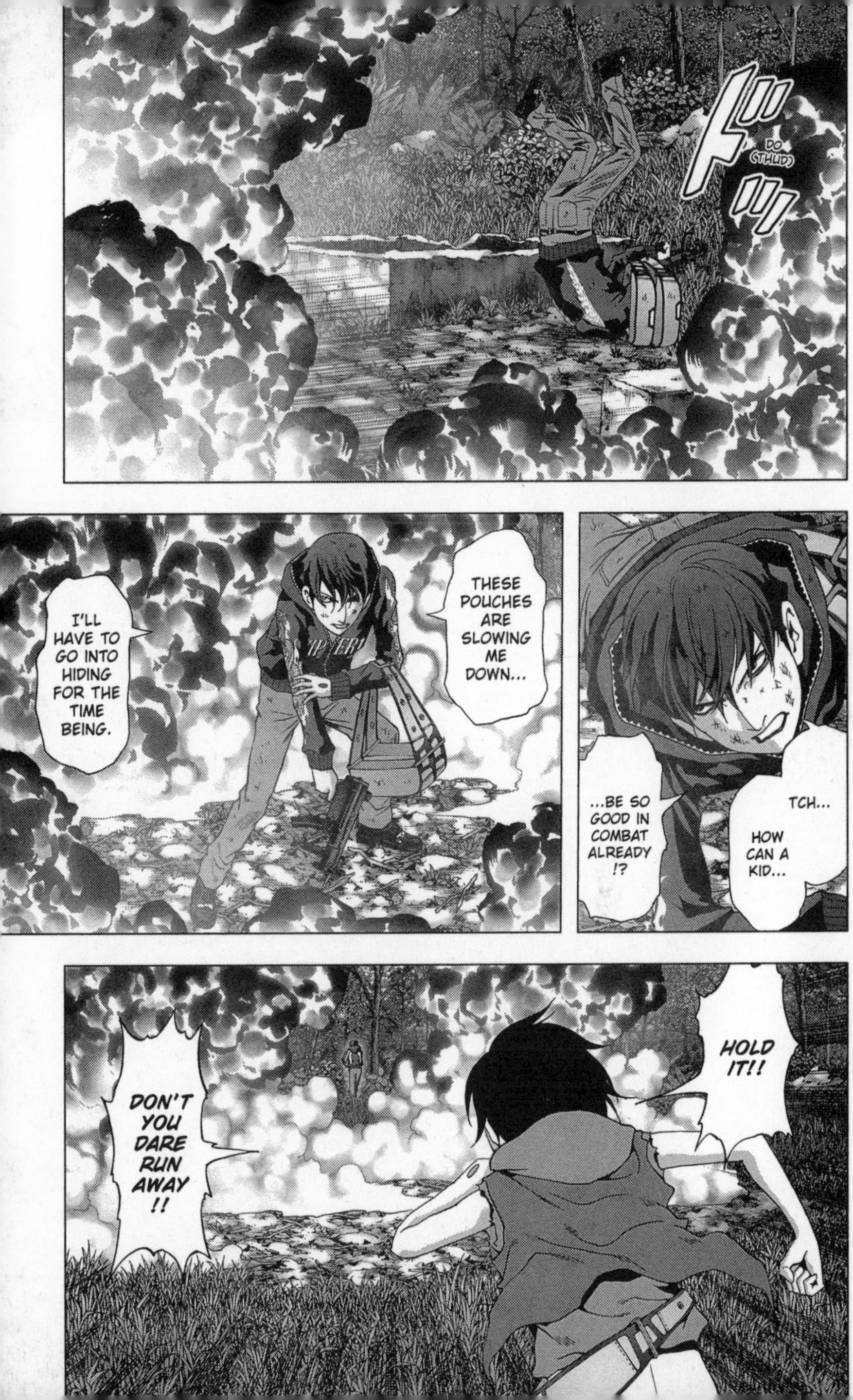
DO (THUD)
TCH...
HOW CAN A KID...
...BE SO GOOD IN COMBAT ALREADY!?
THESE POUCHES ARE SLOWING ME DOWN...
I'LL HAVE TO GO INTO HIDING FOR THE TIME BEING.
HOLD IT!!
DON'T YOU DARE RUN AWAY!!

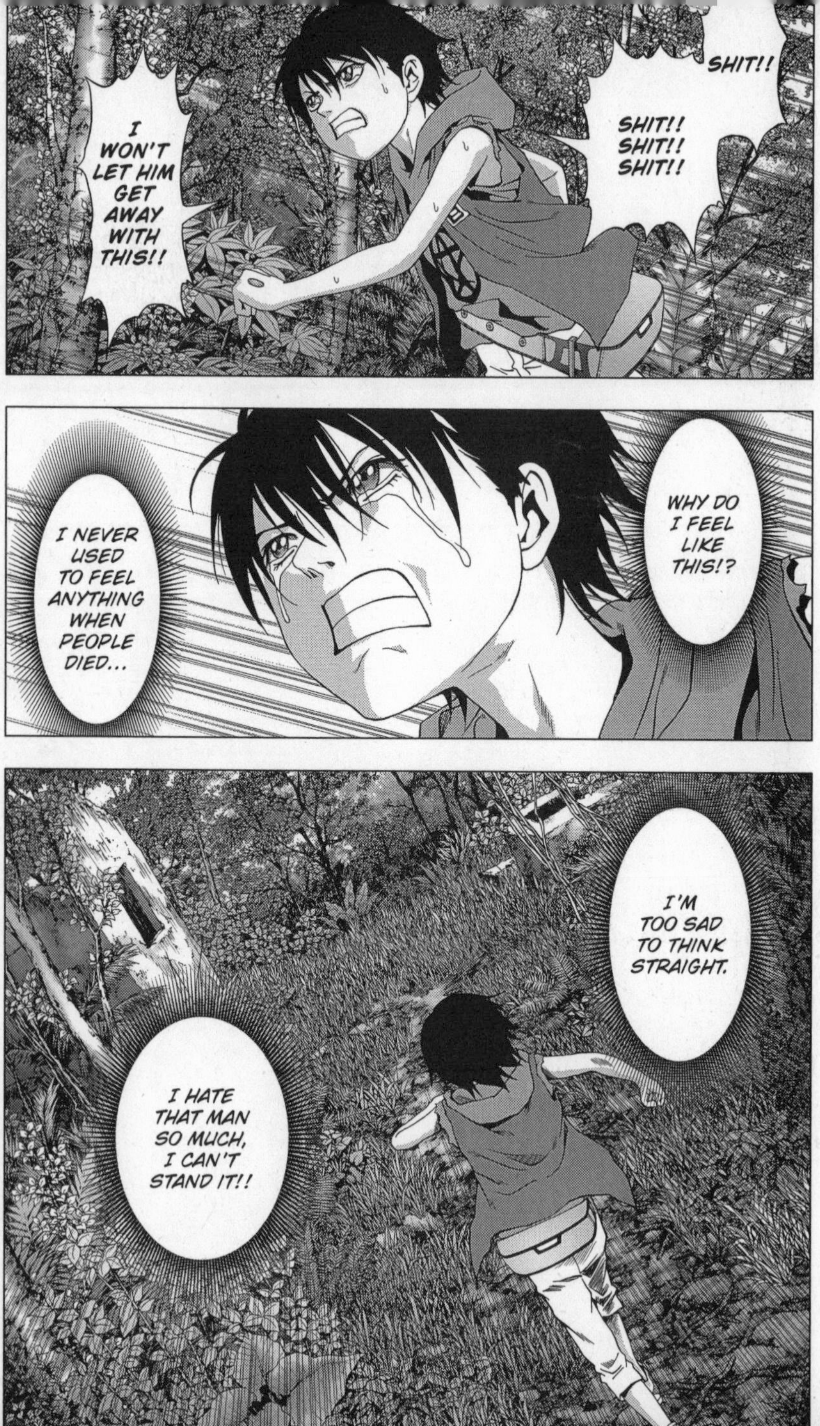
SHIT!!
SHIT!! SHIT!! SHIT!!
I WON'T LET HIM GET AWAY WITH THIS!!
WHY DO I FEEL LIKE THIS!?
I NEVER USED TO FEEL ANYTHING WHEN PEOPLE DIED...
I'M TOO SAD TO THINK STRAIGHT.
I HATE THAT MAN SO MUCH, I CAN'T STAND IT!!

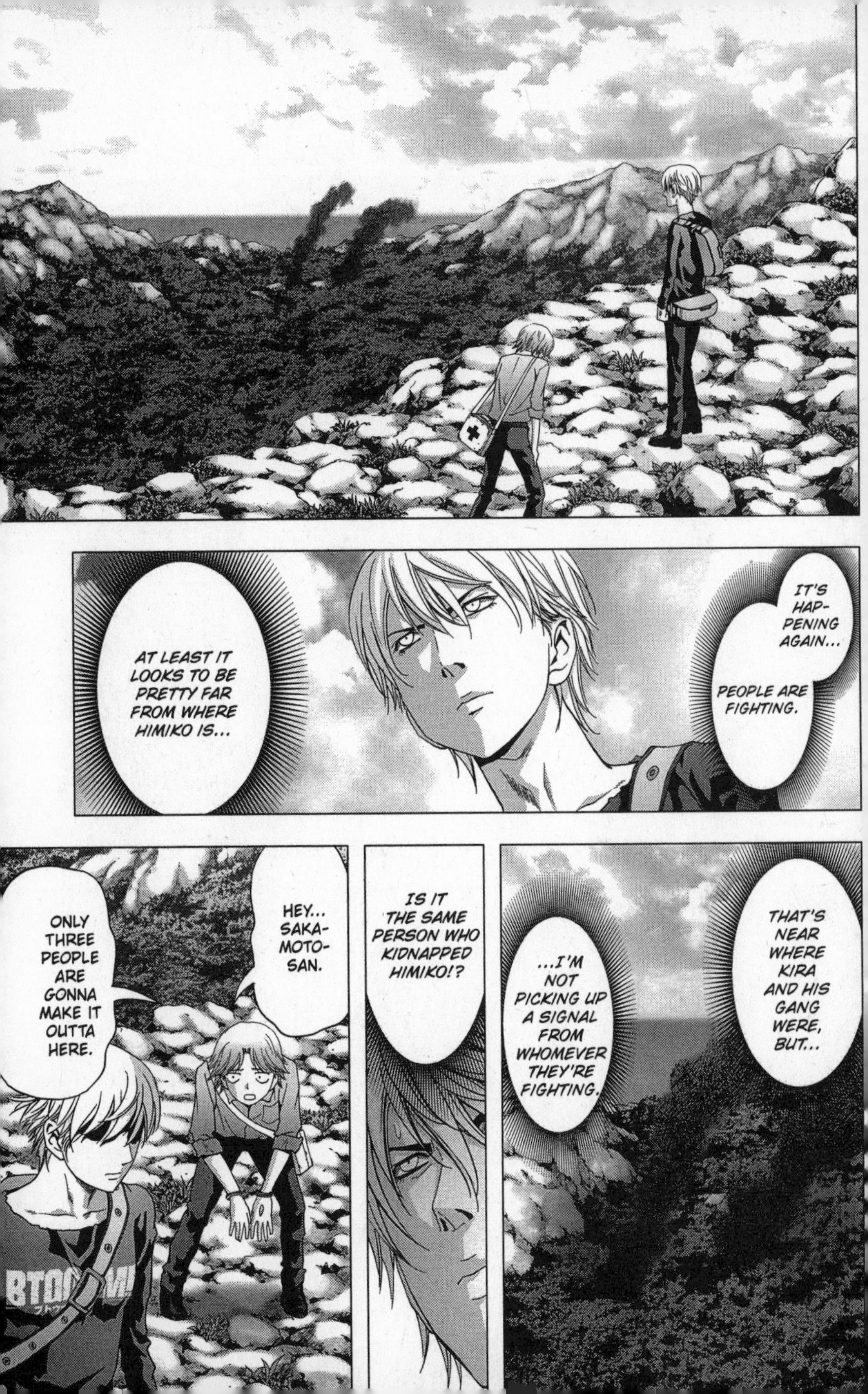
IT'S HAPPENING AGAIN...
PEOPLE ARE FIGHTING.
AT LEAST IT LOOKS TO BE PRETTY FAR FROM WHERE HIMIKO IS...
THAT'S NEAR WHERE KIRA AND HIS GANG WERE, BUT...
...I'M NOT PICKING UP A SIGNAL FROM WHOMEVER THEY'RE FIGHTING.
IS IT THE SAME PERSON WHO KIDNAPPED HIMIKO!?
HEY... SAKAMOTO-SAN.
ONLY THREE PEOPLE ARE GONNA MAKE IT OUTTA HERE.

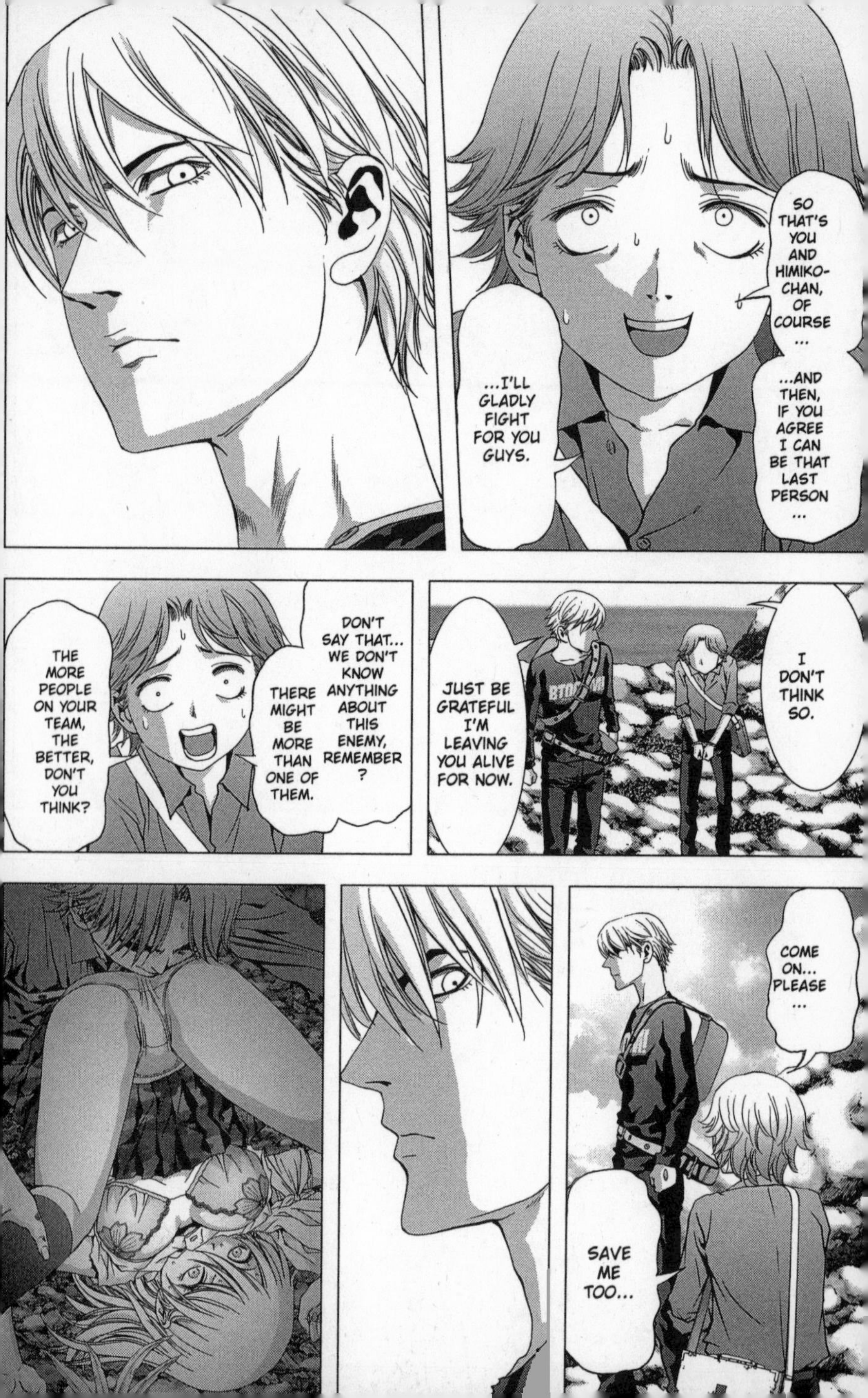
SO THAT'S YOU AND HIMIKO-CHAN, OF COURSE...
...AND THEN, IF YOU AGREE I CAN BE THAT LAST PERSON...
...I'LL GLADLY FIGHT FOR YOU GUYS.
I DON'T THINK SO.
JUST BE GRATEFUL I'M LEAVING YOU ALIVE FOR NOW.
DON'T SAY THAT... WE DON'T KNOW ANYTHING ABOUT THIS ENEMY, REMEMBER?
THERE MIGHT BE MORE THAN ONE OF THEM.
THE MORE PEOPLE ON YOUR TEAM, THE BETTER, DON'T YOU THINK?
COME ON... PLEASE...
SAVE ME TOO...

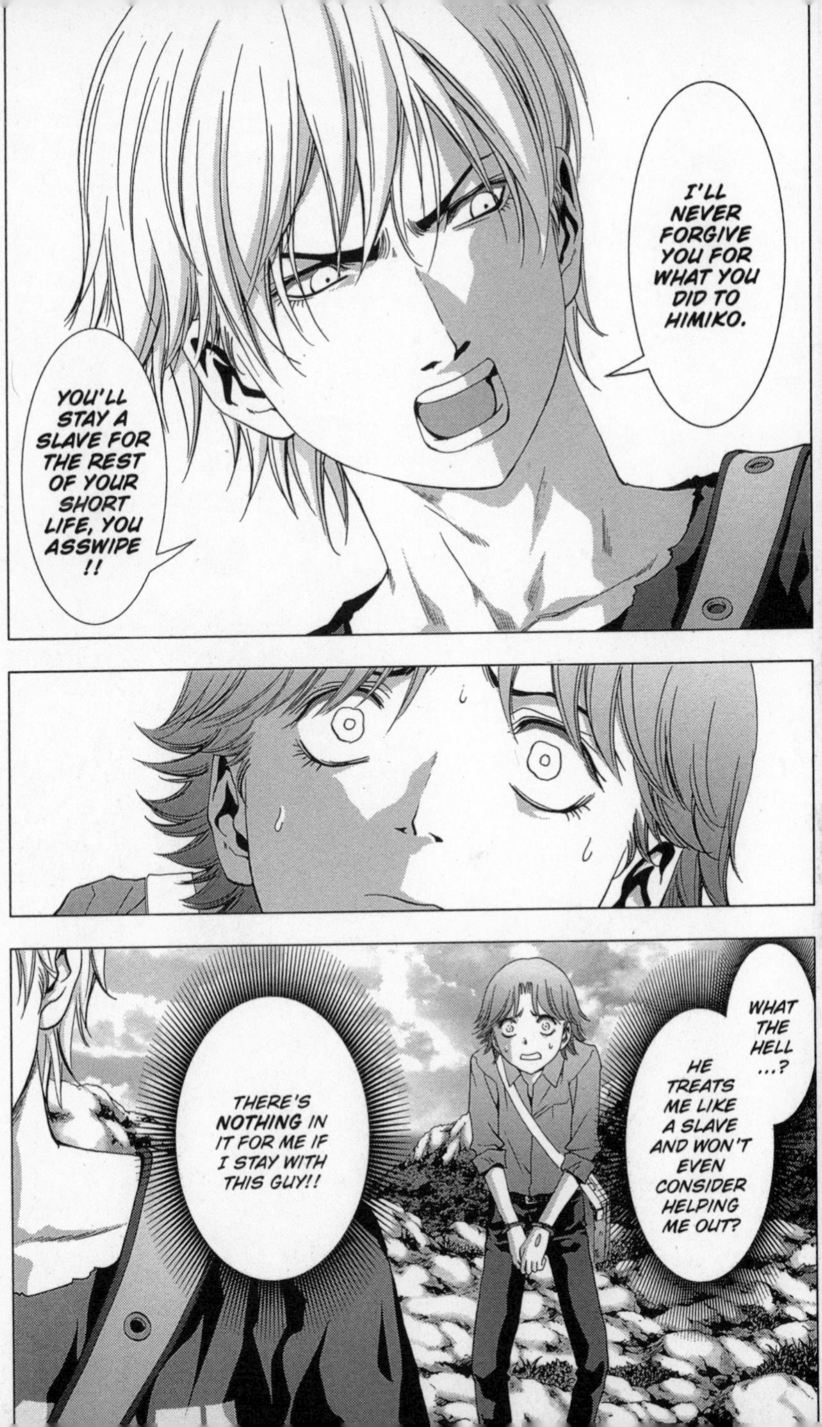
I'LL NEVER FORGIVE YOU FOR WHAT YOU DID TO HIMIKO.
YOU'LL STAY A SLAVE FOR THE REST OF YOUR SHORT LIFE, YOU ASSWIPE!!
WHAT THE HELL...?
HE TREATS ME LIKE A SLAVE AND WON'T EVEN CONSIDER HELPING ME OUT?
THERE'S **NOTHING** IN IT FOR ME IF I STAY WITH THIS GUY!!

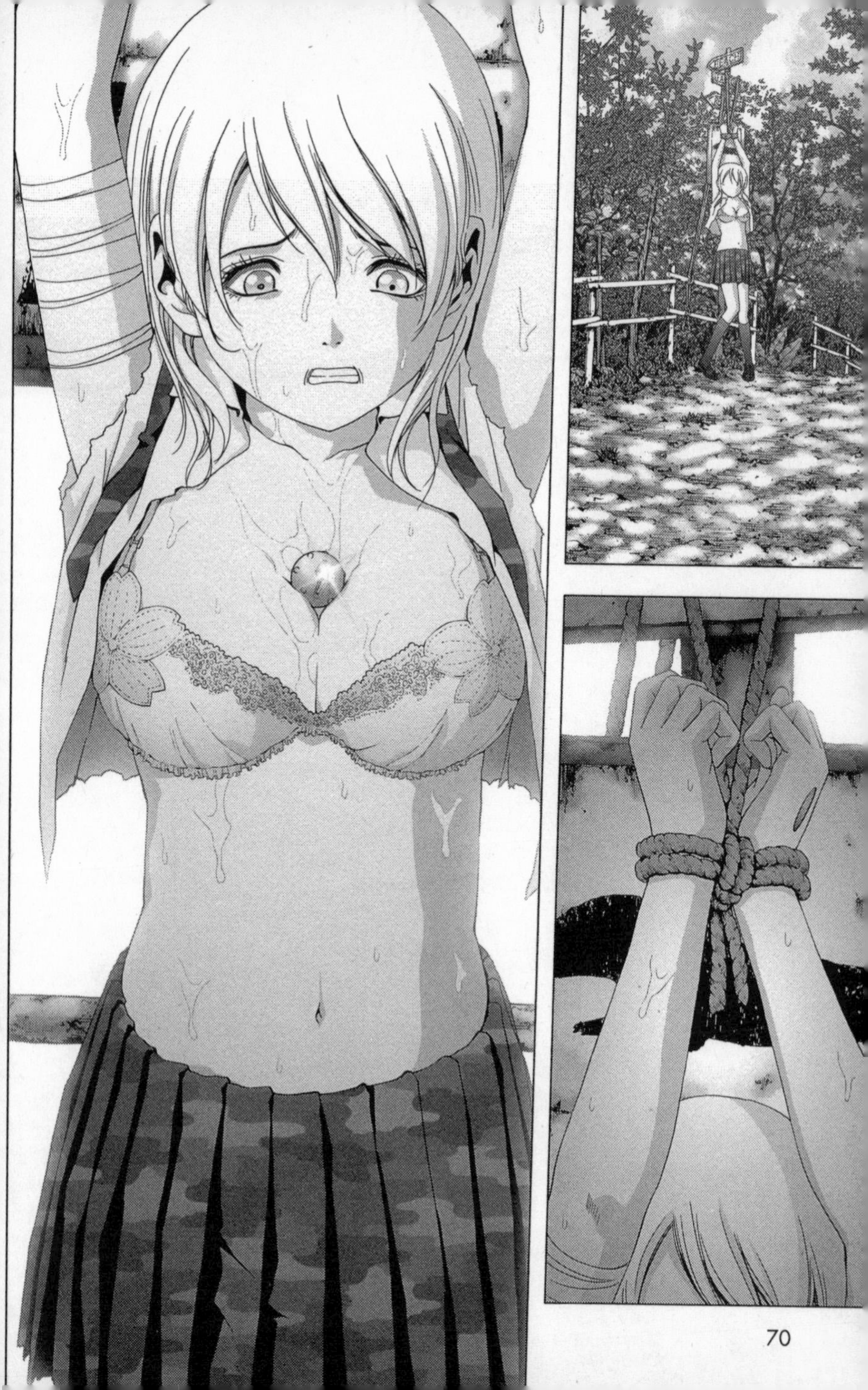

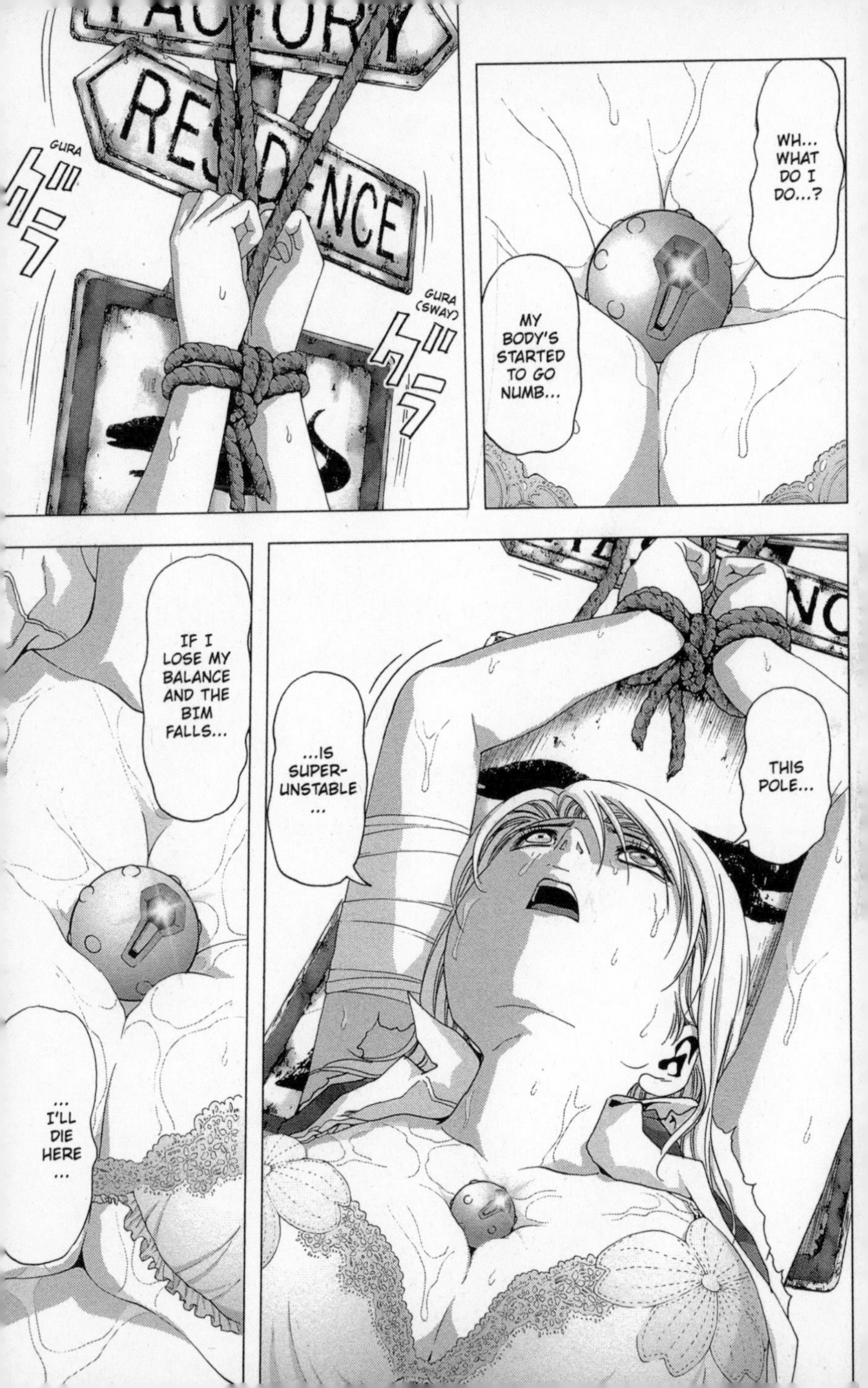
WH... WHAT DO I DO...?
MY BODY'S STARTED TO GO NUMB...
GURA
GURA (SWAY)
THIS POLE...
...IS SUPER-UNSTABLE...
IF I LOSE MY BALANCE AND THE BIM FALLS...
...I'LL DIE HERE...

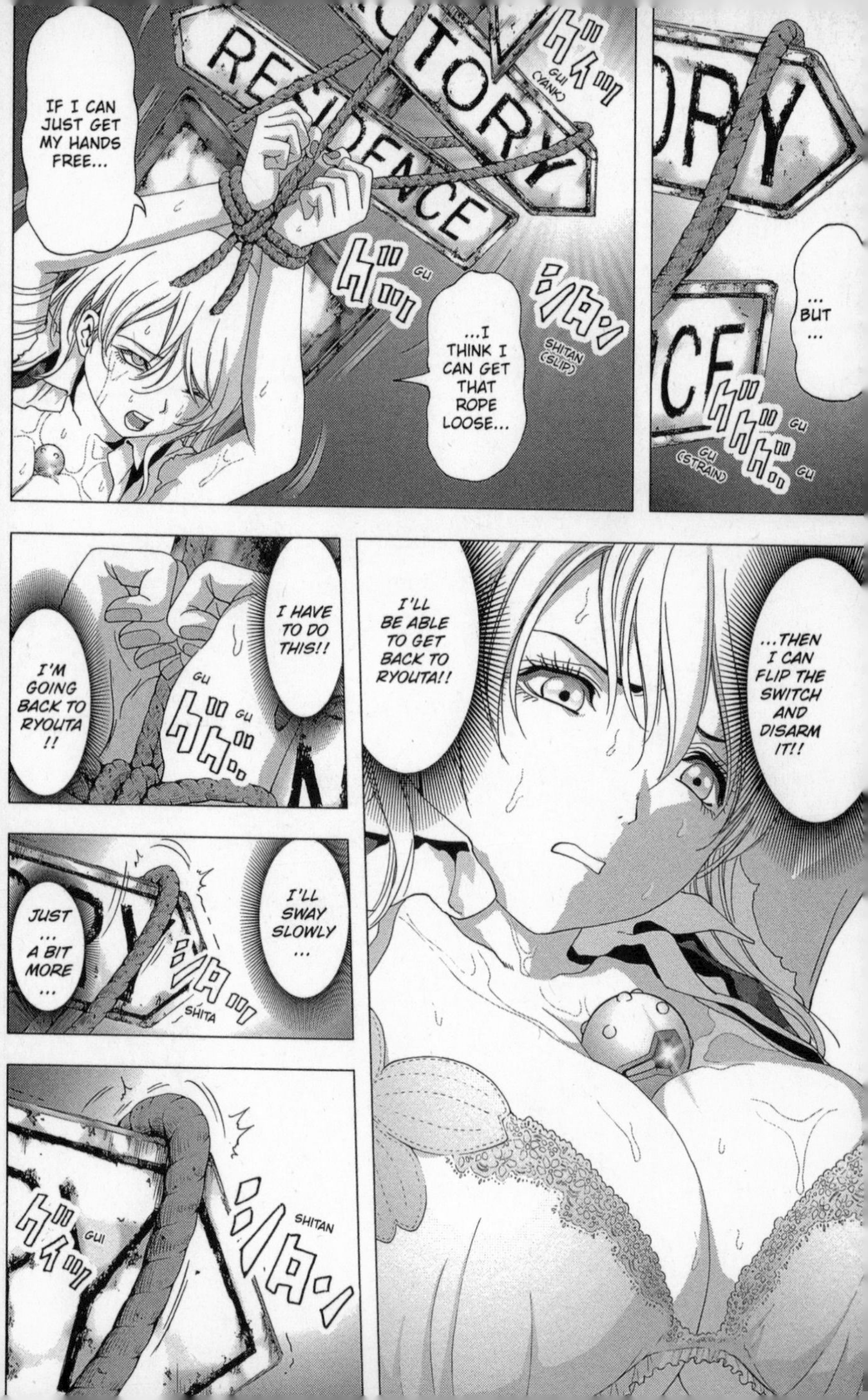
... BUT ...
GU (STRAIN) GU GU
IF I CAN JUST GET MY HANDS FREE...
GUI (YANK)
GU
...I THINK I CAN GET THAT ROPE LOOSE...
SHITAN (SLIP)
...THEN I CAN FLIP THE SWITCH AND DISARM IT!!
I'LL BE ABLE TO GET BACK TO RYOUTA!!
I HAVE TO DO THIS!!
I'M GOING BACK TO RYOUTA!!
GU GU
I'LL SWAY SLOWLY ...
JUST ... A BIT MORE ...
SHITA
SHITAN
GUI

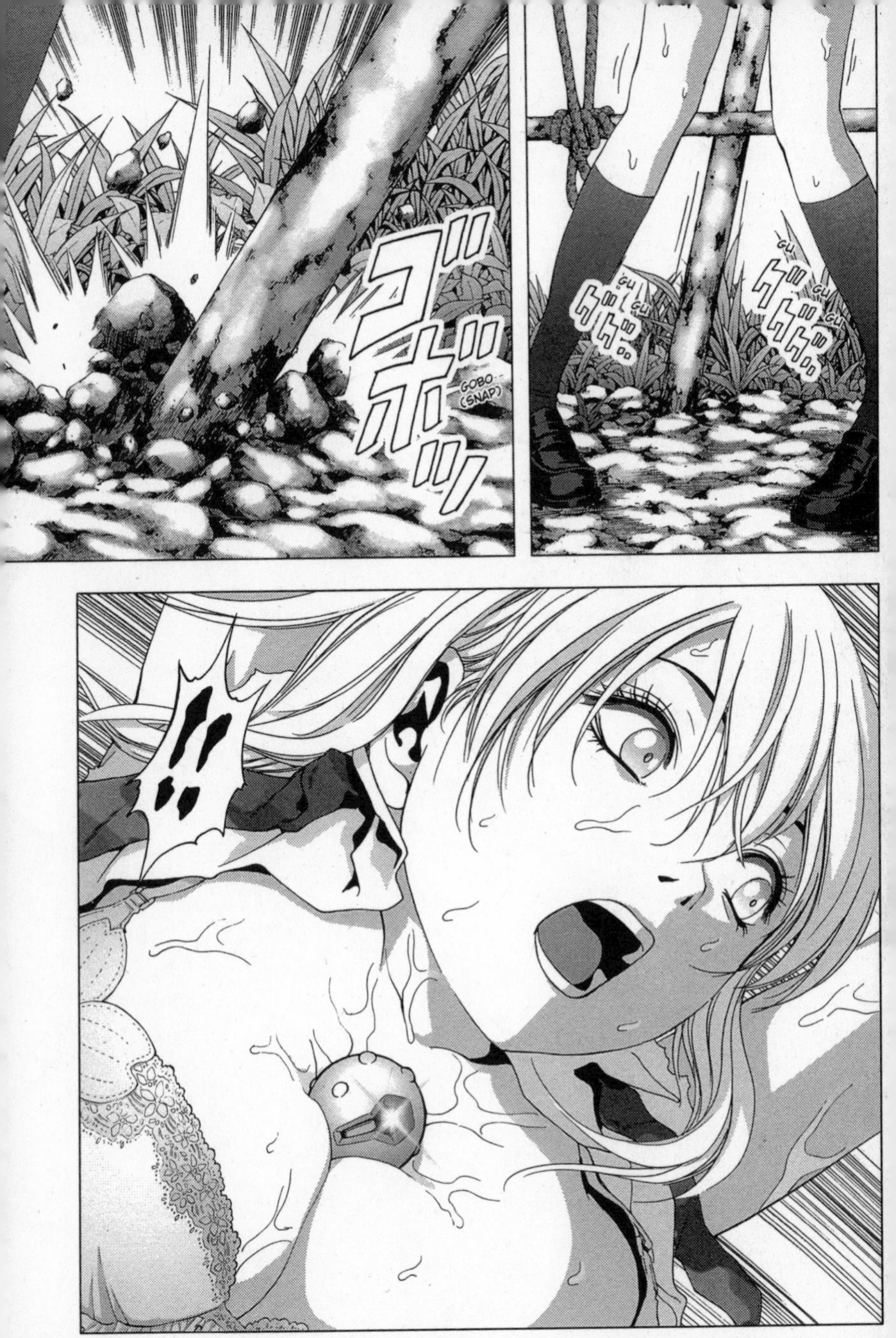
GU GU GU
GU GU
ゴボッ
GOBO (SNAP)

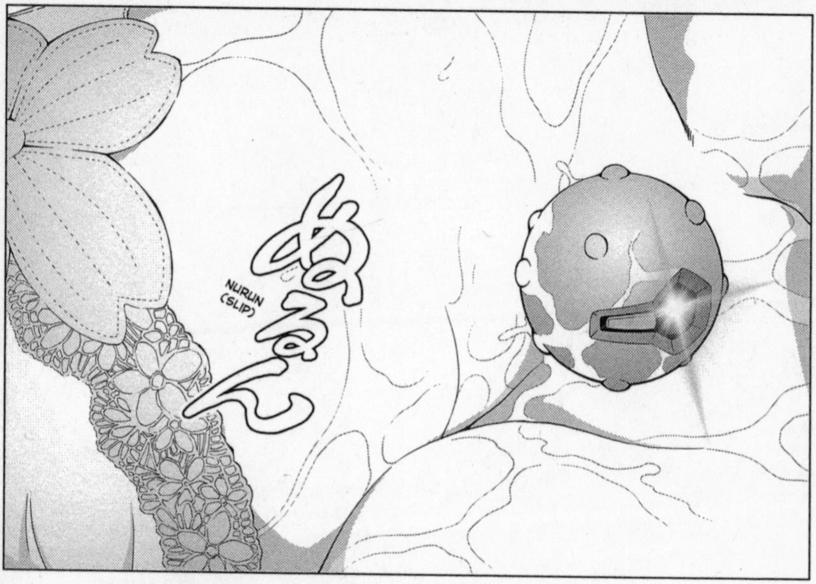
ぬるん
NURUN (SLIP)
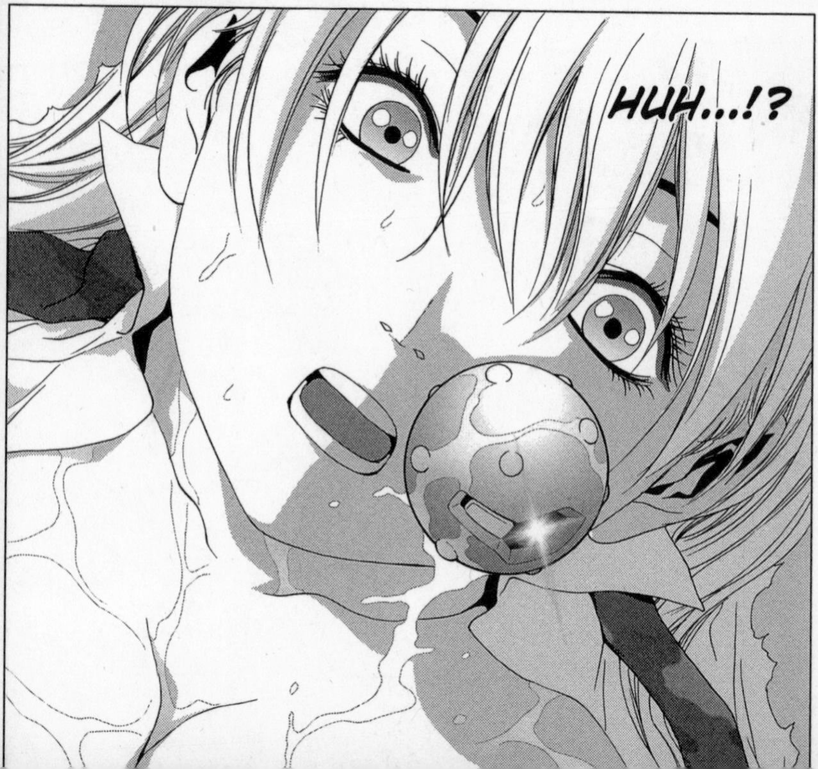
HUH...!?

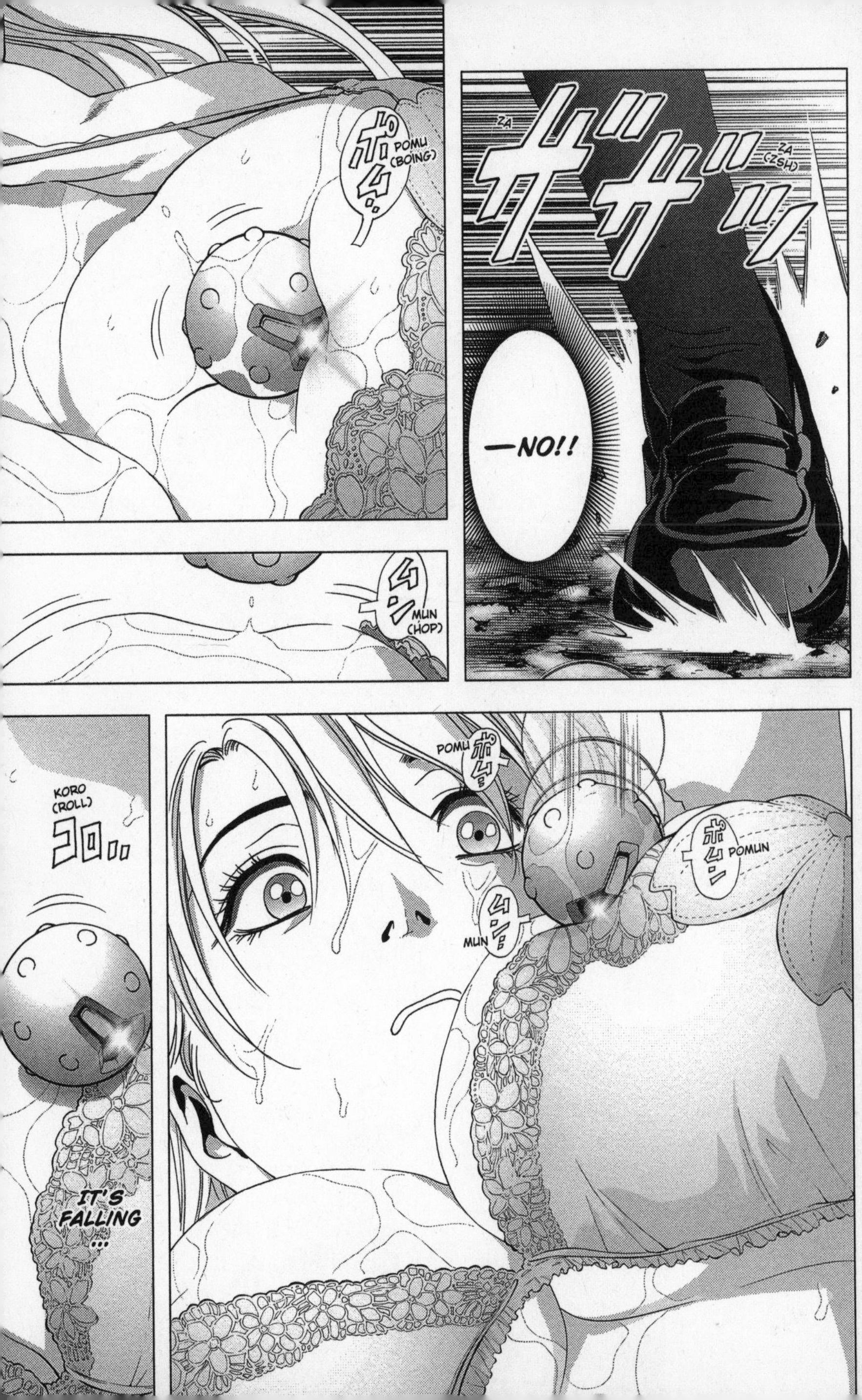
ZA
ザザッ
ZA (ZSH)
—NO!!
ポム
POMU (BOING)
ムン
MUN (HOP)
ポム
POMU
ポムン
POMUN
ムン
MUN
KORO (ROLL)
コロ…
IT'S FALLING…

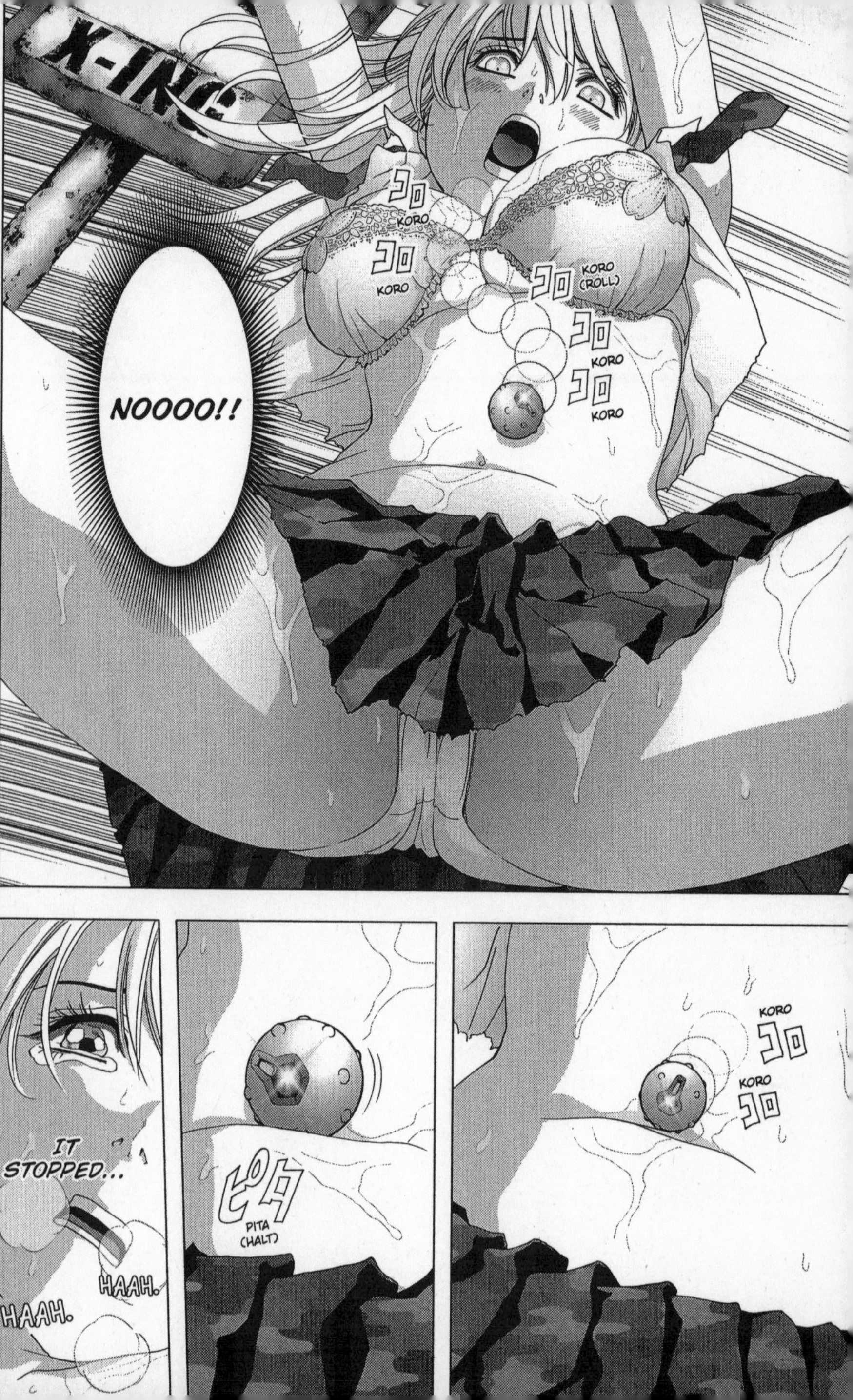
コロ KORO
コロ KORO
コロ KORO (ROLL)
コロ KORO
コロ KORO
NOOOO!!
KORO コロ
KORO コロ
ピタ PITA (HALT)
IT STOPPED...
HAAH.
HAAH.

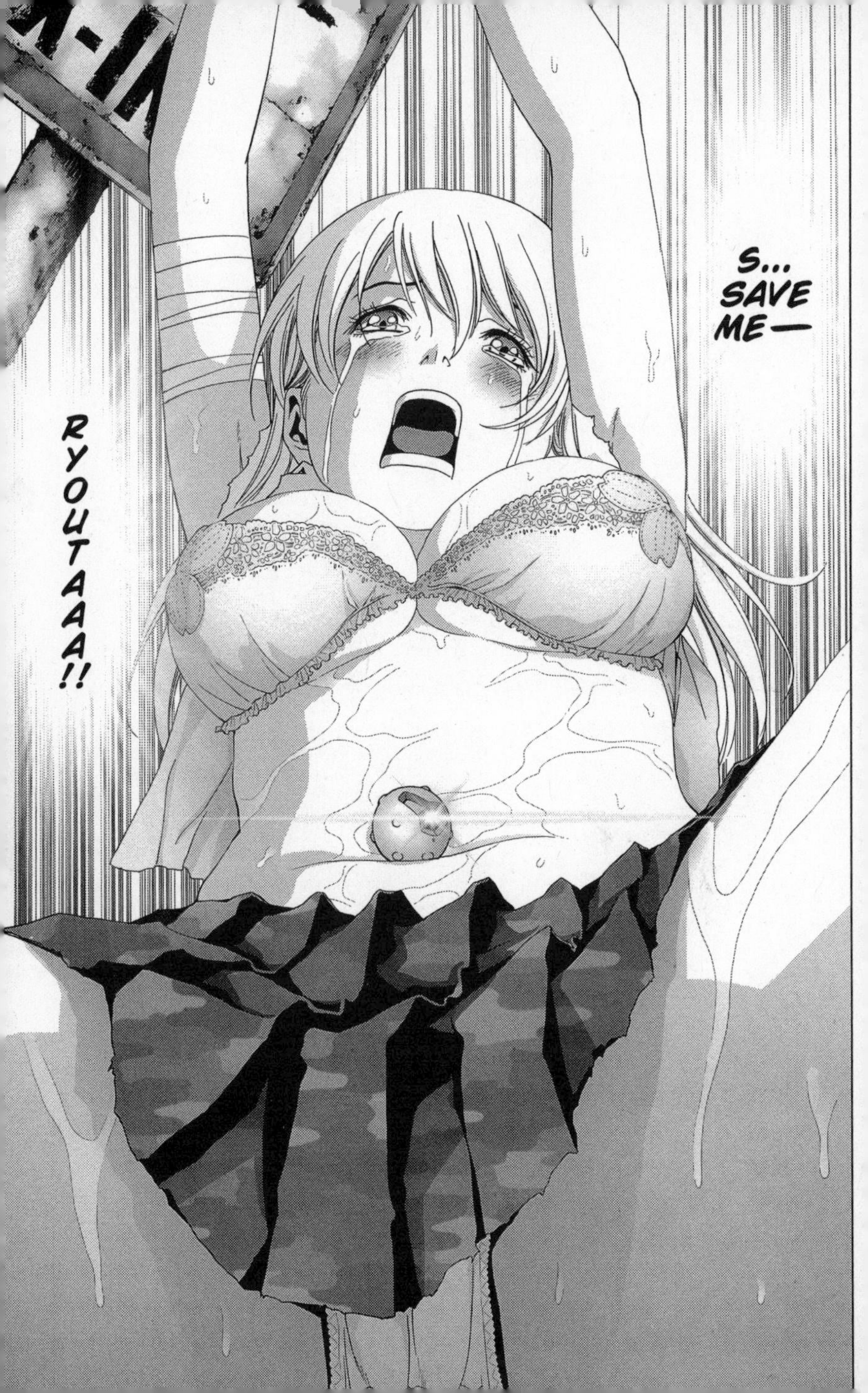
S... SAVE ME—
RYOUTAAA!!

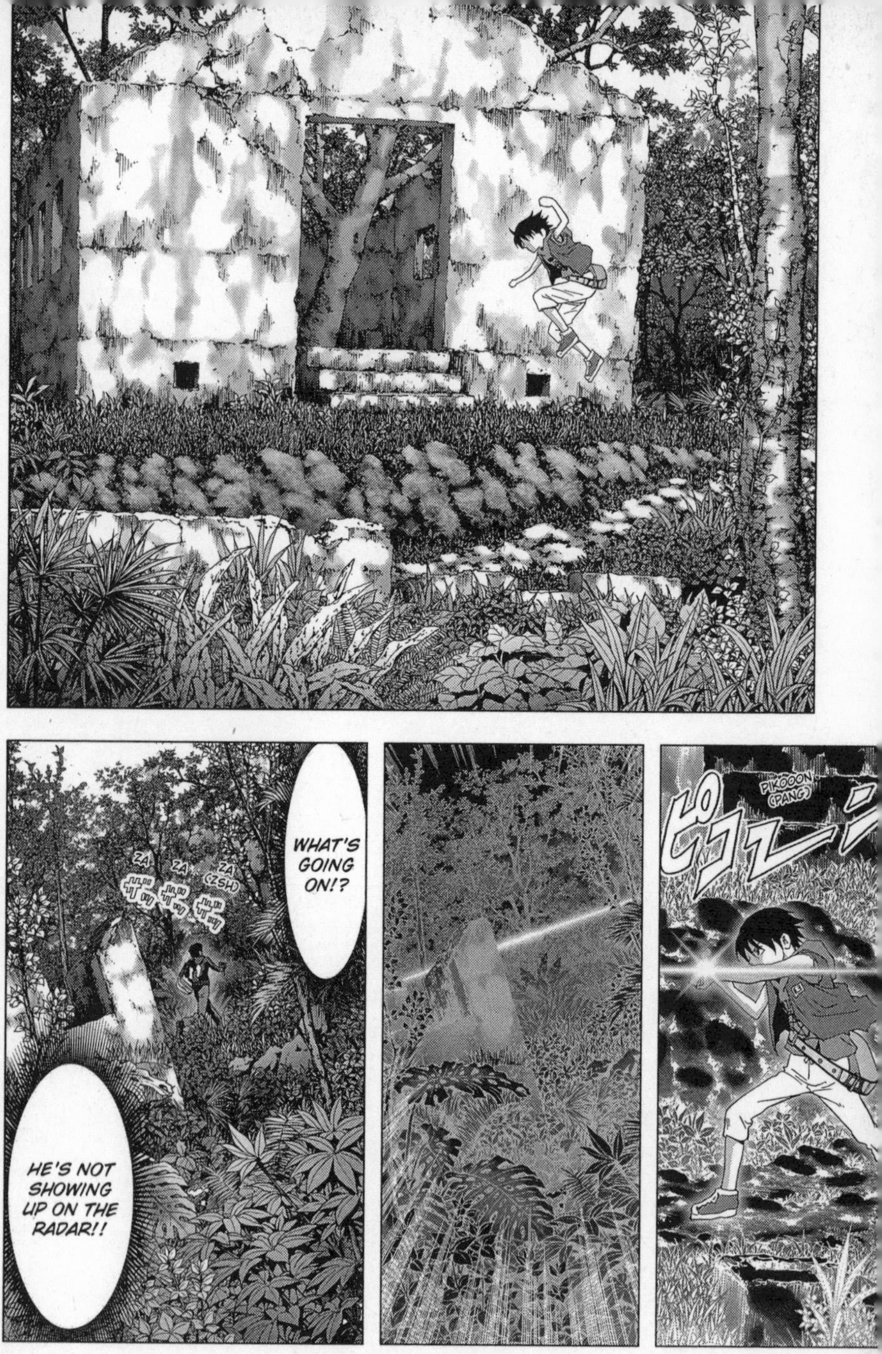
PIKOOON (PANG)
WHAT'S GOING ON!?
HE'S NOT SHOWING UP ON THE RADAR!!
ZA ZA ZA (ZSH)

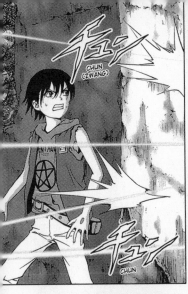

TA TA TA TA TA (RATTA)
ダダダダダ..
チュン
CHUN (ZWANG)
チュン
CHUN
THE RADAR DOESN'T WORK ON HIM.
AND HE'S NOT COUNTERING IT EITHER!!
SO IS HE NOT A PLAYER, THEN!?
GU (GRIP)
グッ
NO MATTER WHO HE IS...
...I SWEAR I'M GONNA KILL HIM!!

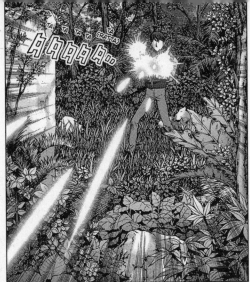

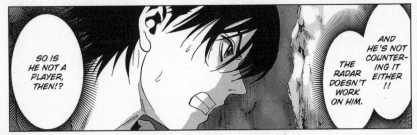

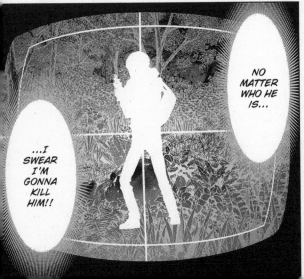

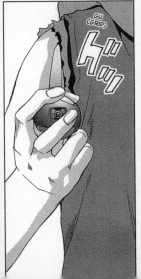

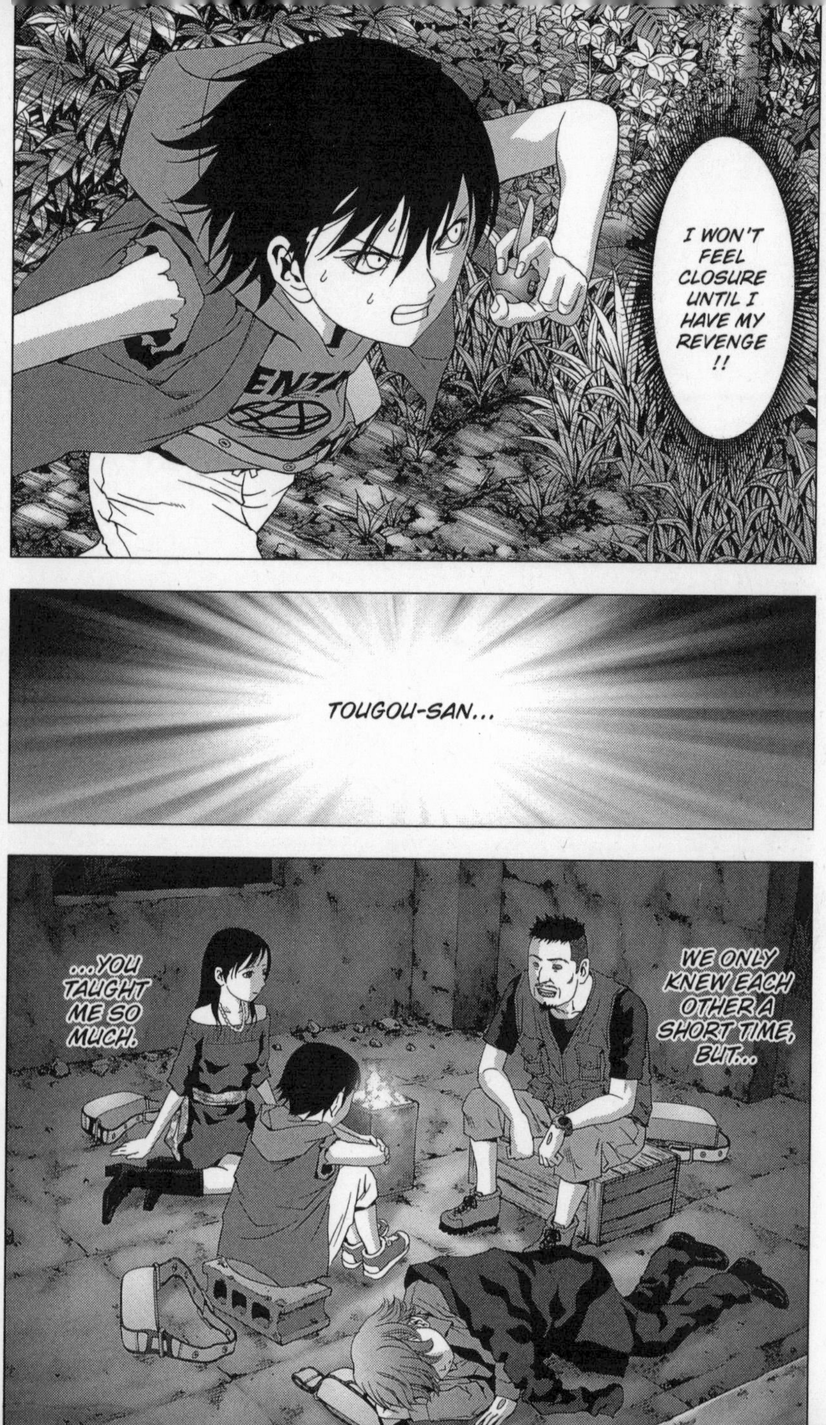
I WON'T FEEL CLOSURE UNTIL I HAVE MY REVENGE !!
TOUGOU-SAN...
WE ONLY KNEW EACH OTHER A SHORT TIME, BUT...
...YOU TAUGHT ME SO MUCH.

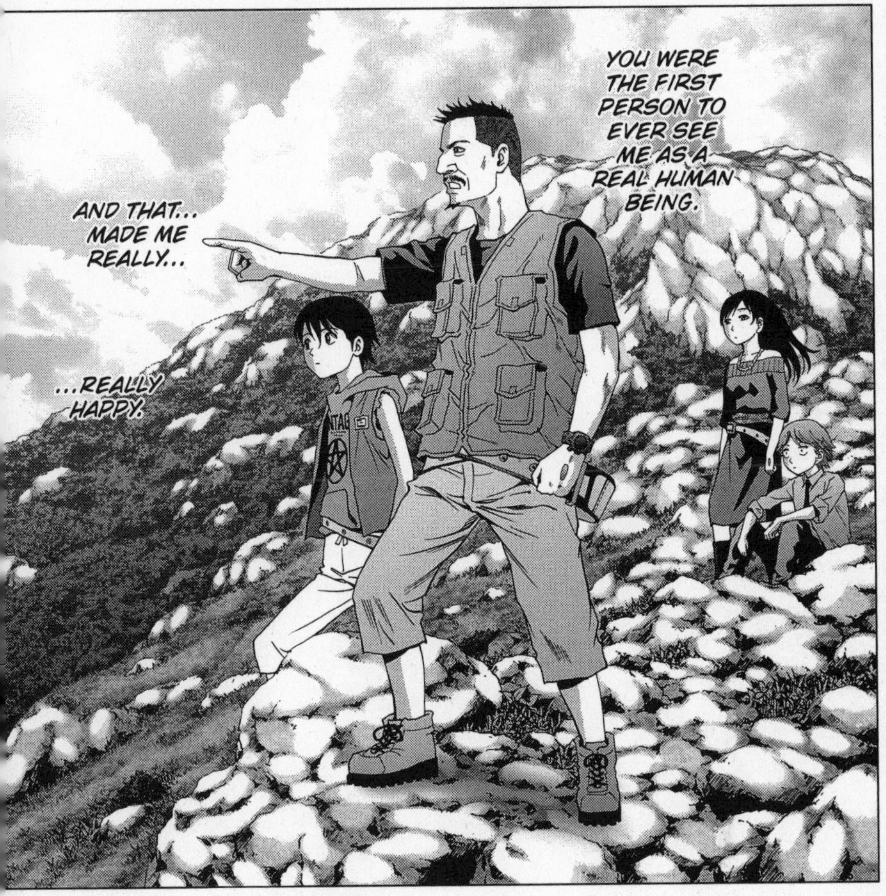
YOU WERE THE FIRST PERSON TO EVER SEE ME AS A REAL HUMAN BEING.
AND THAT... MADE ME REALLY...
...REALLY HAPPY.
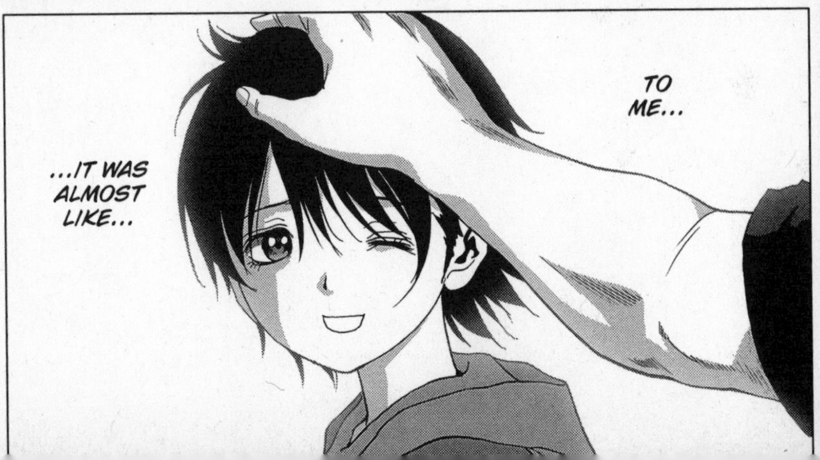
TO ME...
...IT WAS ALMOST LIKE...

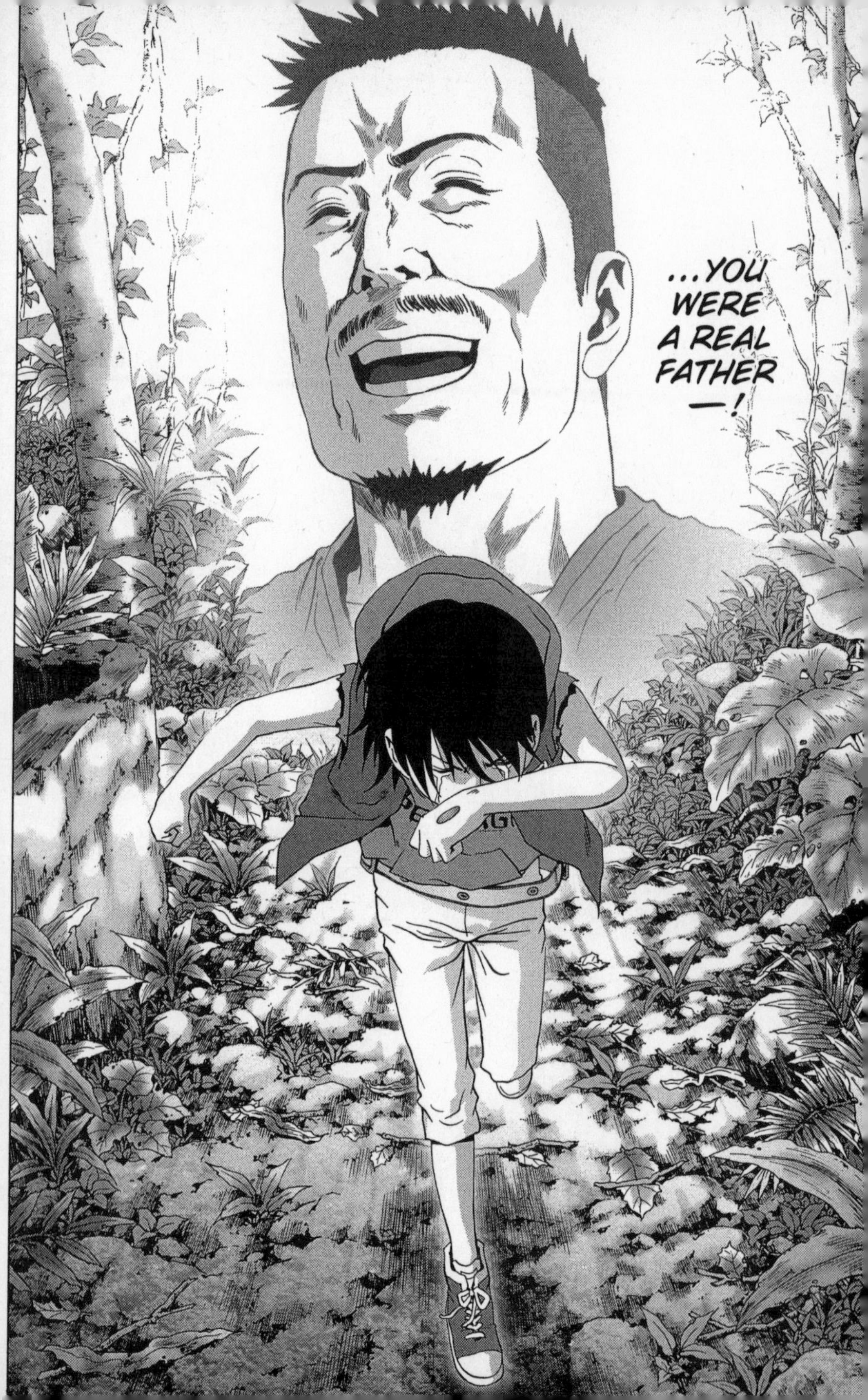
...YOU WERE A REAL FATHER—!

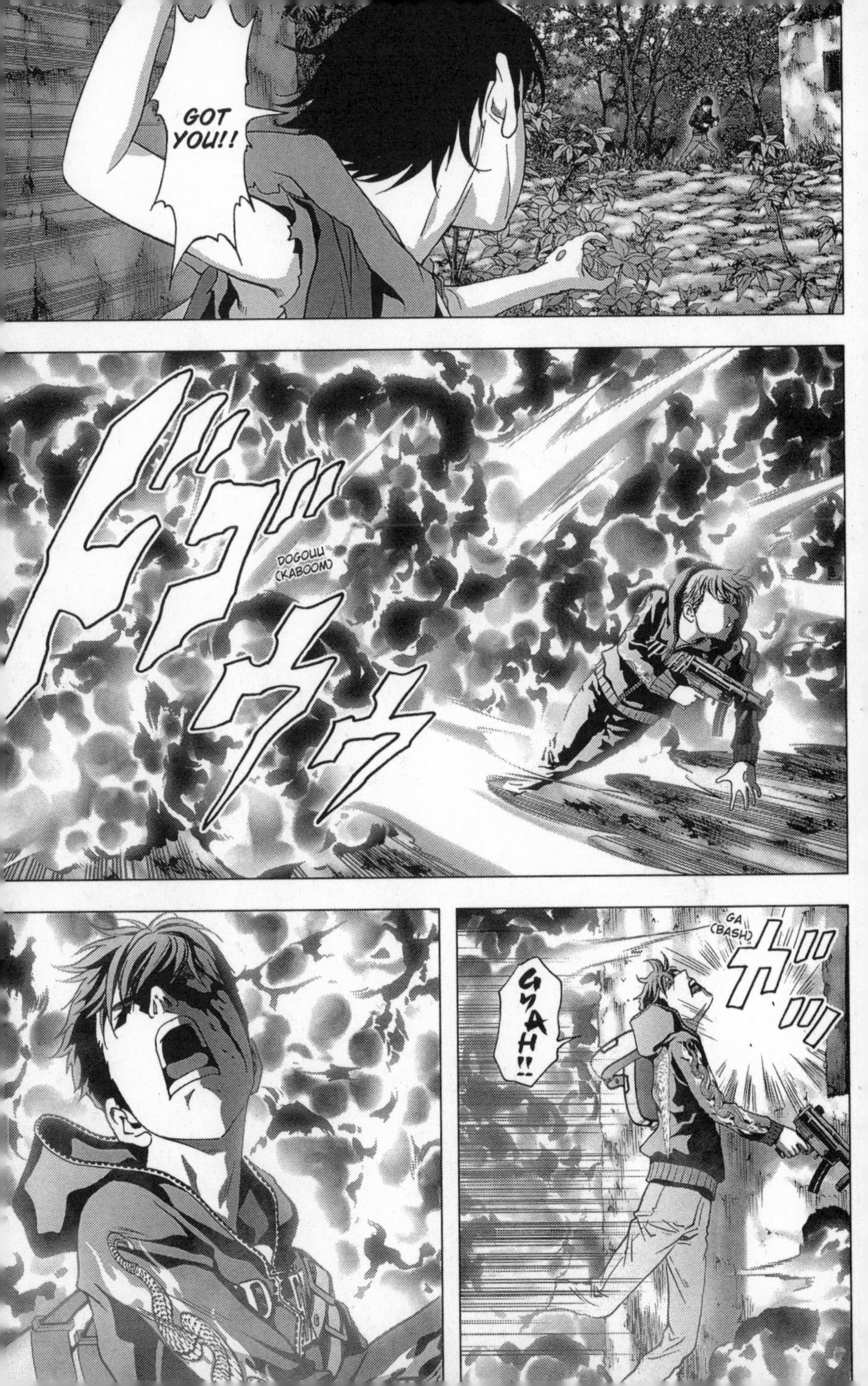
GOT YOU!!
DOGOUU (KABOOM)
GA (BASH)
GYAH!!

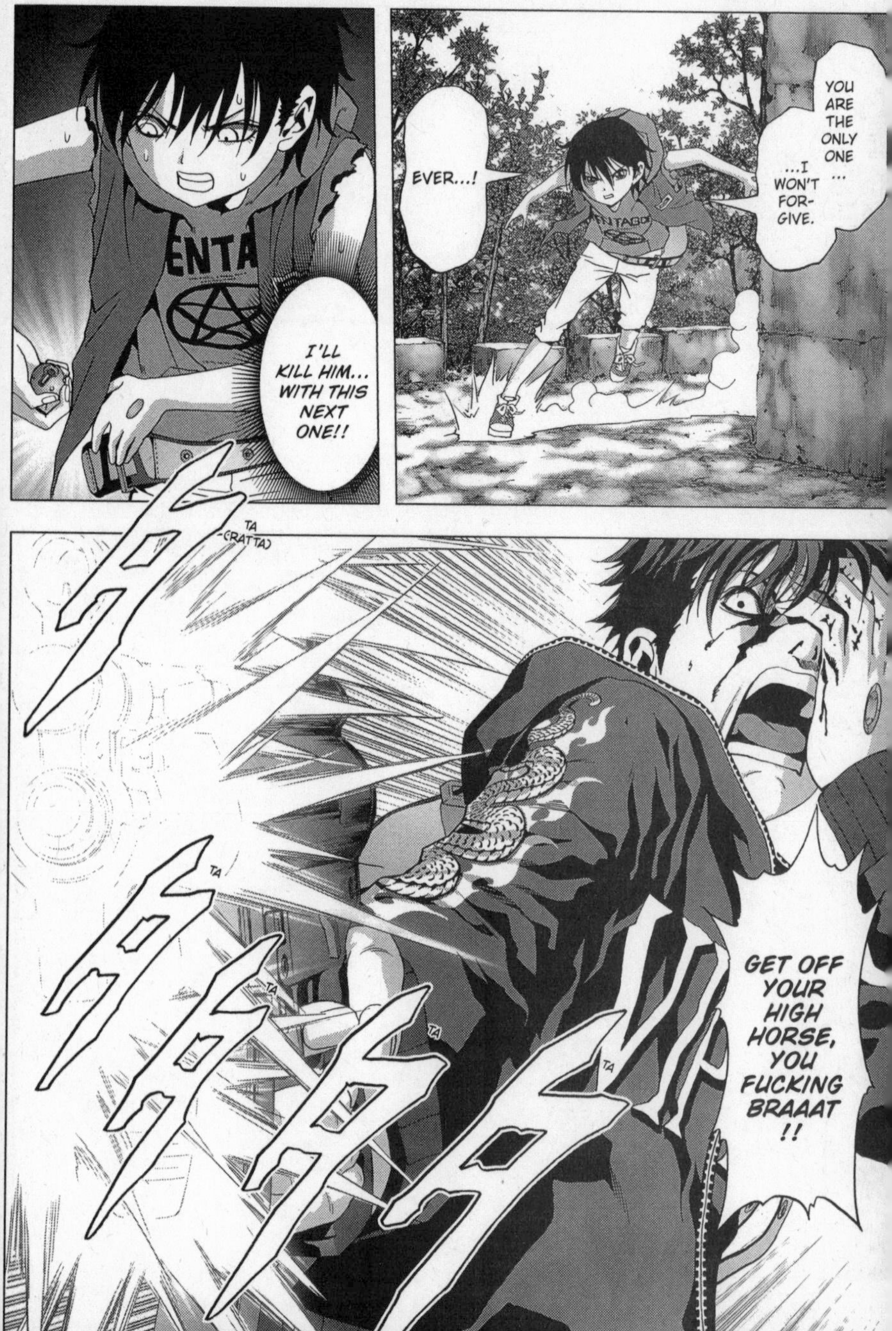
YOU ARE THE ONLY ONE ...
...I WON'T FORGIVE.
EVER...!
I'LL KILL HIM... WITH THIS NEXT ONE!!
GET OFF YOUR HIGH HORSE, YOU FUCKING BRAAAT!!
TA
TA
TA
TA
TA-(RATTA)

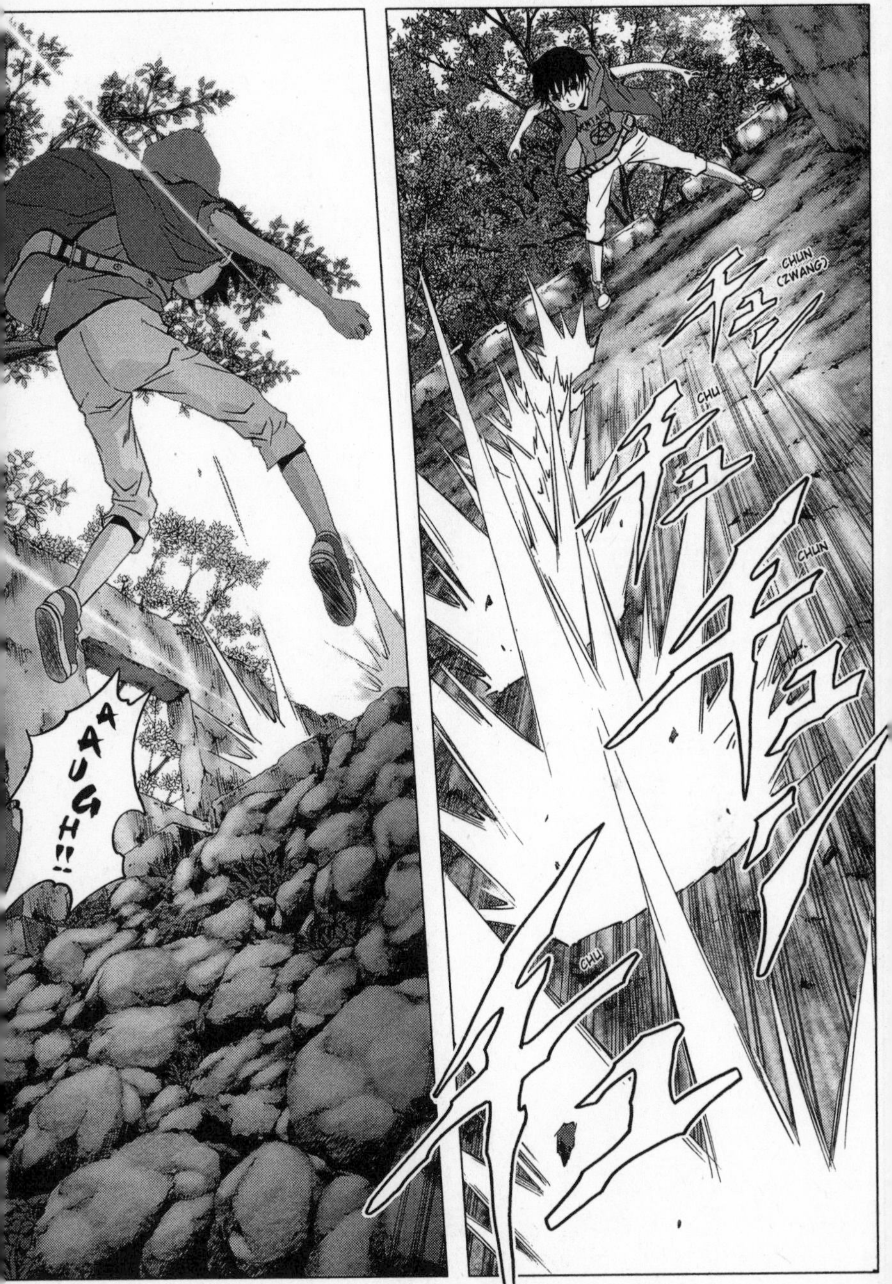
CHUN (ZWANG)
CHU
CHUN
CHU
AAUGH!!

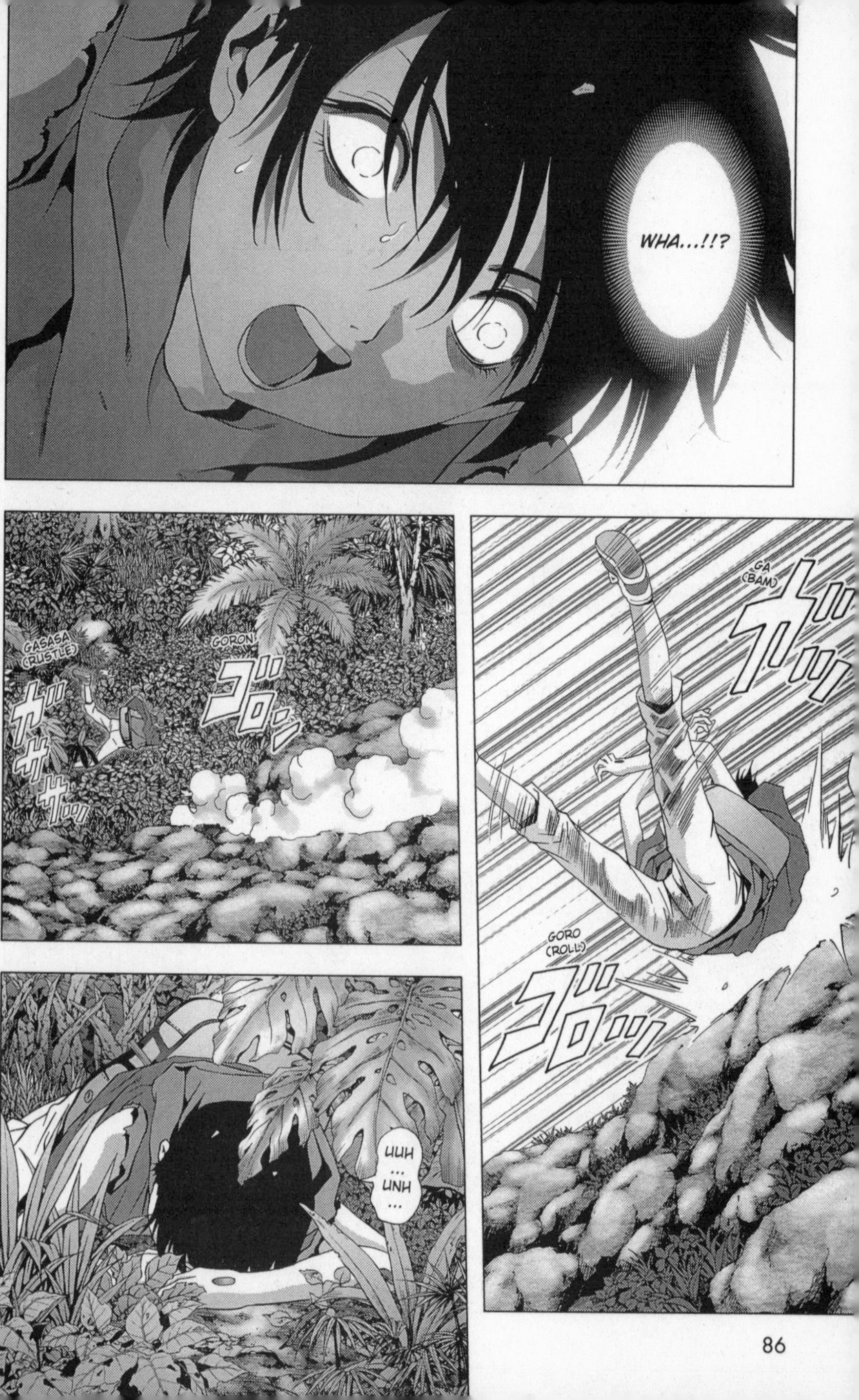
WHA...!!?
GA (BAM)
GORO (ROLL)
GORON
GASASA (RUSTLE)
UUH ... UNH ...

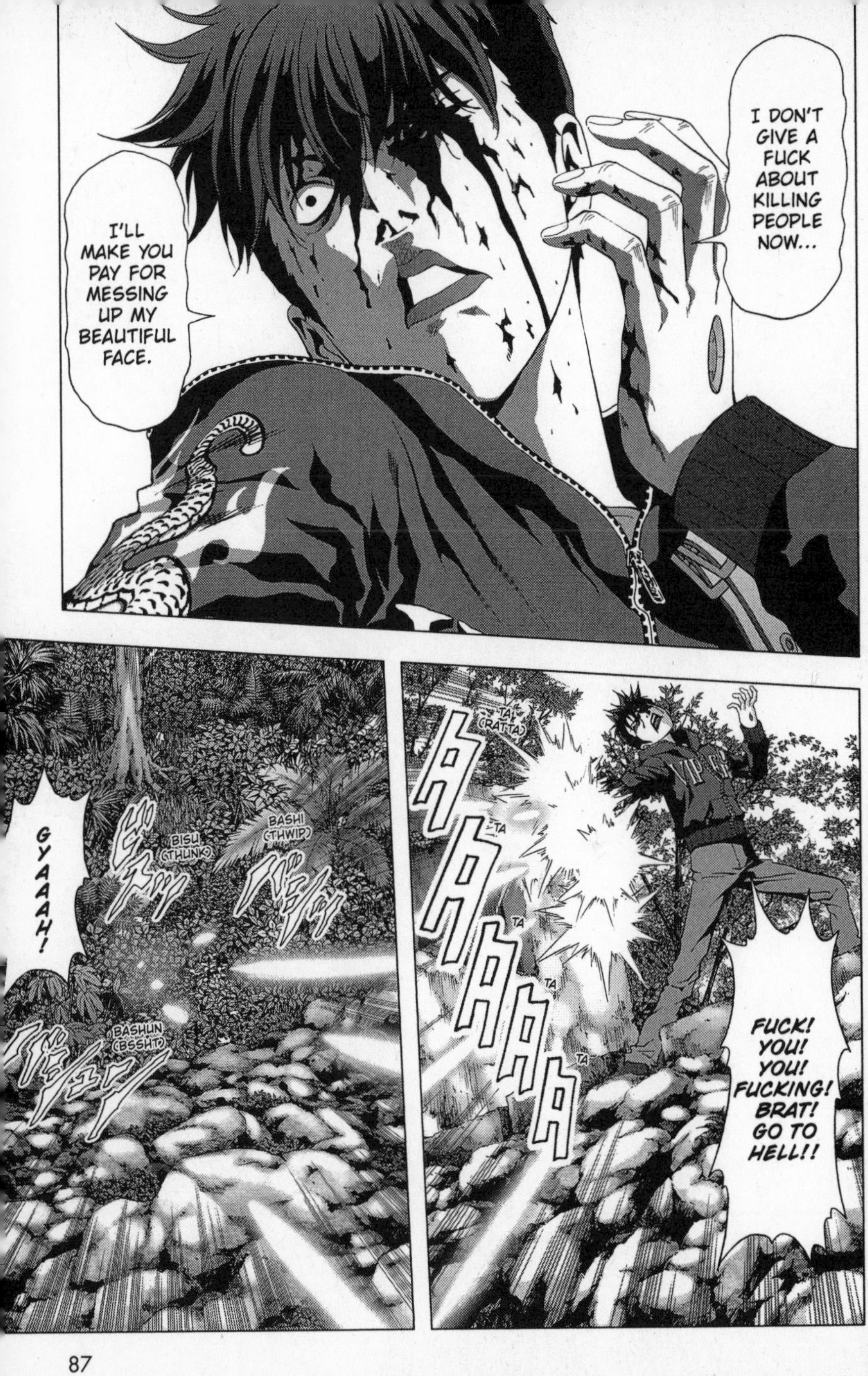
I DON'T GIVE A FUCK ABOUT KILLING PEOPLE NOW...
I'LL MAKE YOU PAY FOR MESSING UP MY BEAUTIFUL FACE.
TA (RAT TA)
TA
TA
TA
TA
FUCK! YOU! YOU! FUCKING! BRAT! GO TO HELL!!
BASHI (THWIP)
BISU (THUNK)
GYAAAAH!
BASHUN (BSSHT)

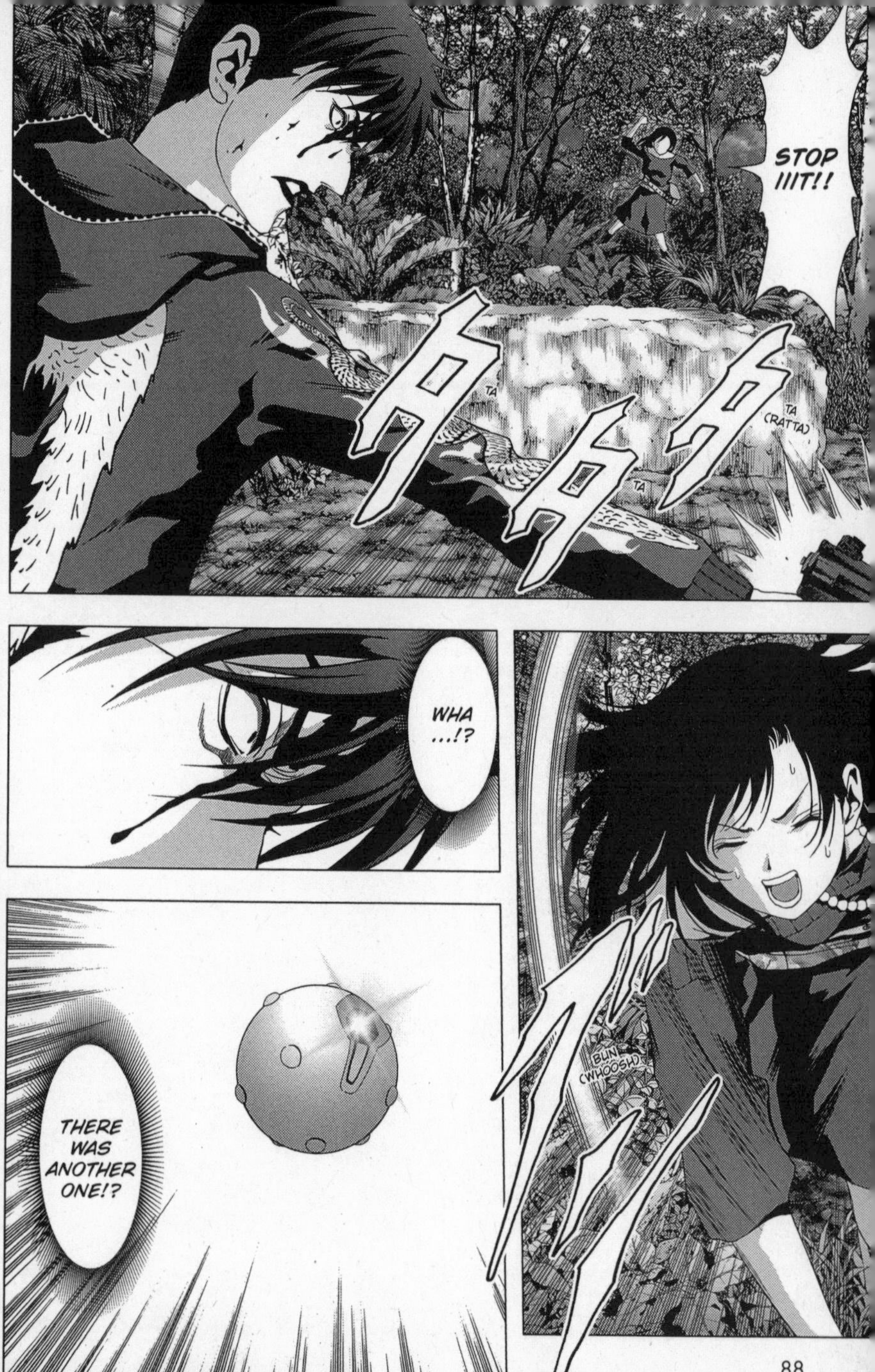
STOP IIIT!!
TA
TA
TA
(RATTA)
BUN
(WHOOSH)
WHA ...!?
THERE WAS ANOTHER ONE!?

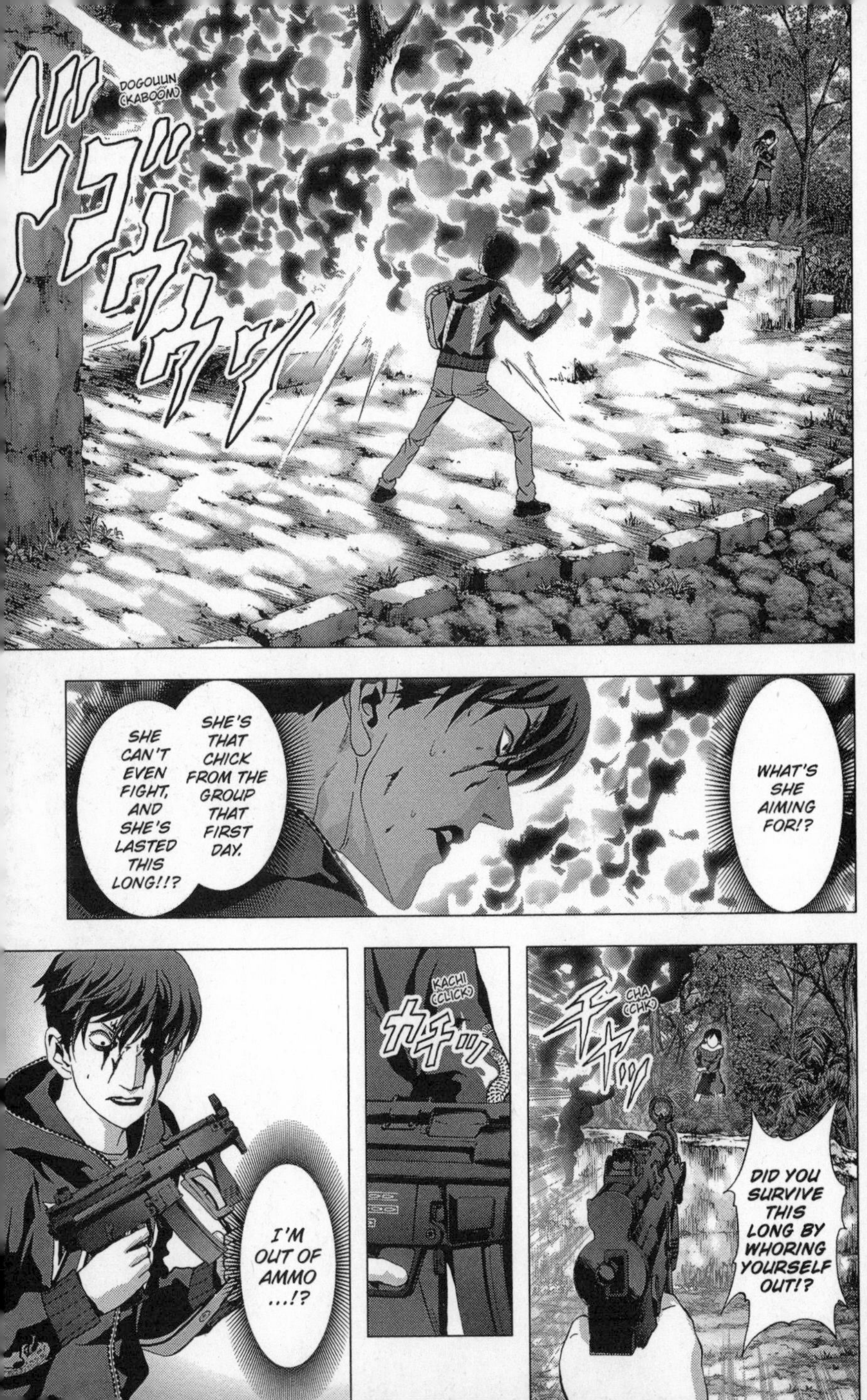
DOGOUUN (KABOOM)
WHAT'S SHE AIMING FOR!?
SHE'S THAT CHICK FROM THE GROUP THAT FIRST DAY.
SHE CAN'T EVEN FIGHT, AND SHE'S LASTED THIS LONG!!?
CHA (CHK)
DID YOU SURVIVE THIS LONG BY WHORING YOURSELF OUT!?
KACHI (CLICK)
I'M OUT OF AMMO ...!?

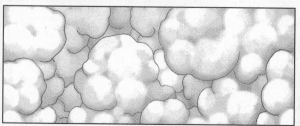

NOT GOOD!! NOW BOTH MY EYES ARE SHOT...

TALK ABOUT BAD TIMING...

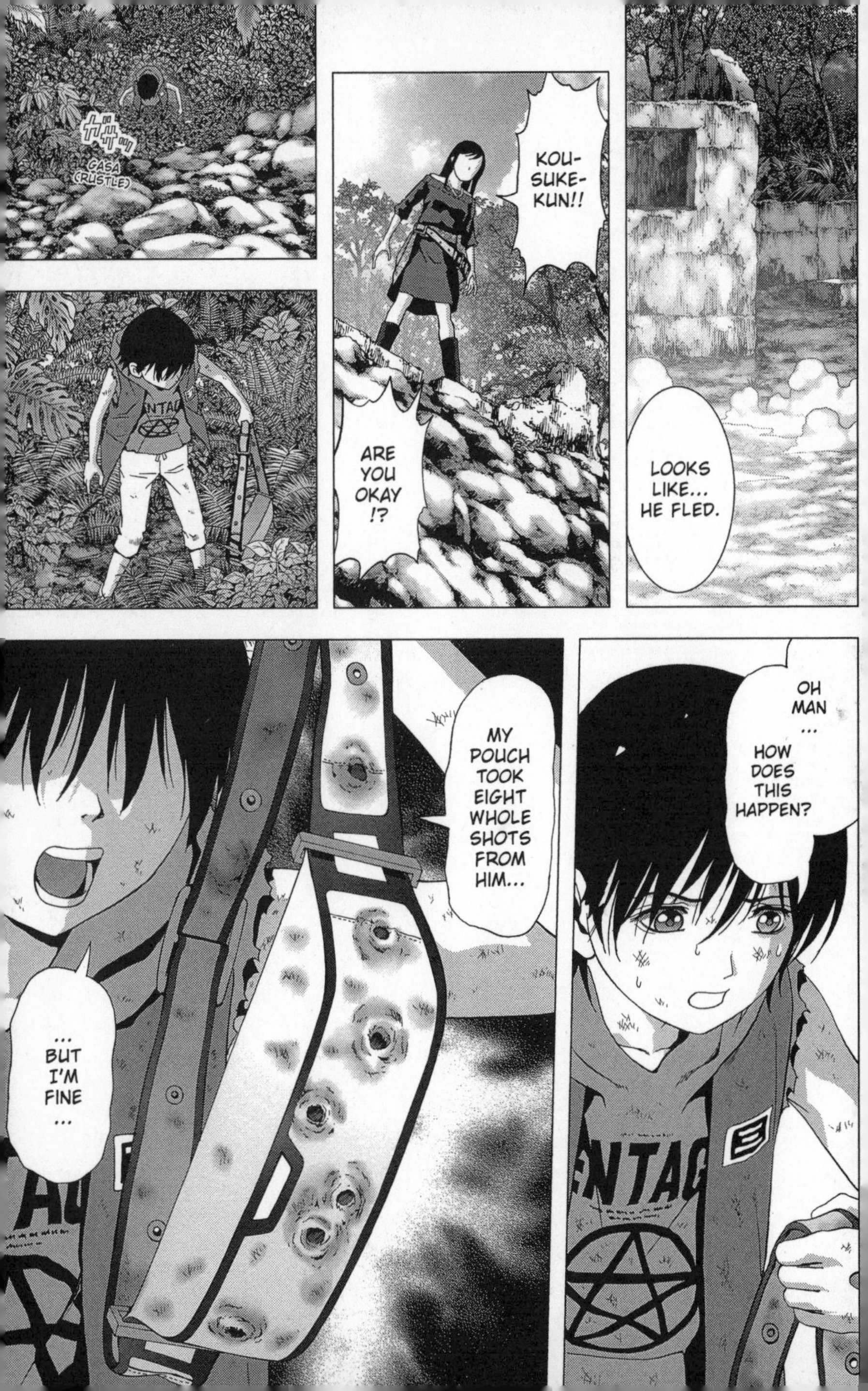
LOOKS LIKE... HE FLED.
KOU-SUKE-KUN!!
ARE YOU OKAY!?
ガサッ
GASA (RUSTLE)
OH MAN...
HOW DOES THIS HAPPEN?
MY POUCH TOOK EIGHT WHOLE SHOTS FROM HIM...
... BUT I'M FINE ...

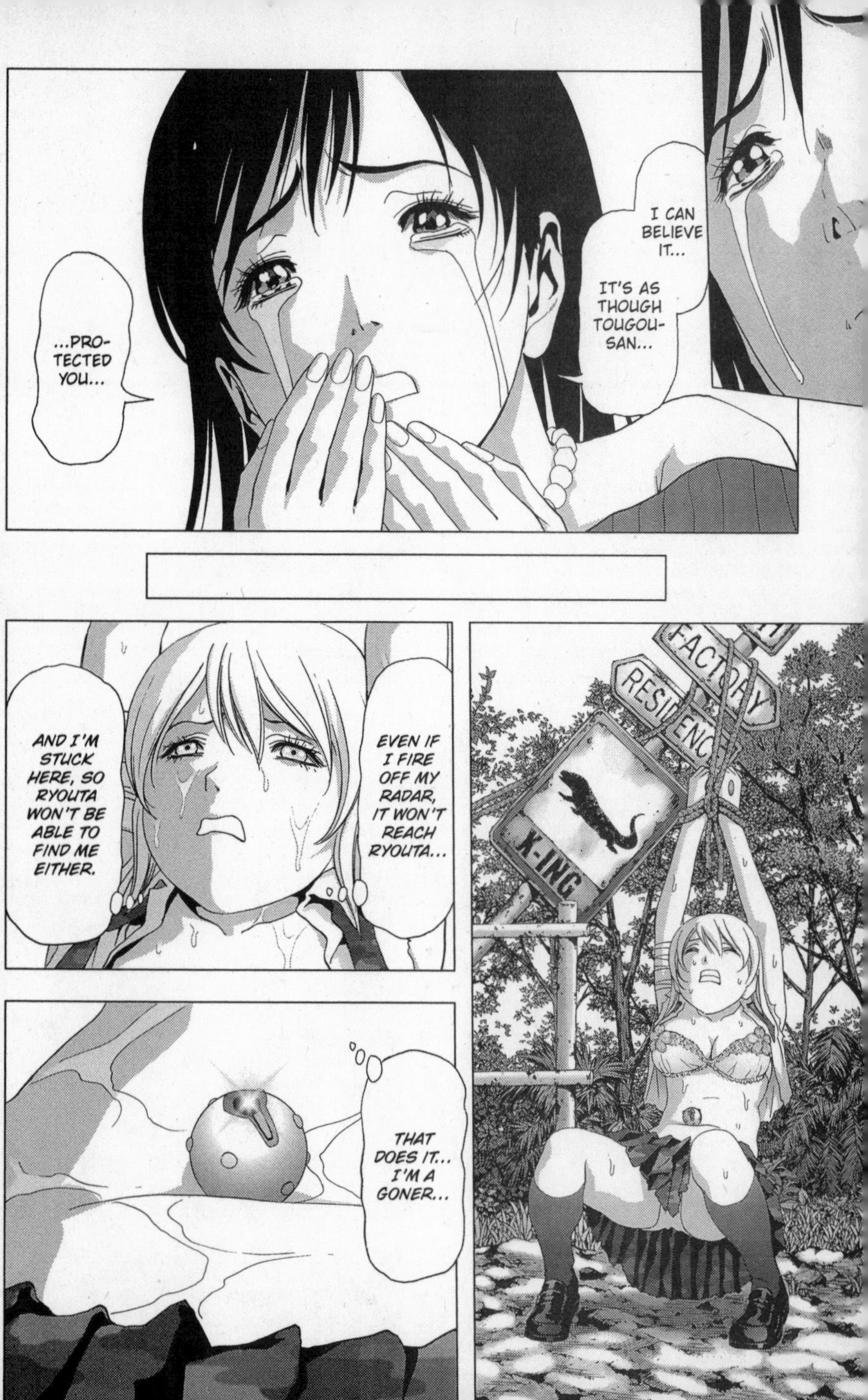
I CAN BELIEVE IT...
IT'S AS THOUGH TOUGOU-SAN...
...PRO-TECTED YOU...
FACTORY
RESIDENC
X-ING
EVEN IF I FIRE OFF MY RADAR, IT WON'T REACH RYOUTA...
AND I'M STUCK HERE, SO RYOUTA WON'T BE ABLE TO FIND ME EITHER.
THAT DOES IT... I'M A GONER...

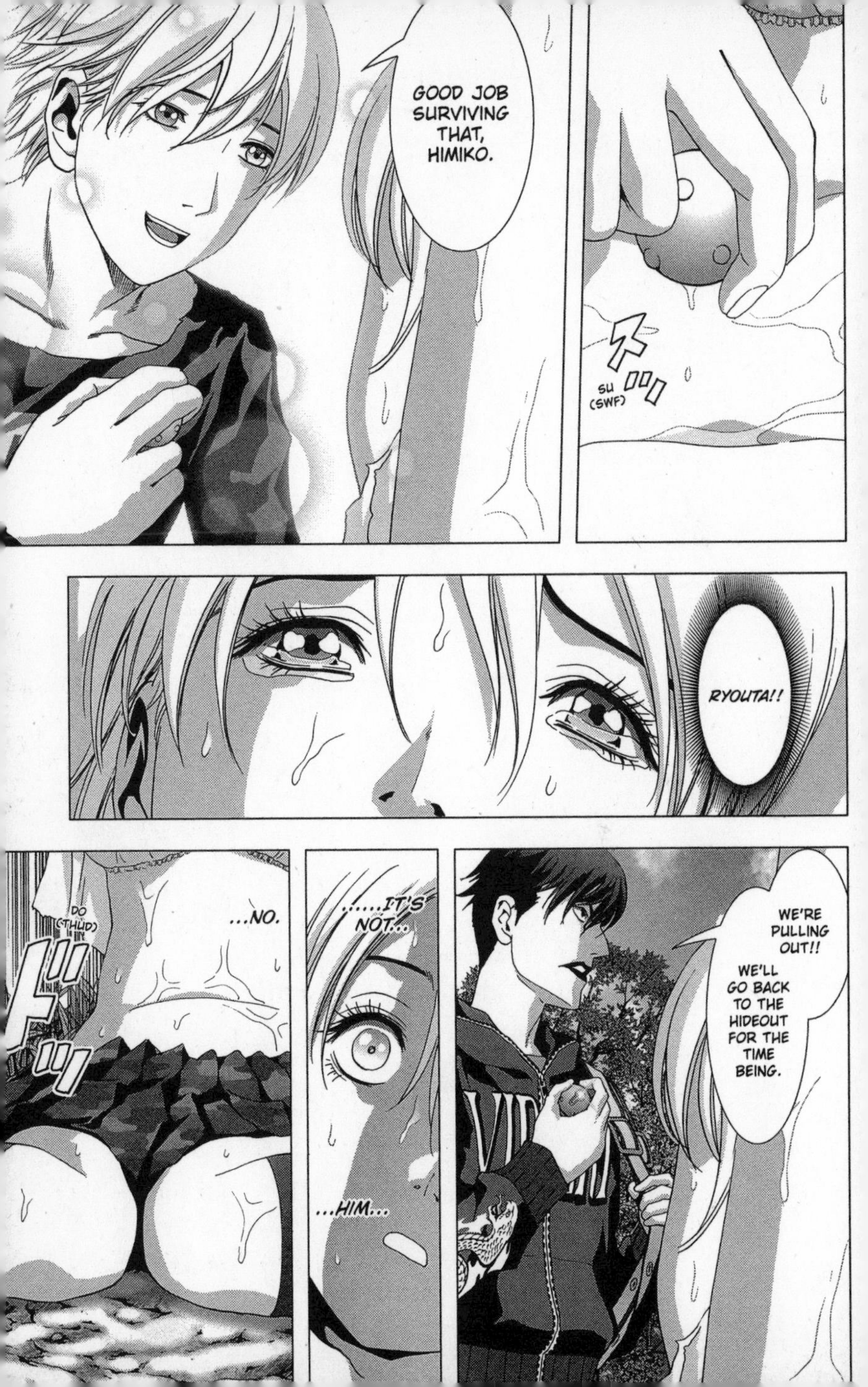
SU (SWF)
GOOD JOB SURVIVING THAT, HIMIKO.
RYOUTA!!
WE'RE PULLING OUT!!
WE'LL GO BACK TO THE HIDEOUT FOR THE TIME BEING.
......IT'S NOT...
...HIM...
DO (THUD)
...NO.

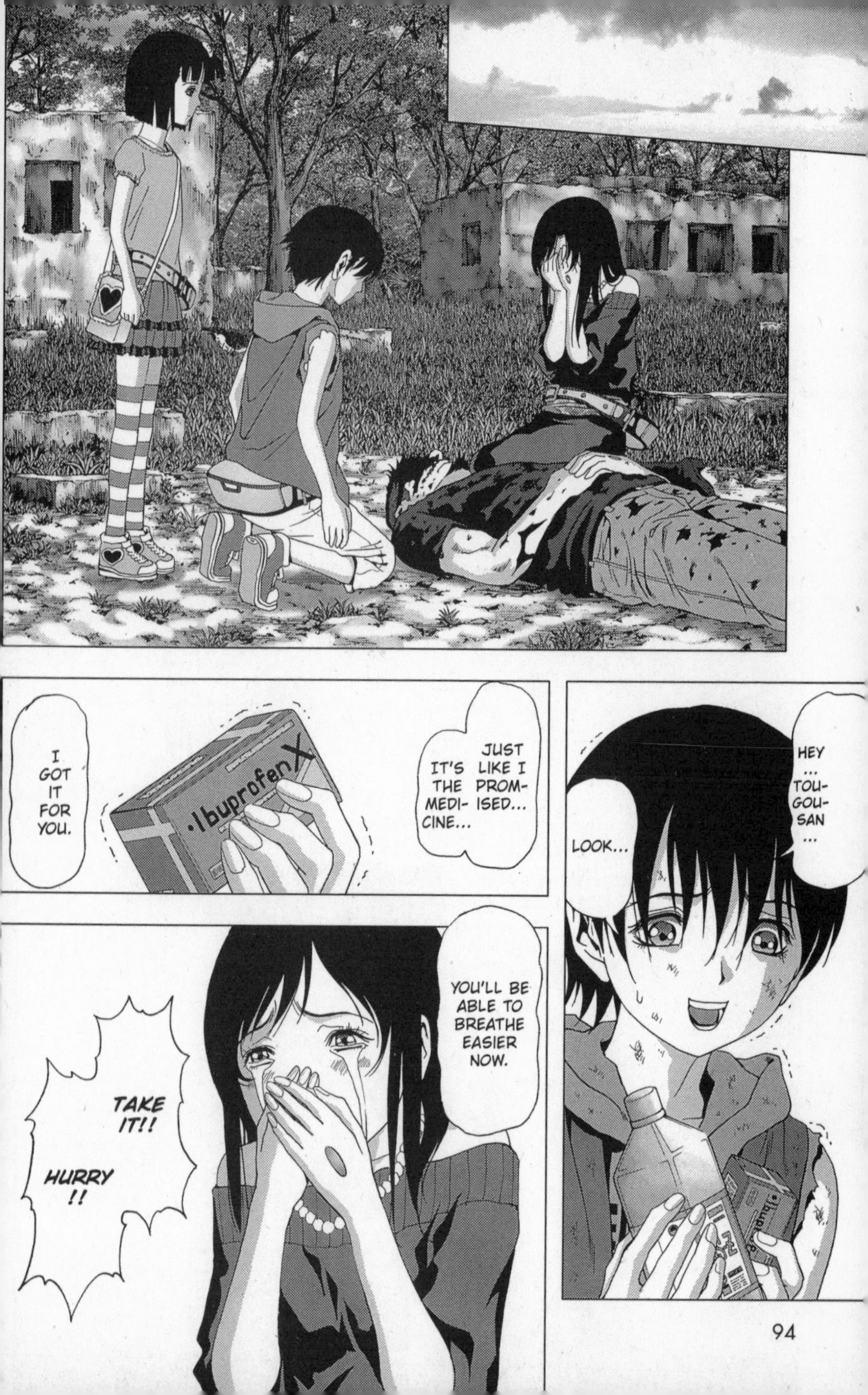
HEY... TOU-GOU-SAN...
LOOK...
JUST LIKE I PROM-ISED...
IT'S THE MEDI-CINE...
I GOT IT FOR YOU.
Ibuprofen X
YOU'LL BE ABLE TO BREATHE EASIER NOW.
TAKE IT!!
HURRY!!

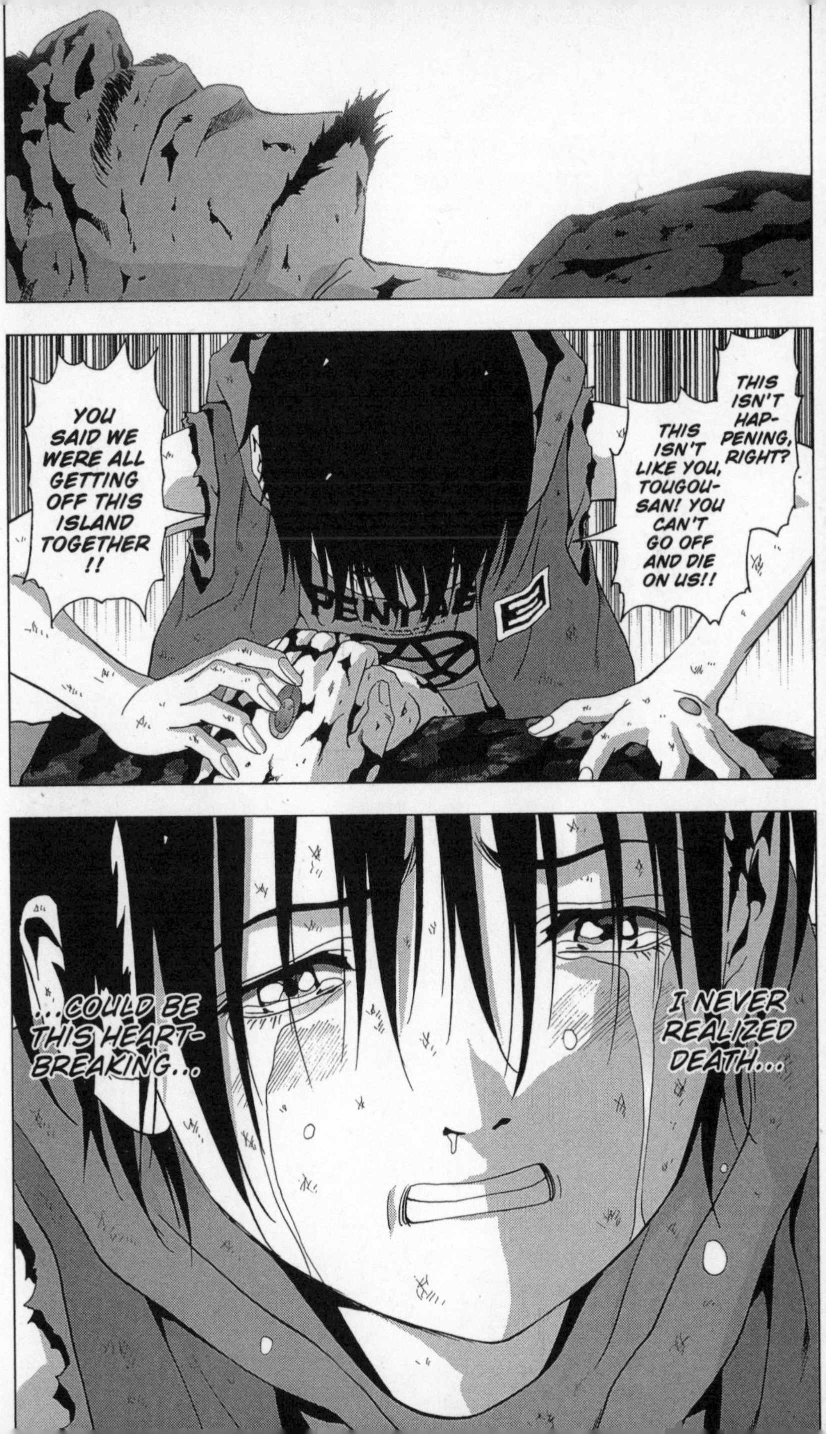
THIS ISN'T HAPPENING, RIGHT?
THIS ISN'T LIKE YOU, TOUGOU-SAN! YOU CAN'T GO OFF AND DIE ON US!!
YOU SAID WE WERE ALL GETTING OFF THIS ISLAND TOGETHER!!
I NEVER REALIZED DEATH...
...COULD BE THIS HEART-BREAKING...

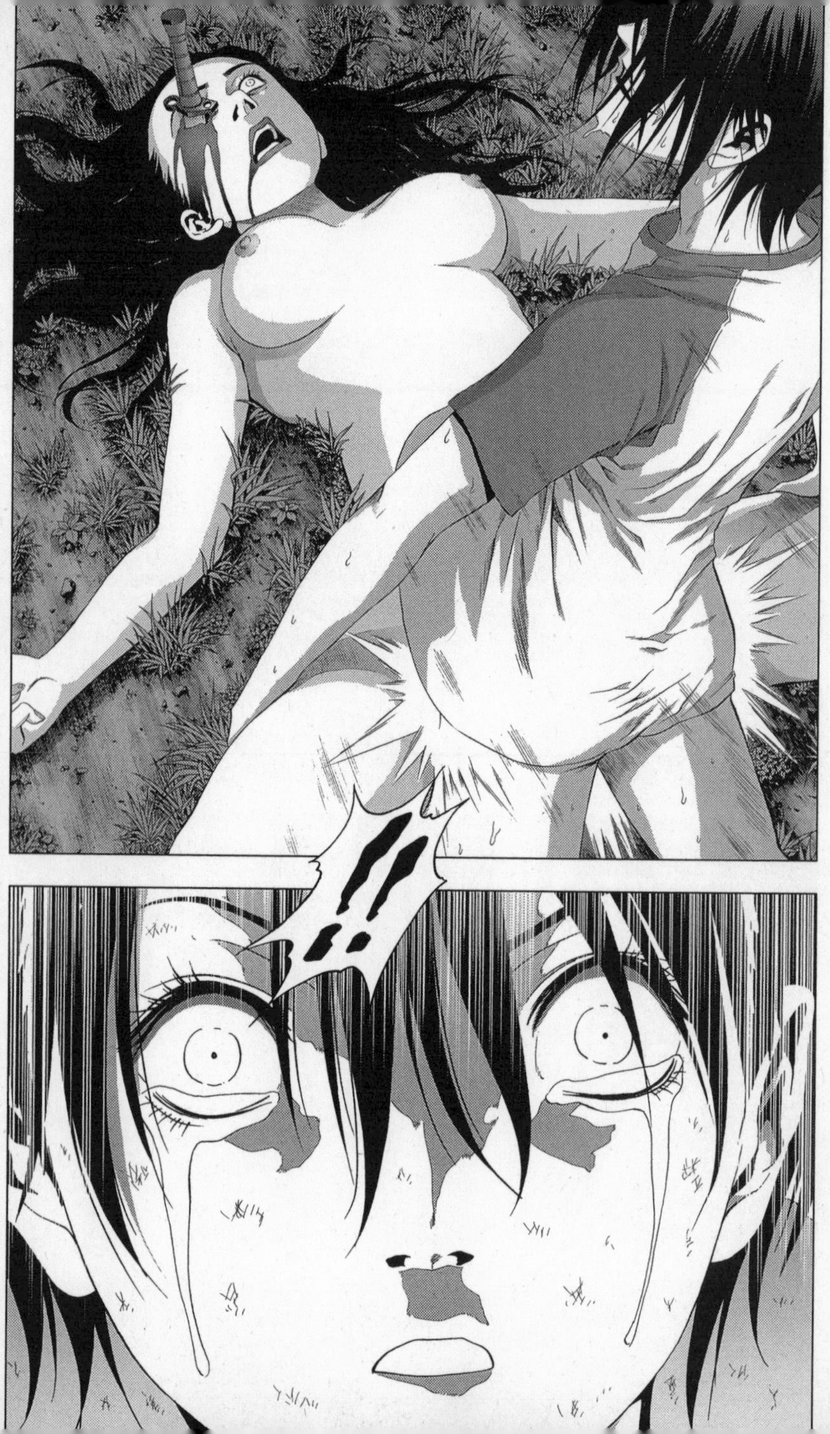
!!

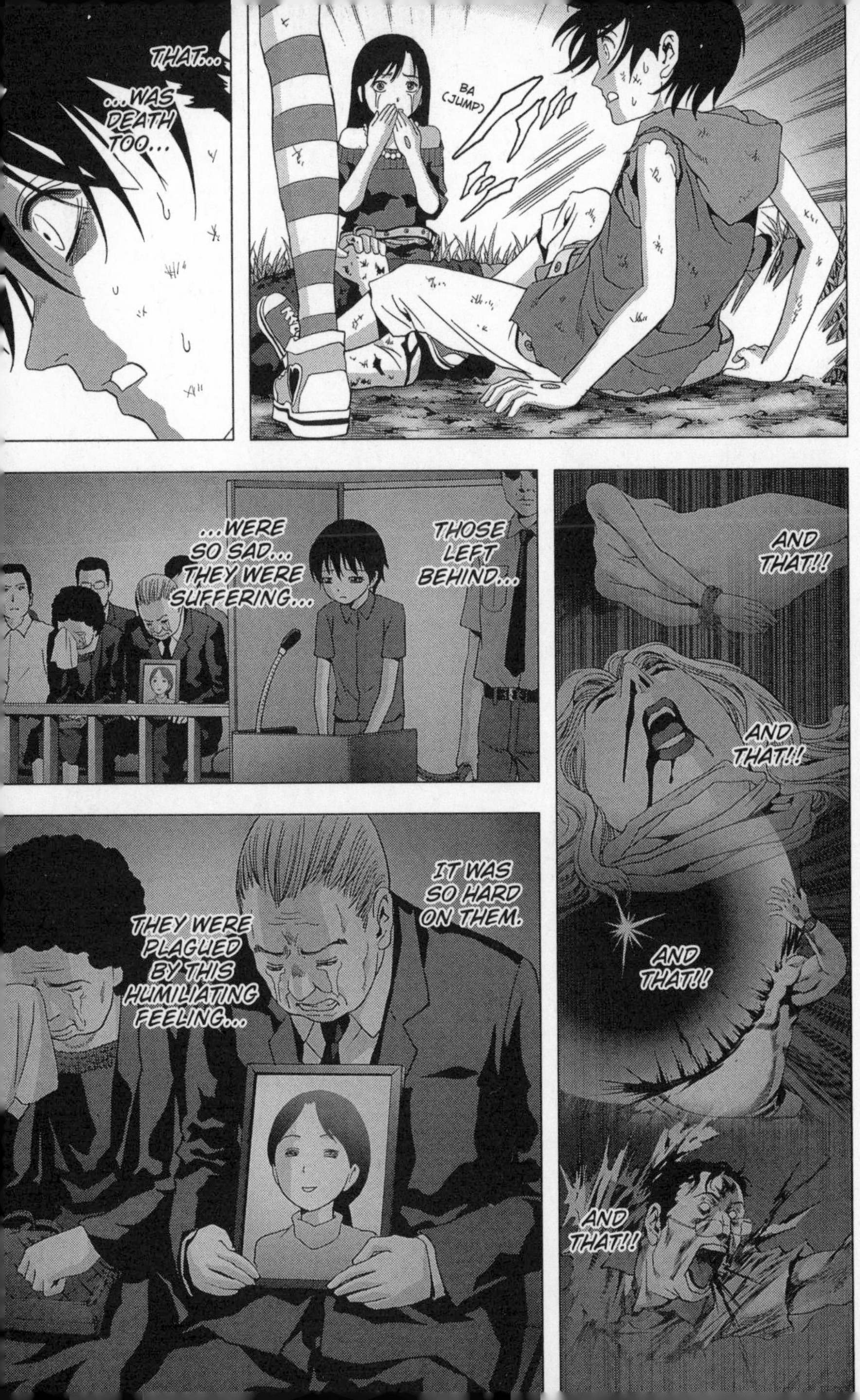
BA (JUMP)
THAT...
...WAS DEATH TOO...
AND THAT!!
AND THAT!!
AND THAT!!
AND THAT!!
THOSE LEFT BEHIND...
...WERE SO SAD... THEY WERE SUFFERING...
IT WAS SO HARD ON THEM.
THEY WERE PLAGUED BY THIS HUMILIATING FEELING...

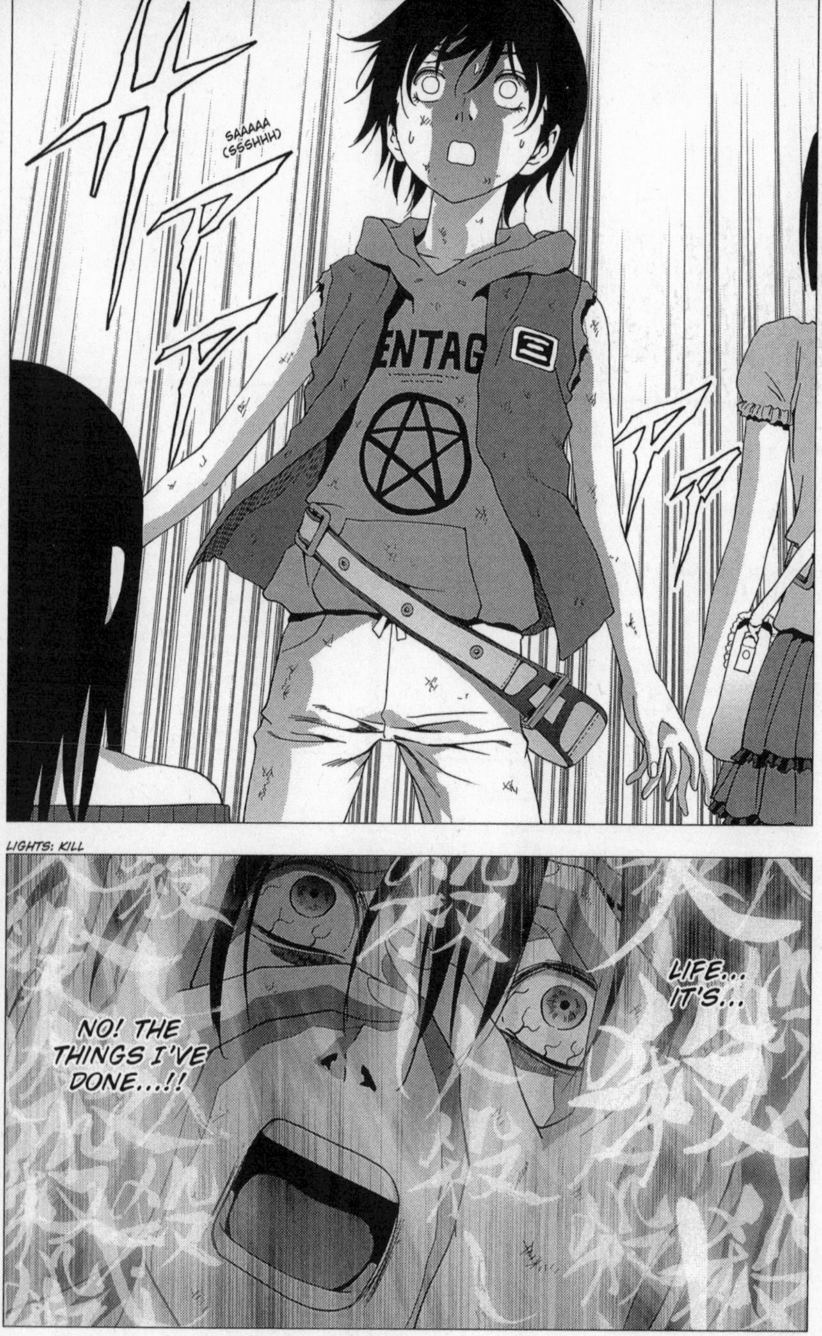
SAAAAA (SSSHHH)
ENTAG
LIGHTS: KILL
LIFE... IT'S...
NO! THE THINGS I'VE DONE...!!

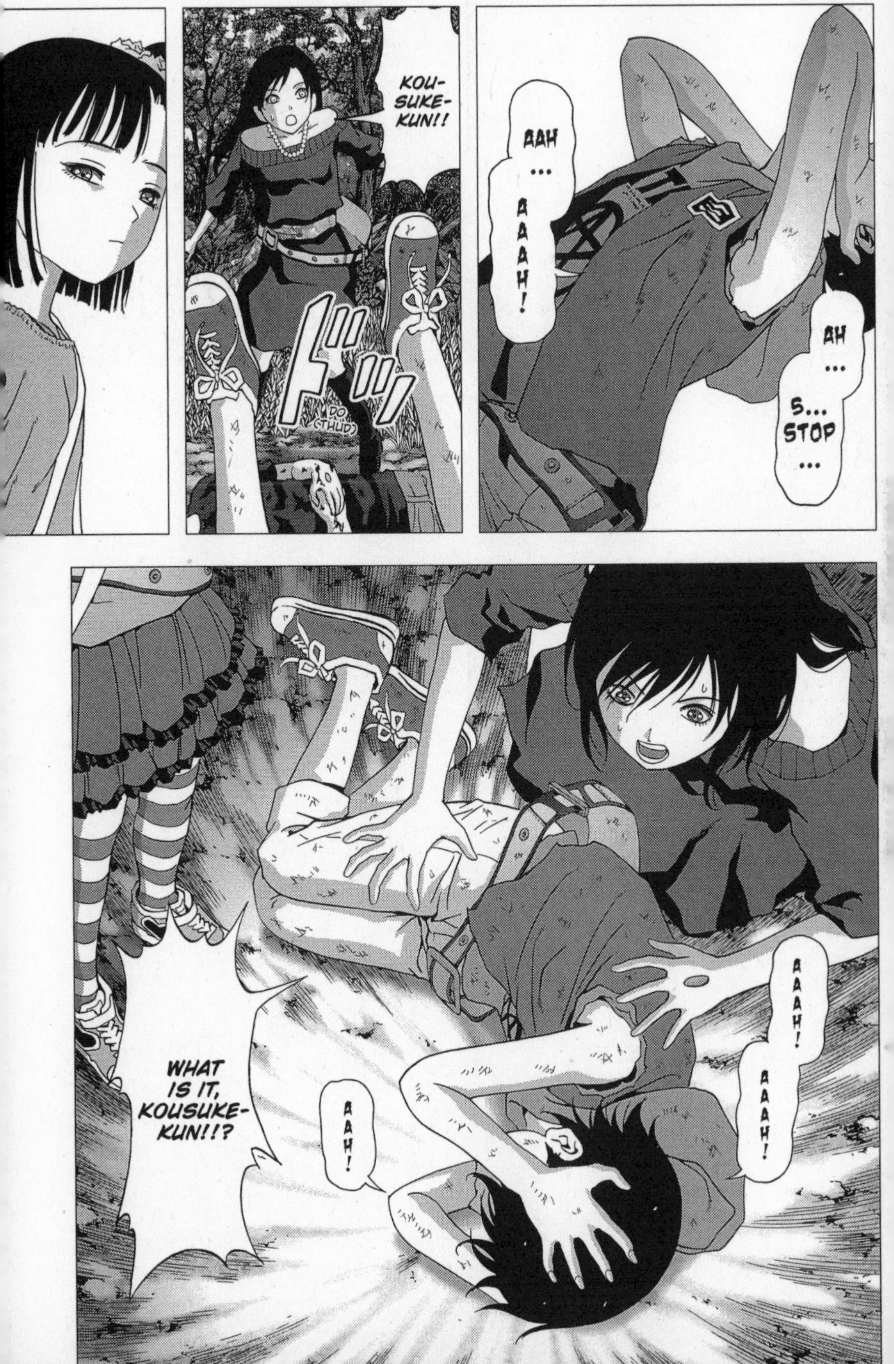

AAH ... AAAAH!
AH ... S... STOP ...
KOU-SUKE-KUN!!
DO (THUD)
AAAH!
AAAAH!
AAAH!
WHAT IS IT, KOUSUKE-KUN!!?

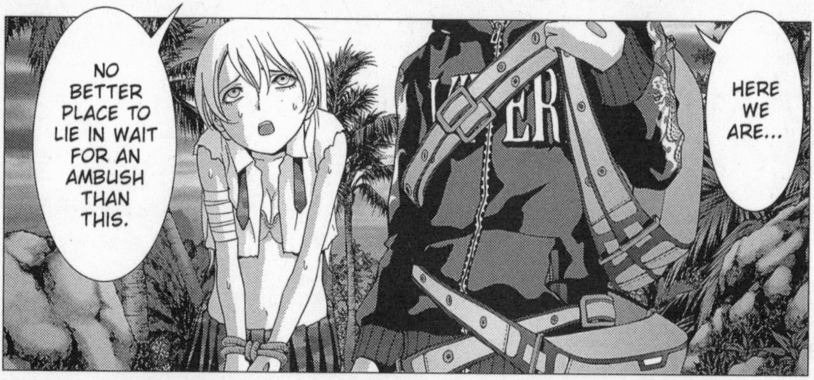
HERE WE ARE...
NO BETTER PLACE TO LIE IN WAIT FOR AN AMBUSH THAN THIS.

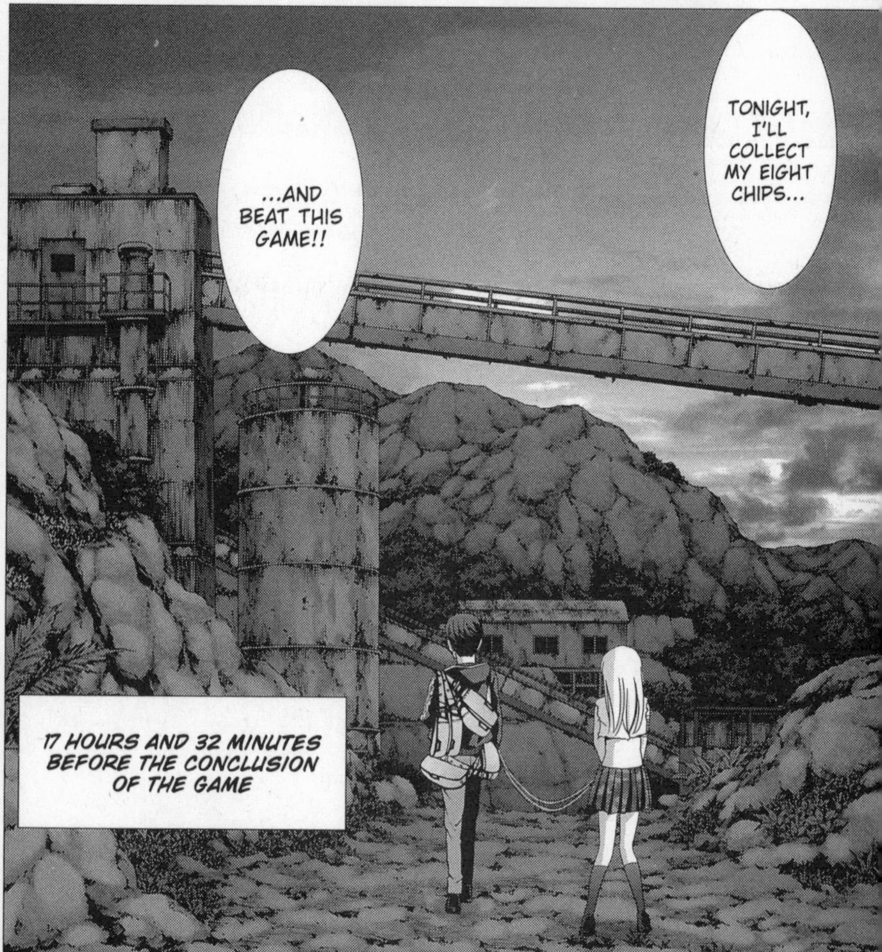
TONIGHT, I'LL COLLECT MY EIGHT CHIPS...
...AND BEAT THIS GAME!!
17 HOURS AND 32 MINUTES BEFORE THE CONCLUSION OF THE GAME

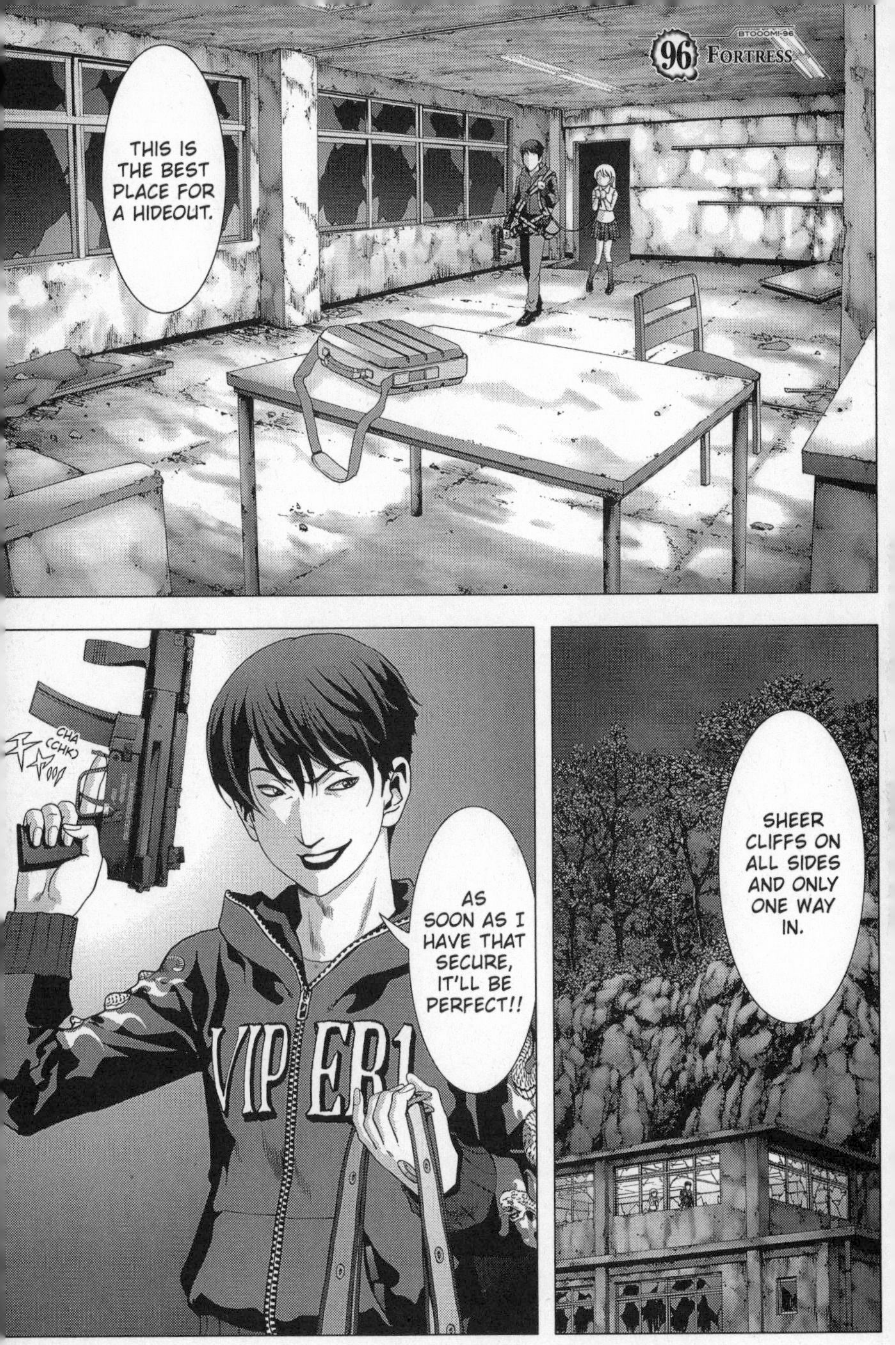
BTOOOM!-96
96 FORTRESS
THIS IS THE BEST PLACE FOR A HIDEOUT.
SHEER CLIFFS ON ALL SIDES AND ONLY ONE WAY IN.
CHA (CHK)
AS SOON AS I HAVE THAT SECURE, IT'LL BE PERFECT!!
VIP ER1

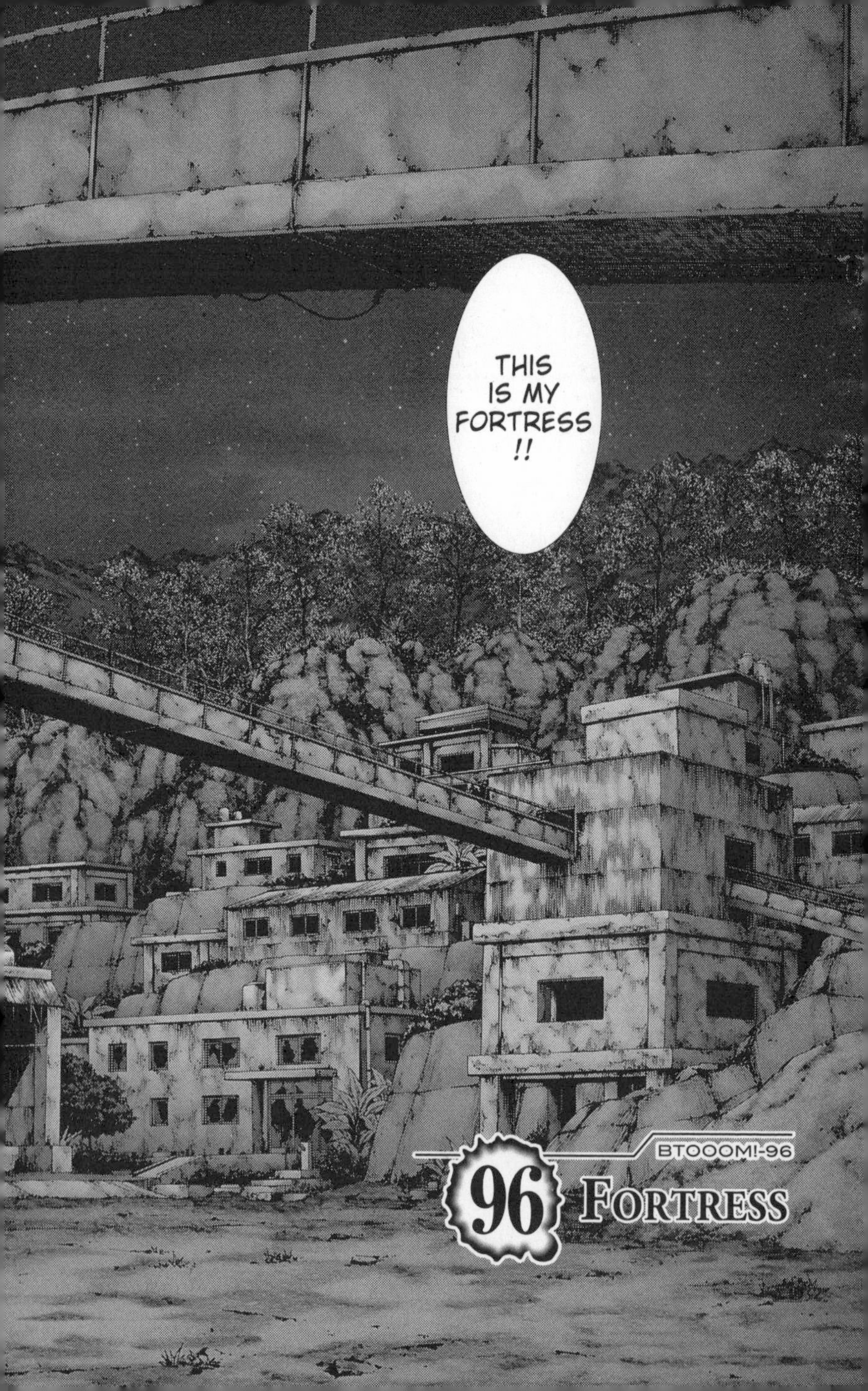
THIS IS MY FORTRESS !!
BTOOOM!-96
96 FORTRESS

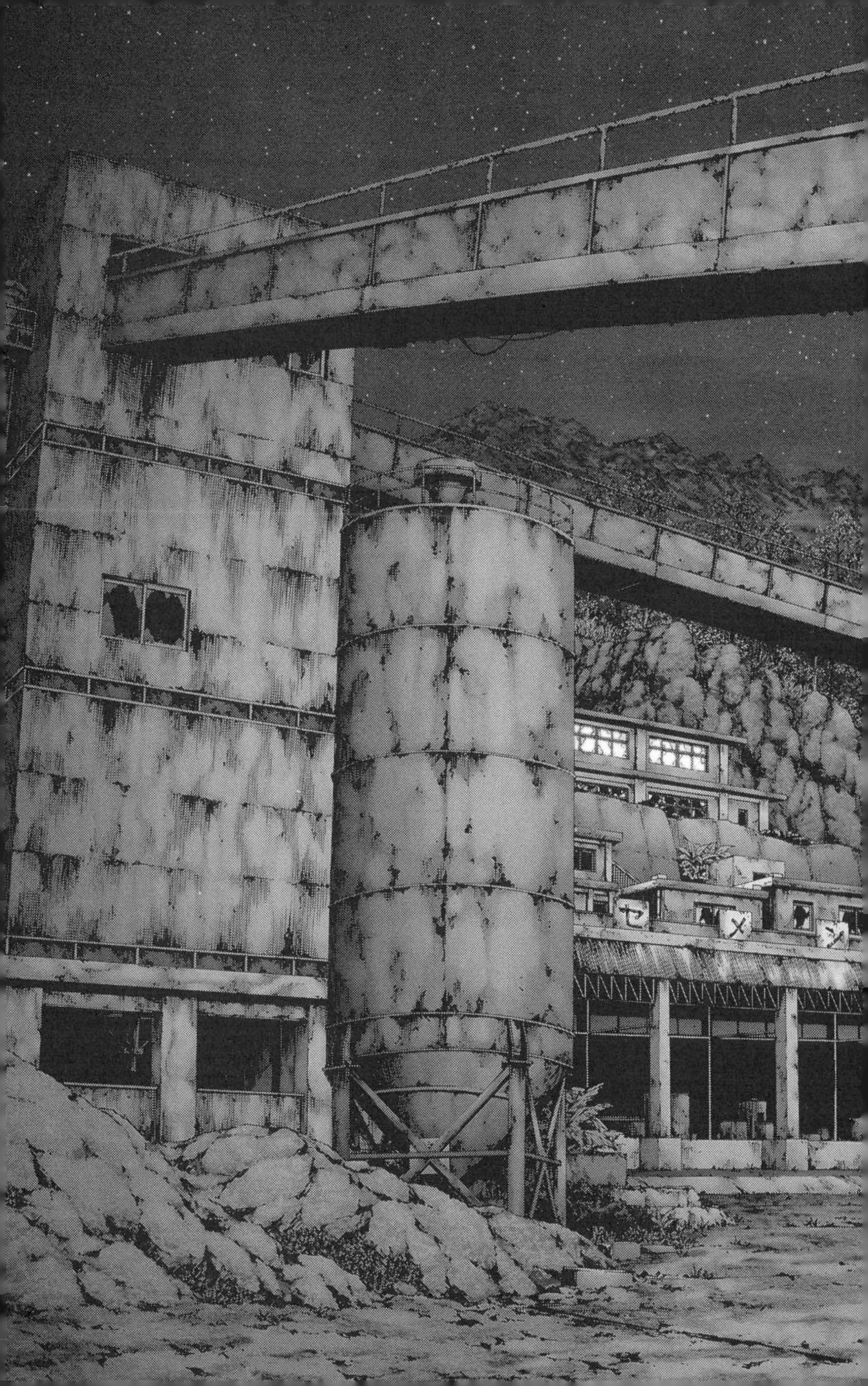
セメン

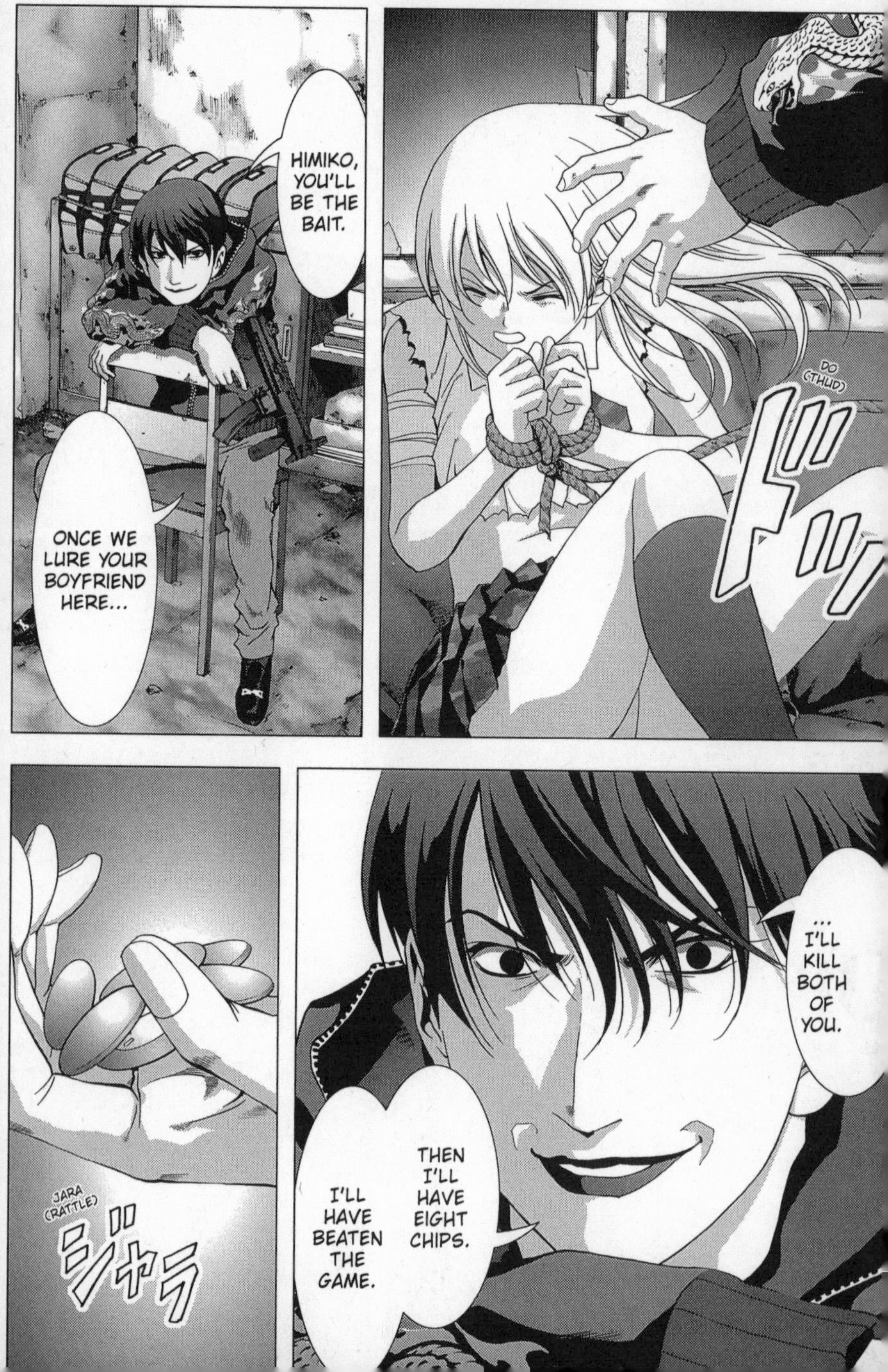
DO (THUD)
ドッ
HIMIKO, YOU'LL BE THE BAIT.
ONCE WE LURE YOUR BOYFRIEND HERE...
... I'LL KILL BOTH OF YOU.
THEN I'LL HAVE EIGHT CHIPS.
I'LL HAVE BEATEN THE GAME.
JARA (RATTLE)
ジャラ

RYOUTA ...!!

...OH!

BUT...

I WISH YOU'D COME SAVE ME...

...I HAVE TO LET HIM KNOW IT'S A TRAP...

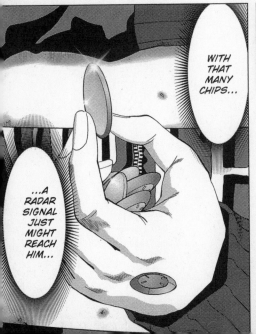

WITH THAT MANY CHIPS...

...A RADAR SIGNAL JUST MIGHT REACH HIM...

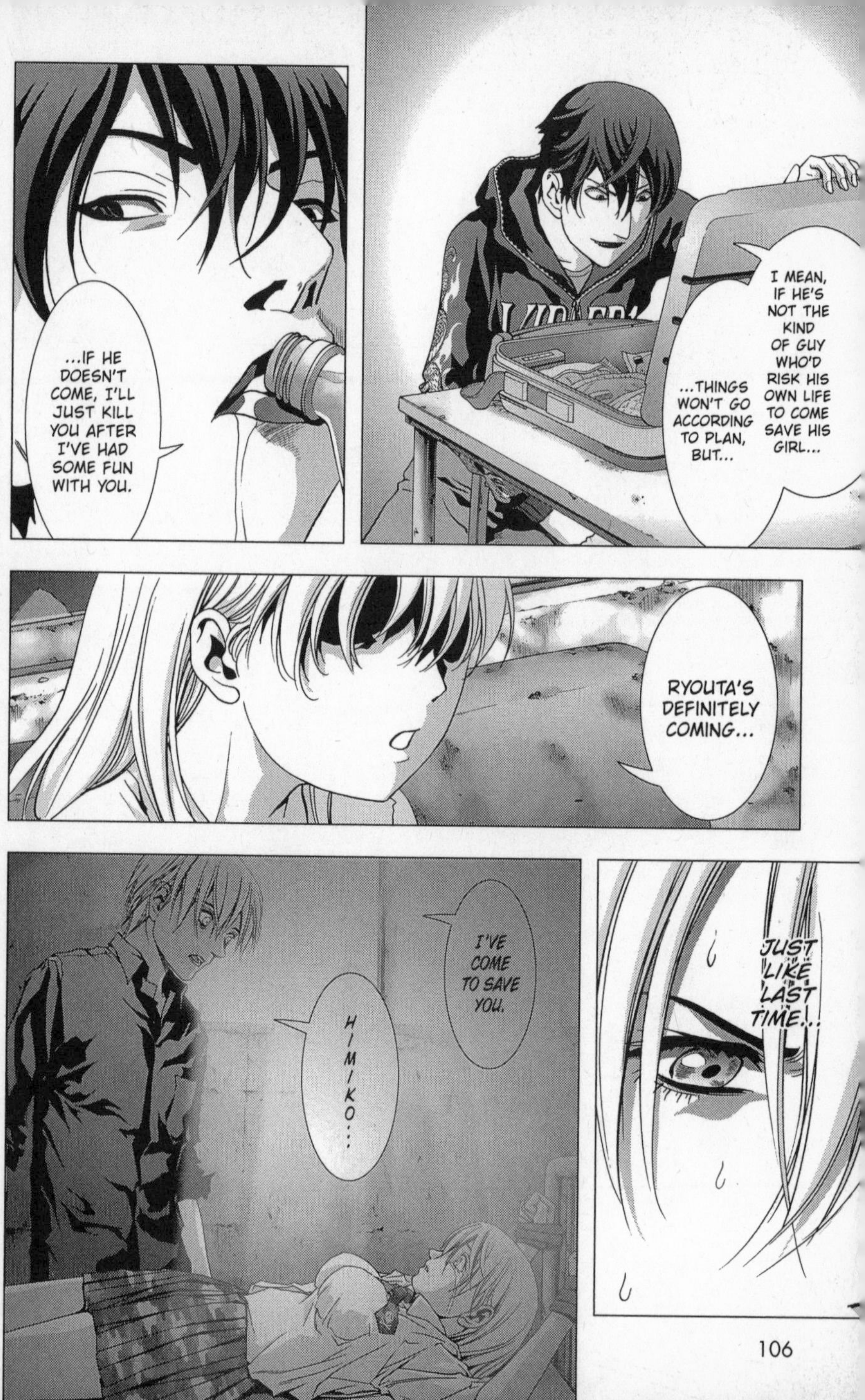
I MEAN, IF HE'S NOT THE KIND OF GUY WHO'D RISK HIS OWN LIFE TO COME SAVE HIS GIRL...
...THINGS WON'T GO ACCORDING TO PLAN, BUT...
...IF HE DOESN'T COME, I'LL JUST KILL YOU AFTER I'VE HAD SOME FUN WITH YOU.
RYOUTA'S DEFINITELY COMING...
JUST LIKE LAST TIME...
I'VE COME TO SAVE YOU.
HIMIKO...

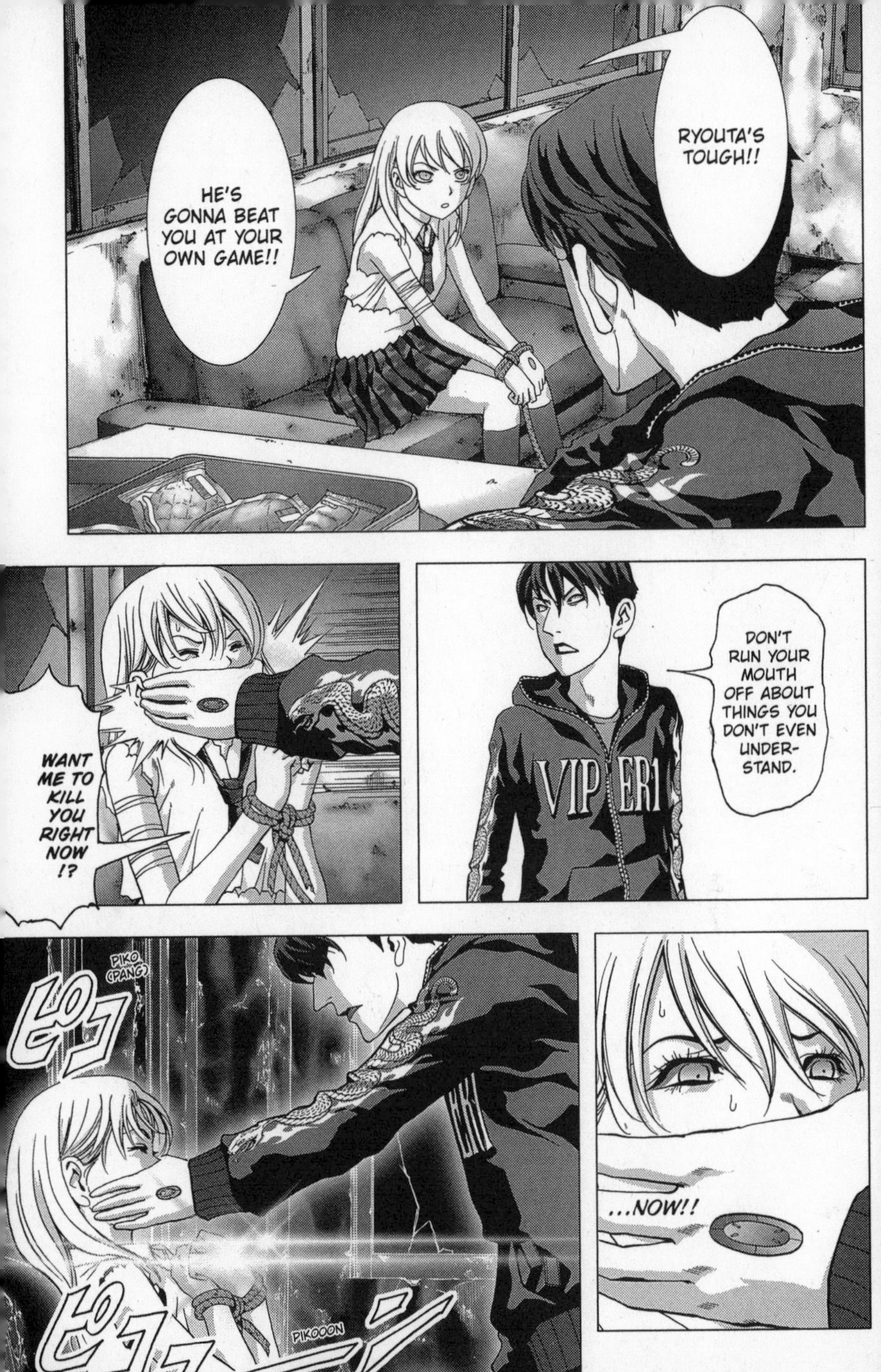
RYOUTA'S TOUGH!!
HE'S GONNA BEAT YOU AT YOUR OWN GAME!!
DON'T RUN YOUR MOUTH OFF ABOUT THINGS YOU DON'T EVEN UNDER-STAND.
VIPER1
WANT ME TO KILL YOU RIGHT NOW!?
...NOW!!
PIKO (PANG)
PIKOOON

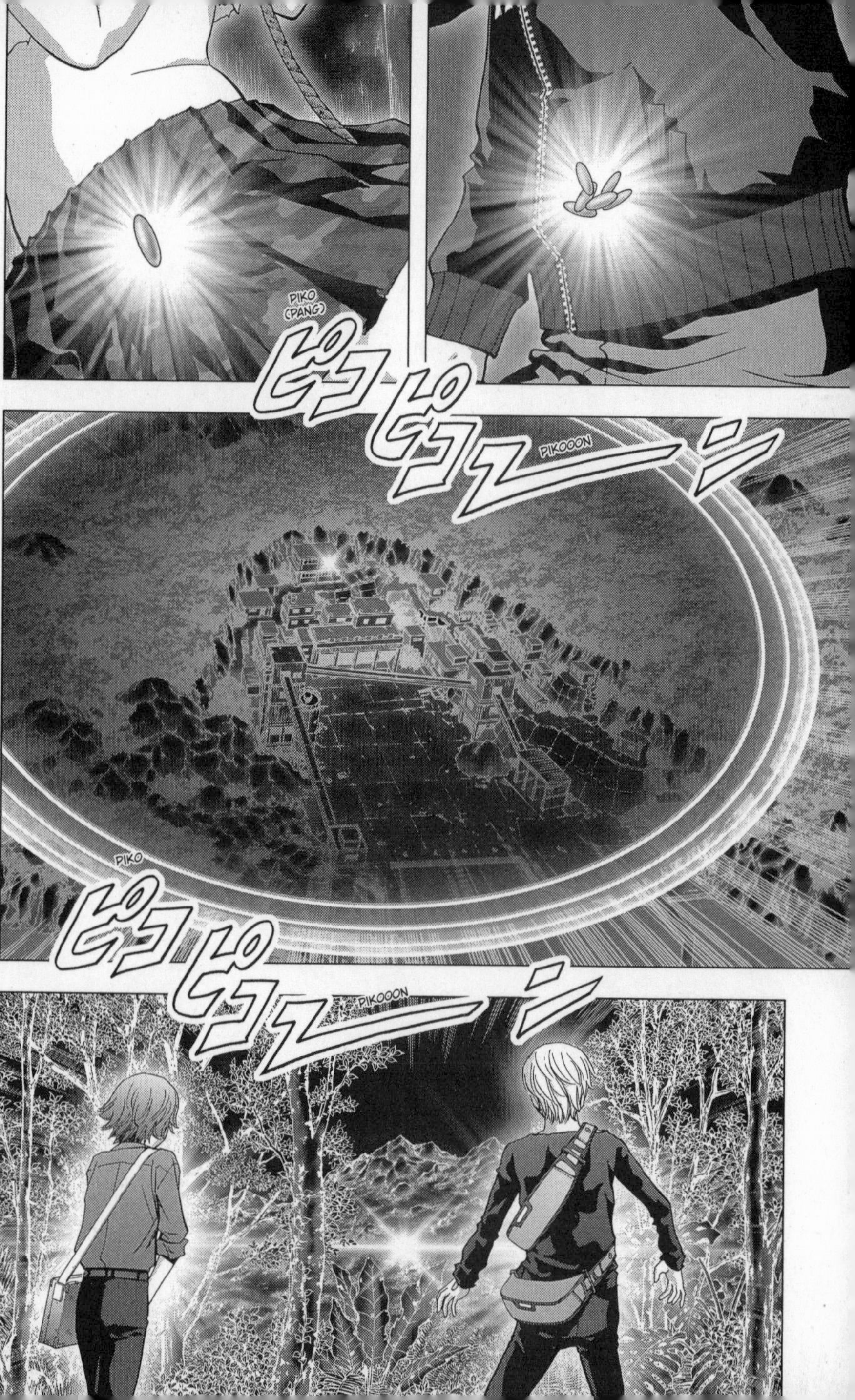
PIKO (PANG)
PIKOOON
PIKO
PIKOOON

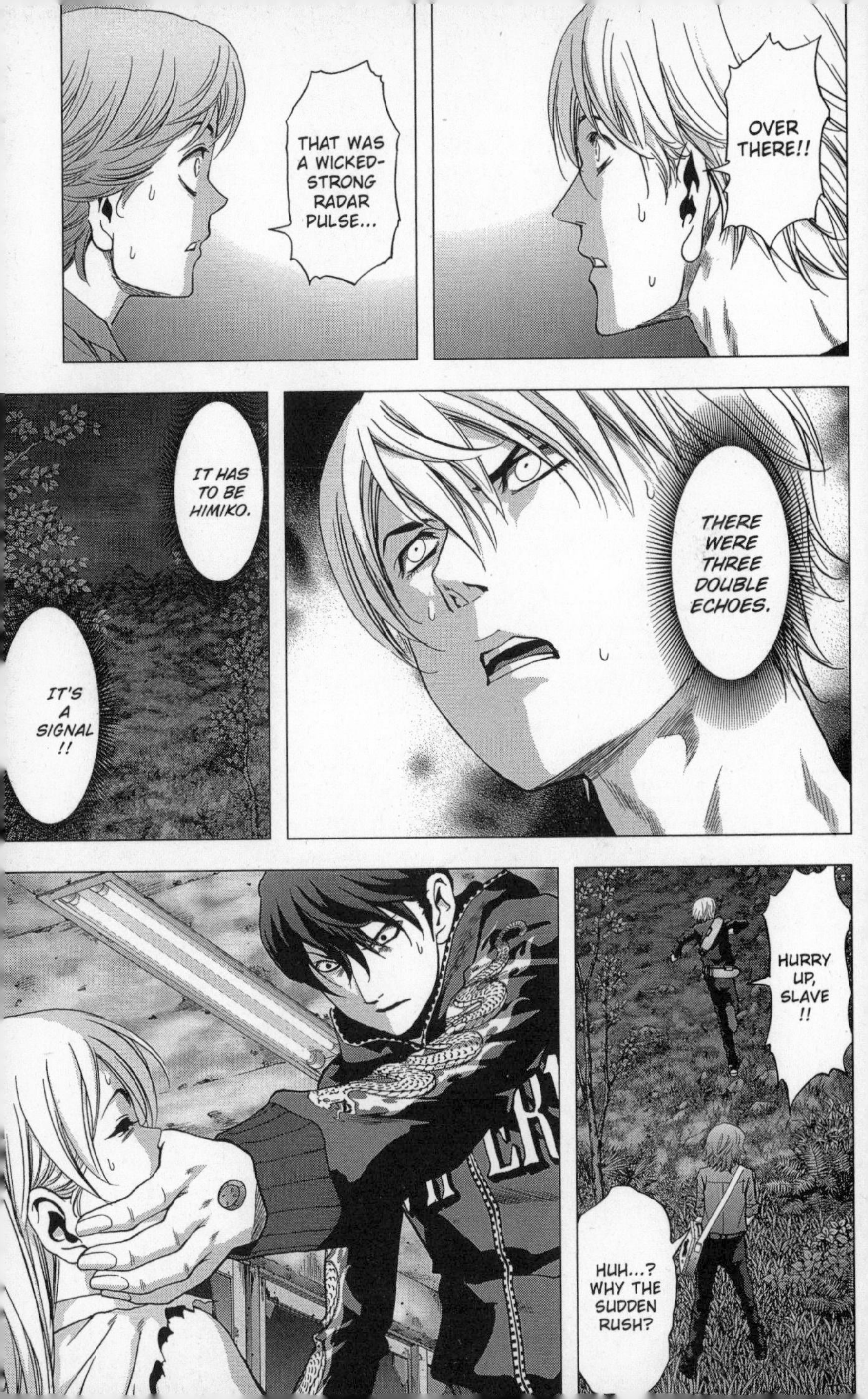
OVER THERE!!
THAT WAS A WICKED-STRONG RADAR PULSE...
THERE WERE THREE DOUBLE ECHOES.
IT HAS TO BE HIMIKO.
IT'S A SIGNAL!!
HURRY UP, SLAVE!!
HUH...? WHY THE SUDDEN RUSH?

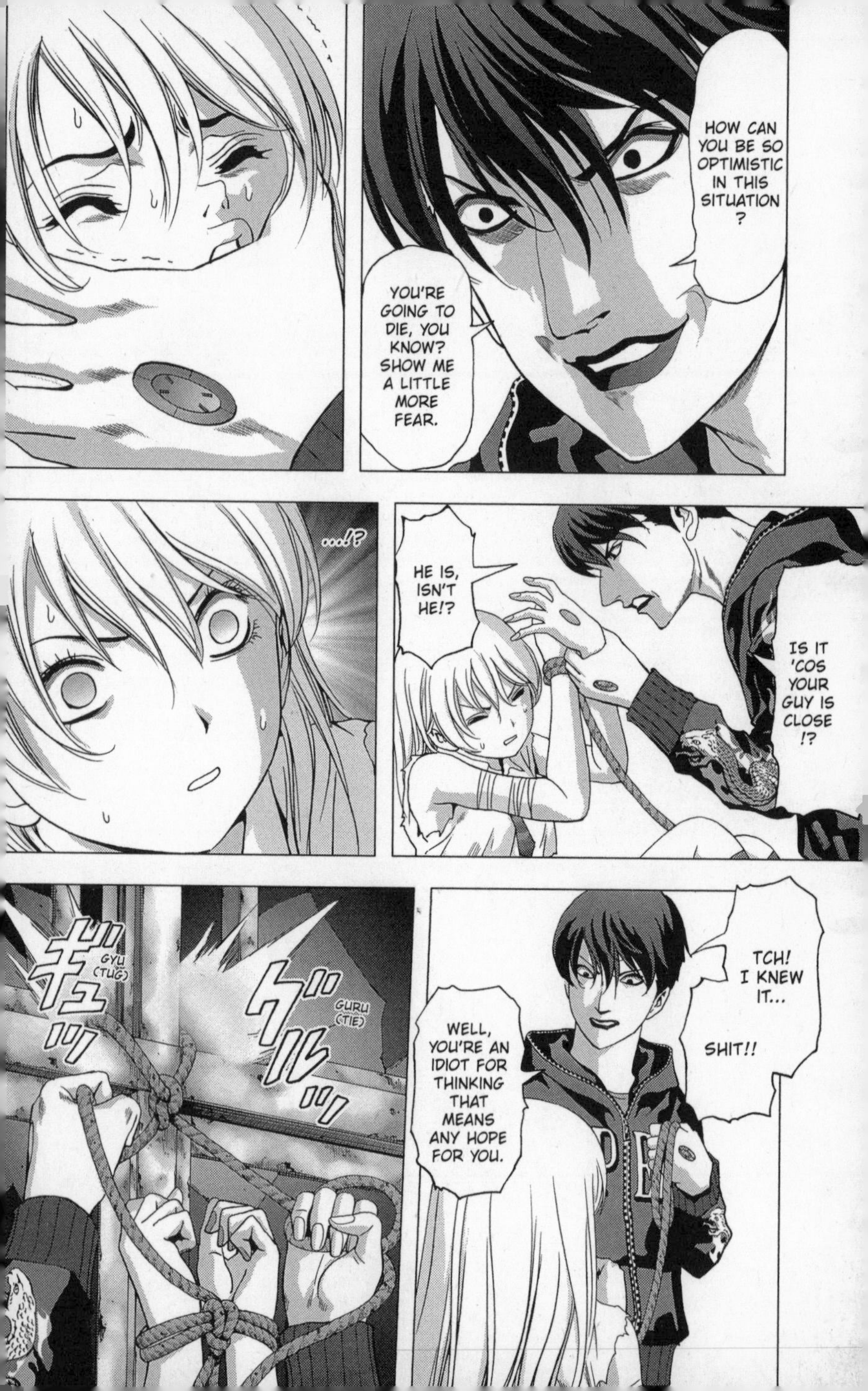
HOW CAN YOU BE SO OPTIMISTIC IN THIS SITUATION?
YOU'RE GOING TO DIE, YOU KNOW? SHOW ME A LITTLE MORE FEAR.
IS IT 'COS YOUR GUY IS CLOSE!?
HE IS, ISN'T HE!?
...!?
TCH! I KNEW IT...
SHIT!!
WELL, YOU'RE AN IDIOT FOR THINKING THAT MEANS ANY HOPE FOR YOU.
GURU (TIE)
GYU (TUG)

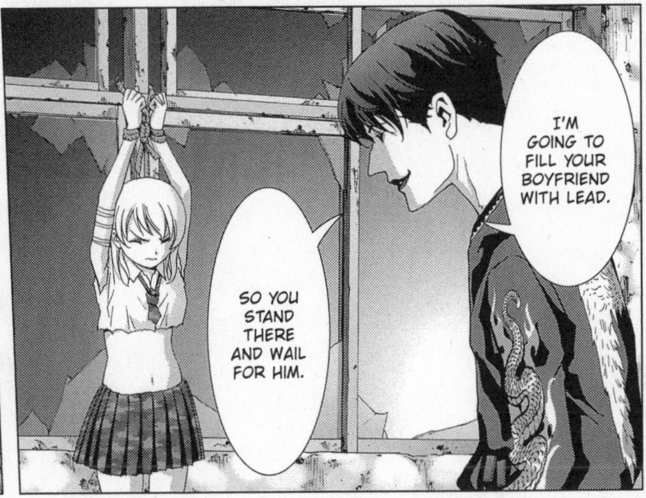
I'M GOING TO FILL YOUR BOYFRIEND WITH LEAD.
SO YOU STAND THERE AND WAIL FOR HIM.
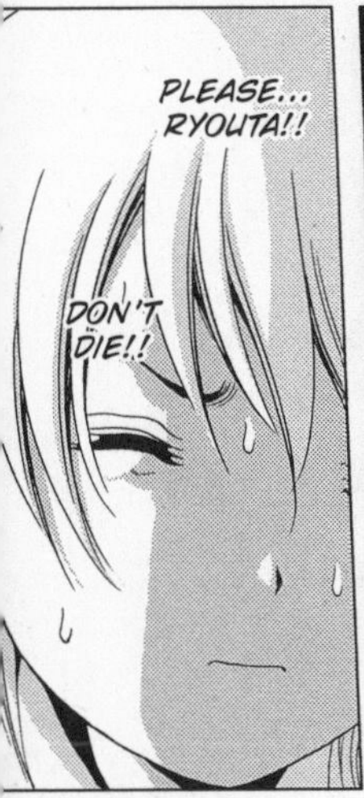
PLEASE... RYOUTA!!
DON'T DIE!!
LIGHTS: KILL
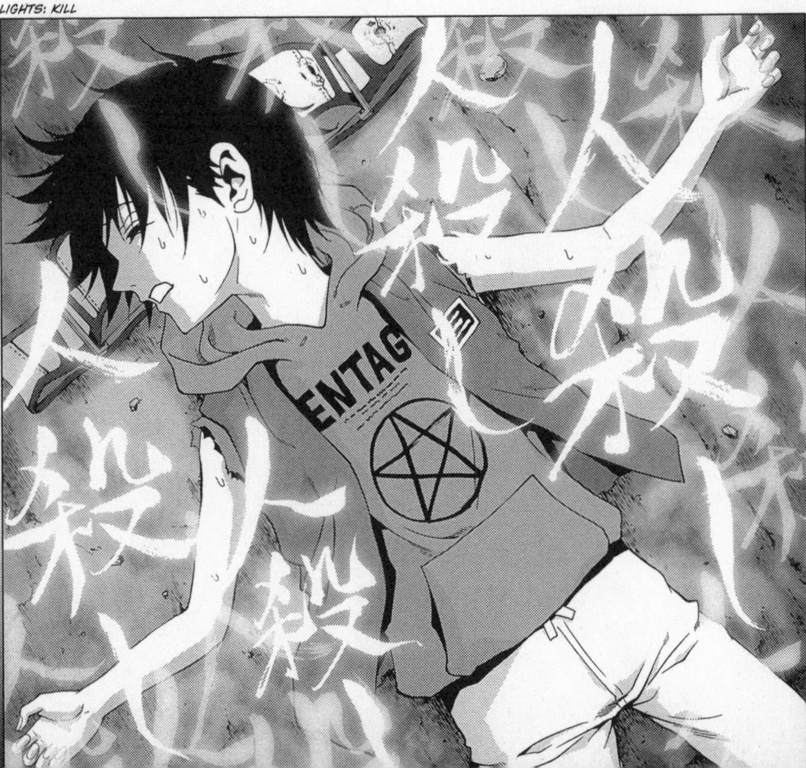

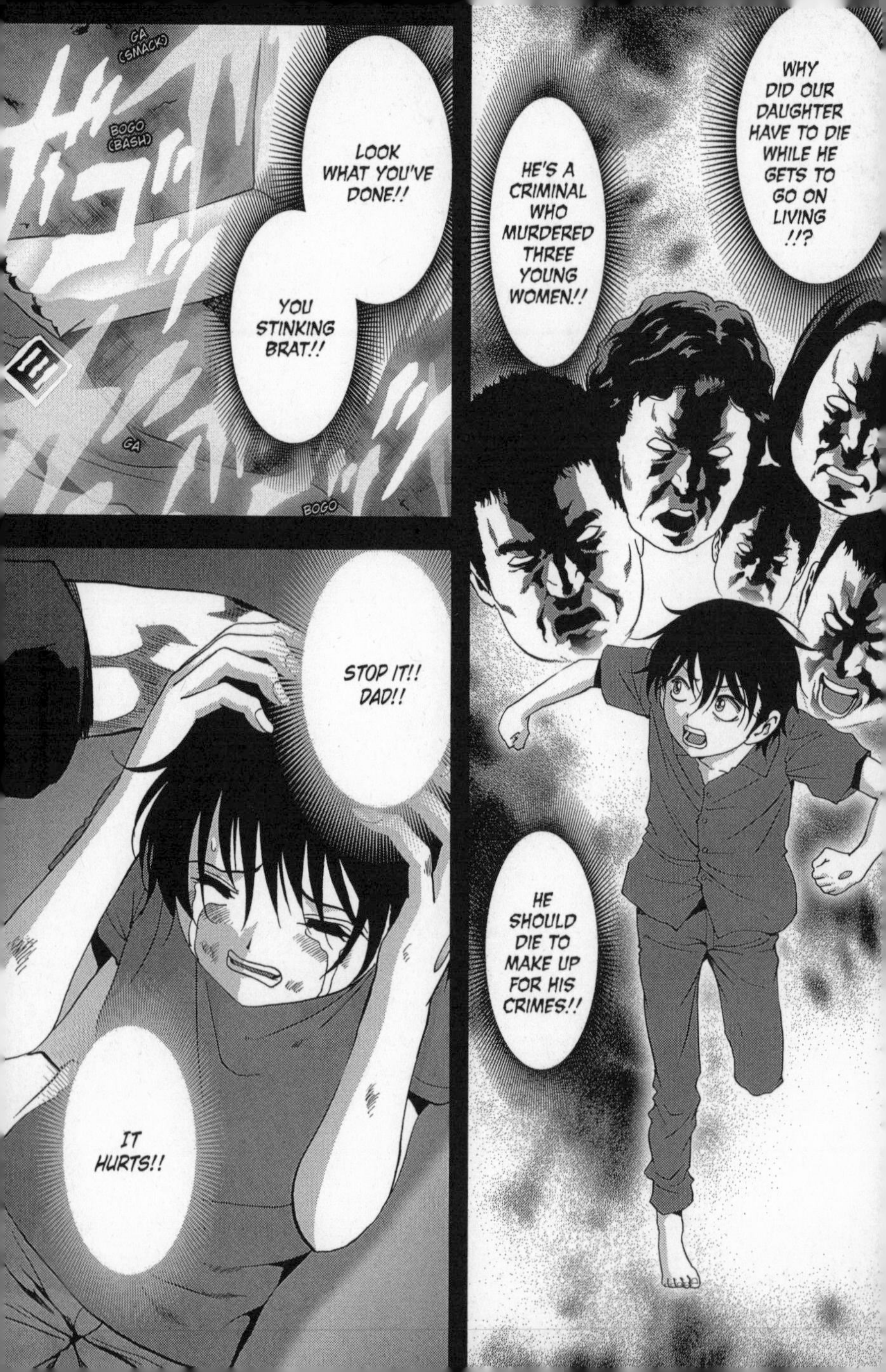
WHY DID OUR DAUGHTER HAVE TO DIE WHILE HE GETS TO GO ON LIVING!!?
HE'S A CRIMINAL WHO MURDERED THREE YOUNG WOMEN!!
HE SHOULD DIE TO MAKE UP FOR HIS CRIMES!!
GA (SMACK)
BOGO (BASH)
LOOK WHAT YOU'VE DONE!!
YOU STINKING BRAT!!
GA
BOGO
STOP IT!! DAD!!
IT HURTS!!

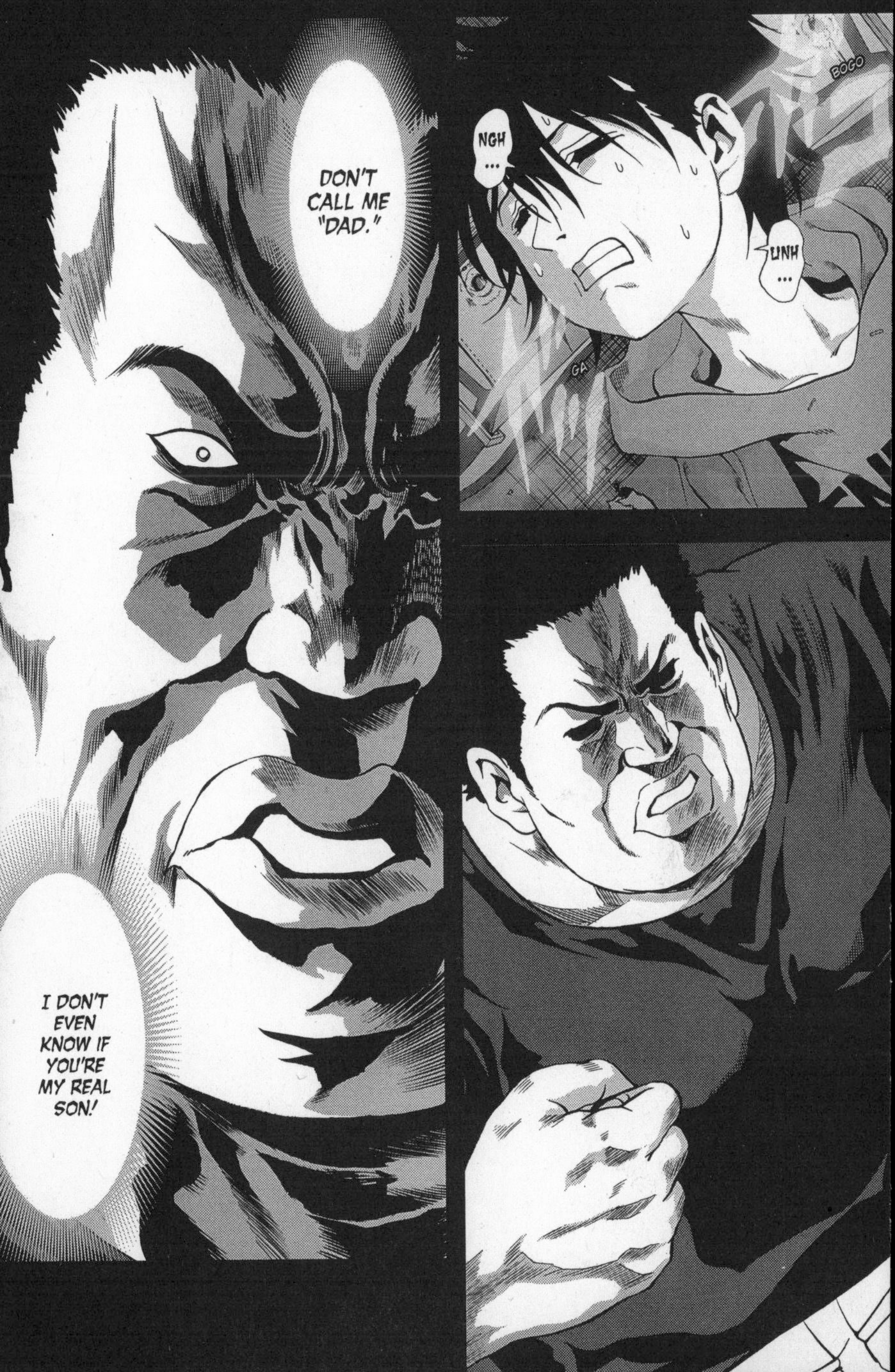
BOGO
UNH ...
NGH ...
GA
DON'T CALL ME "DAD."
I DON'T EVEN KNOW IF YOU'RE MY REAL SON!

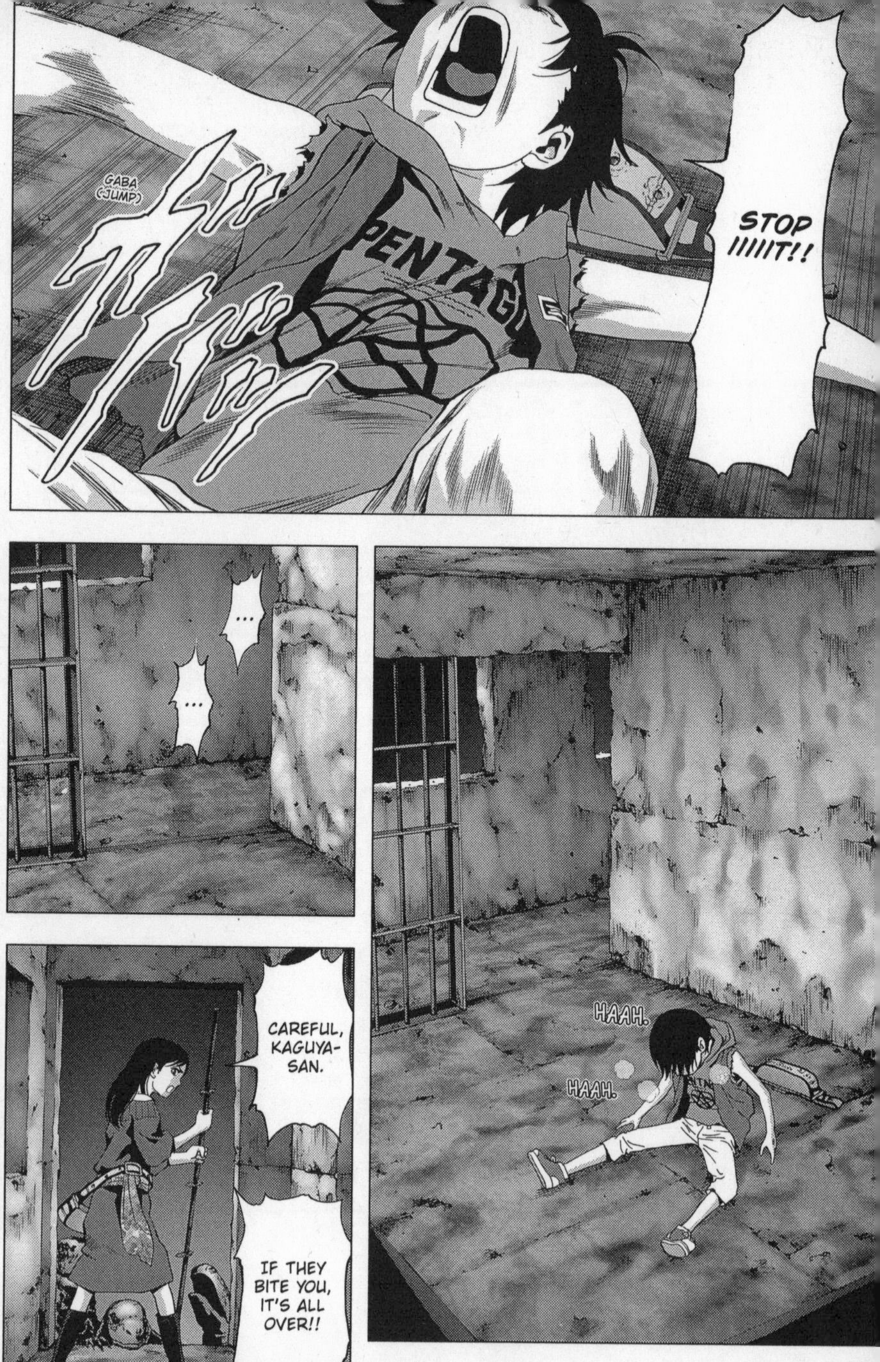
STOP IIIIIT!!
GABA (JUMP)
HAAH.
HAAH.
...
...
CAREFUL, KAGUYA-SAN.
IF THEY BITE YOU, IT'S ALL OVER!!

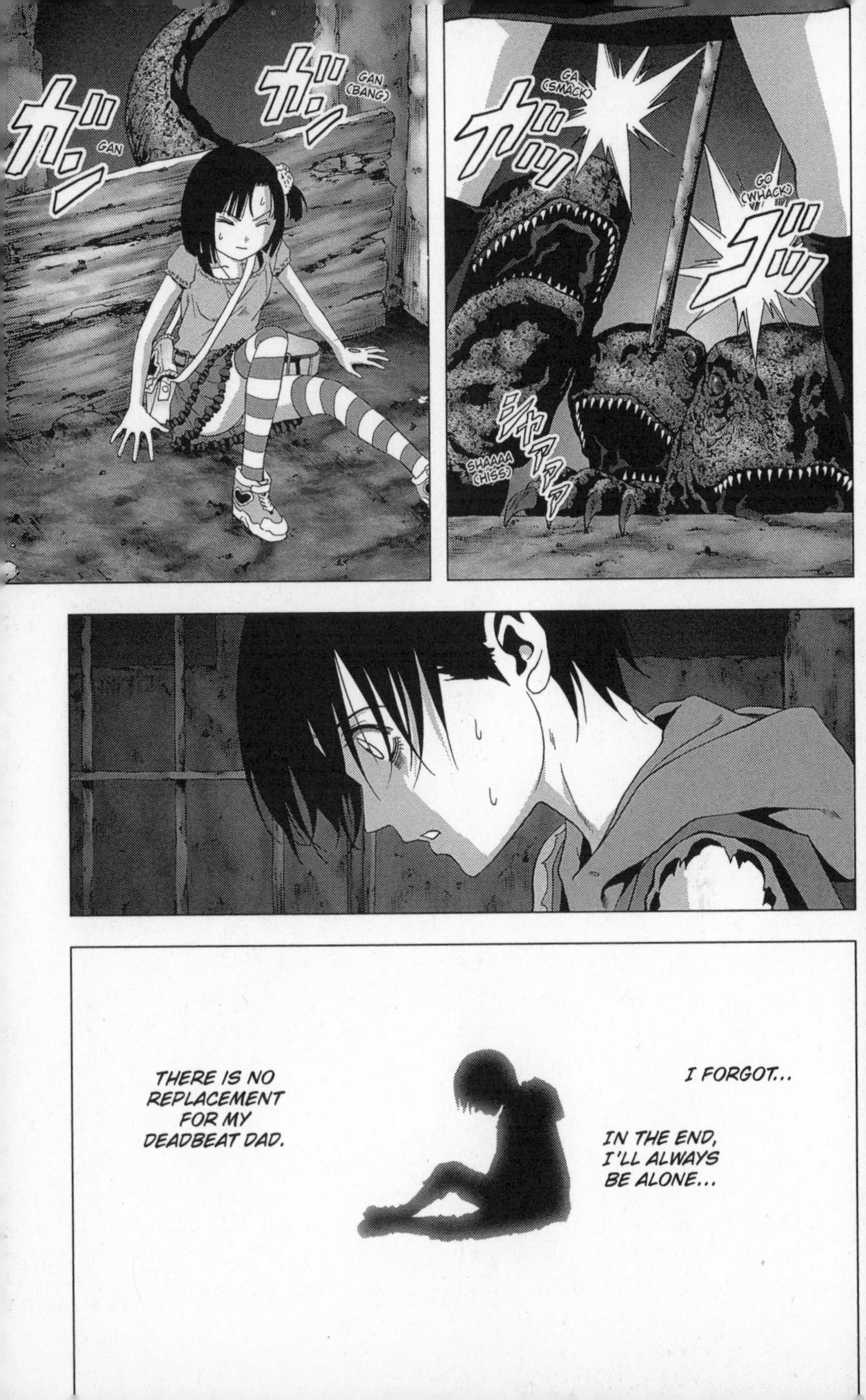
GA (SMACK)
GO (WHACK)
SHAAAA (HISS)
GAN (BANG)
GAN
I FORGOT...
IN THE END, I'LL ALWAYS BE ALONE...
THERE IS NO REPLACEMENT FOR MY DEADBEAT DAD.

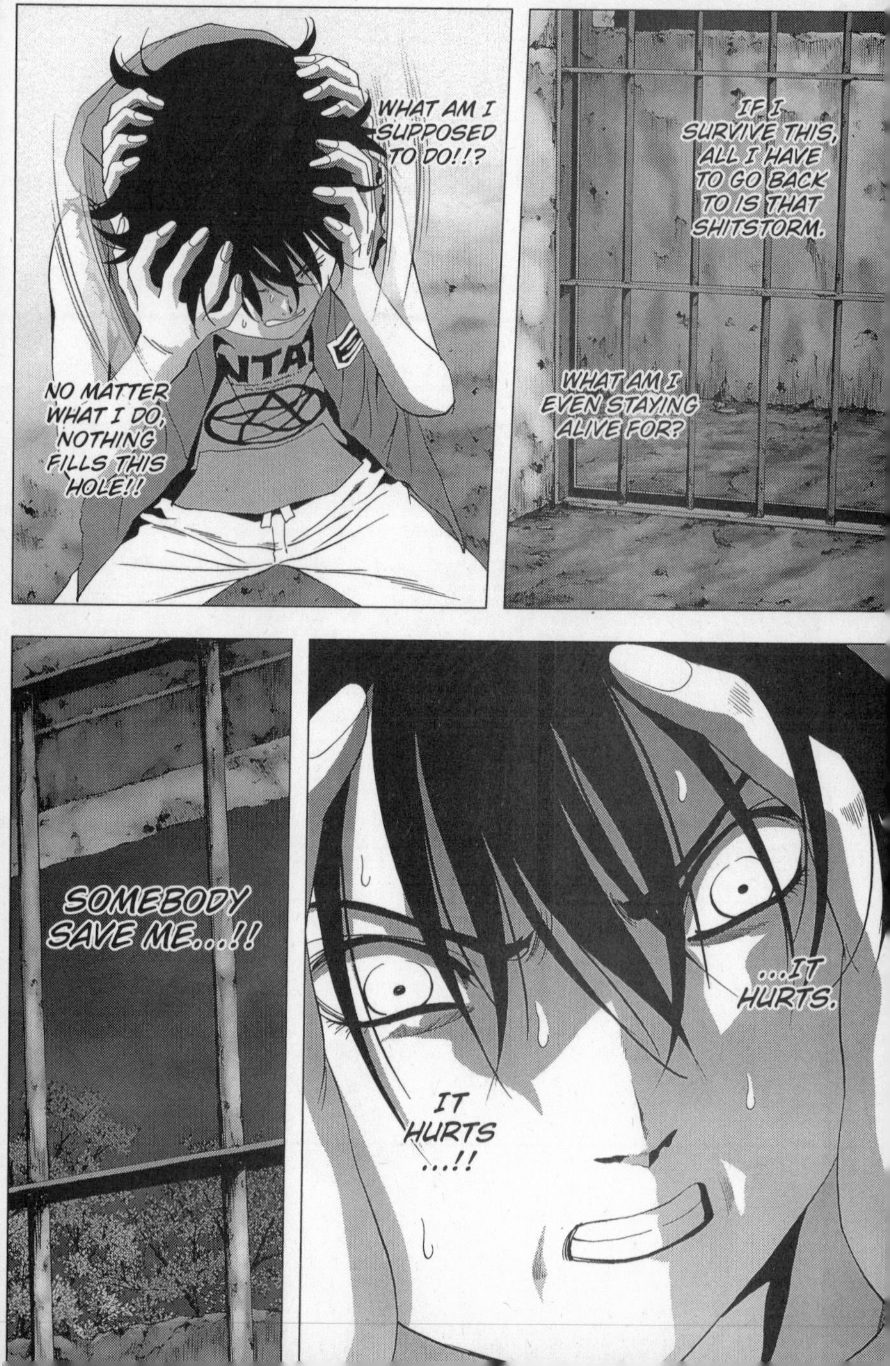
IF I SURVIVE THIS, ALL I HAVE TO GO BACK TO IS THAT SHITSTORM.
WHAT AM I EVEN STAYING ALIVE FOR?
WHAT AM I SUPPOSED TO DO!!?
NO MATTER WHAT I DO, NOTHING FILLS THIS HOLE!!
...IT HURTS.
IT HURTS ...!!
SOMEBODY SAVE ME...!!

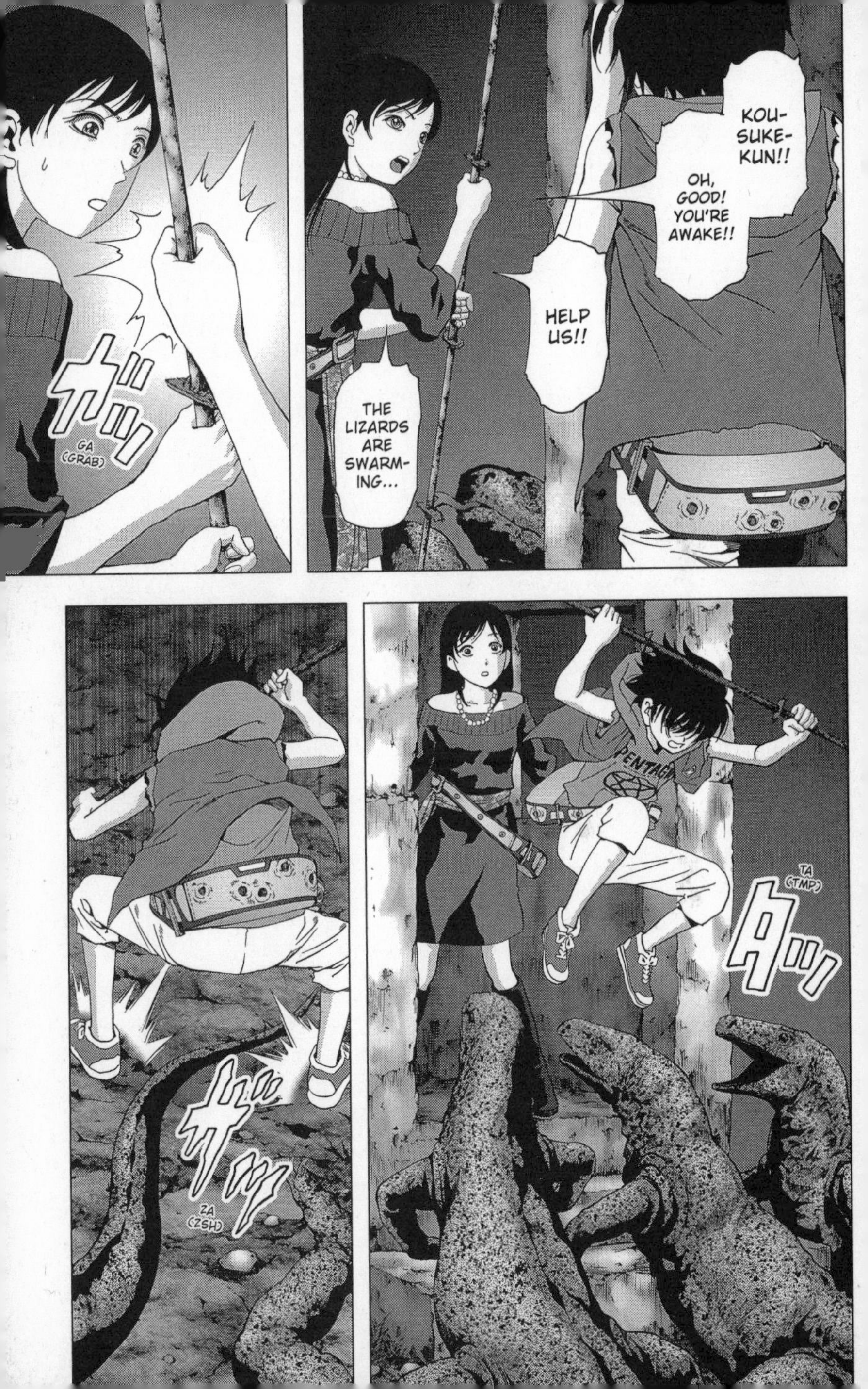
KOU-SUKE-KUN!!
OH, GOOD! YOU'RE AWAKE!!
HELP US!!
THE LIZARDS ARE SWARMING...
GA (GRAB)
TA (TMP)
ZA (ZSH)

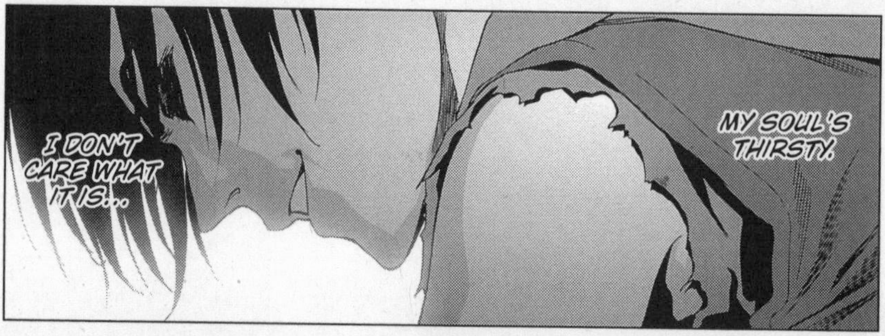
MY SOUL'S THIRSTY.
I DON'T CARE WHAT IT IS...
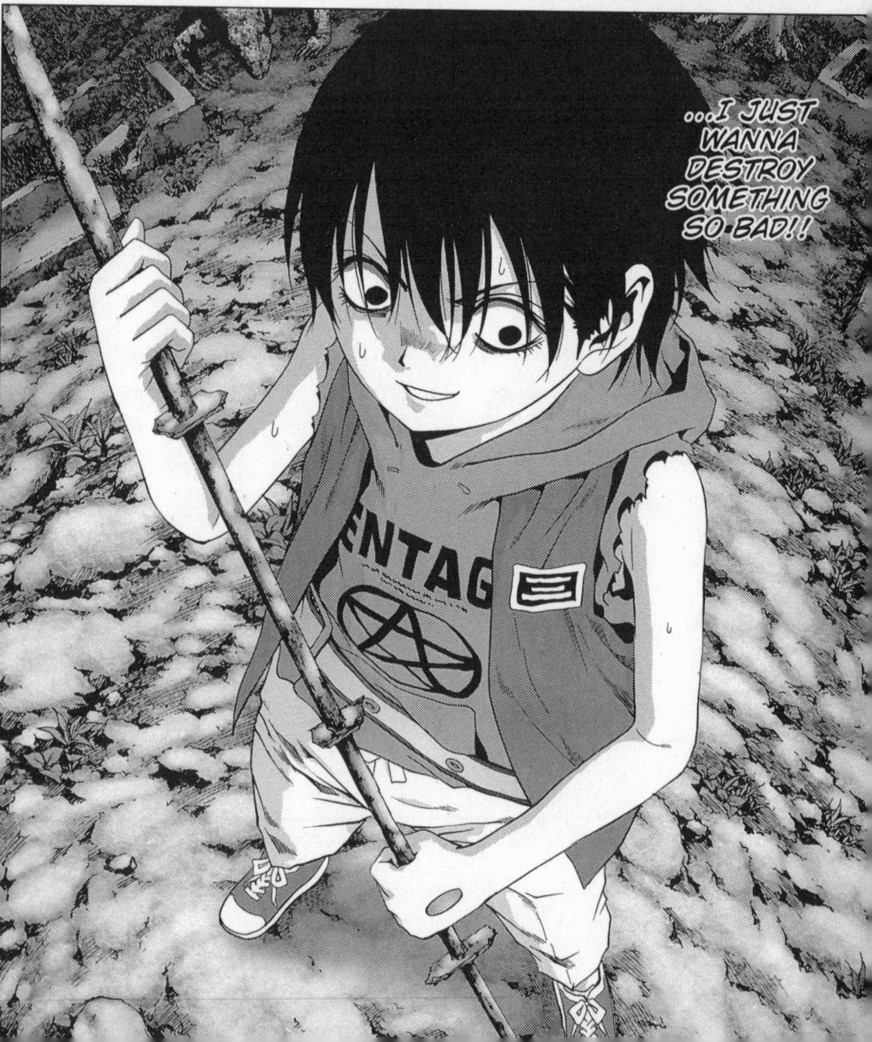
...I JUST WANNA DESTROY SOMETHING SO BAD!!

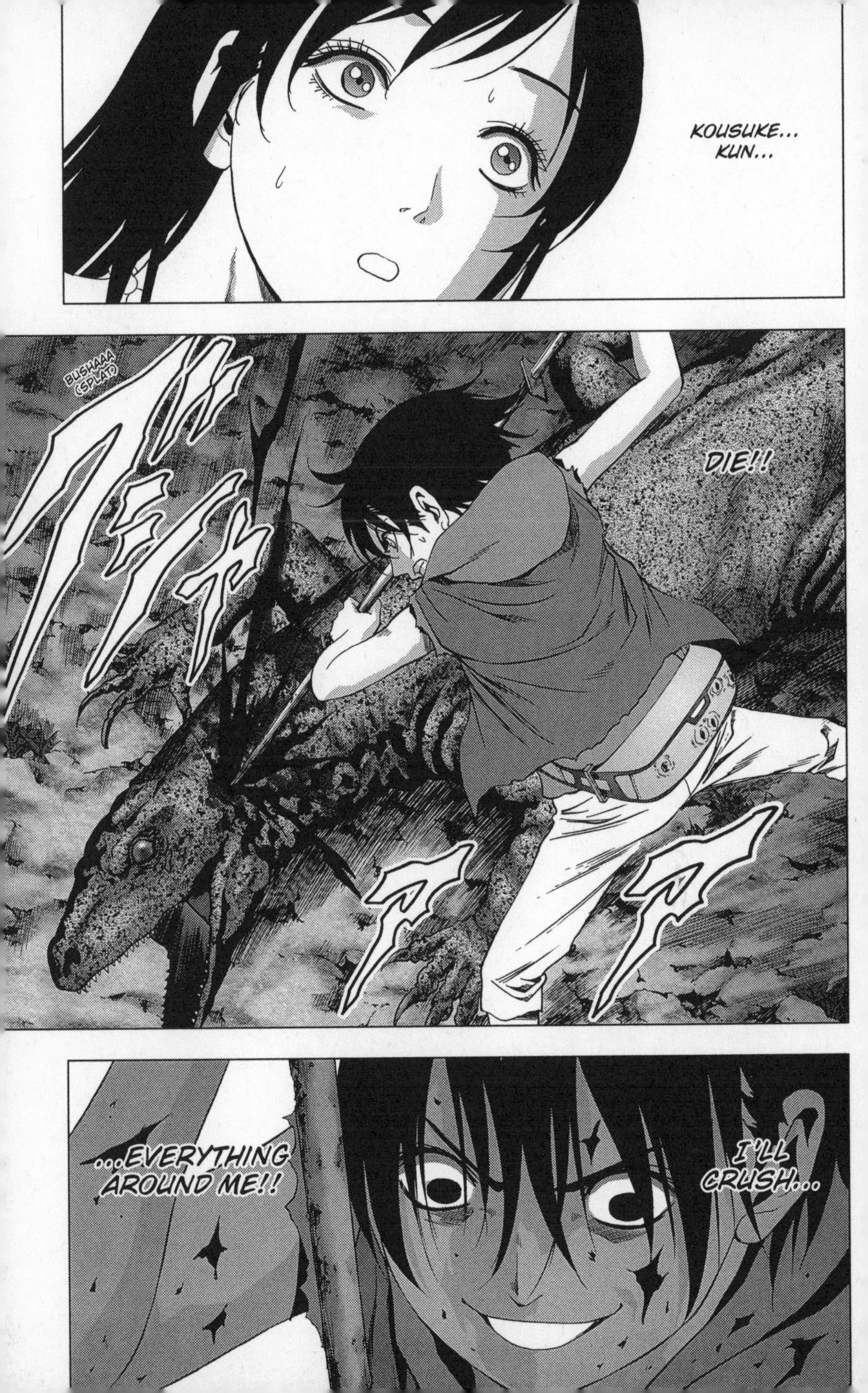
KOUSUKE... KUN...
BUSHAAA (SPLAT)
DIE!!
I'LL CRUSH...
...EVERYTHING AROUND ME!!

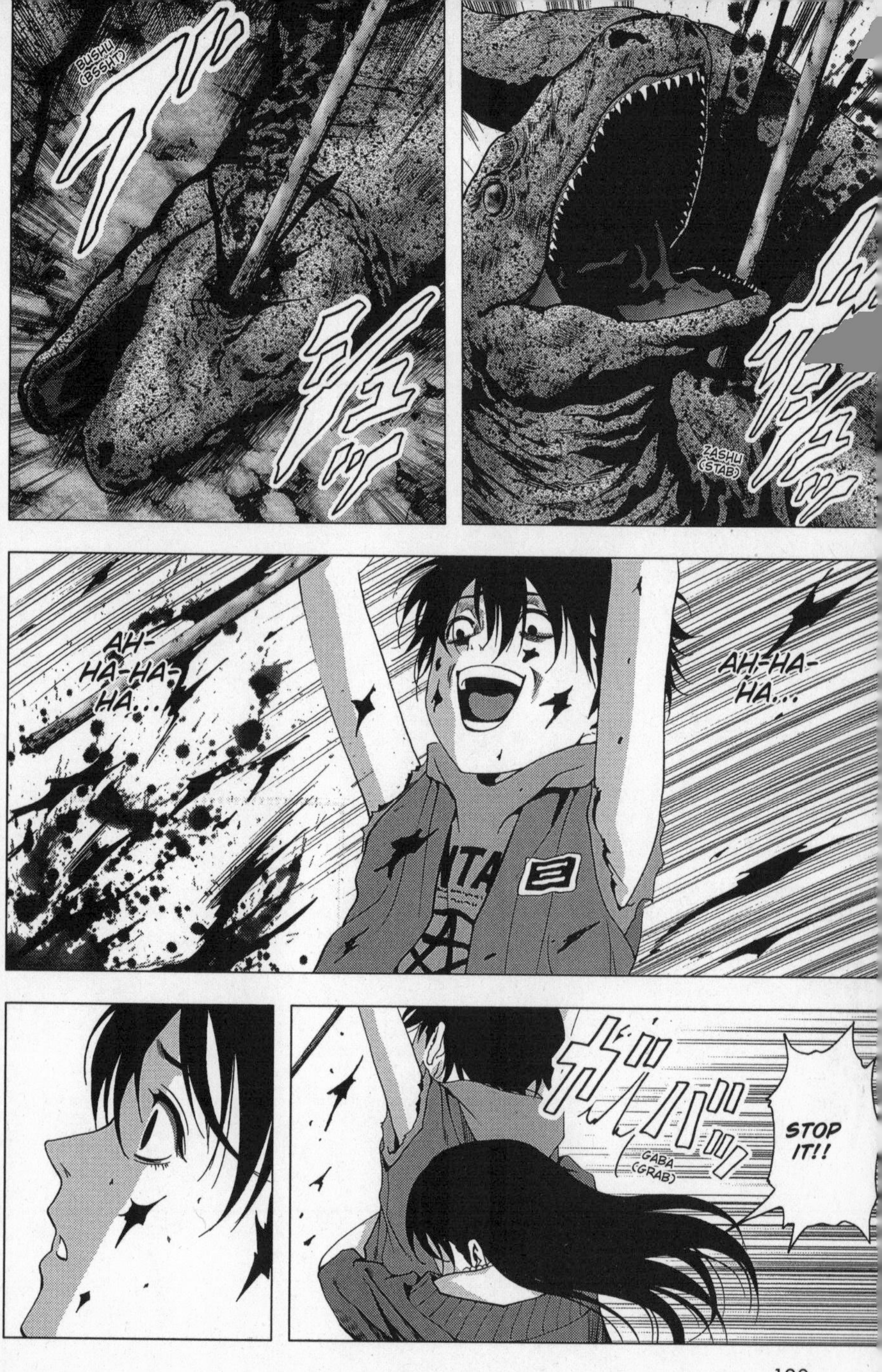
ZASHU
(STAB)
BUSHU
(BSSHT)
AH-HA-HA...
AH-HA-HA-HA...
STOP IT!!
GABA
(GRAB)

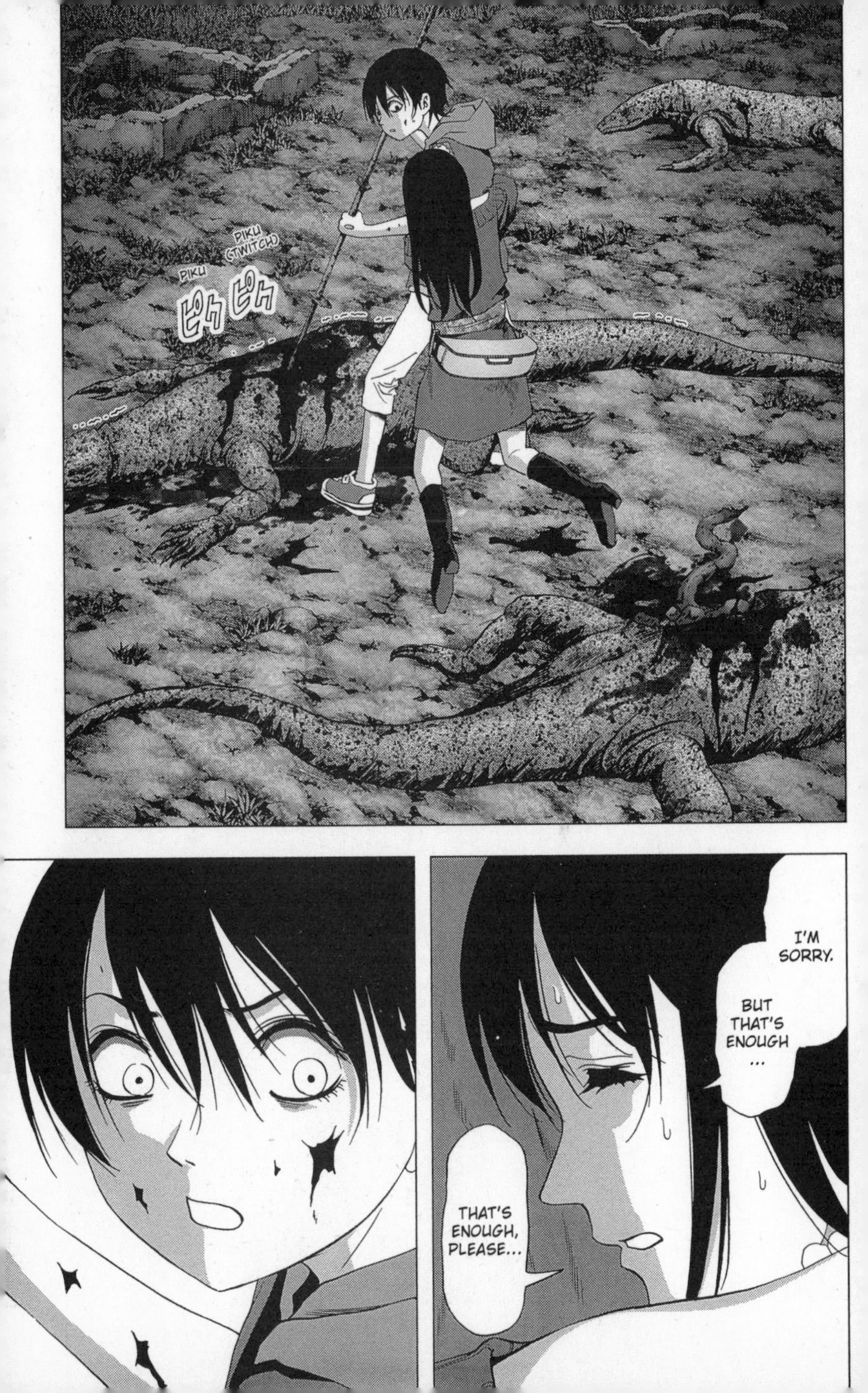
ピク ピク
PIKU (TWITCH)
PIKU
I'M SORRY.
BUT THAT'S ENOUGH ...
THAT'S ENOUGH, PLEASE...

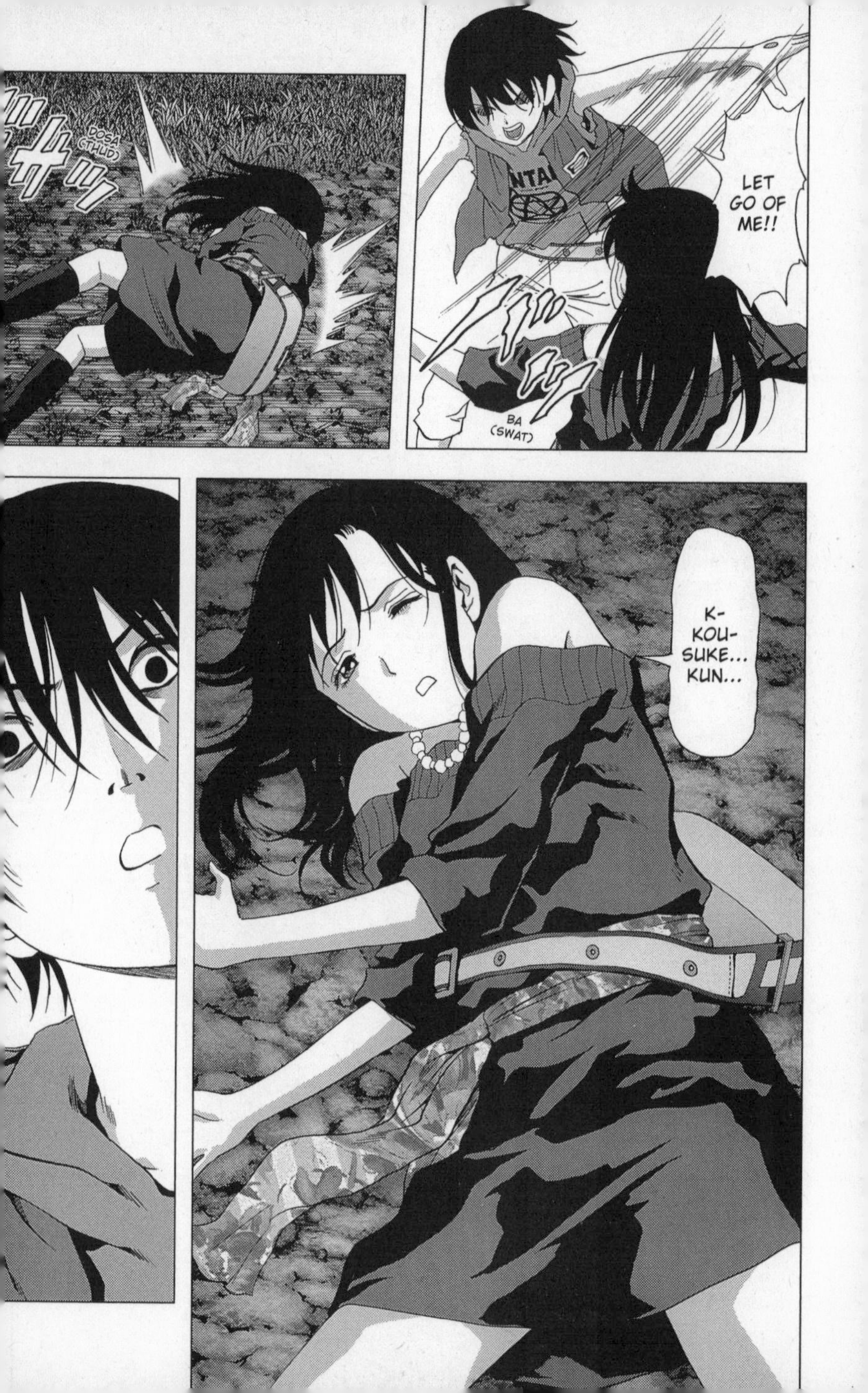
LET GO OF ME!!
BA (SWAT)
DOSA (THUD)
K-KOU-SUKE... KUN...

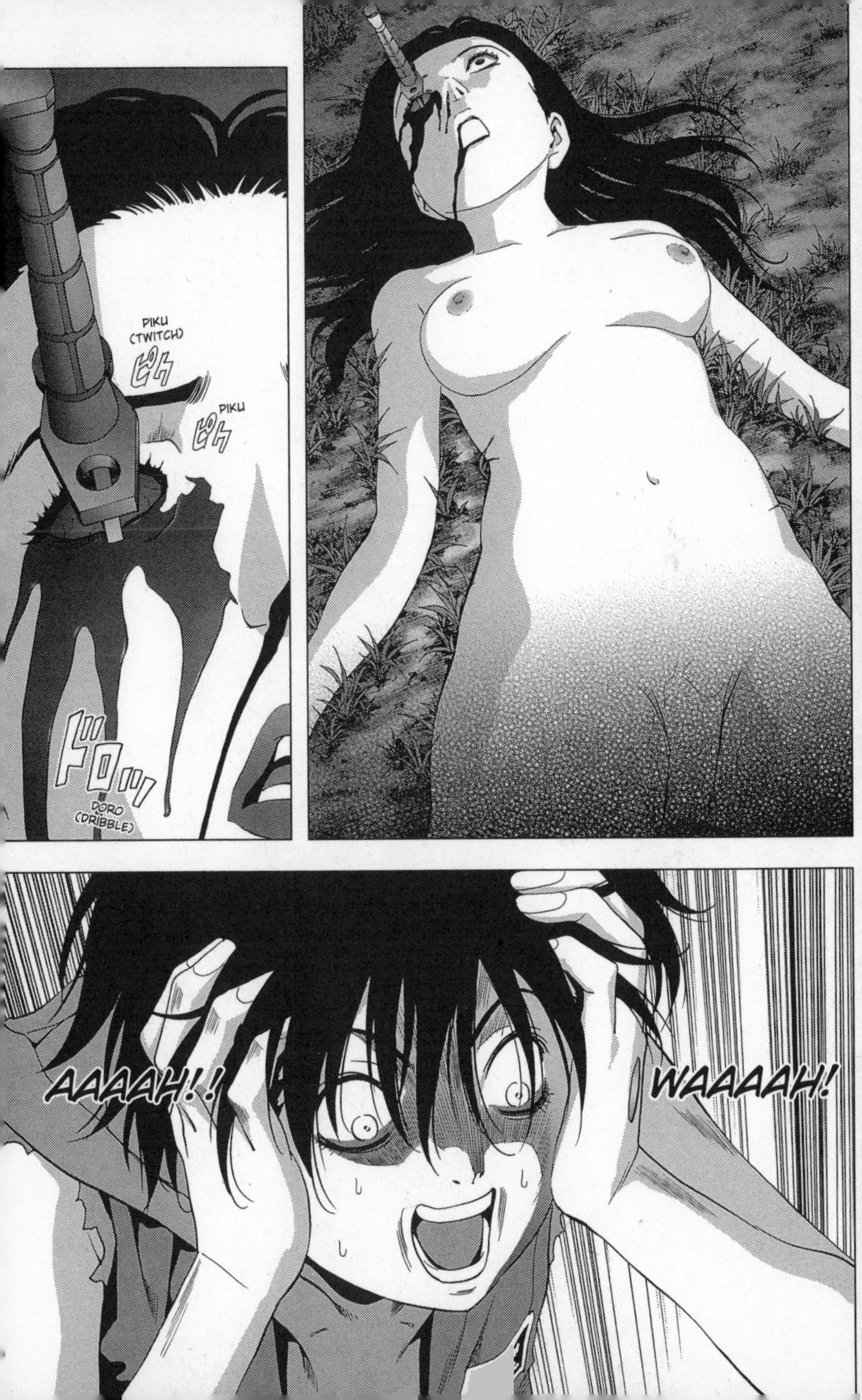
PIKU (TWITCH)
ピク
PIKU
ピク
ドロッ
DORO (DRIBBLE)
WAAAAH!
AAAAH!!

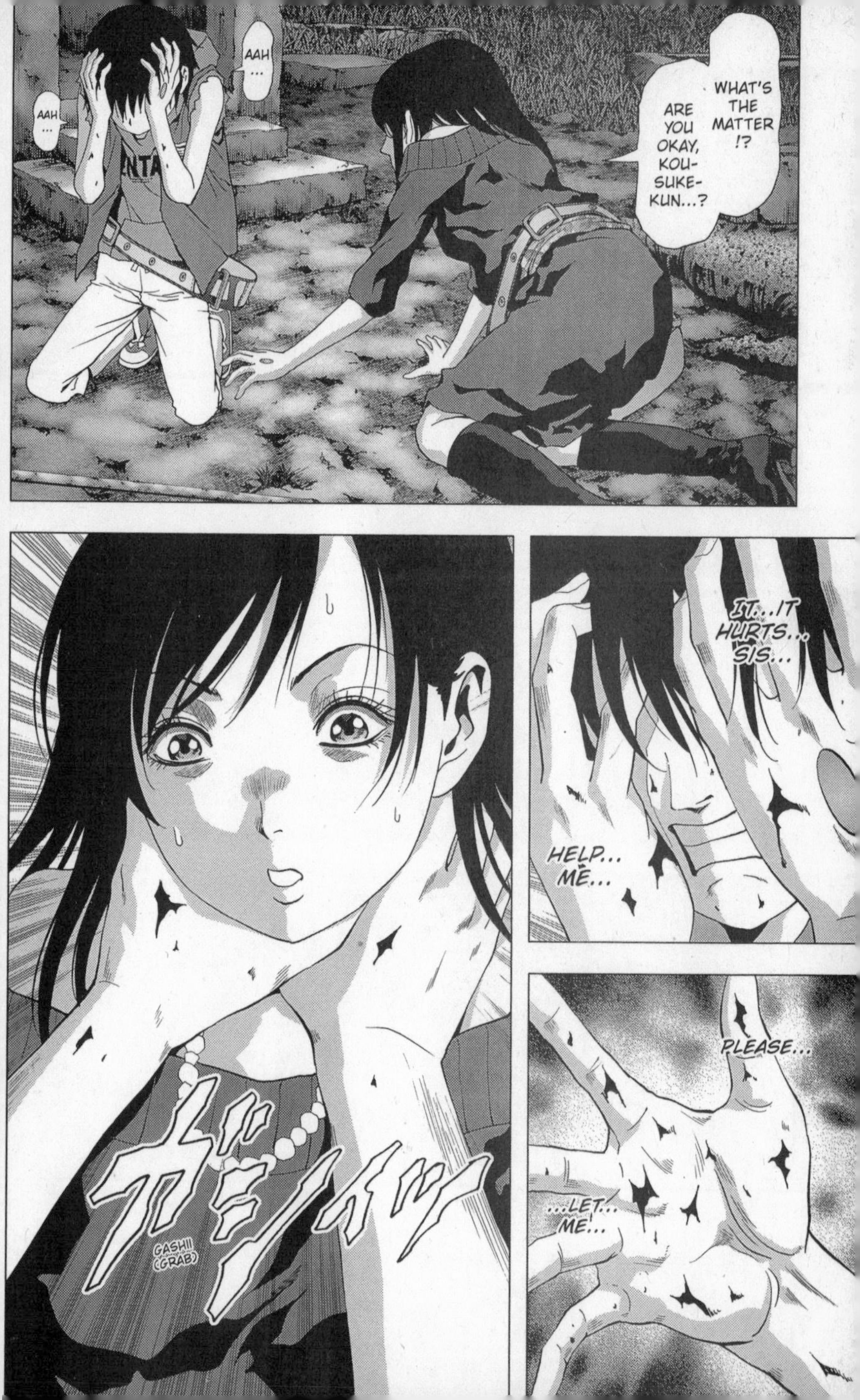
WHAT'S THE MATTER !?
ARE YOU OKAY, KOU-SUKE-KUN...?
AAH ...
AAH ...
IT...IT HURTS... SIS...
HELP... ME...
PLEASE...
...LET... ME...
GASHII (GRAB)

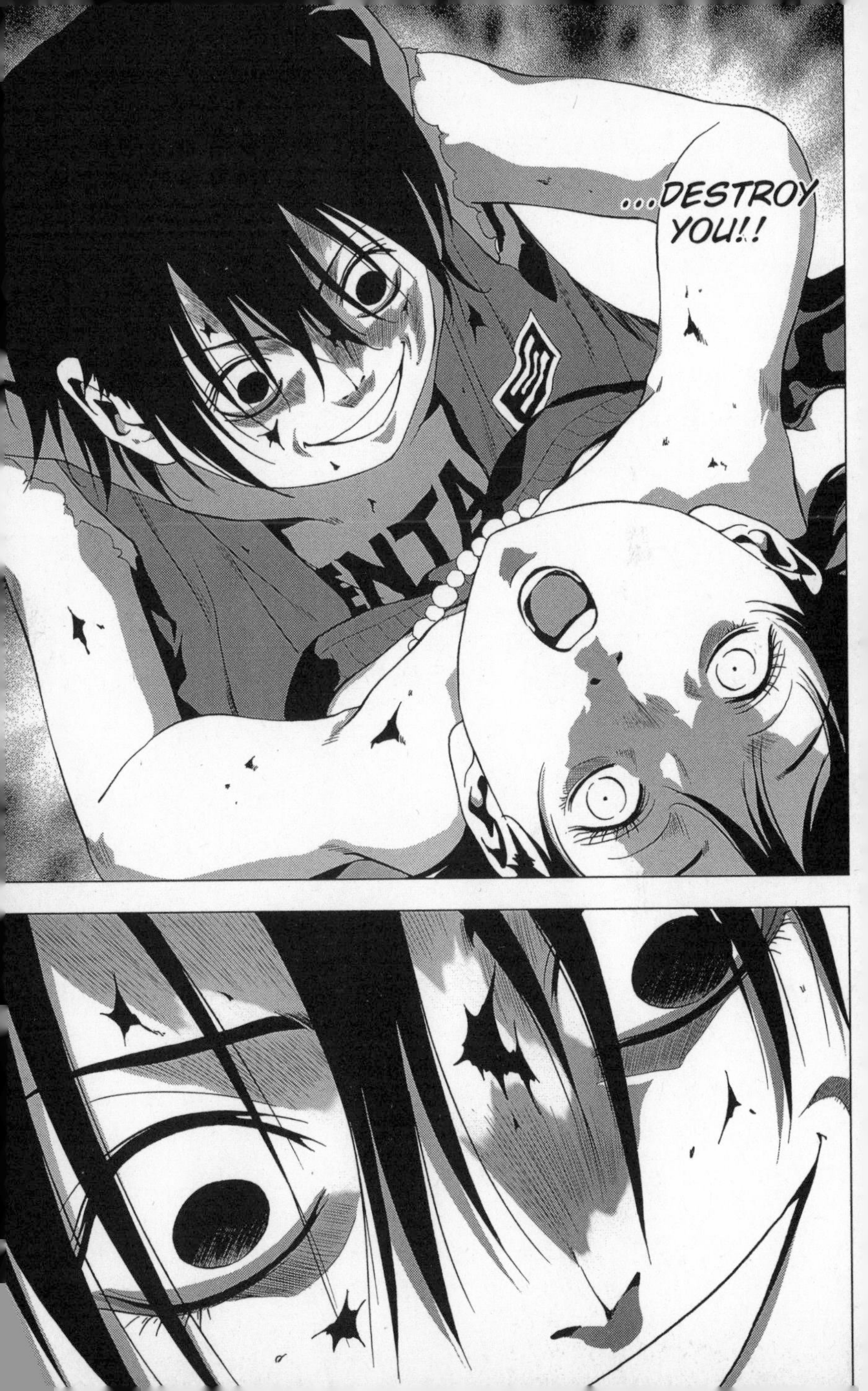
...DESTROY YOU!!

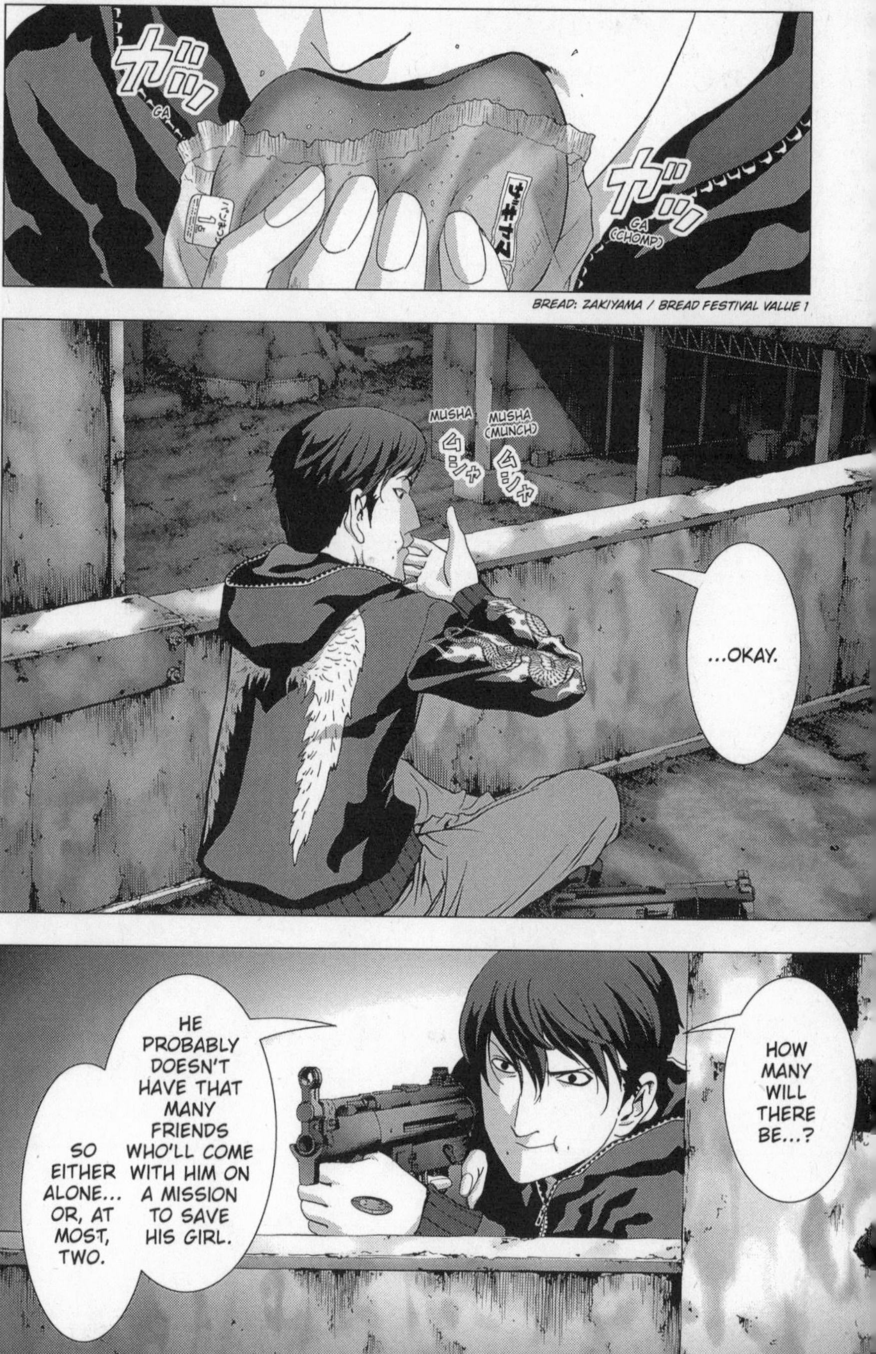
GA (CHOMP)
GA
BREAD: ZAKIYAMA / BREAD FESTIVAL VALUE 1
MUSHA (MUNCH)
MUSHA
...OKAY.
HOW MANY WILL THERE BE...?
HE PROBABLY DOESN'T HAVE THAT MANY FRIENDS WHO'LL COME WITH HIM ON A MISSION TO SAVE HIS GIRL.
SO EITHER ALONE... OR, AT MOST, TWO.

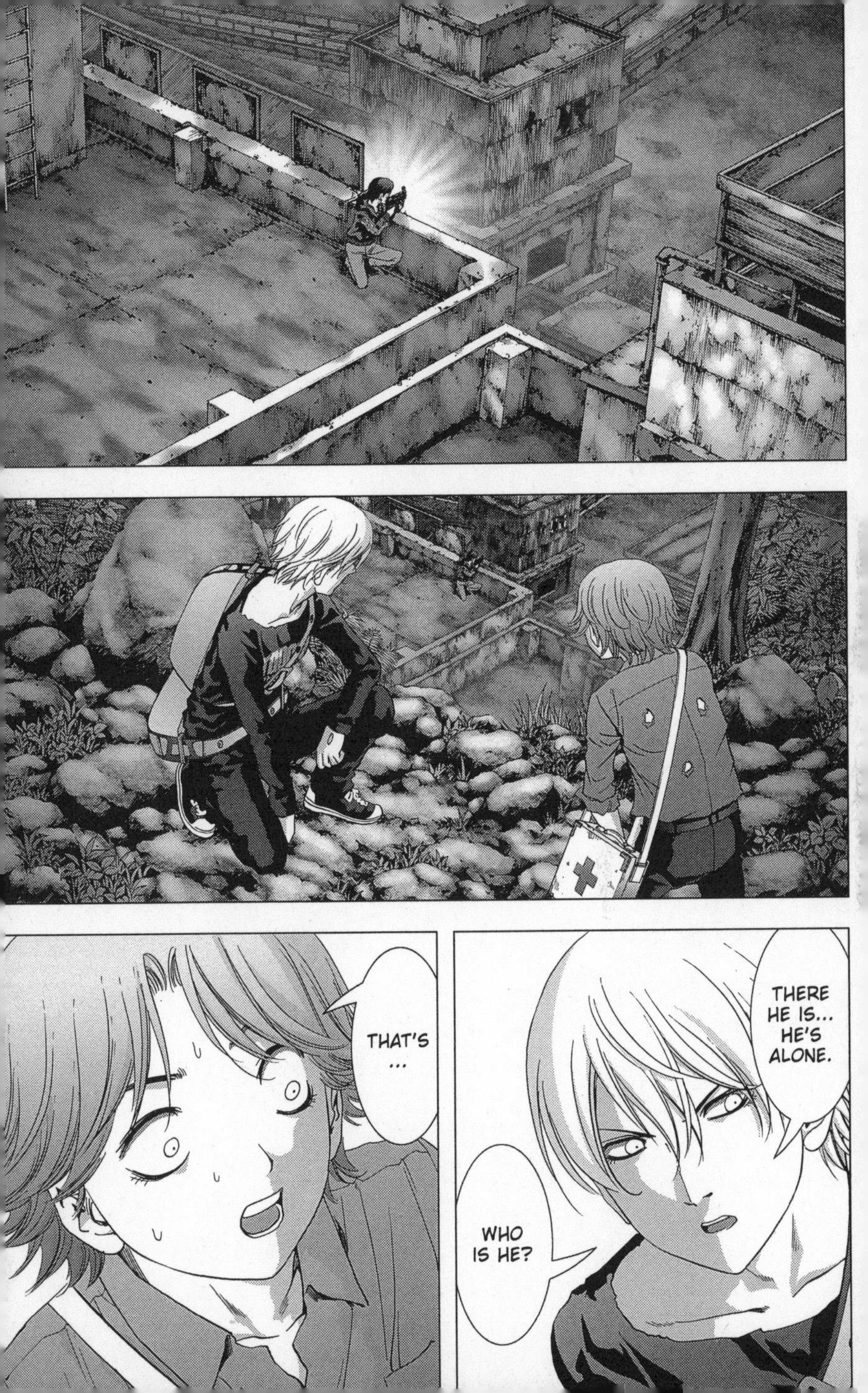
THERE HE IS... HE'S ALONE.
WHO IS HE?
THAT'S ...

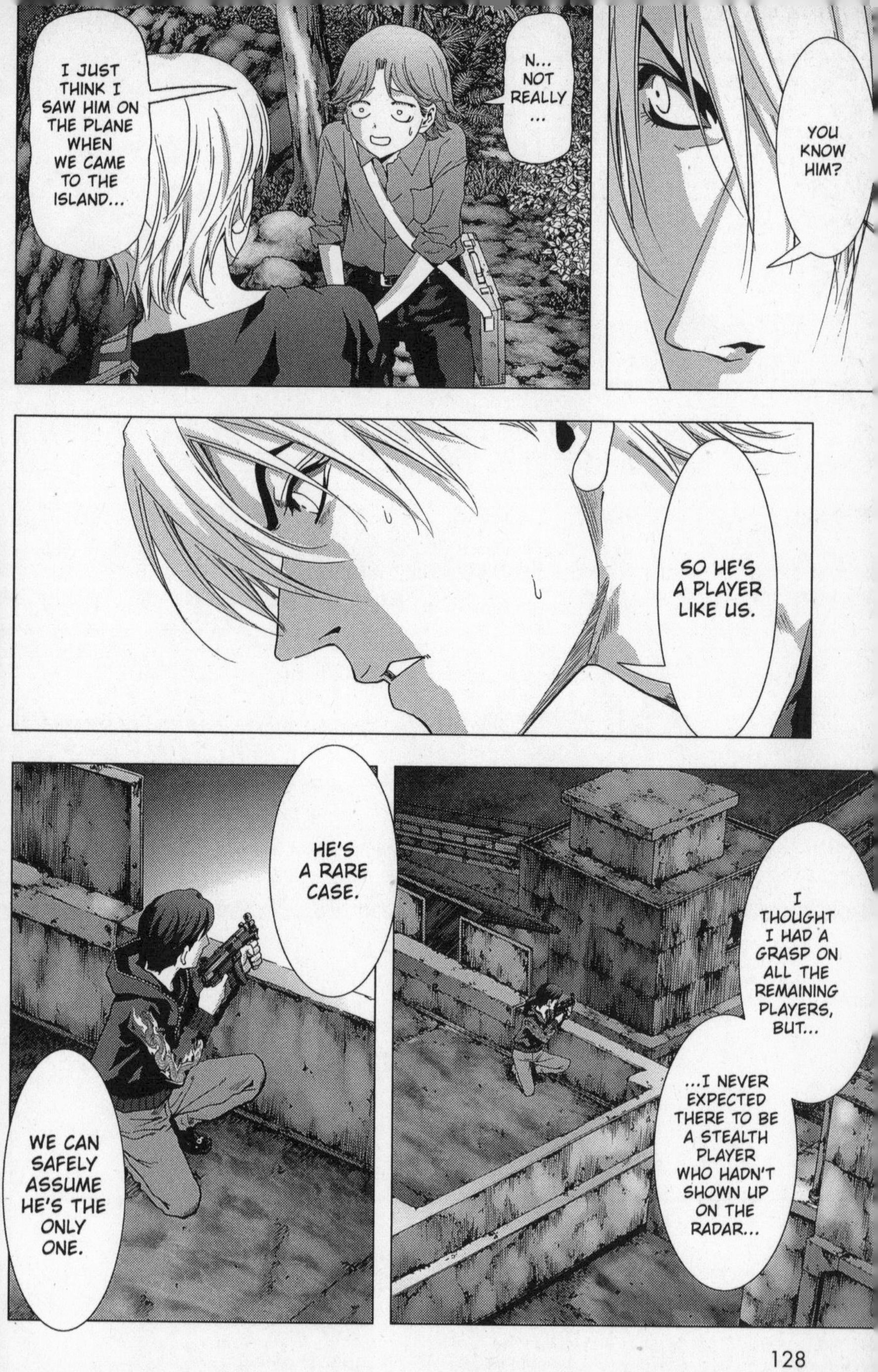
YOU KNOW HIM?
N... NOT REALLY...
I JUST THINK I SAW HIM ON THE PLANE WHEN WE CAME TO THE ISLAND...
SO HE'S A PLAYER LIKE US.
I THOUGHT I HAD A GRASP ON ALL THE REMAINING PLAYERS, BUT...
...I NEVER EXPECTED THERE TO BE A STEALTH PLAYER WHO HADN'T SHOWN UP ON THE RADAR...
HE'S A RARE CASE.
WE CAN SAFELY ASSUME HE'S THE ONLY ONE.

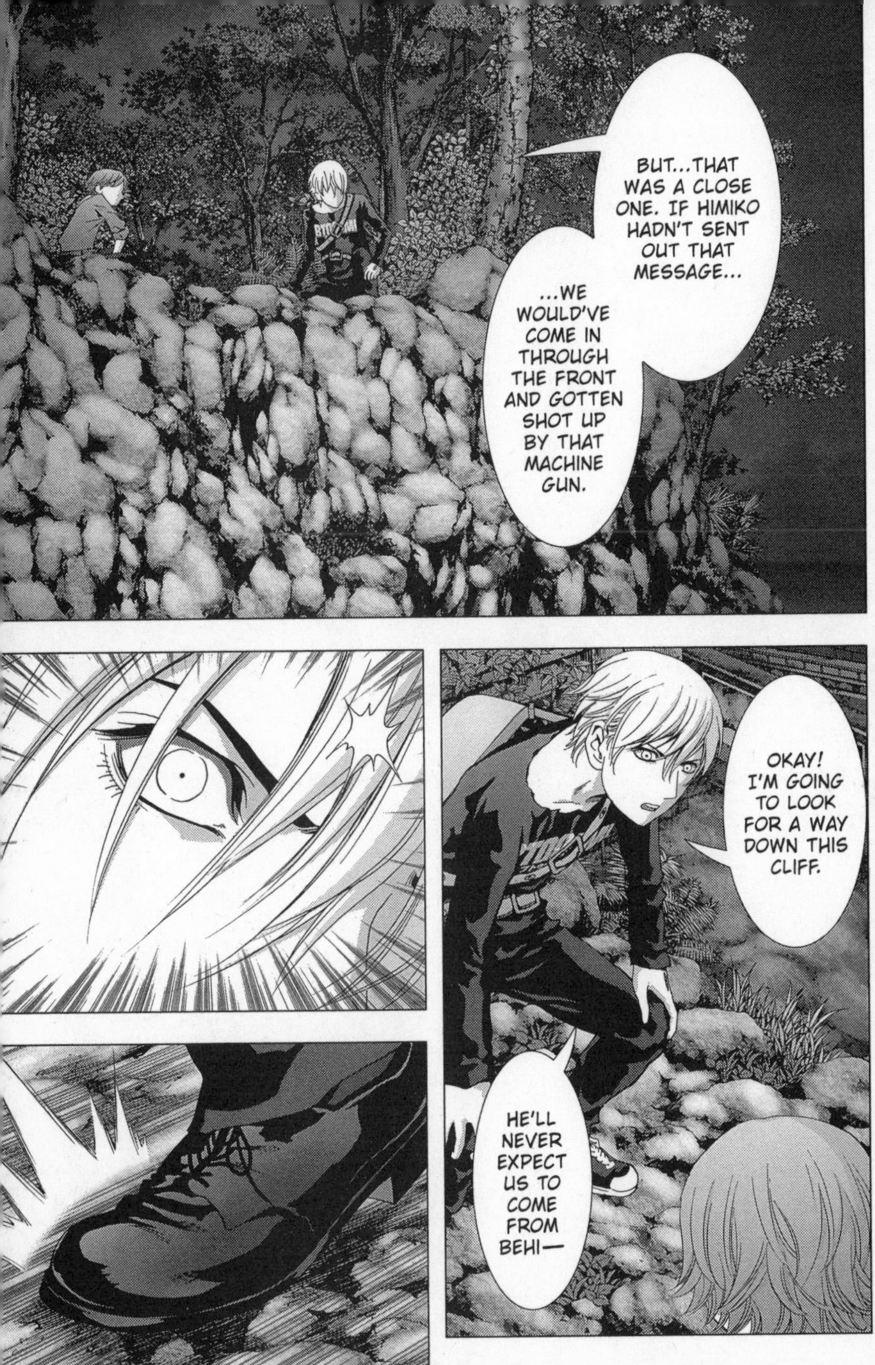
BUT...THAT WAS A CLOSE ONE. IF HIMIKO HADN'T SENT OUT THAT MESSAGE...
...WE WOULD'VE COME IN THROUGH THE FRONT AND GOTTEN SHOT UP BY THAT MACHINE GUN.
OKAY! I'M GOING TO LOOK FOR A WAY DOWN THIS CLIFF.
HE'LL NEVER EXPECT US TO COME FROM BEHI—

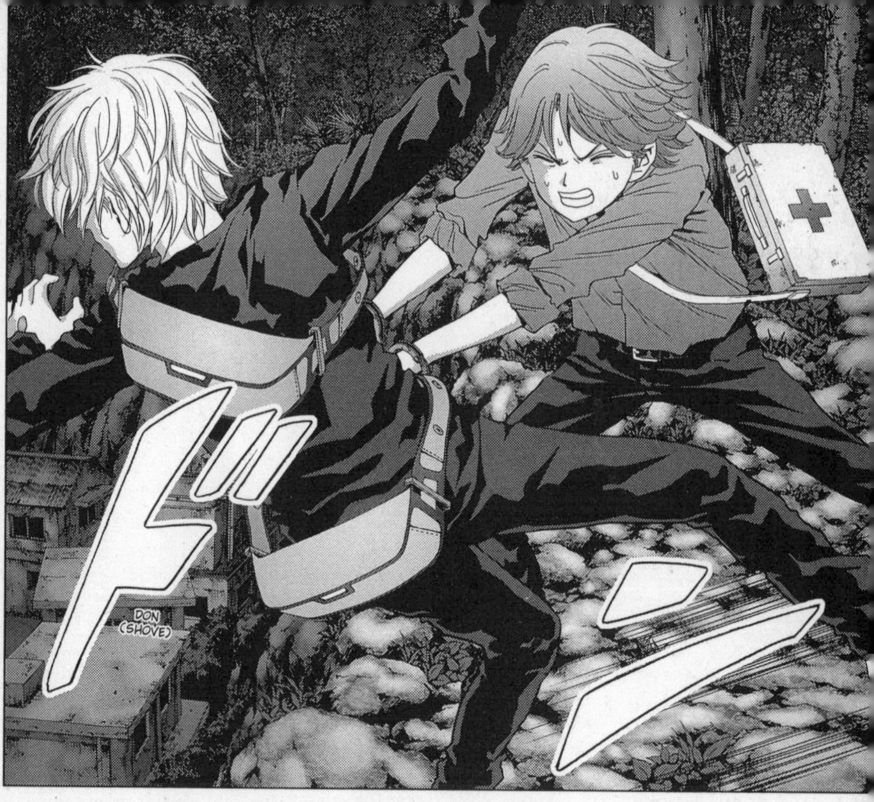
DON
(SHOVE)
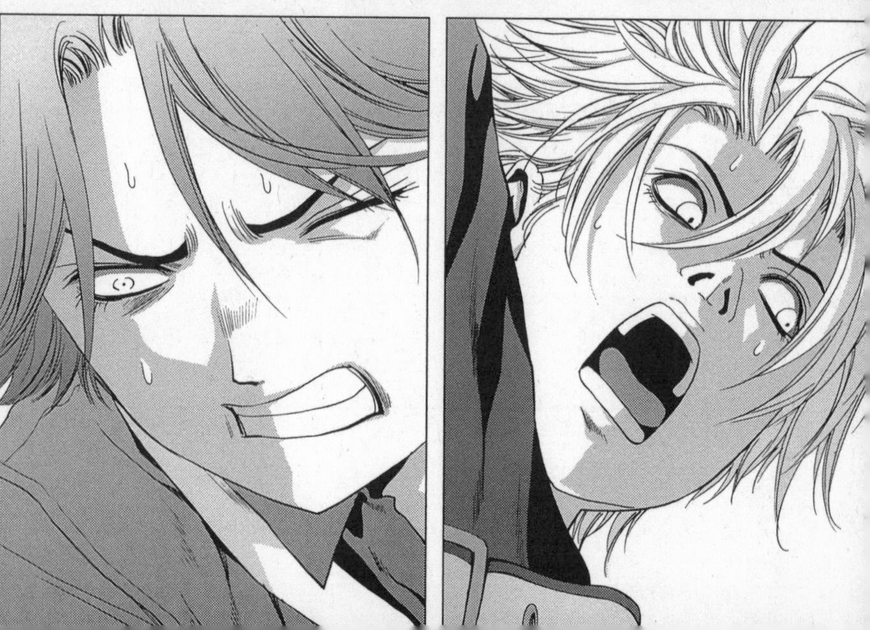

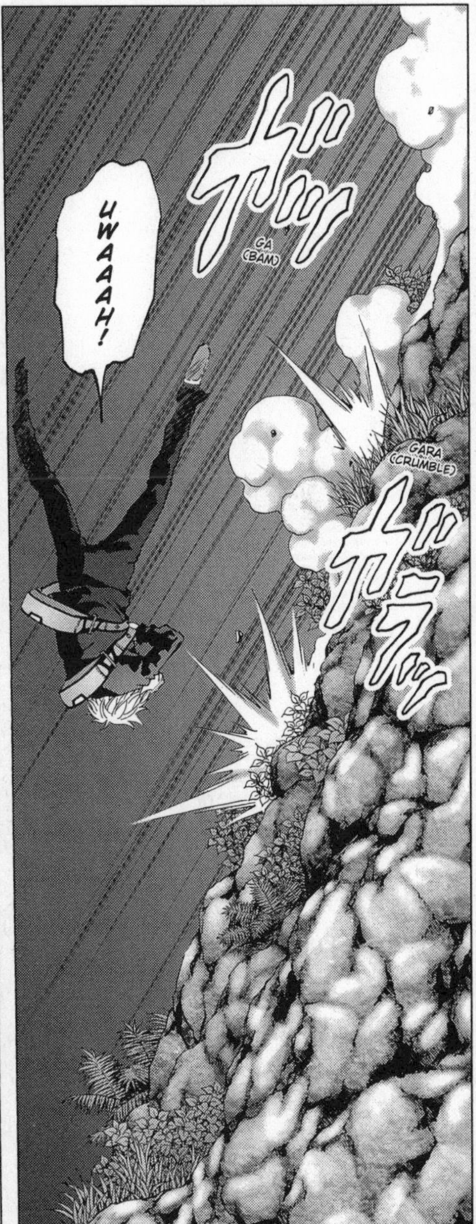
GA (BAM)
UWAAAAH!
GARA (CRUMBLE)

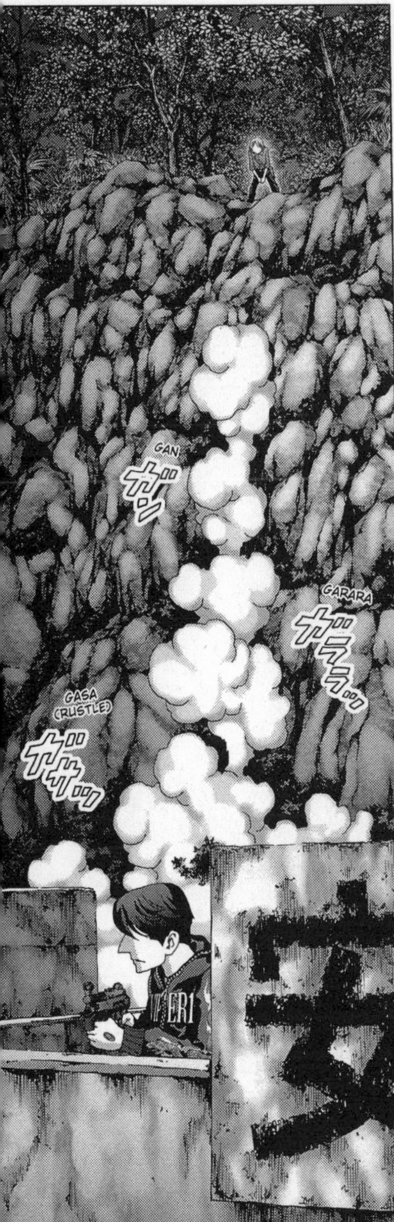
GAN
GARARA
GASA (RUSTLE)

IT...IT'S YOUR OWN FAULT...

AFTER ALL...

...THERE WAS *NOTHING* IN IT FOR ME IF I STUCK WITH YOU...

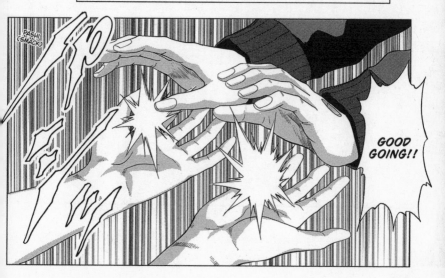

PASH! (SMACK)

GOOD GOING!!

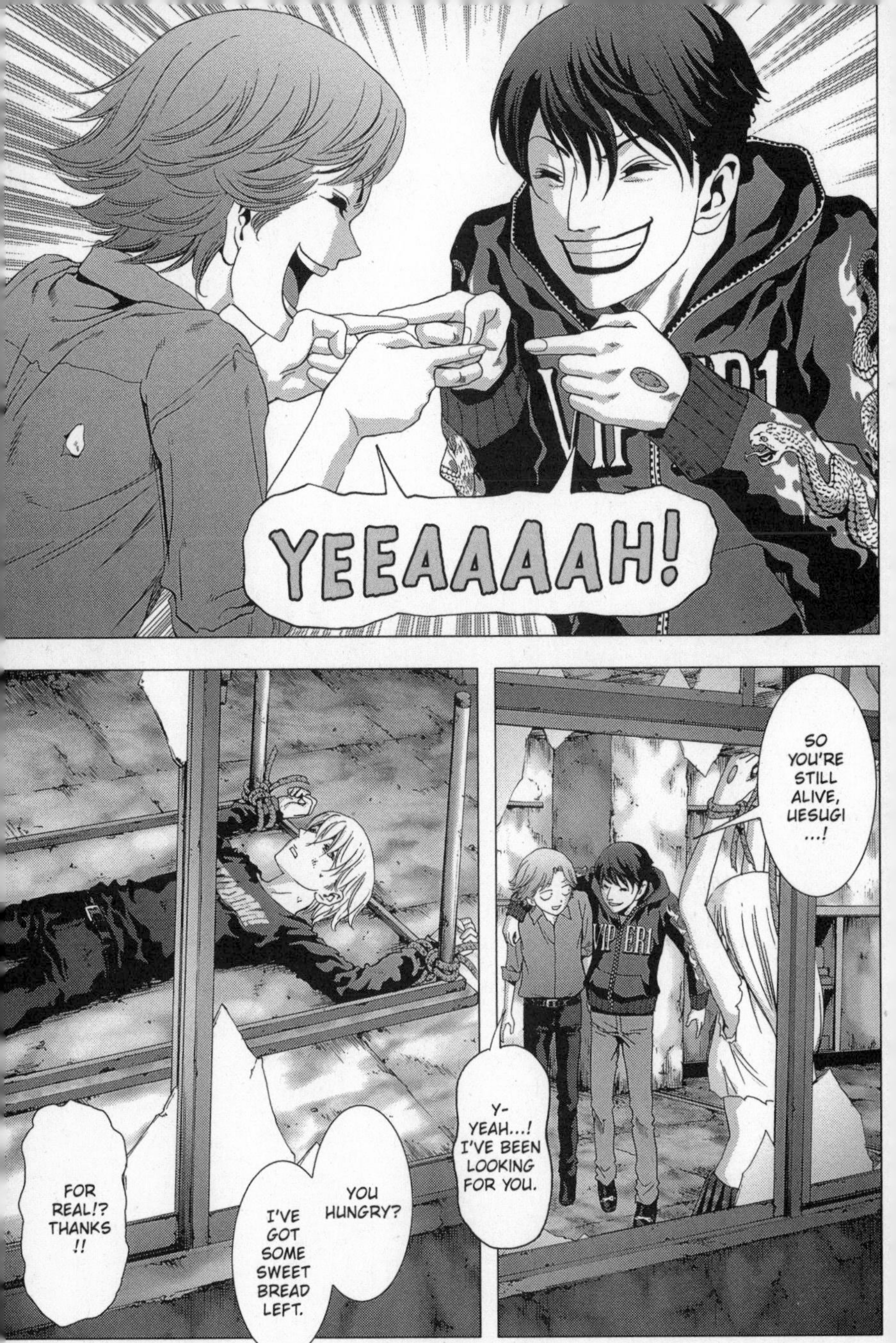
YEEAAAAH!
SO YOU'RE STILL ALIVE, UESUGI ...!
Y- YEAH...! I'VE BEEN LOOKING FOR YOU.
YOU HUNGRY?
I'VE GOT SOME SWEET BREAD LEFT.
FOR REAL!? THANKS !!

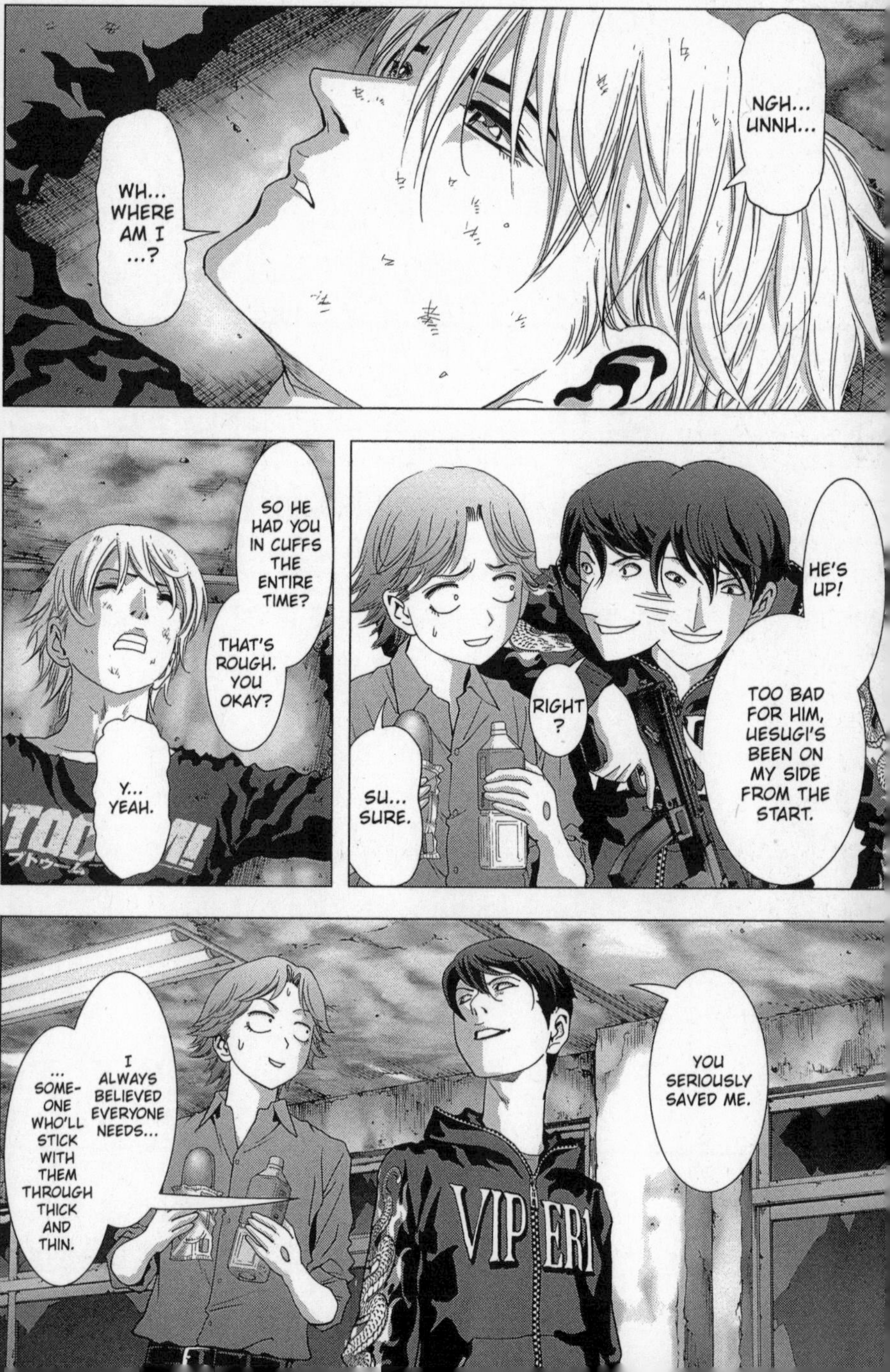
NGH... UNNH...
WH... WHERE AM I ...?
HE'S UP!
TOO BAD FOR HIM, UESUGI'S BEEN ON MY SIDE FROM THE START.
RIGHT?
SU... SURE.
SO HE HAD YOU IN CUFFS THE ENTIRE TIME?
THAT'S ROUGH. YOU OKAY?
Y... YEAH.
YOU SERIOUSLY SAVED ME.
I ALWAYS BELIEVED EVERYONE NEEDS...
... SOMEONE WHO'LL STICK WITH THEM THROUGH THICK AND THIN.
VIPER1

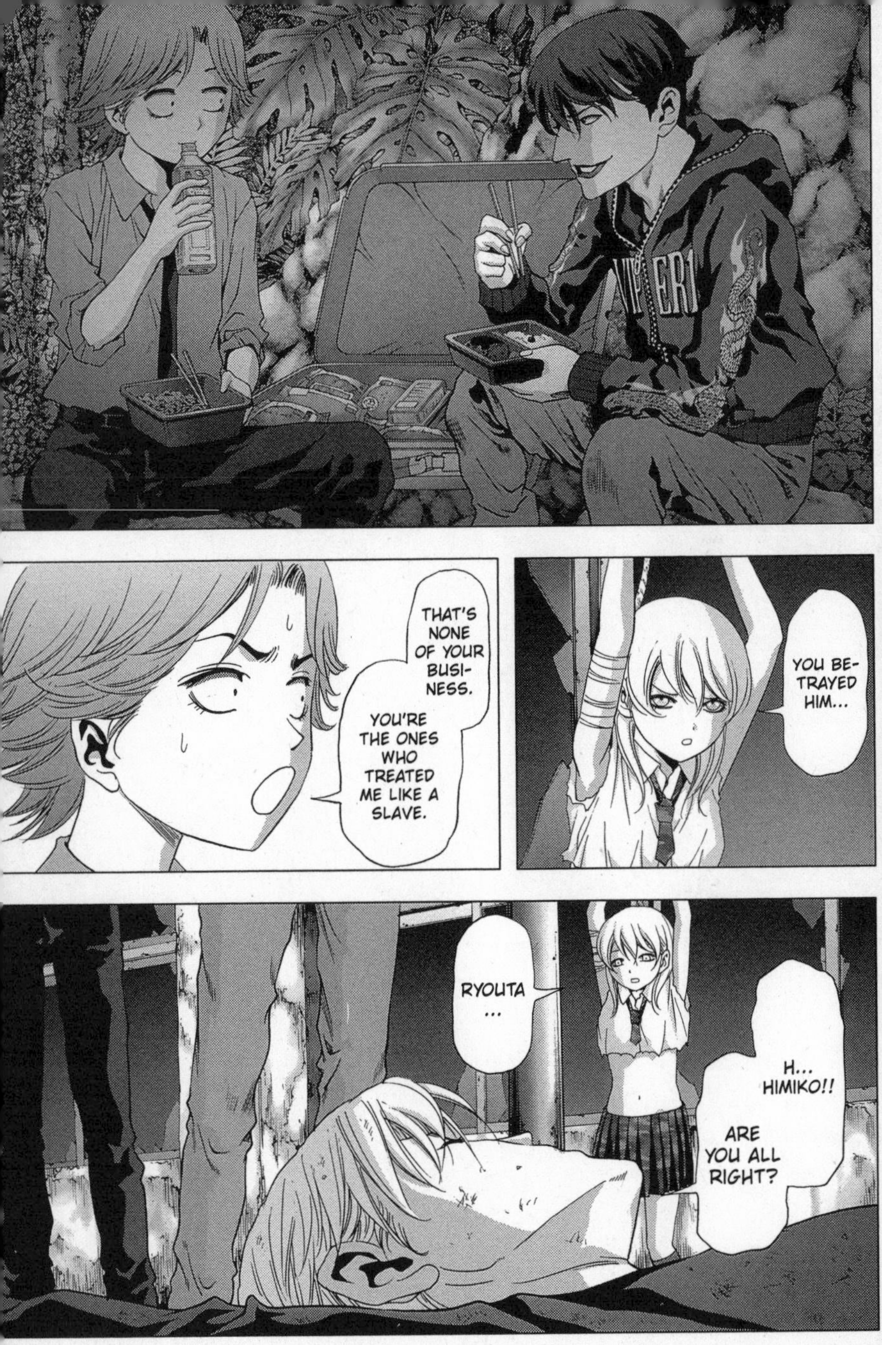
YOU BE-TRAYED HIM...
THAT'S NONE OF YOUR BUSI-NESS.
YOU'RE THE ONES WHO TREATED ME LIKE A SLAVE.
H... HIMIKO!!
ARE YOU ALL RIGHT?
RYOUTA ...

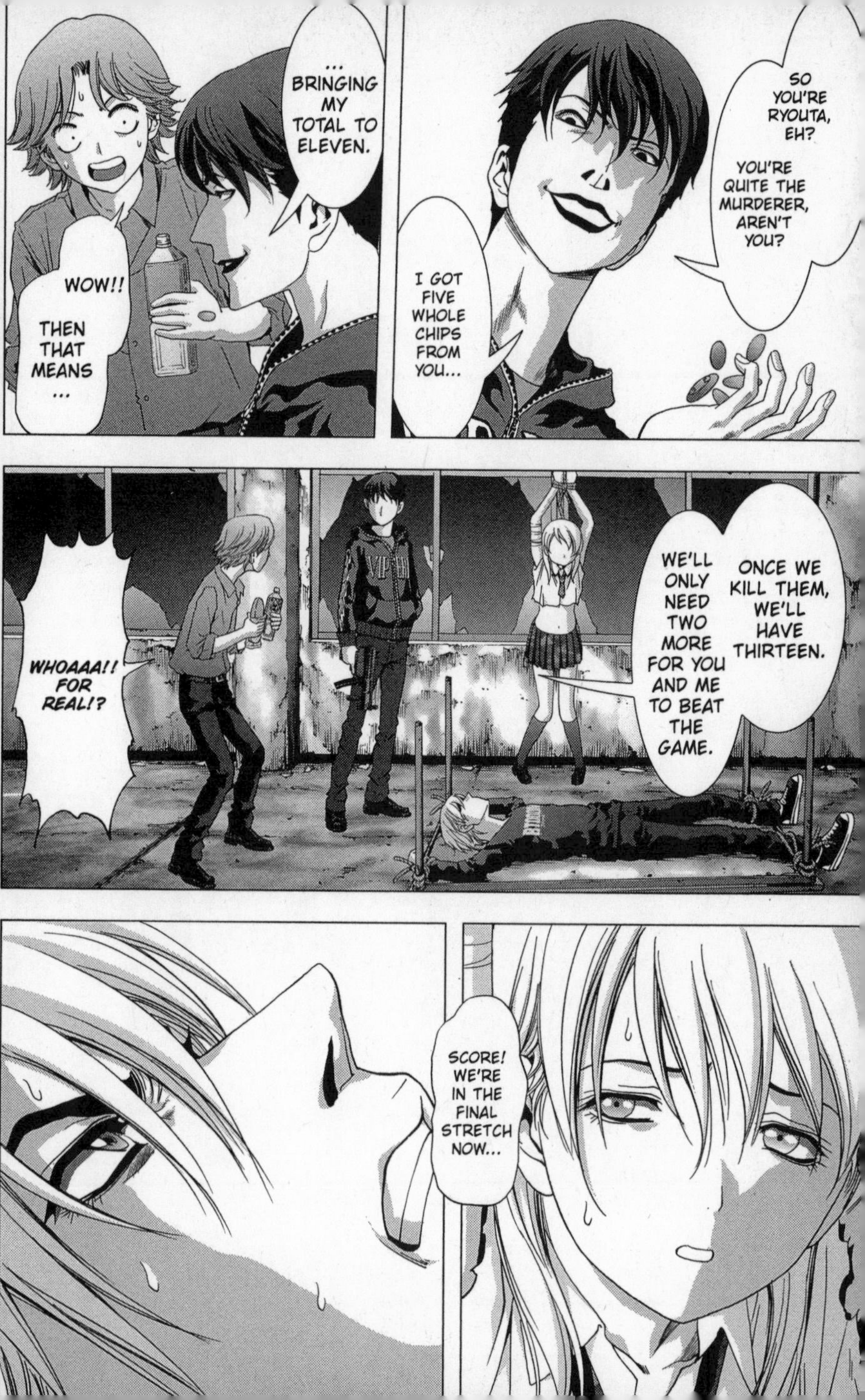
SO YOU'RE RYOUTA, EH?
YOU'RE QUITE THE MURDERER, AREN'T YOU?
I GOT FIVE WHOLE CHIPS FROM YOU...
...BRINGING MY TOTAL TO ELEVEN.
WOW!!
THEN THAT MEANS ...
ONCE WE KILL THEM, WE'LL HAVE THIRTEEN.
WE'LL ONLY NEED TWO MORE FOR YOU AND ME TO BEAT THE GAME.
WHOAAA!! FOR REAL!?
SCORE! WE'RE IN THE FINAL STRETCH NOW...

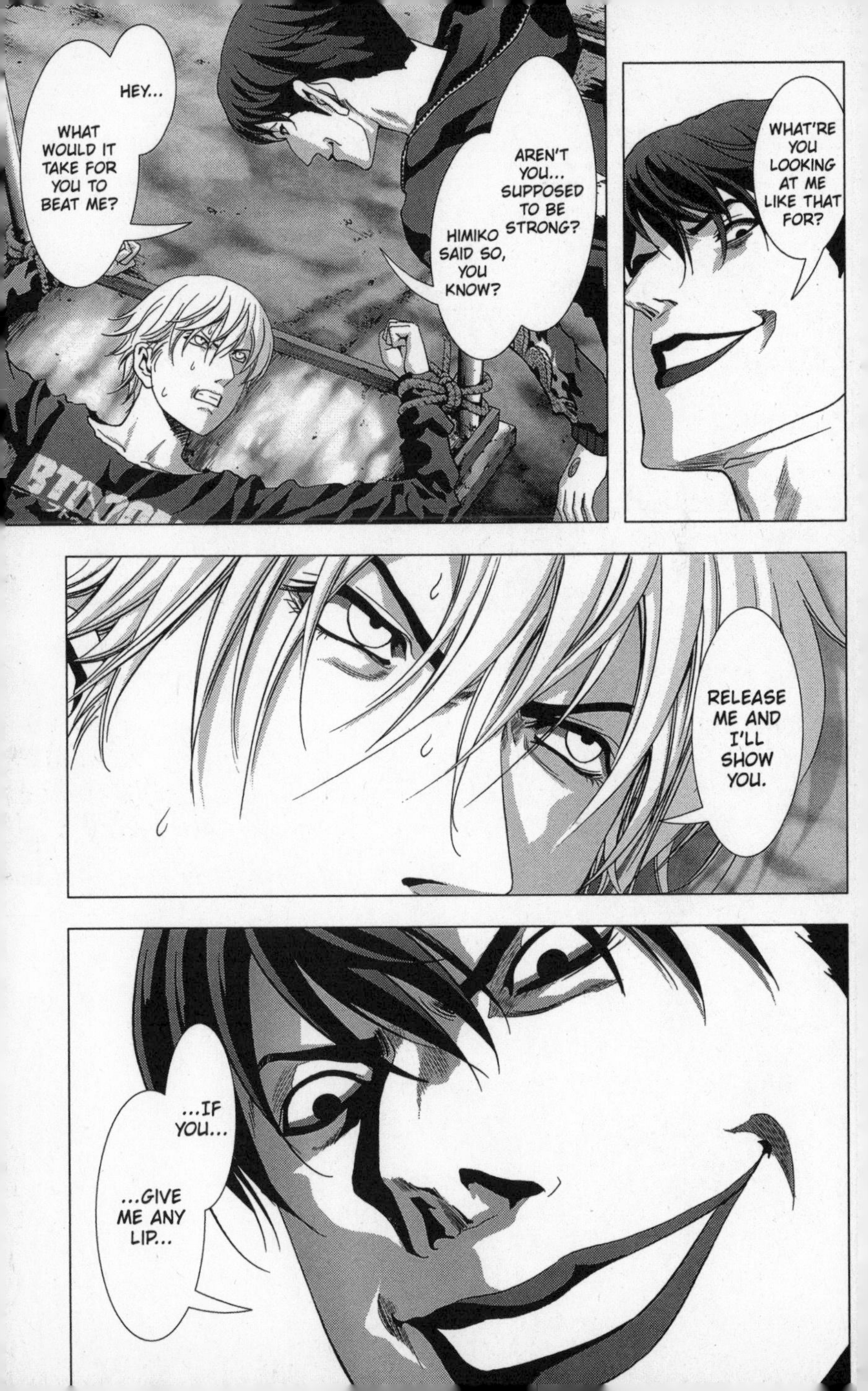
WHAT'RE YOU LOOKING AT ME LIKE THAT FOR?
AREN'T YOU... SUPPOSED TO BE STRONG?
HIMIKO SAID SO, YOU KNOW?
HEY...
WHAT WOULD IT TAKE FOR YOU TO BEAT ME?
RELEASE ME AND I'LL SHOW YOU.
...IF YOU...
...GIVE ME ANY LIP...

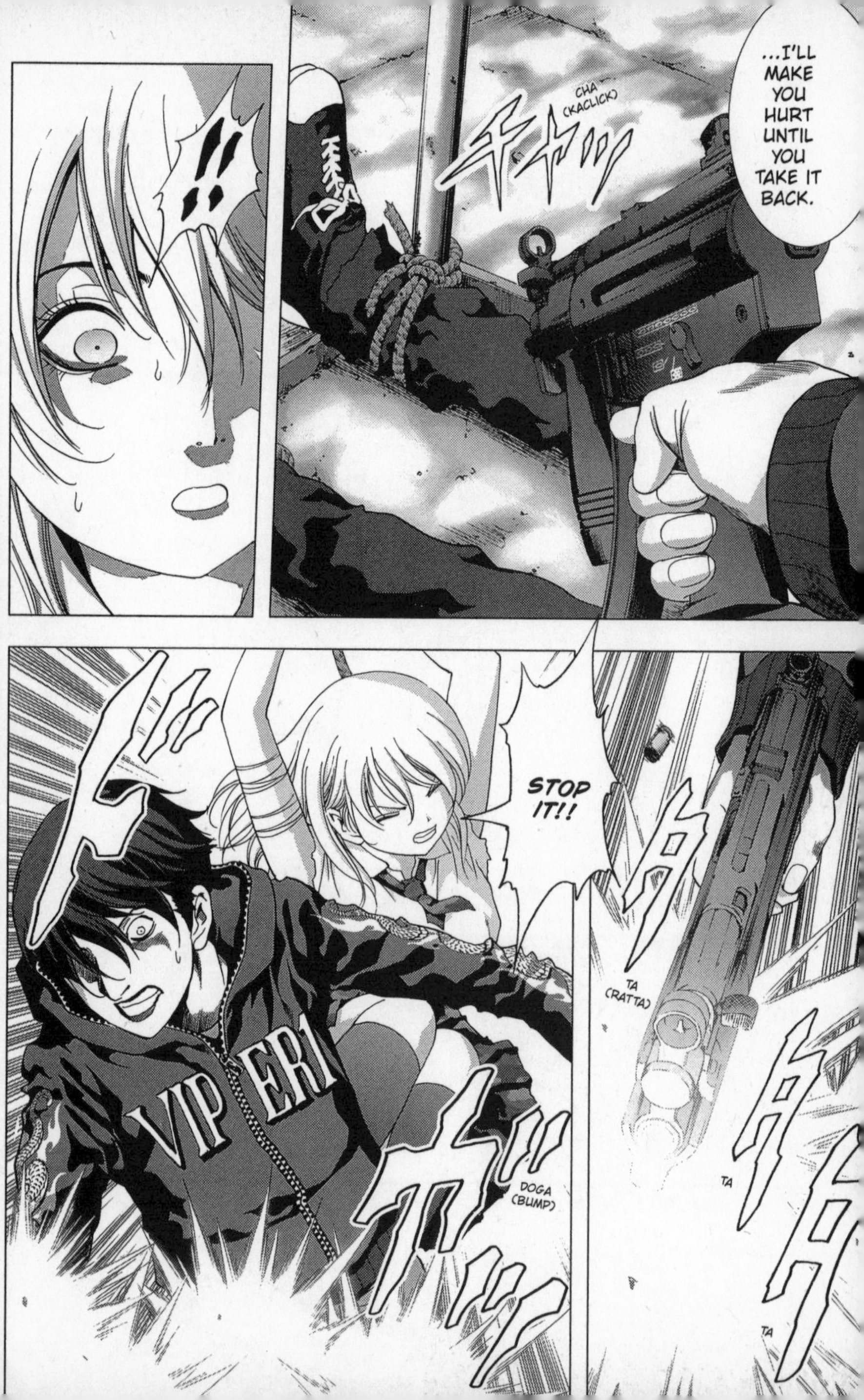
...I'LL MAKE YOU HURT UNTIL YOU TAKE IT BACK.
CHA (KACLICK)
TA (RATTA)
TA
TA
STOP IT!!
VIPER1
DOGA (BUMP)

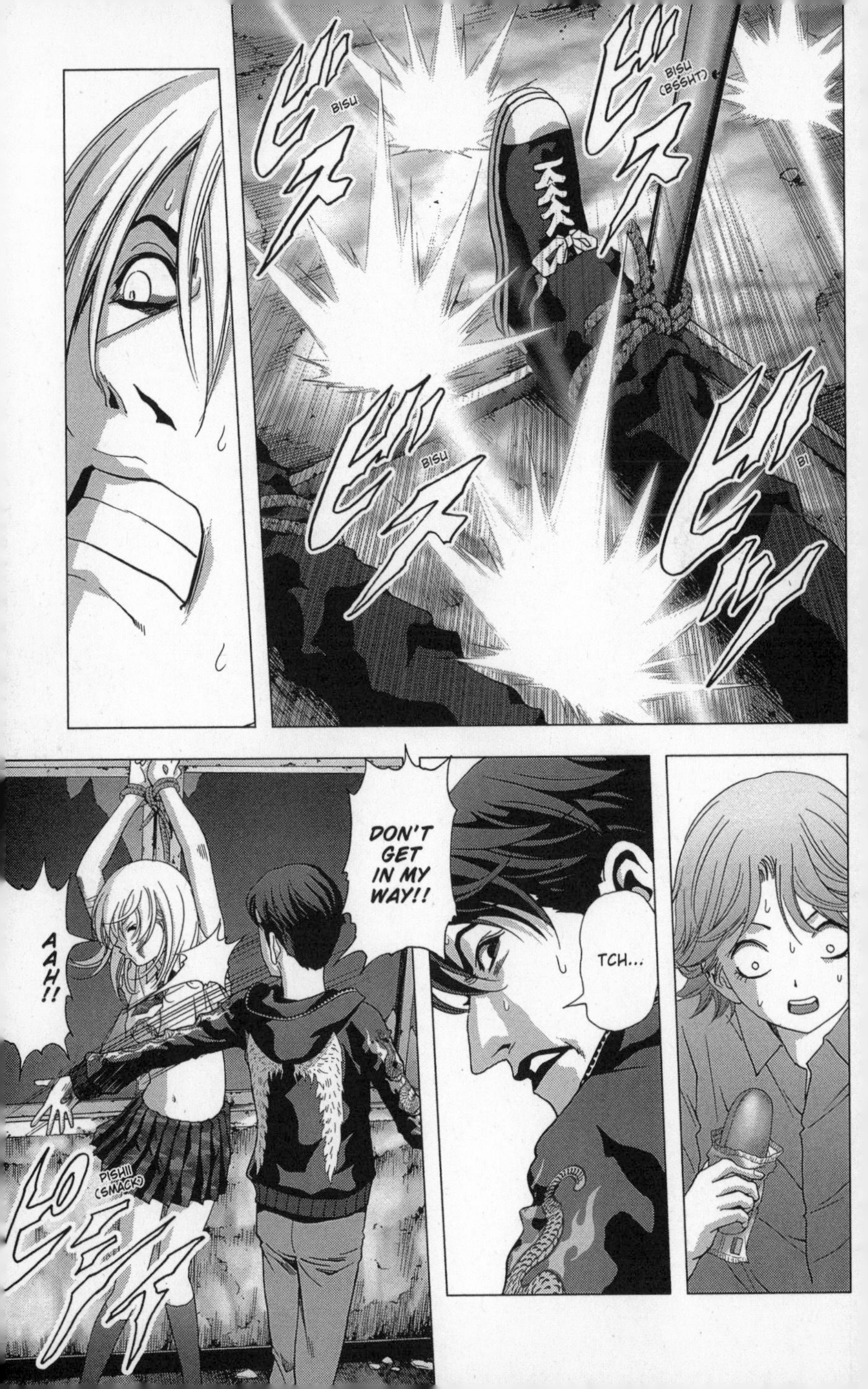
BISU (BSSHT)
BISU
BI
BISU
TCH...
DON'T GET IN MY WAY!!
AAAH!!
PISHII (SMACK)

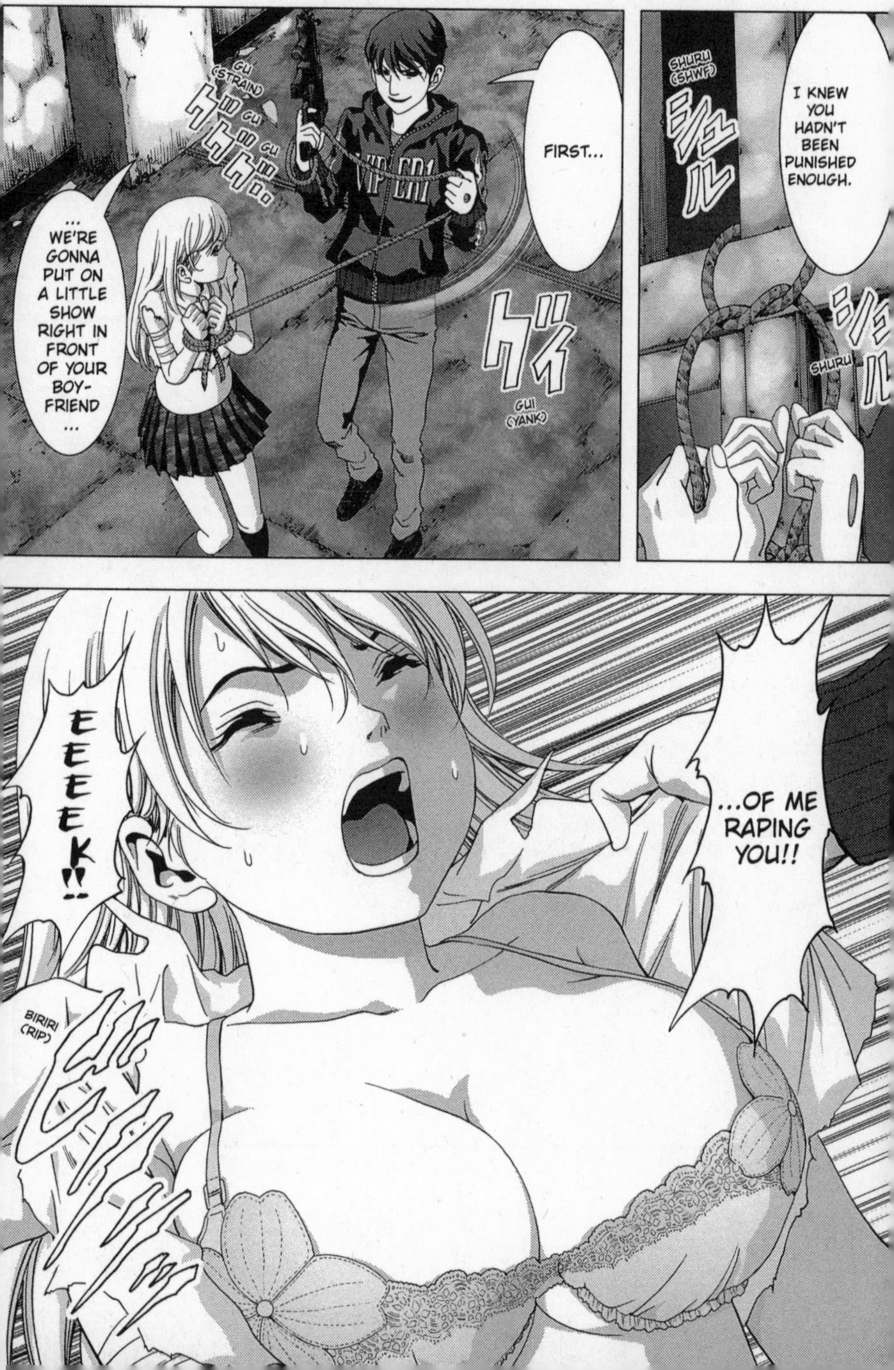
SHURU (SHWF)
I KNEW YOU HADN'T BEEN PUNISHED ENOUGH.
SHURU
FIRST...
GU (STRAIN) GU GU
... WE'RE GONNA PUT ON A LITTLE SHOW RIGHT IN FRONT OF YOUR BOY-FRIEND ...
GUI (YANK)
...OF ME RAPING YOU!!
EEEEEK!!
BIRIRI (RIP)

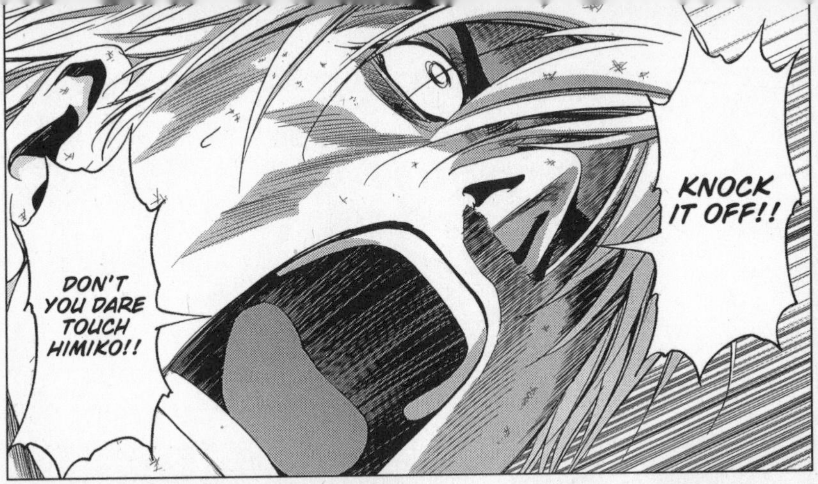
KNOCK IT OFF!!
DON'T YOU DARE TOUCH HIMIKO!!
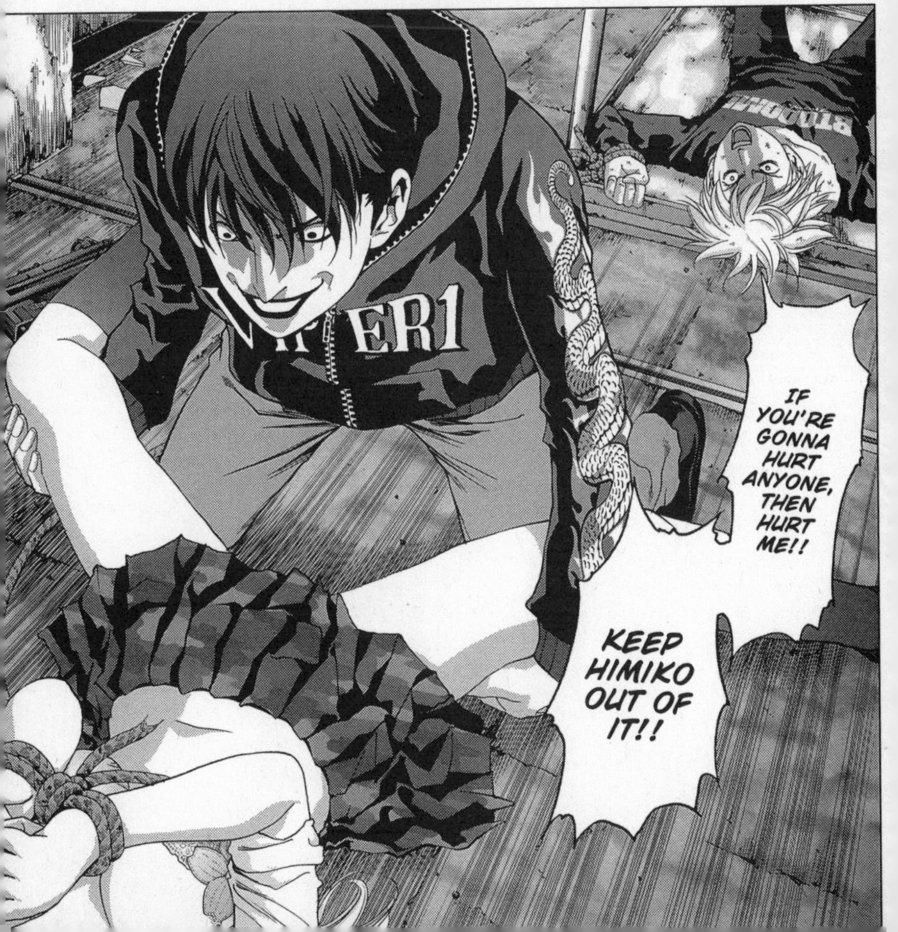
IF YOU'RE GONNA HURT ANYONE, THEN HURT ME!!
KEEP HIMIKO OUT OF IT!!

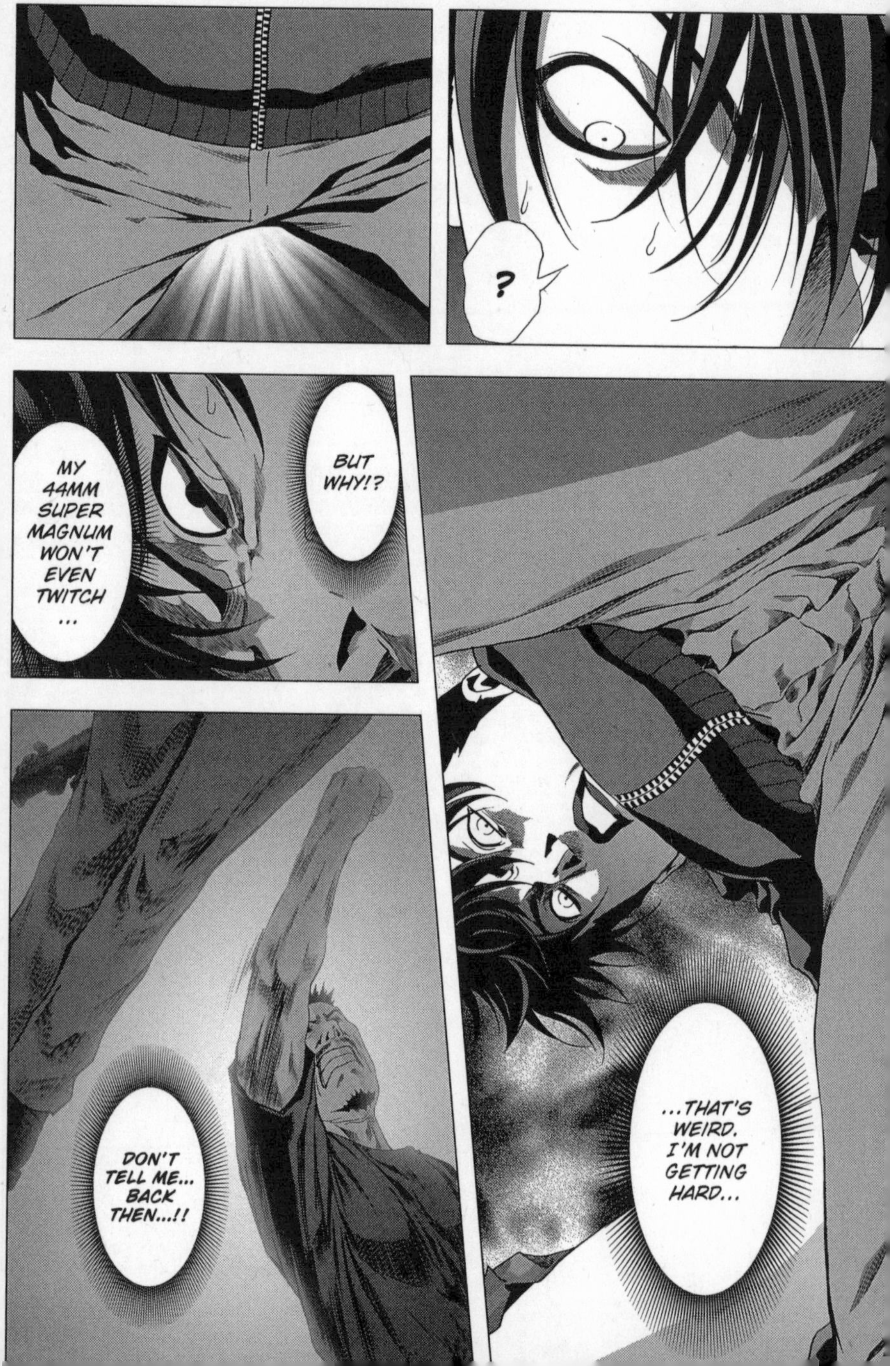
?
...THAT'S WEIRD. I'M NOT GETTING HARD...
BUT WHY!?
MY 44MM SUPER MAGNUM WON'T EVEN TWITCH...
DON'T TELL ME... BACK THEN...!!

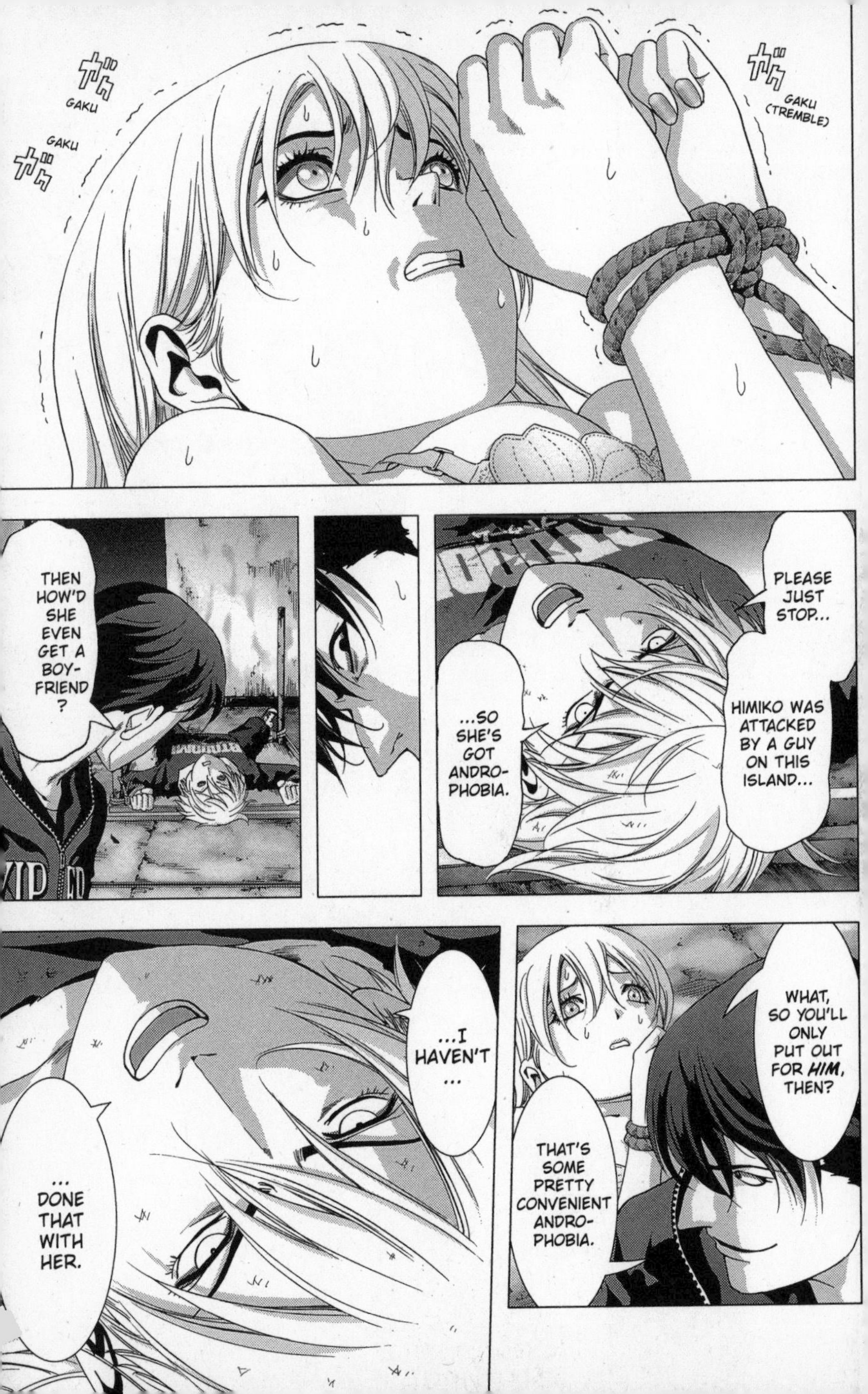
ガク
GAKU (TREMBLE)
ガク
GAKU
GAKU
ガク
PLEASE JUST STOP...
HIMIKO WAS ATTACKED BY A GUY ON THIS ISLAND...
...SO SHE'S GOT ANDROPHOBIA.
THEN HOW'D SHE EVEN GET A BOYFRIEND?
WHAT, SO YOU'LL ONLY PUT OUT FOR *HIM*, THEN?
THAT'S SOME PRETTY CONVENIENT ANDROPHOBIA.
...I HAVEN'T ...
... DONE THAT WITH HER.

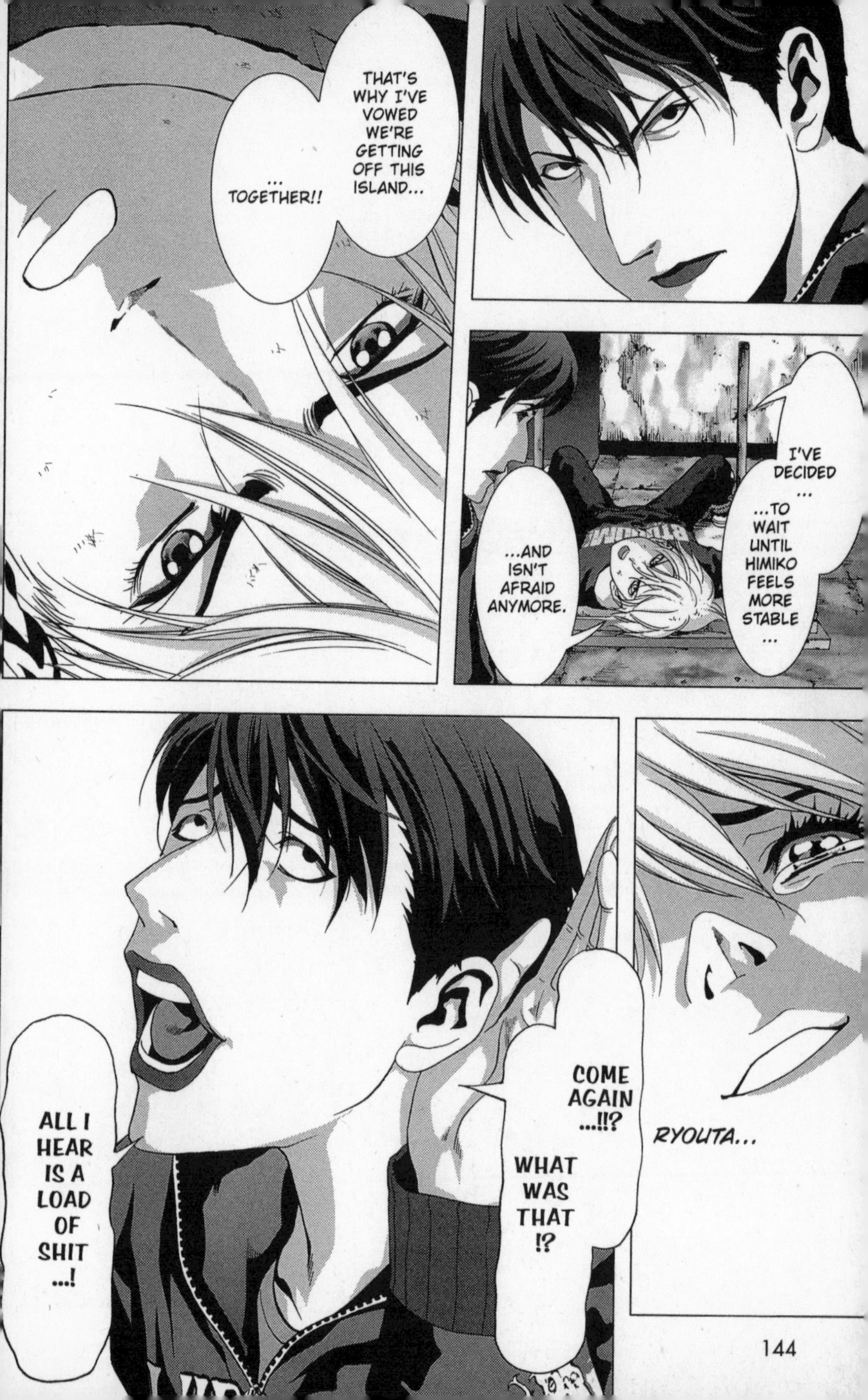
I'VE DECIDED...
...TO WAIT UNTIL HIMIKO FEELS MORE STABLE...
...AND ISN'T AFRAID ANYMORE.
THAT'S WHY I'VE VOWED WE'RE GETTING OFF THIS ISLAND...
...TOGETHER!!
RYOUTA...
COME AGAIN...!!?
WHAT WAS THAT!?
ALL I HEAR IS A LOAD OF SHIT...!

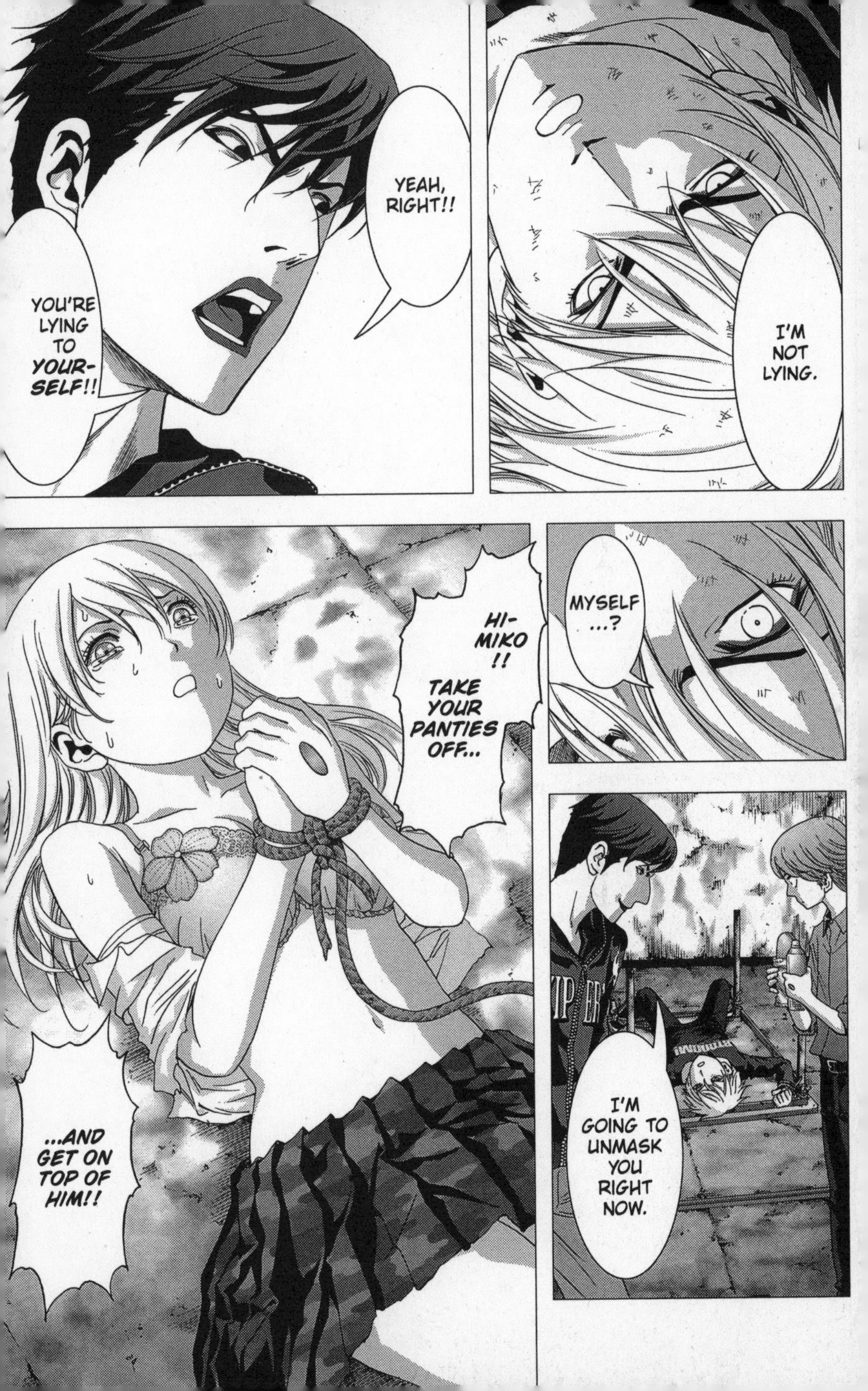
I'M NOT LYING.
YEAH, RIGHT!!
YOU'RE LYING TO YOURSELF!!
MYSELF ...?
I'M GOING TO UNMASK YOU RIGHT NOW.
HI-MIKO!!
TAKE YOUR PANTIES OFF...
...AND GET ON TOP OF HIM!!

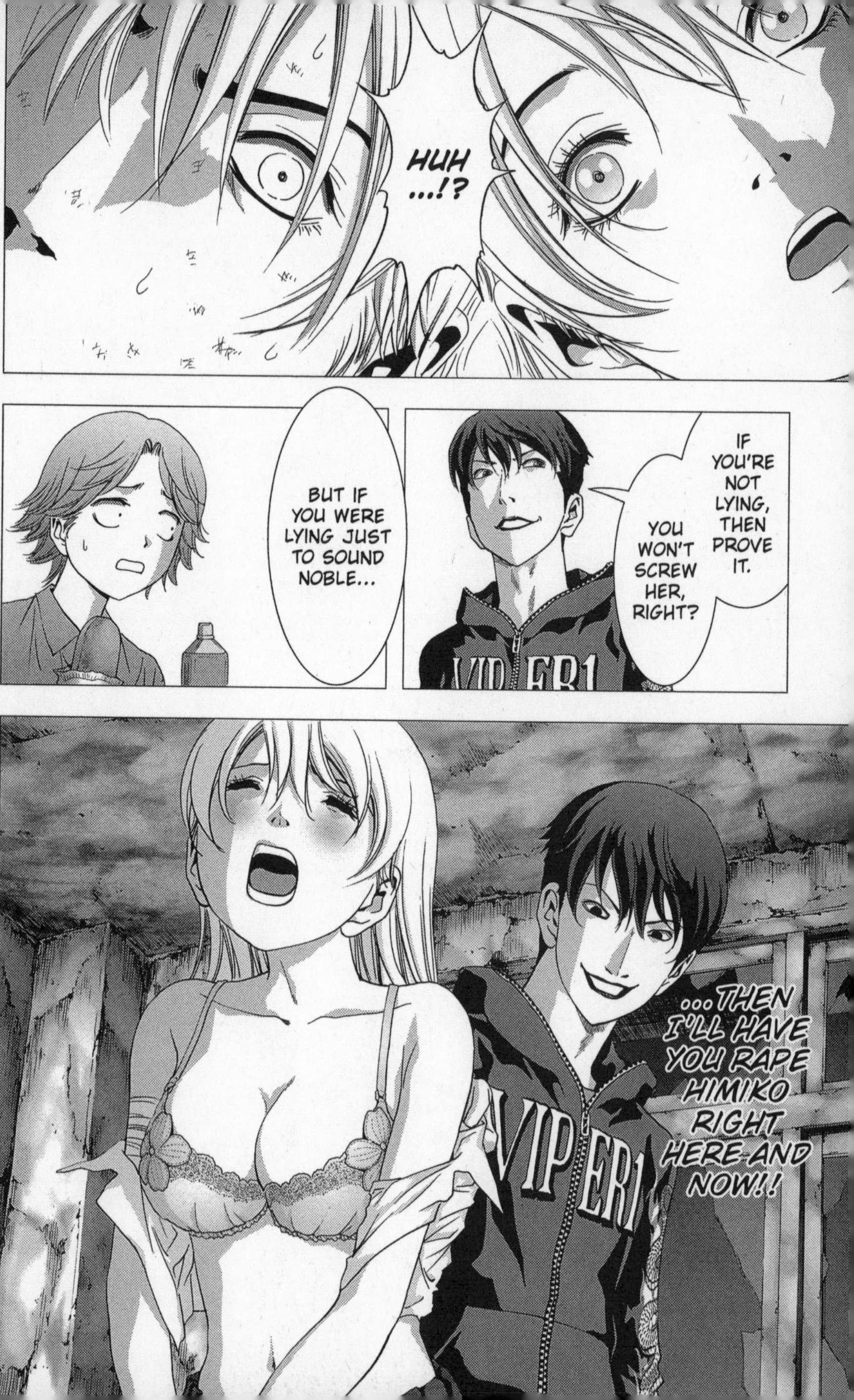
HUH ...!?
IF YOU'RE NOT LYING, THEN PROVE IT.
YOU WON'T SCREW HER, RIGHT?
BUT IF YOU WERE LYING JUST TO SOUND NOBLE...
...THEN I'LL HAVE YOU RAPE HIMIKO RIGHT HERE AND NOW!!
VIPER1

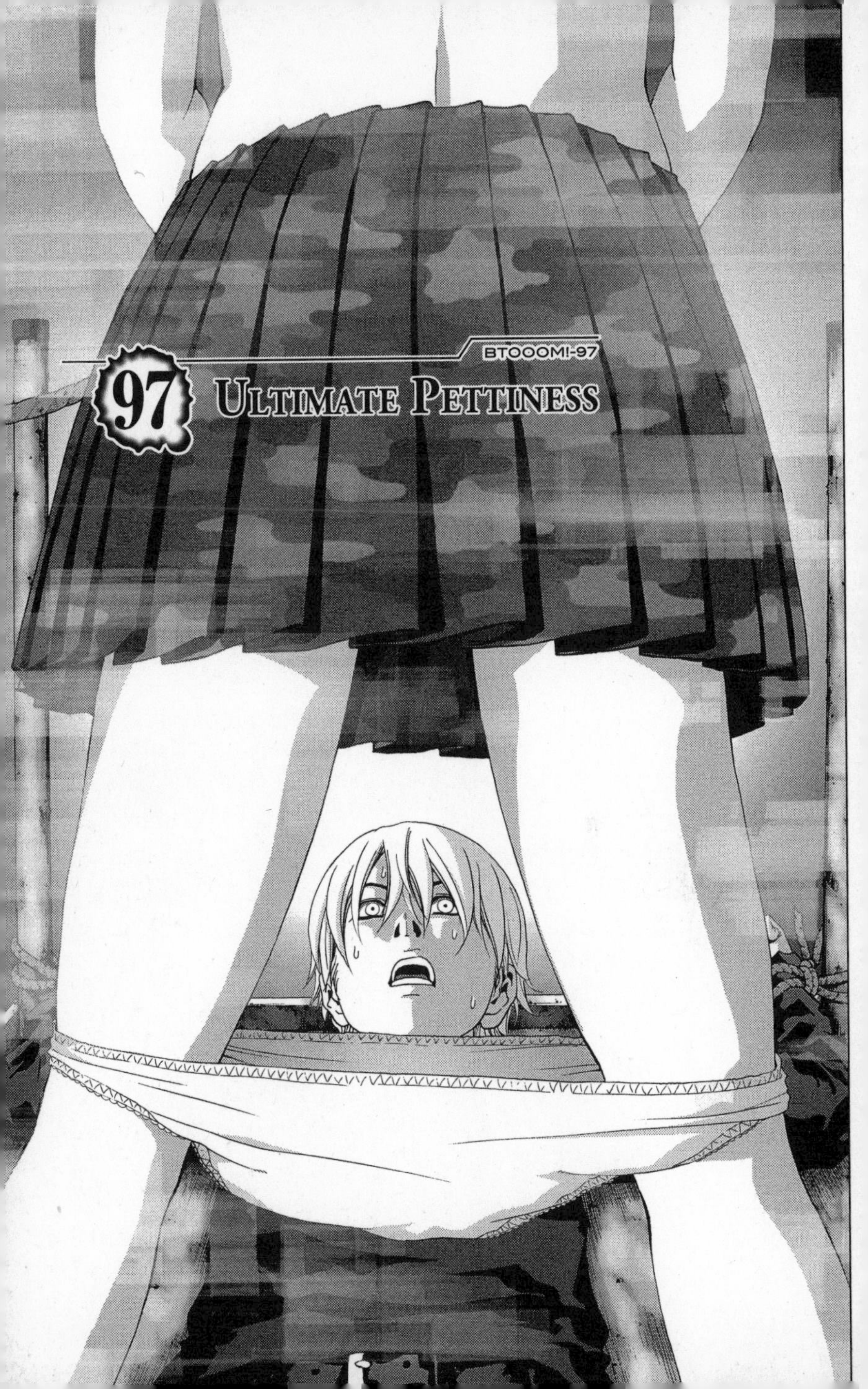
BTOOOM!-97
97 Ultimate Pettiness

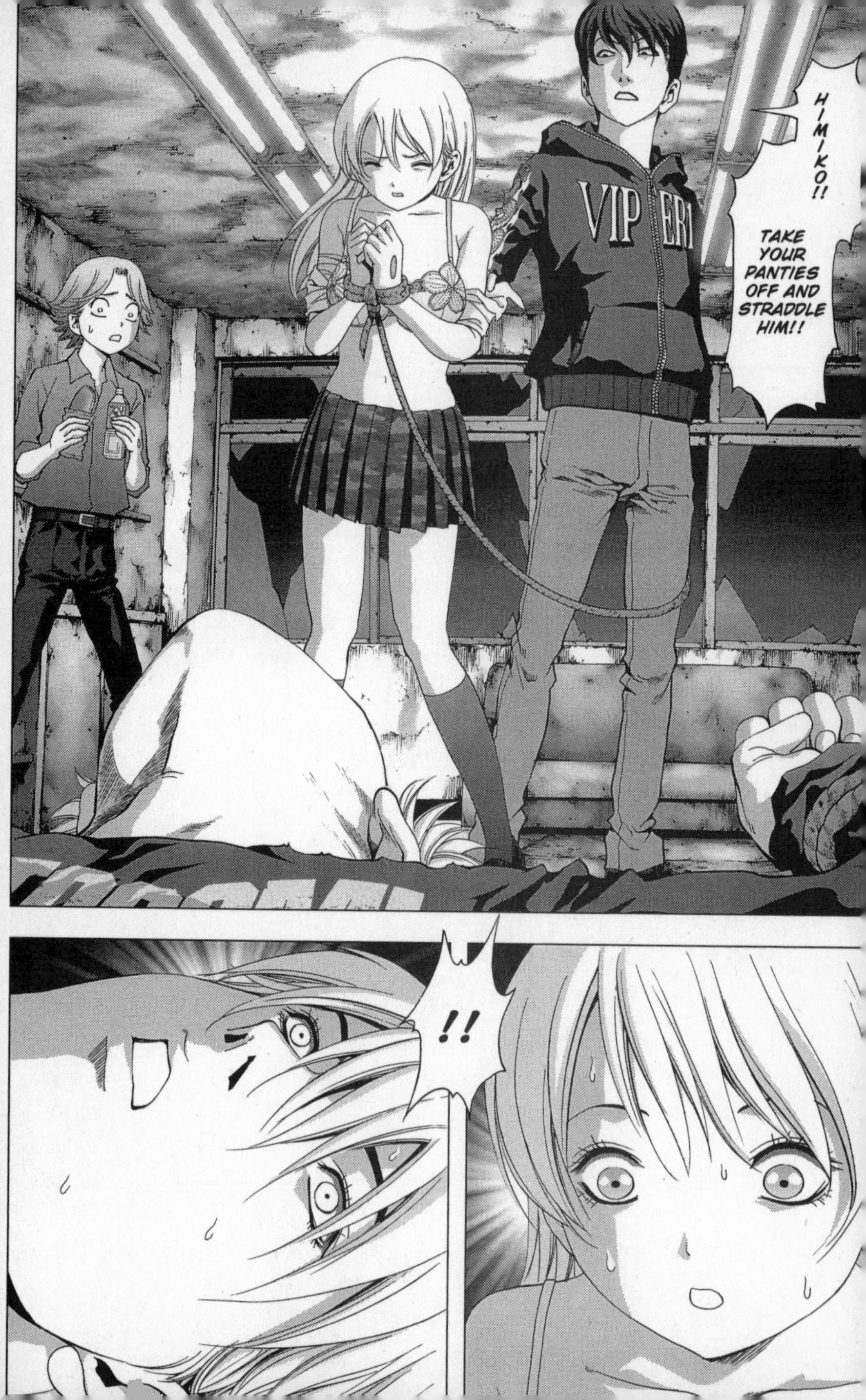
HIMIKO!!
TAKE YOUR PANTIES OFF AND STRADDLE HIM!!
!!

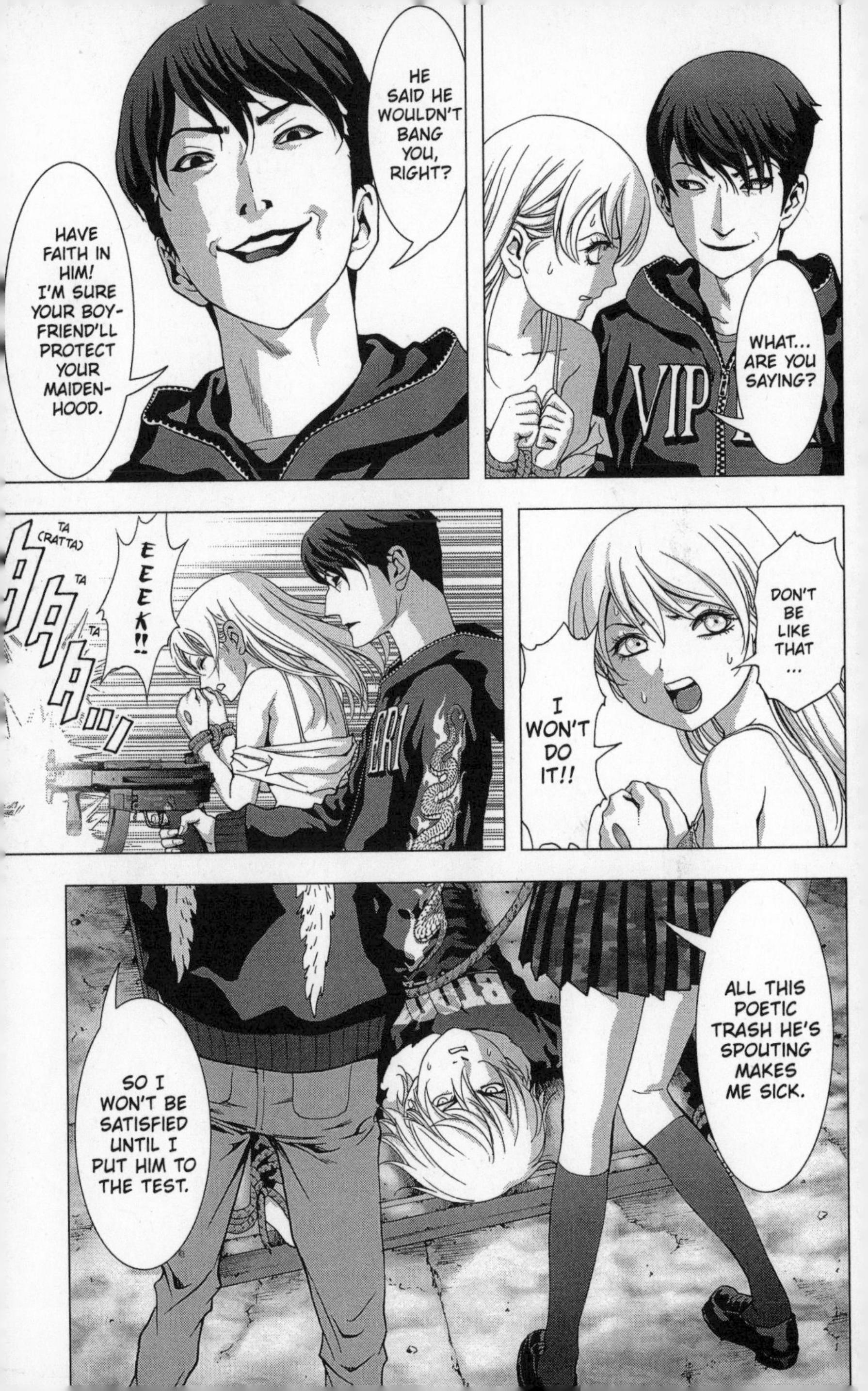
WHAT... ARE YOU SAYING?
HE SAID HE WOULDN'T BANG YOU, RIGHT?
HAVE FAITH IN HIM! I'M SURE YOUR BOY-FRIEND'LL PROTECT YOUR MAIDEN-HOOD.
DON'T BE LIKE THAT...
I WON'T DO IT!!
EEEEK!!
TA (RATTA)
TA
TA
ALL THIS POETIC TRASH HE'S SPOUTING MAKES ME SICK.
SO I WON'T BE SATISFIED UNTIL I PUT HIM TO THE TEST.

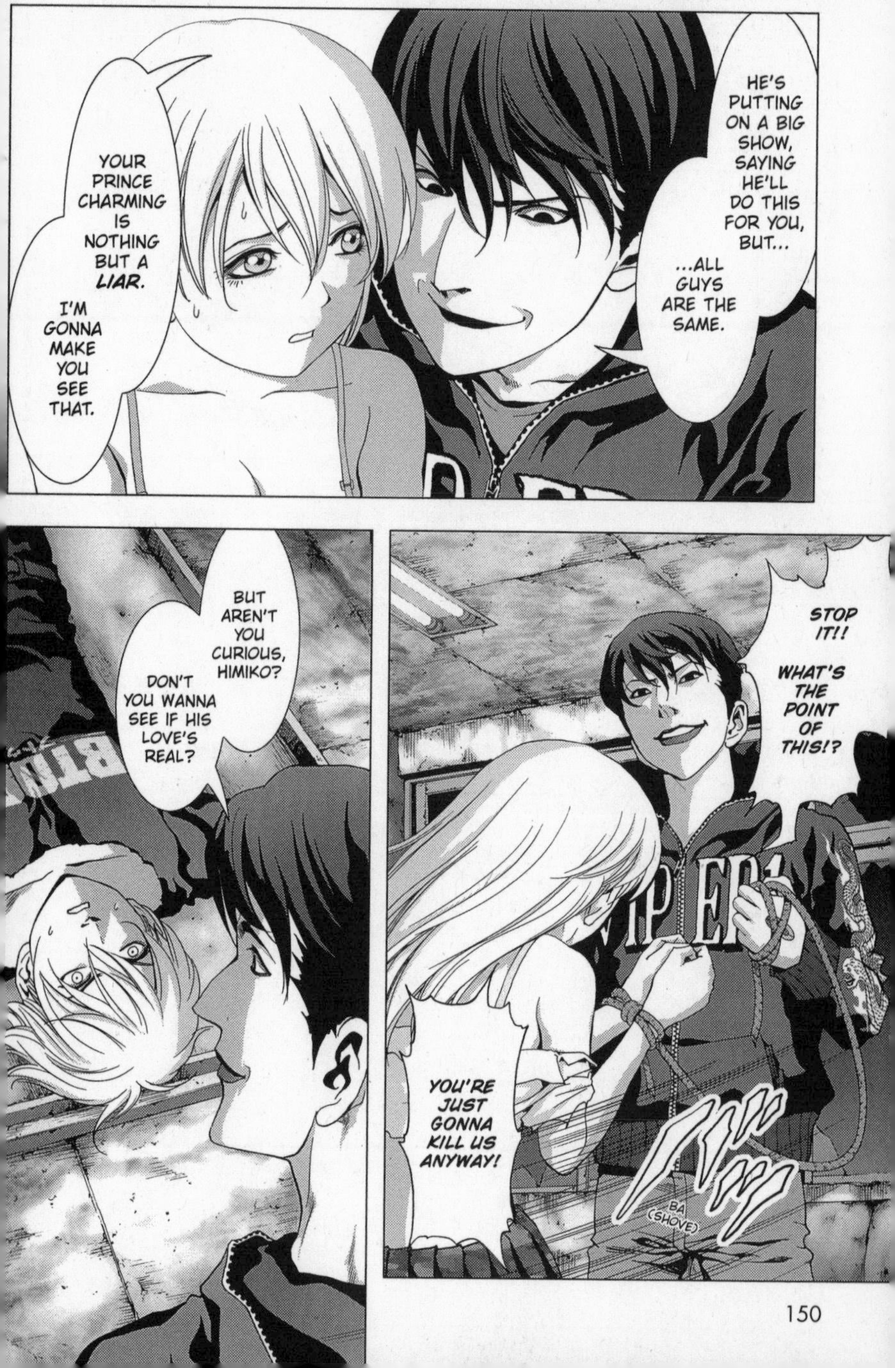
HE'S PUTTING ON A BIG SHOW, SAYING HE'LL DO THIS FOR YOU, BUT...
...ALL GUYS ARE THE SAME.
YOUR PRINCE CHARMING IS NOTHING BUT A *LIAR*.
I'M GONNA MAKE YOU SEE THAT.
STOP IT!!
WHAT'S THE POINT OF THIS!?
YOU'RE JUST GONNA KILL US ANYWAY!
BA (SHOVE)
BUT AREN'T YOU CURIOUS, HIMIKO?
DON'T YOU WANNA SEE IF HIS LOVE'S REAL?

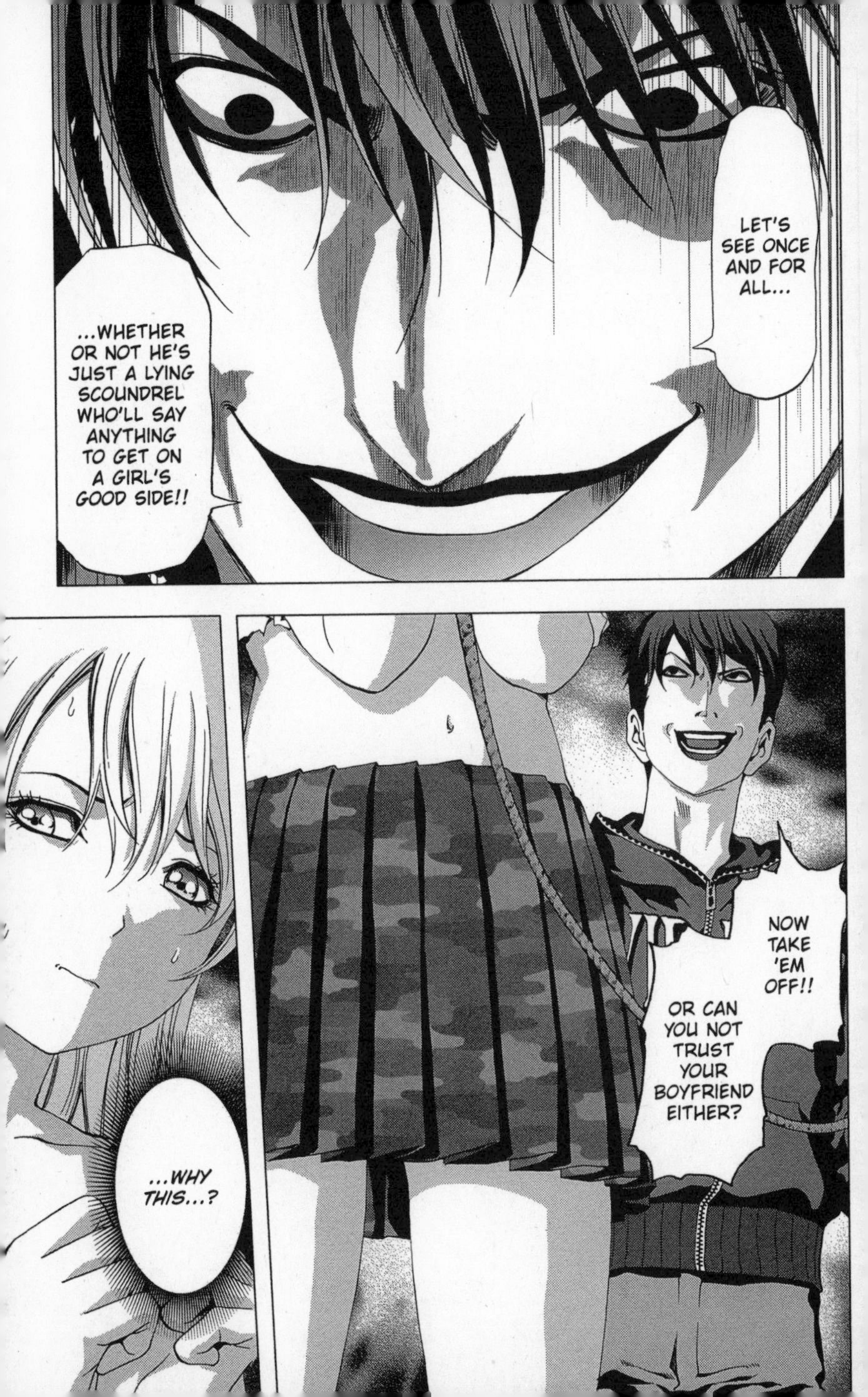
LET'S SEE ONCE AND FOR ALL...
...WHETHER OR NOT HE'S JUST A LYING SCOUNDREL WHO'LL SAY ANYTHING TO GET ON A GIRL'S GOOD SIDE!!
NOW TAKE 'EM OFF!!
OR CAN YOU NOT TRUST YOUR BOYFRIEND EITHER?
...WHY THIS...?

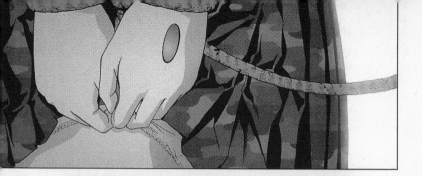

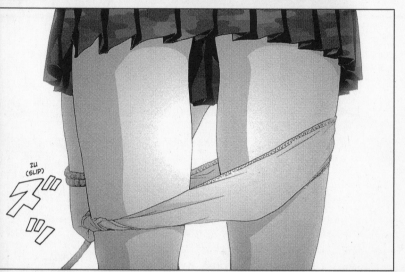

ZU
(SLIP)

HERE WE GO.

NOW STRADDLE HIM.

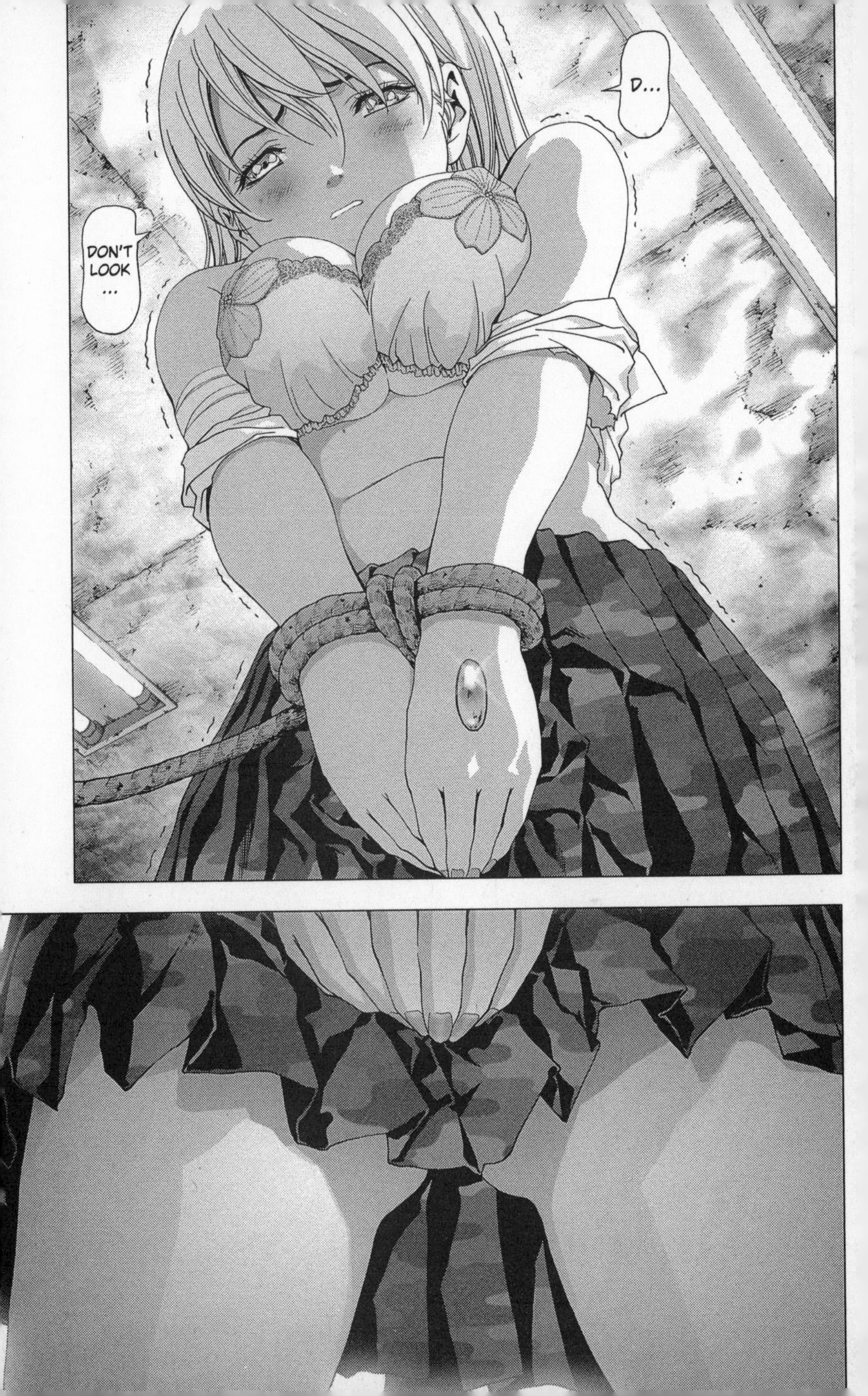
D...
DON'T LOOK ...

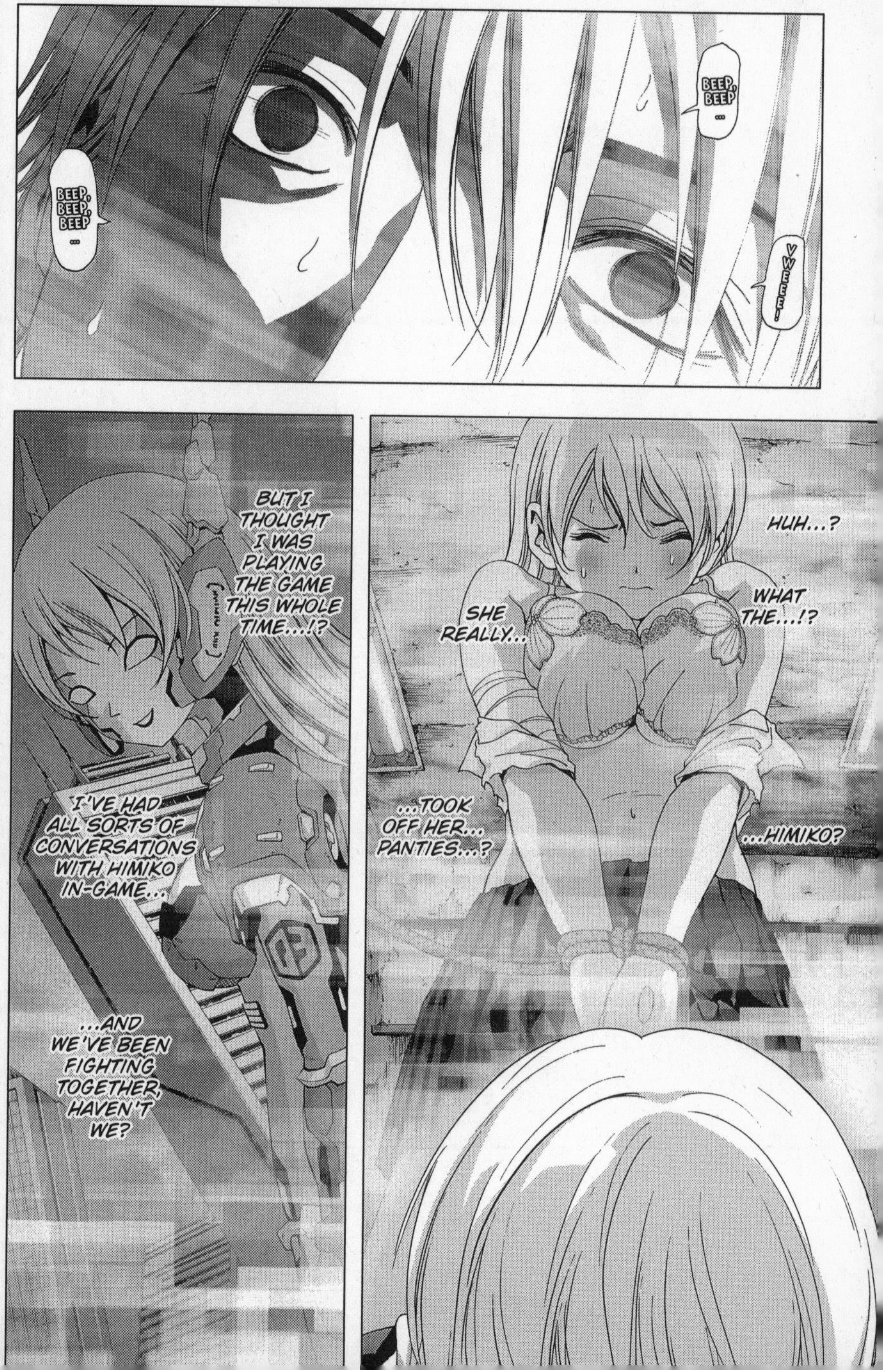
BEEP, BEEP ...
VWEEE!
BEEP, BEEP, BEEP ...
HUH...?
WHAT THE...!?
SHE REALLY...
...TOOK OFF HER... PANTIES...?
...HIMIKO?
BUT I THOUGHT I WAS PLAYING THE GAME THIS WHOLE TIME...!?
I'VE HAD ALL SORTS OF CONVERSATIONS WITH HIMIKO IN-GAME...
...AND WE'VE BEEN FIGHTING TOGETHER, HAVEN'T WE?

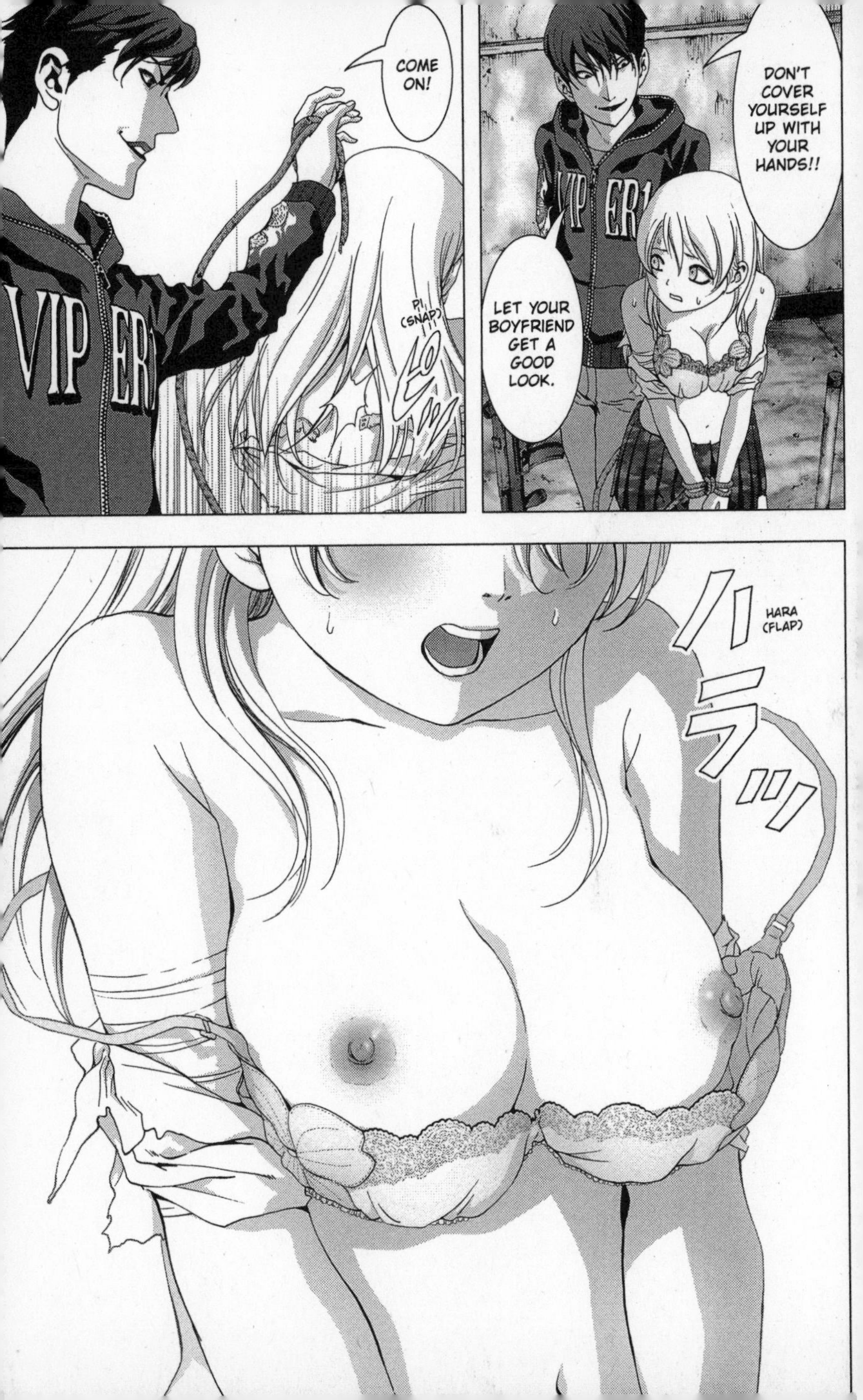
DON'T COVER YOURSELF UP WITH YOUR HANDS!!
LET YOUR BOYFRIEND GET A GOOD LOOK.
COME ON!
PI (SNAP)
HARA (FLAP)

FUSAA
(FWSH)

NO!!

BA
(BLOCK)

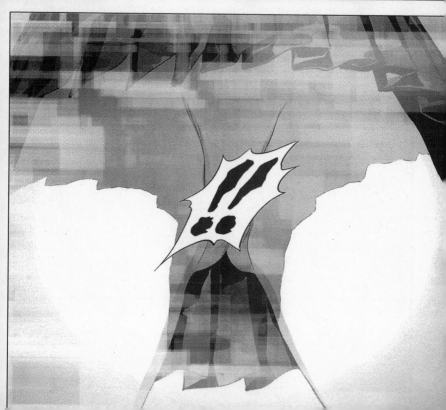

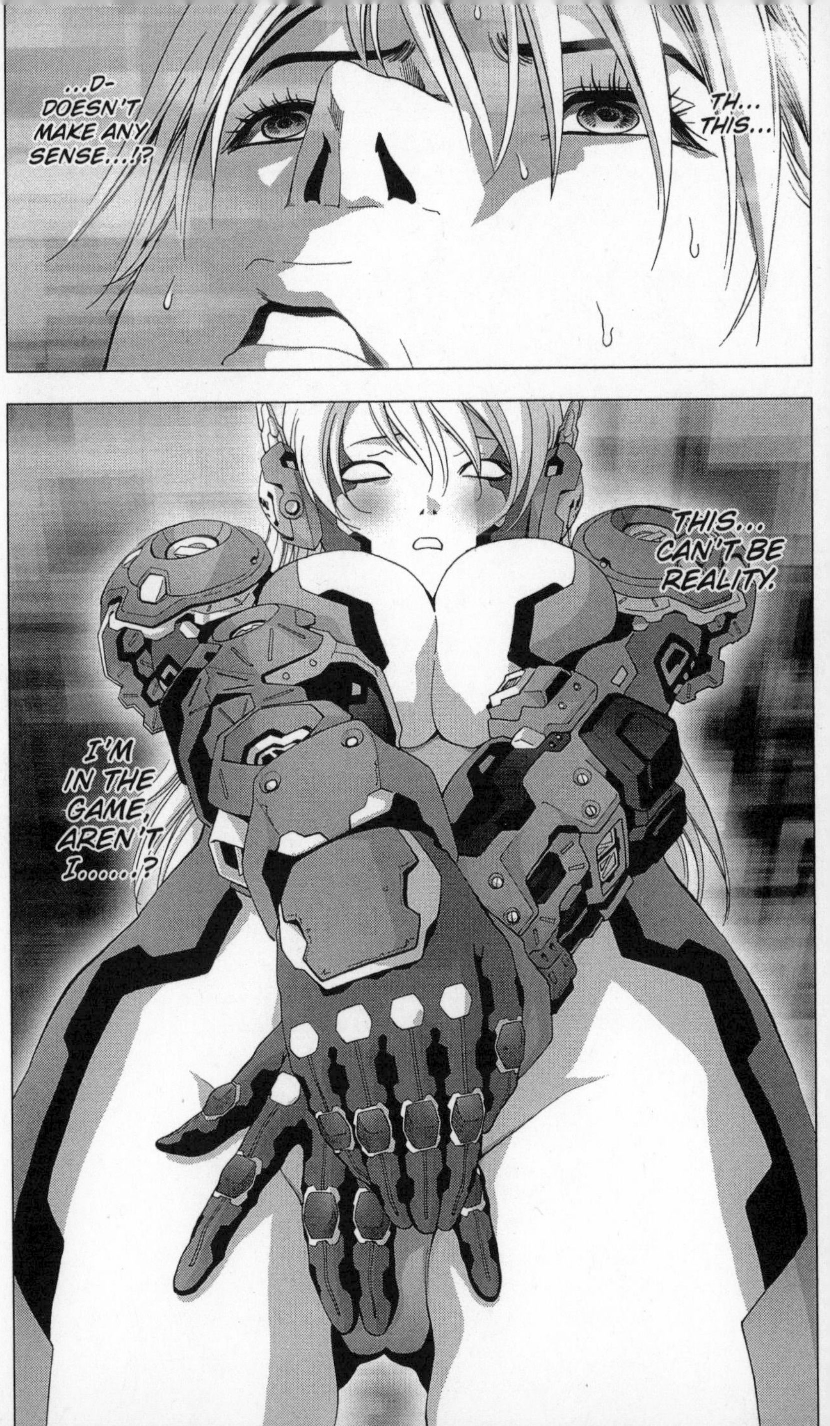
TH... THIS...
...D-DOESN'T MAKE ANY SENSE...!?
THIS... CAN'T BE REALITY.
I'M IN THE GAME, AREN'T I.......?

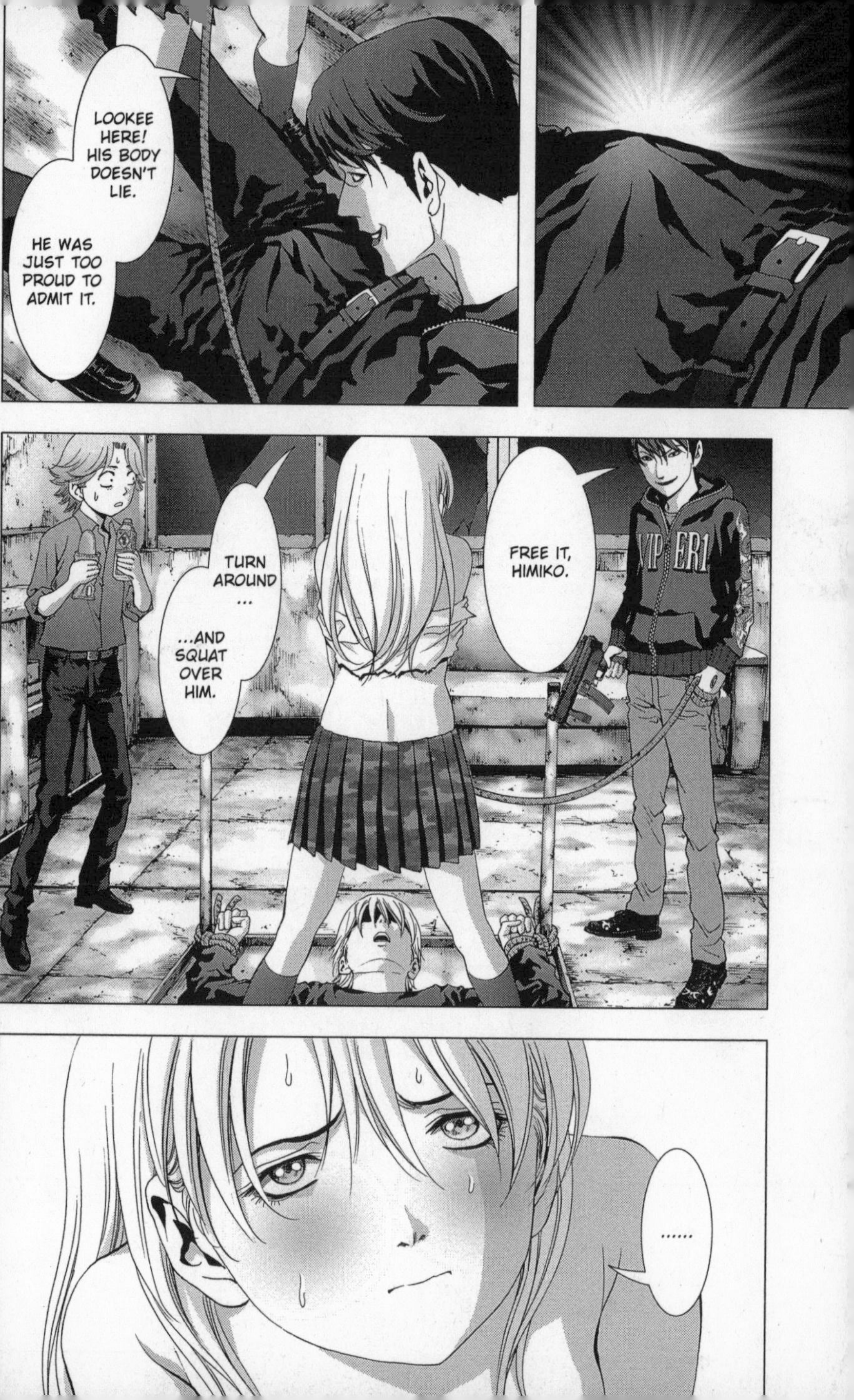
LOOKEE HERE! HIS BODY DOESN'T LIE.
HE WAS JUST TOO PROUD TO ADMIT IT.
FREE IT, HIMIKO.
TURN AROUND ...
...AND SQUAT OVER HIM.
......
VIPER1

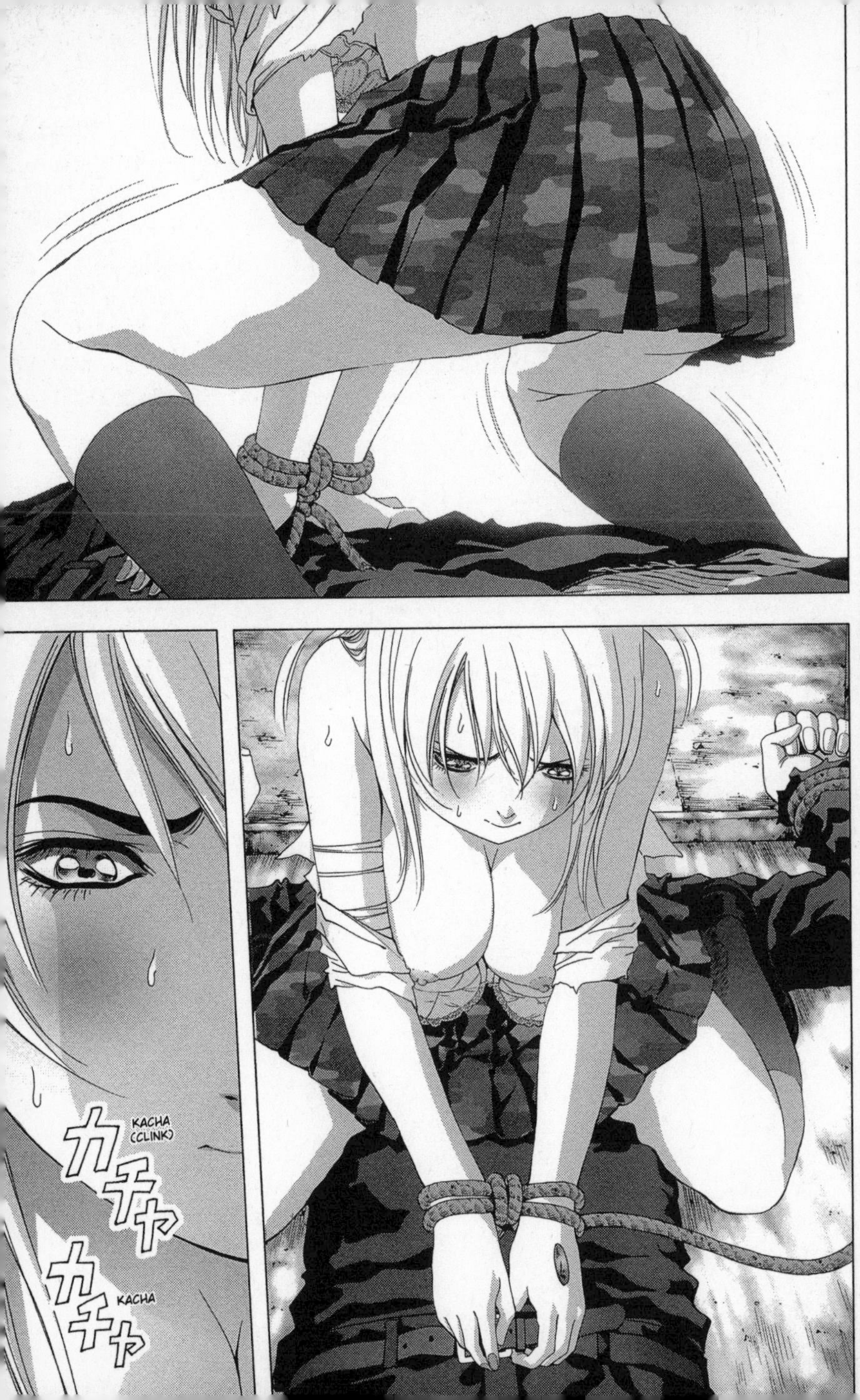
カチャ
KACHA (CLINK)
カチャ
KACHA

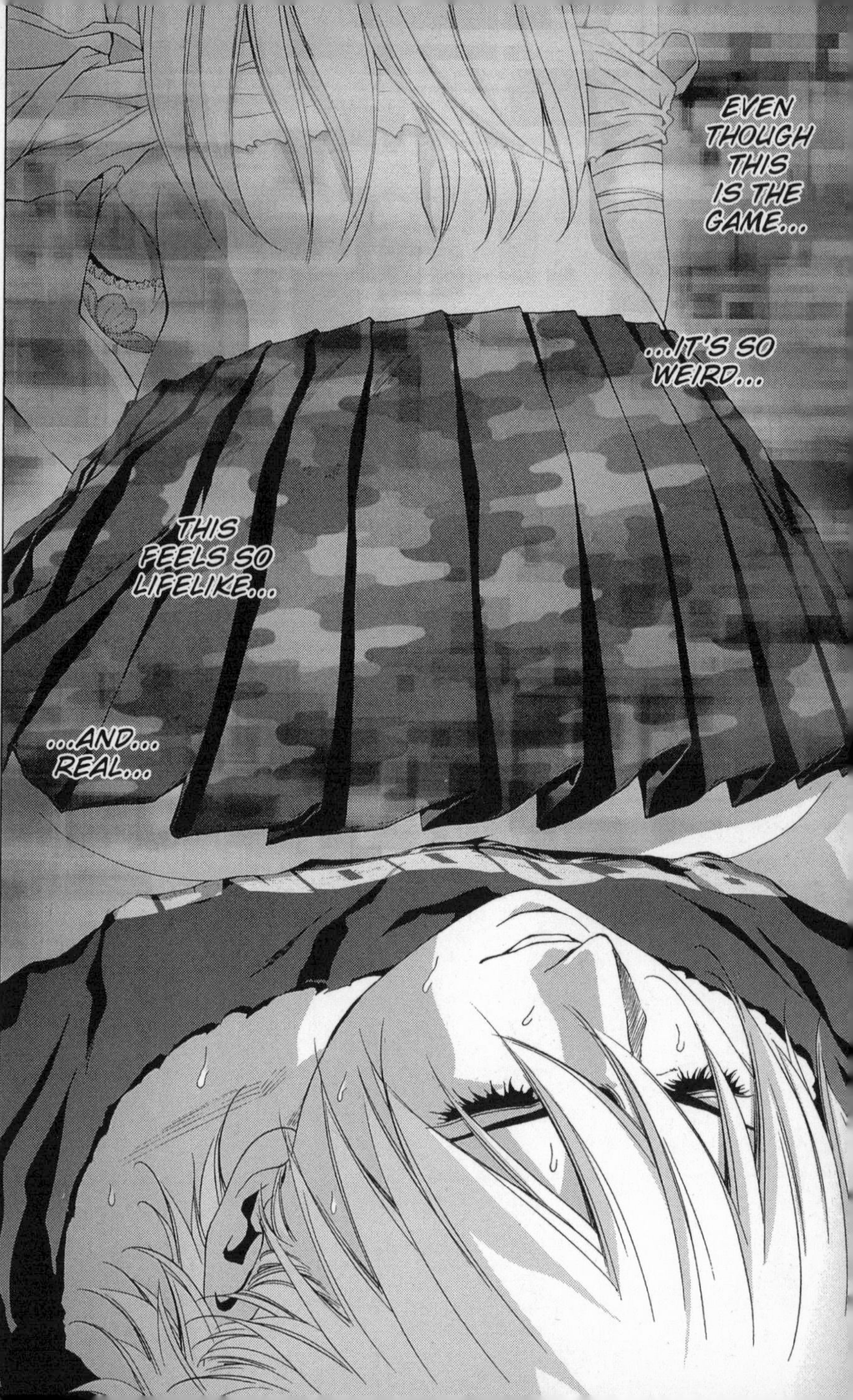
EVEN THOUGH THIS IS THE GAME...
...IT'S SO WEIRD...
THIS FEELS SO LIFELIKE...
...AND... REAL...

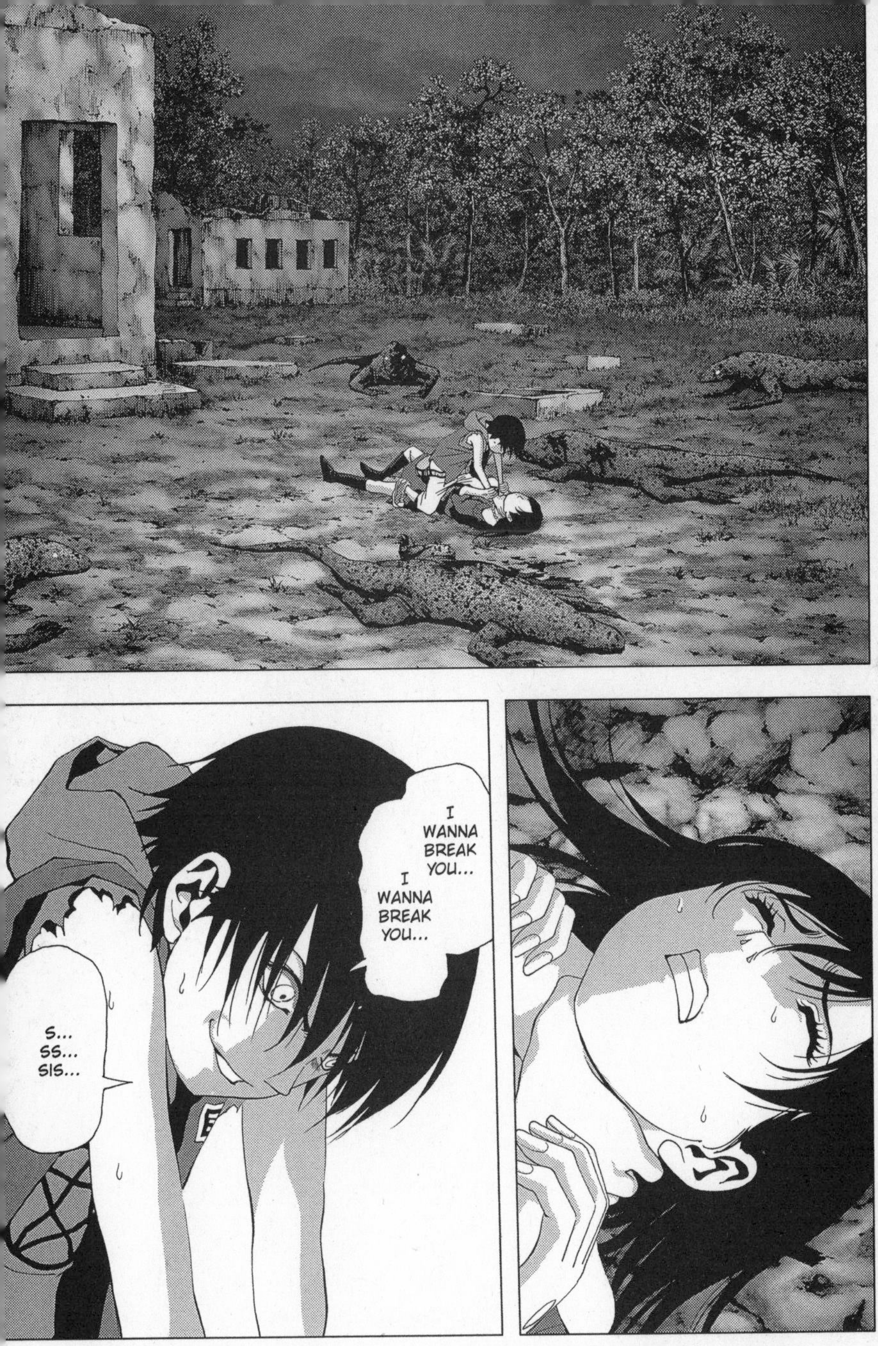
I WANNA BREAK YOU... I WANNA BREAK YOU...
S... SS... SIS...

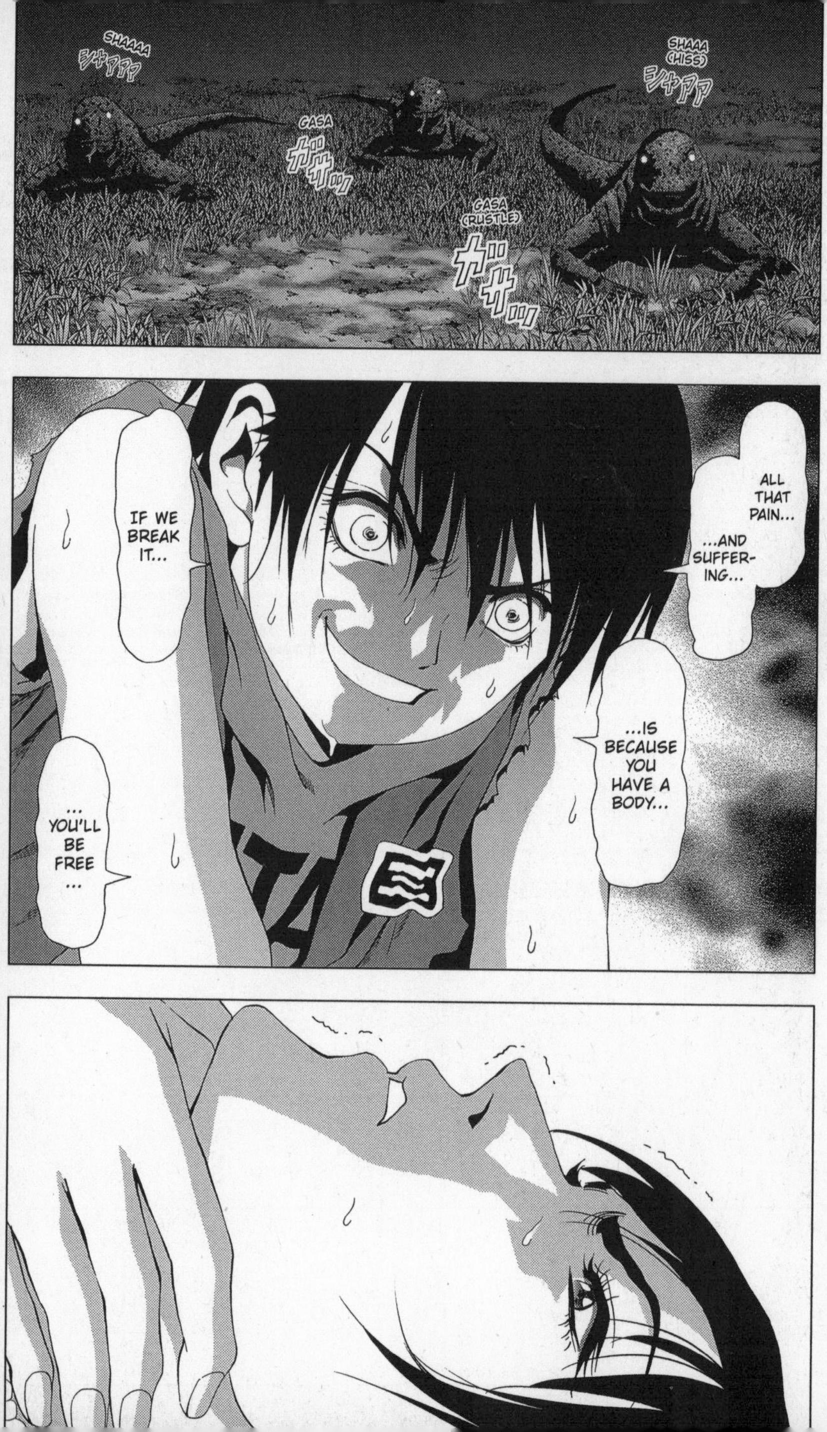
SHAAA (HISS)
シャアア
GASA (RUSTLE)
ガサッ
GASA
ガサッ
SHAAA
シャアア
ALL THAT PAIN...
...AND SUFFERING...
...IS BECAUSE YOU HAVE A BODY...
IF WE BREAK IT...
...YOU'LL BE FREE...

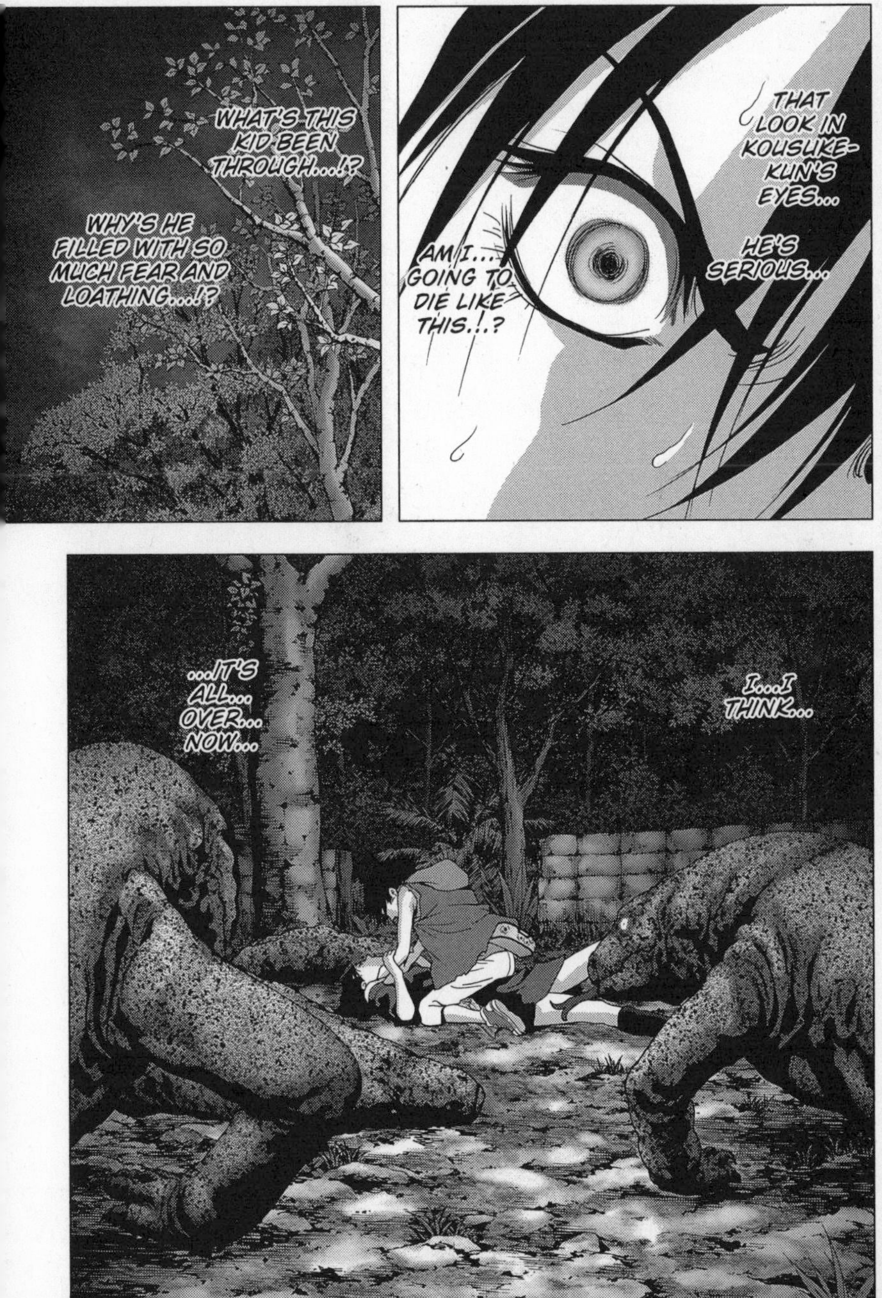
THAT LOOK IN KOUSUKE-KUN'S EYES...
HE'S SERIOUS...
AM I... GOING TO DIE LIKE THIS...!?
WHAT'S THIS KID BEEN THROUGH...!?
WHY'S HE FILLED WITH SO MUCH FEAR AND LOATHING...!?
I...I THINK...
...IT'S ALL... OVER... NOW...

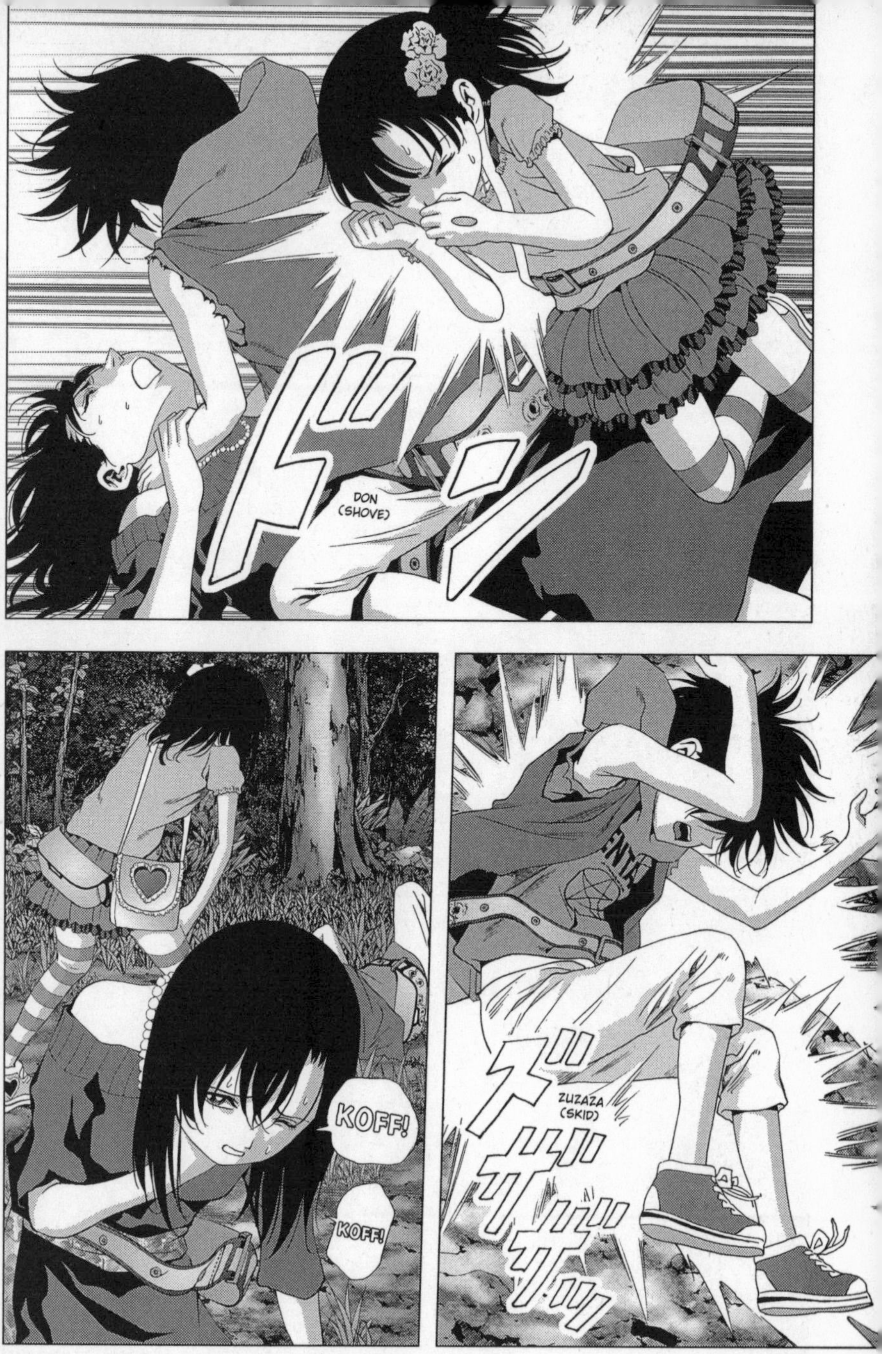
DON (SHOVE)
ZUZAZA (SKID)
KOFF!
KOFF!

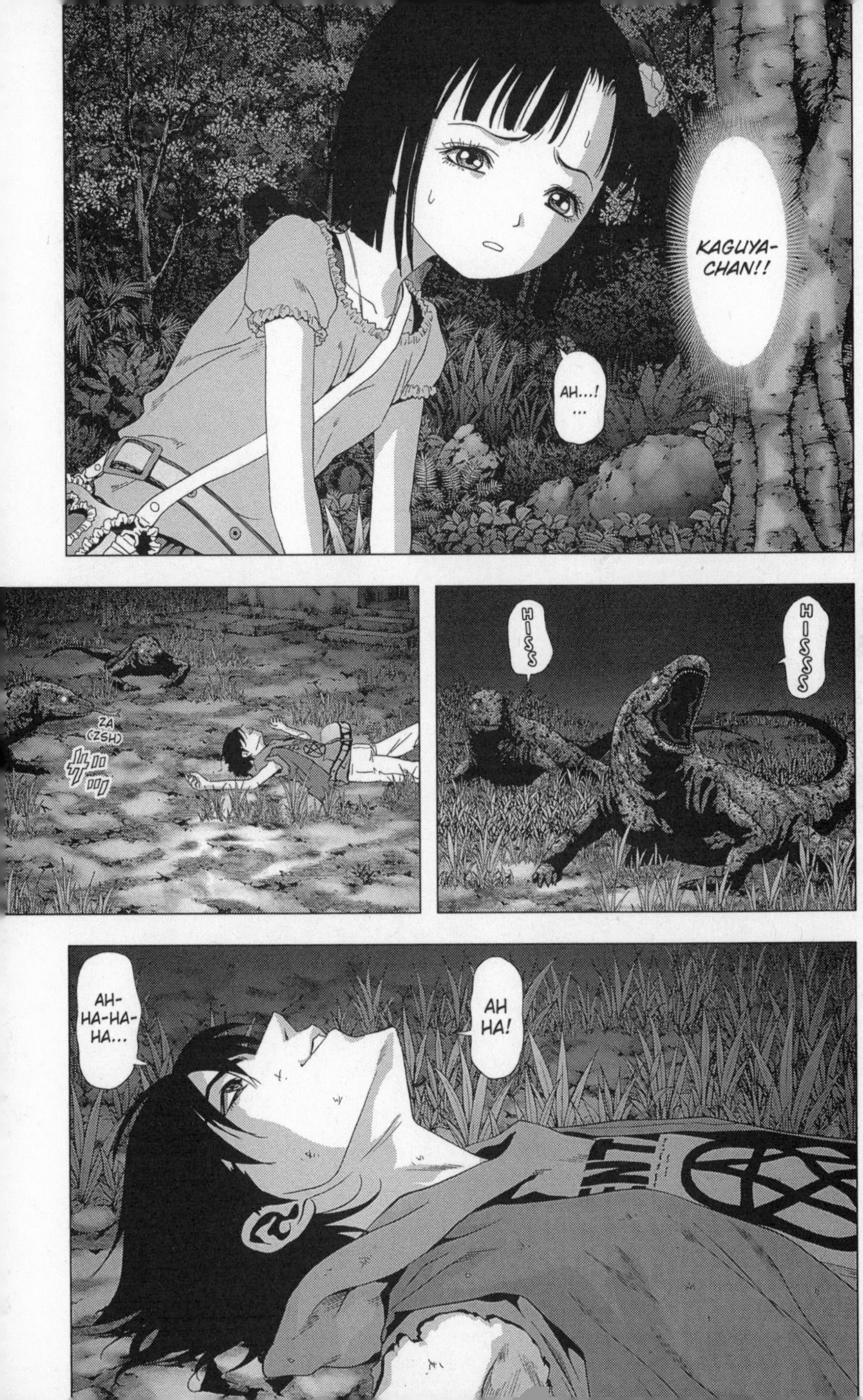
KAGUYA-CHAN!!
AH...! ...
HISS
HISS
ZA (ZSH)
AH HA!
AH-HA-HA-HA...

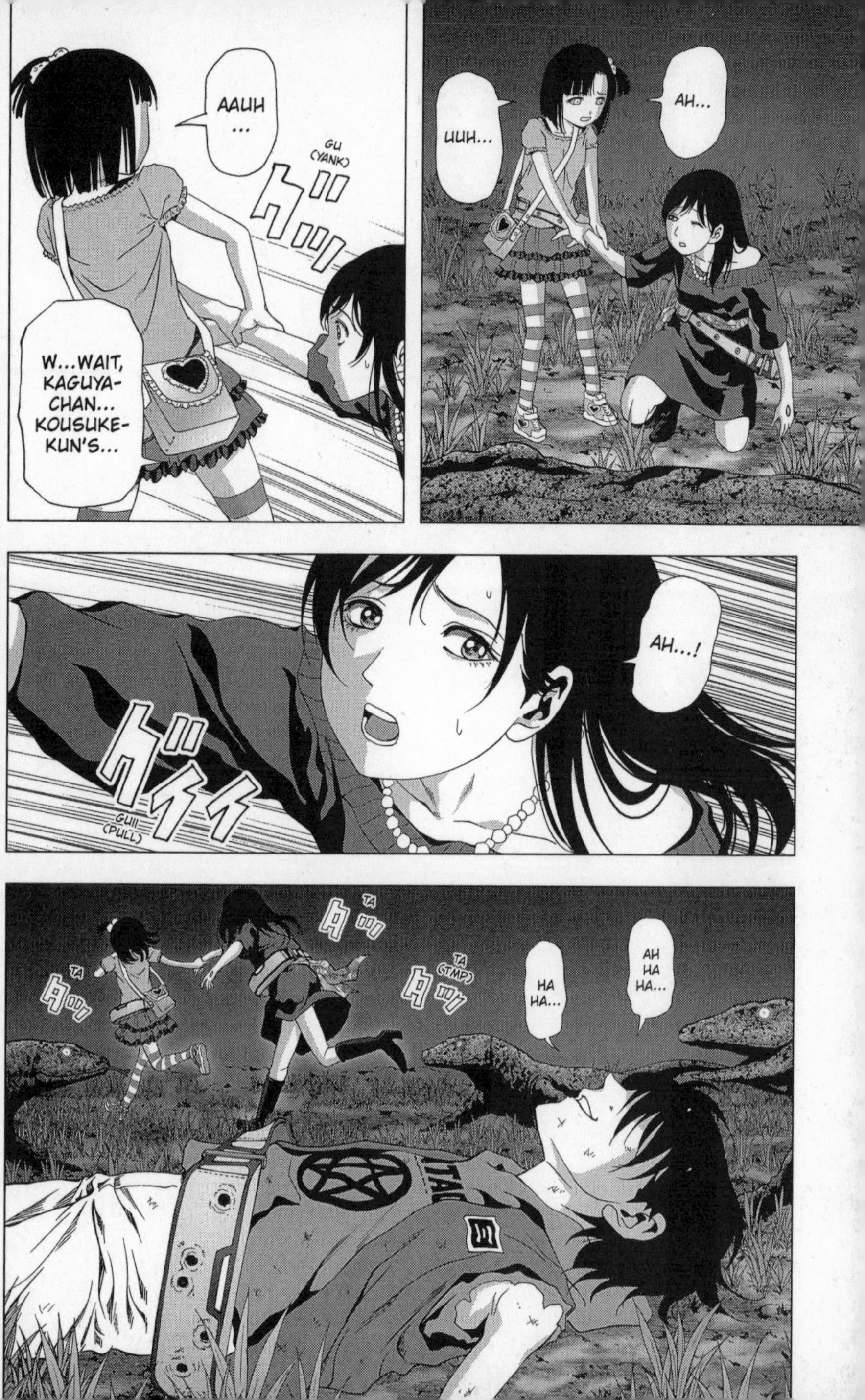
AH...
UUH...
AAUH ...
GU (YANK)
W...WAIT, KAGUYA-CHAN... KOUSUKE-KUN'S...
AH...!
GUII (PULL)
AH HA HA...
HA HA...
TA
TA (TMP)
TA

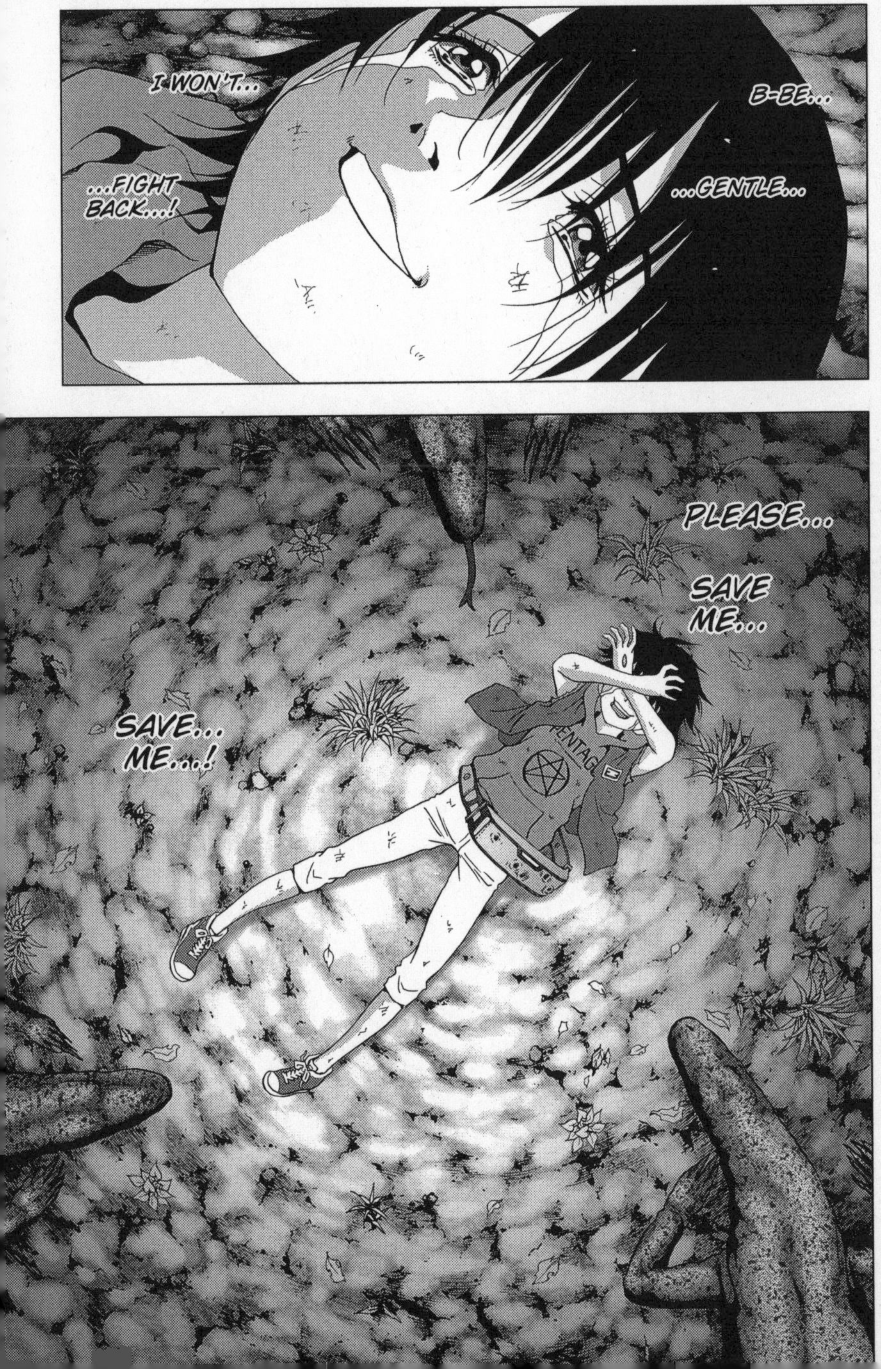
B-BE...
...GENTLE...
I WON'T...
...FIGHT BACK...!
PLEASE...
SAVE ME...
SAVE... ME...!

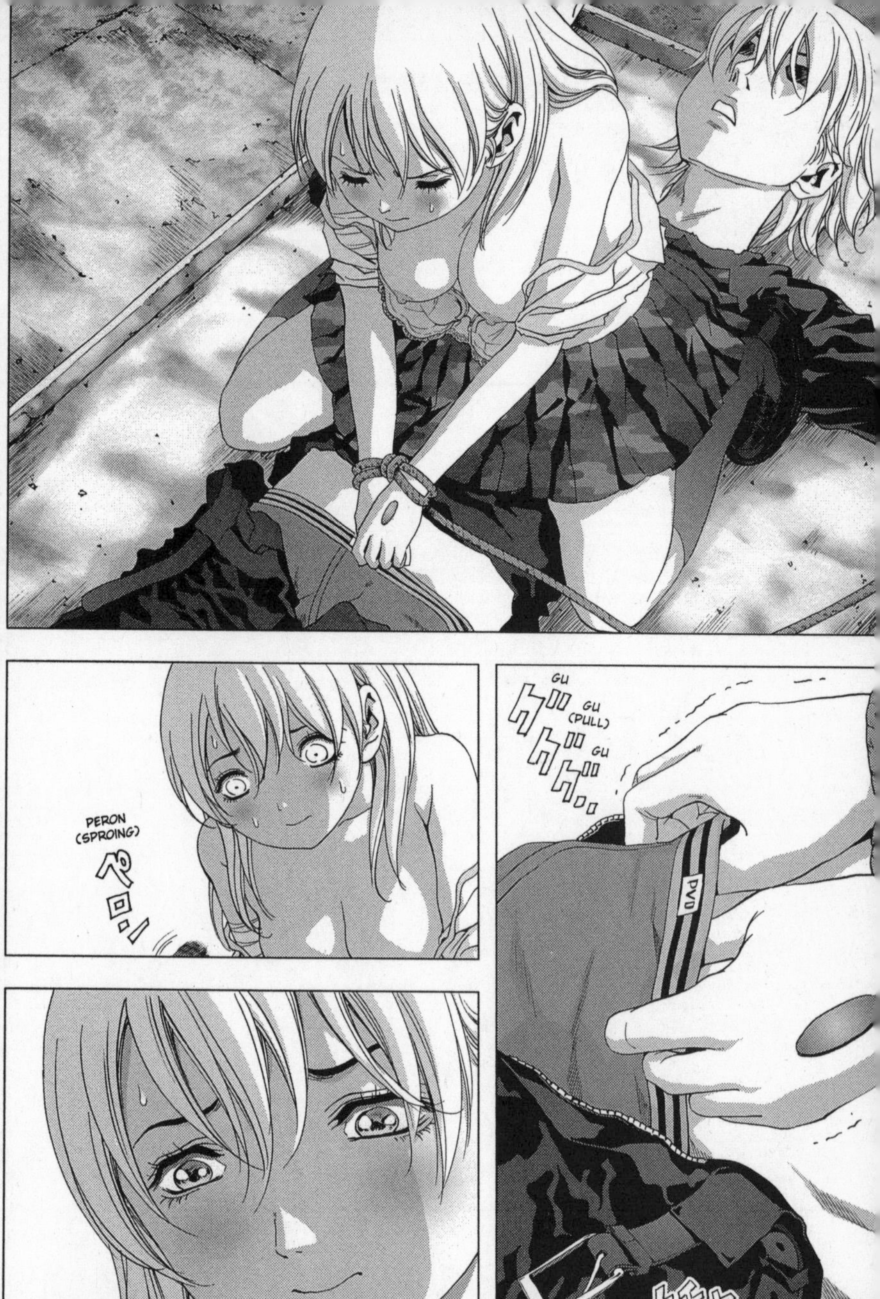
GU
GU
(PULL)
GU
カチャ
KACHA
(CLINK)
PERON
(SPROING)

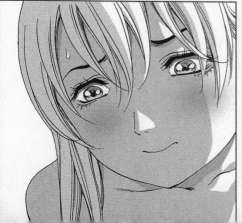

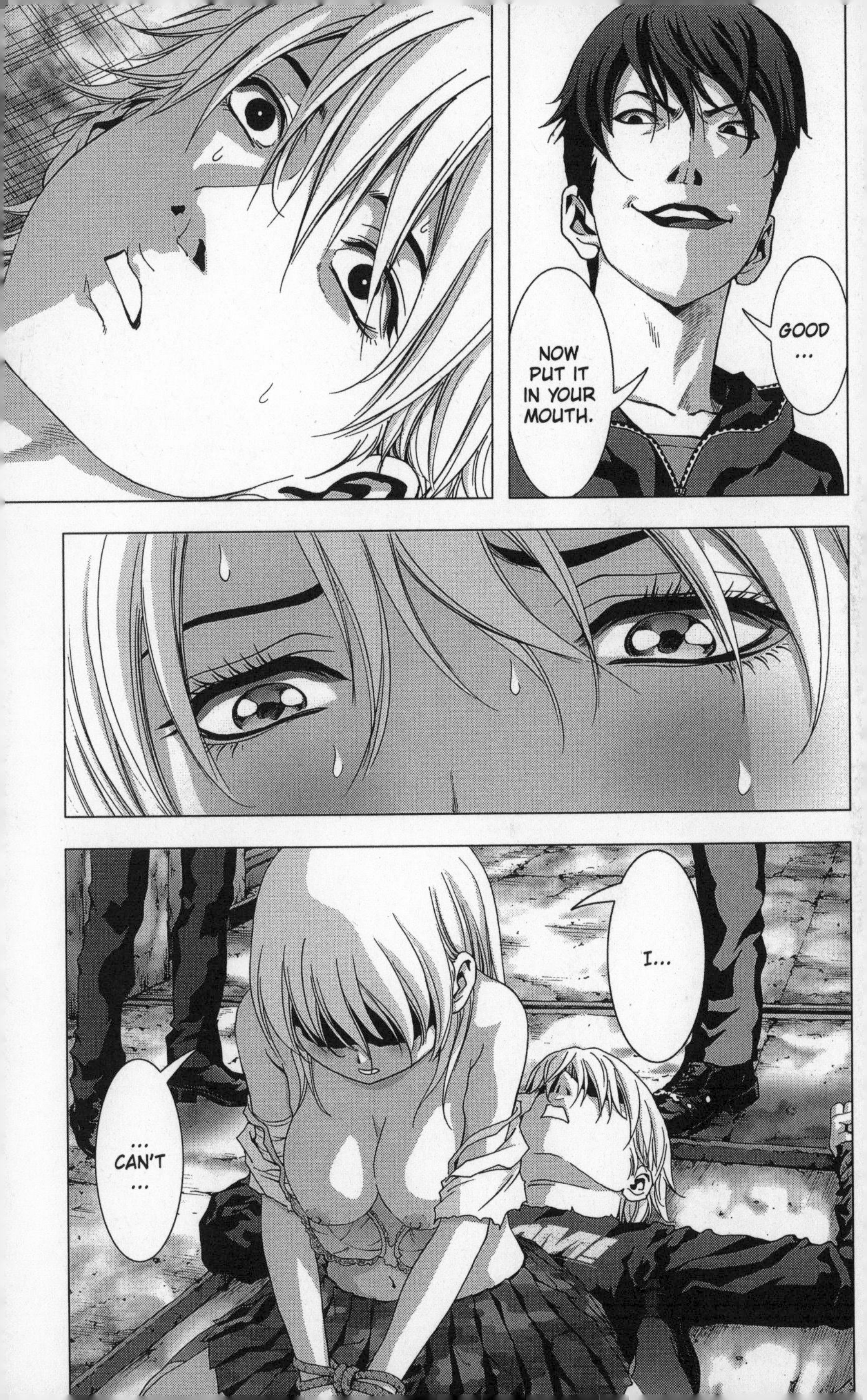
GOOD ...
NOW PUT IT IN YOUR MOUTH.
I...
... CAN'T ...

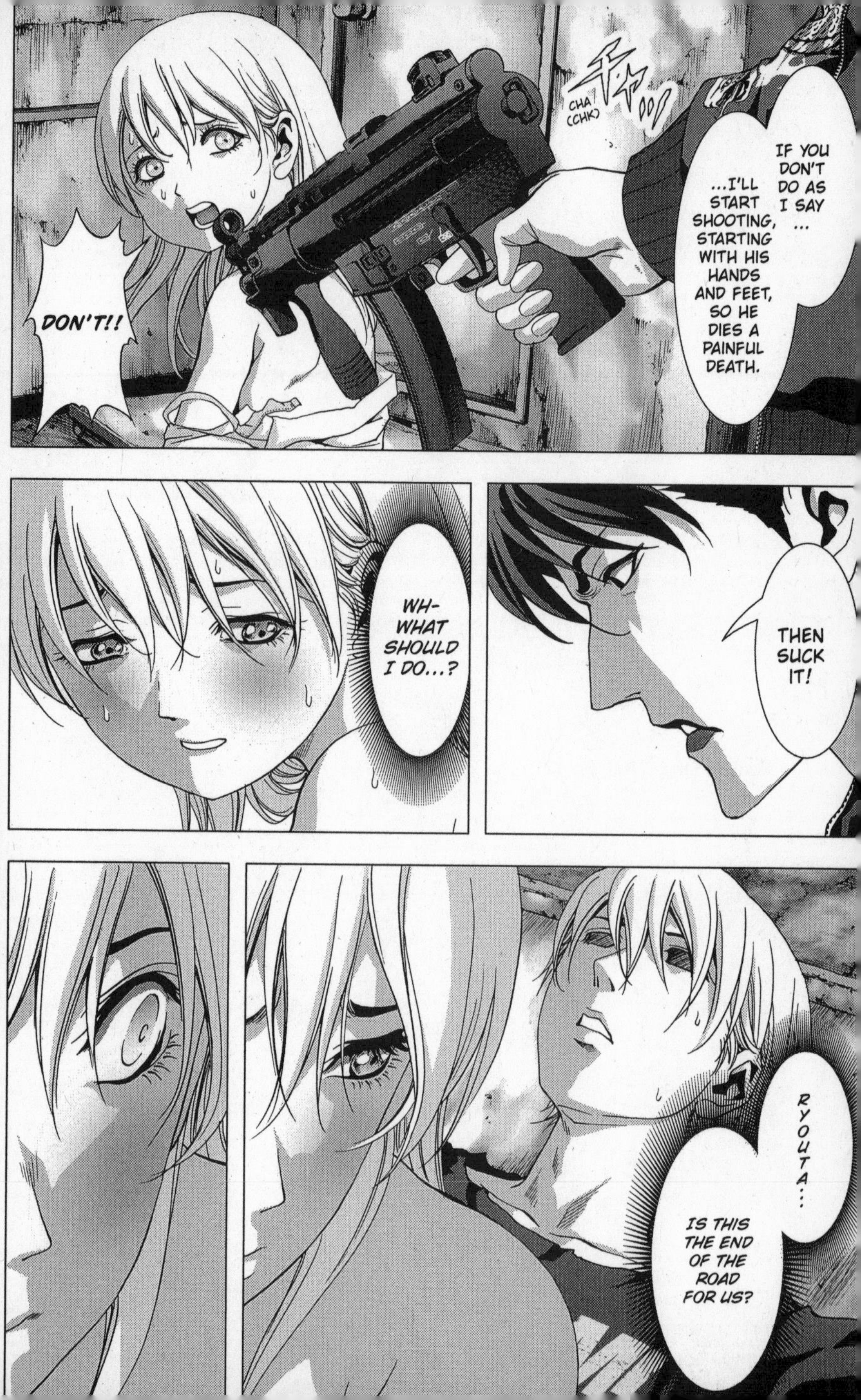
CHA (CHK)
IF YOU DON'T DO AS I SAY ...
...I'LL START SHOOTING, STARTING WITH HIS HANDS AND FEET, SO HE DIES A PAINFUL DEATH.
DON'T!!
THEN SUCK IT!
WH- WHAT SHOULD I DO...?
RYOUTA...
IS THIS THE END OF THE ROAD FOR US?

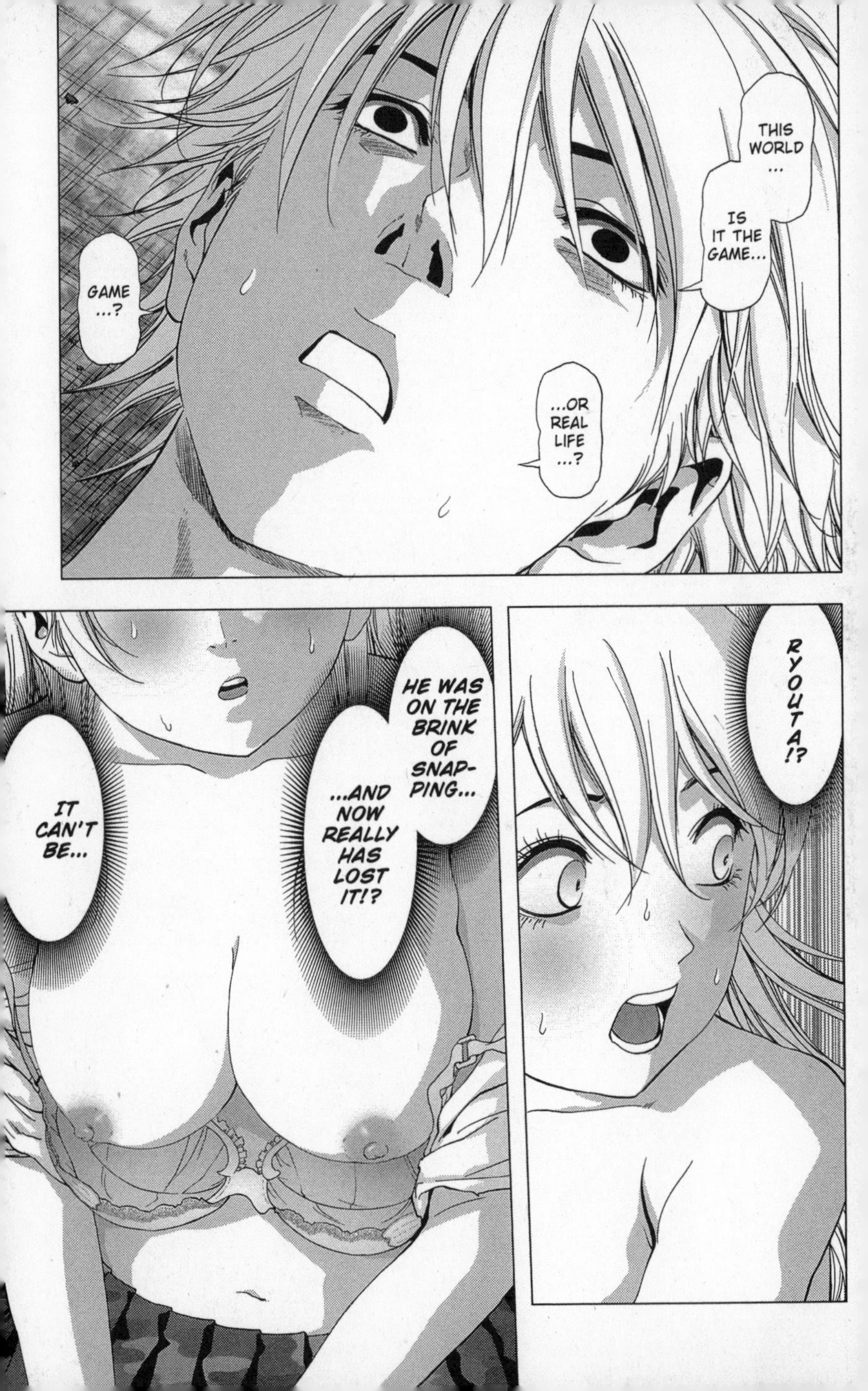
THIS WORLD ...
IS IT THE GAME...
...OR REAL LIFE ...?
GAME ...?
RYOUTA!?
HE WAS ON THE BRINK OF SNAP-PING...
...AND NOW REALLY HAS LOST IT!?
IT CAN'T BE...

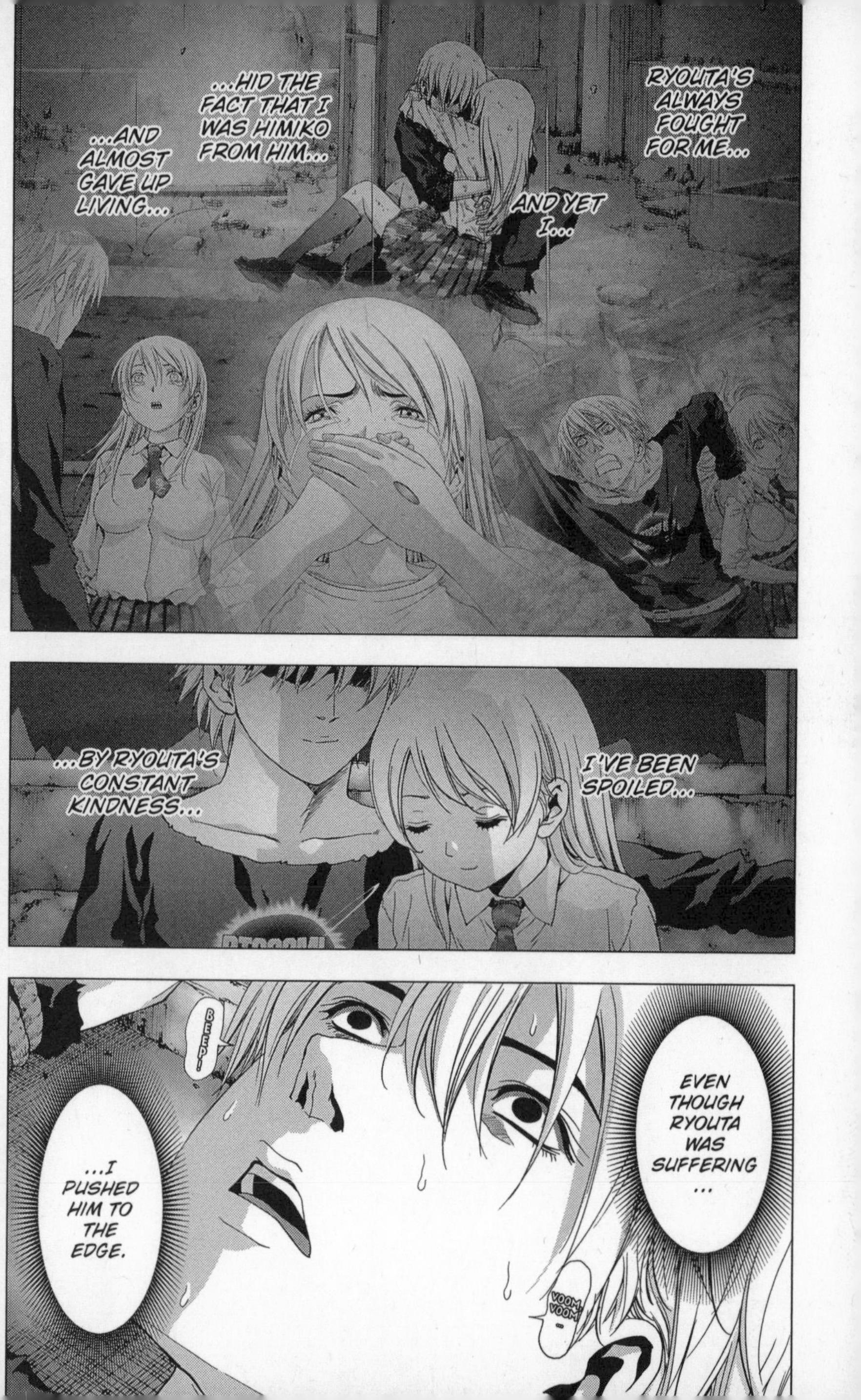
RYOUTA'S ALWAYS FOUGHT FOR ME...
AND YET I...
...HID THE FACT THAT I WAS HIMIKO FROM HIM...
...AND ALMOST GAVE UP LIVING...
I'VE BEEN SPOILED...
...BY RYOUTA'S CONSTANT KINDNESS...
EVEN THOUGH RYOUTA WAS SUFFERING...
BEEP!
VOOM VOOM...
...I PUSHED HIM TO THE EDGE.

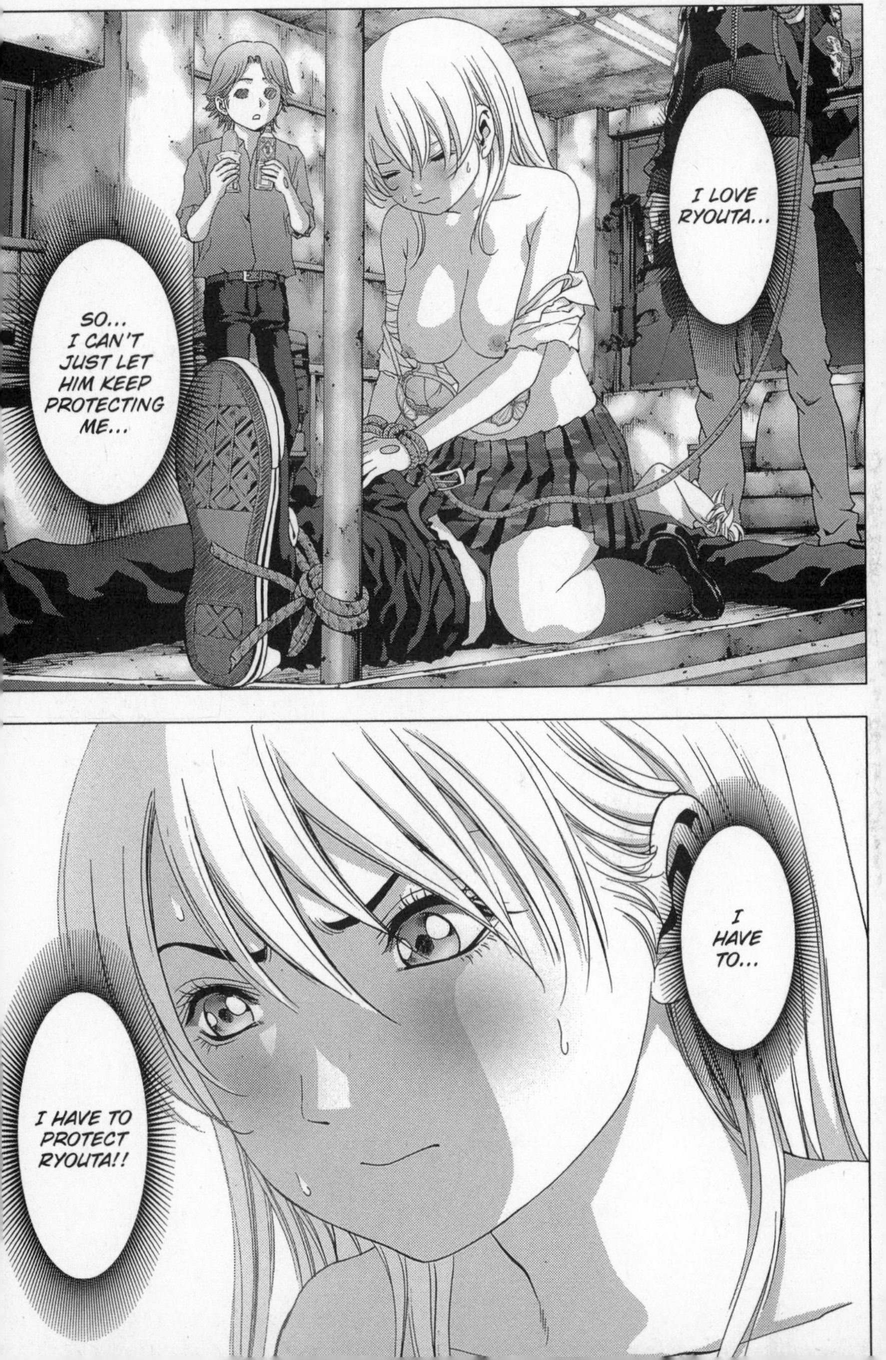
I LOVE RYOUTA...
SO... I CAN'T JUST LET HIM KEEP PROTECTING ME...
I HAVE TO...
I HAVE TO PROTECT RYOUTA!!

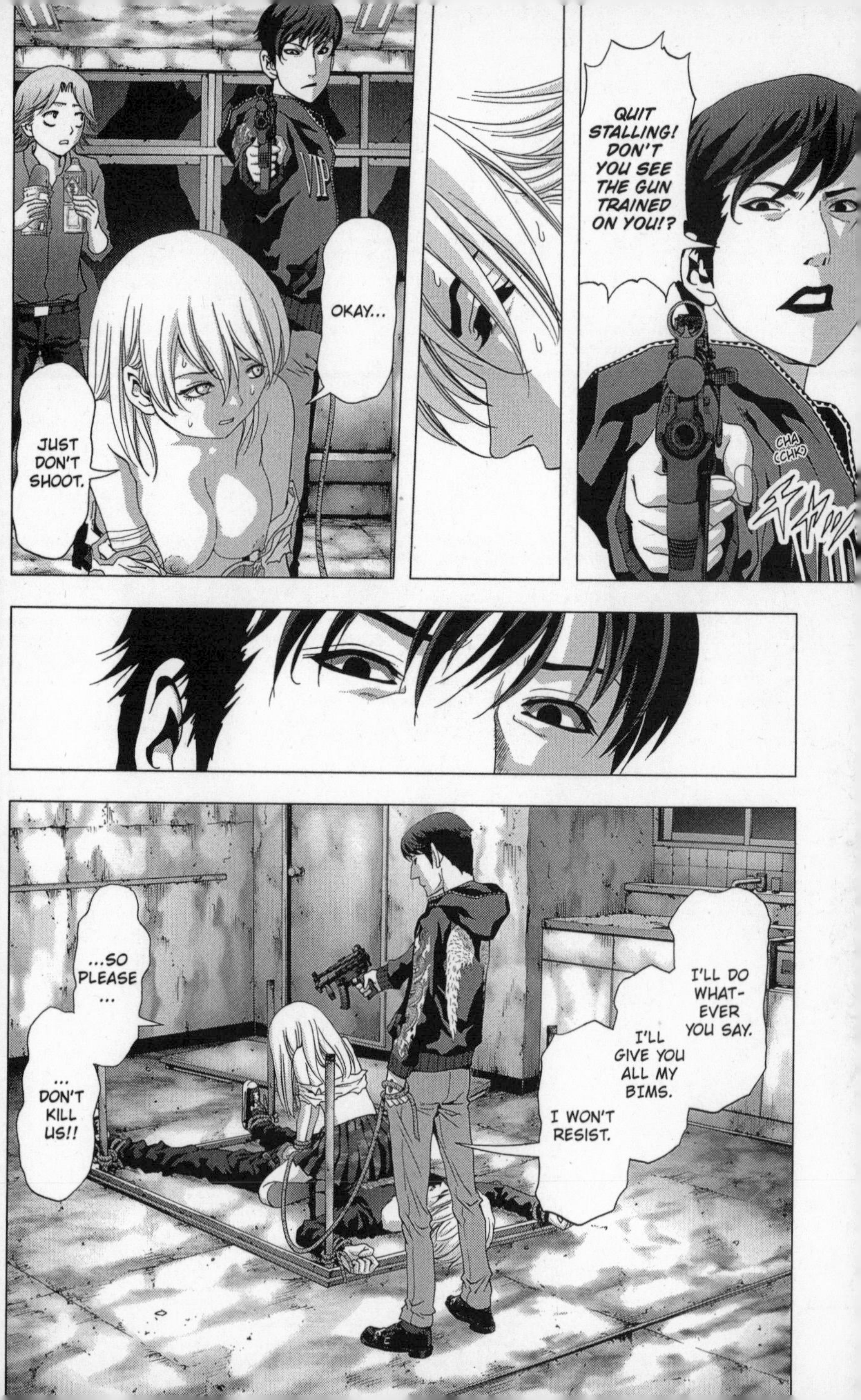
QUIT STALLING! DON'T YOU SEE THE GUN TRAINED ON YOU!?
CHA (CHK)
OKAY...
JUST DON'T SHOOT.
I'LL DO WHAT-EVER YOU SAY.
I'LL GIVE YOU ALL MY BIMS.
I WON'T RESIST.
...SO PLEASE...
...DON'T KILL US!!

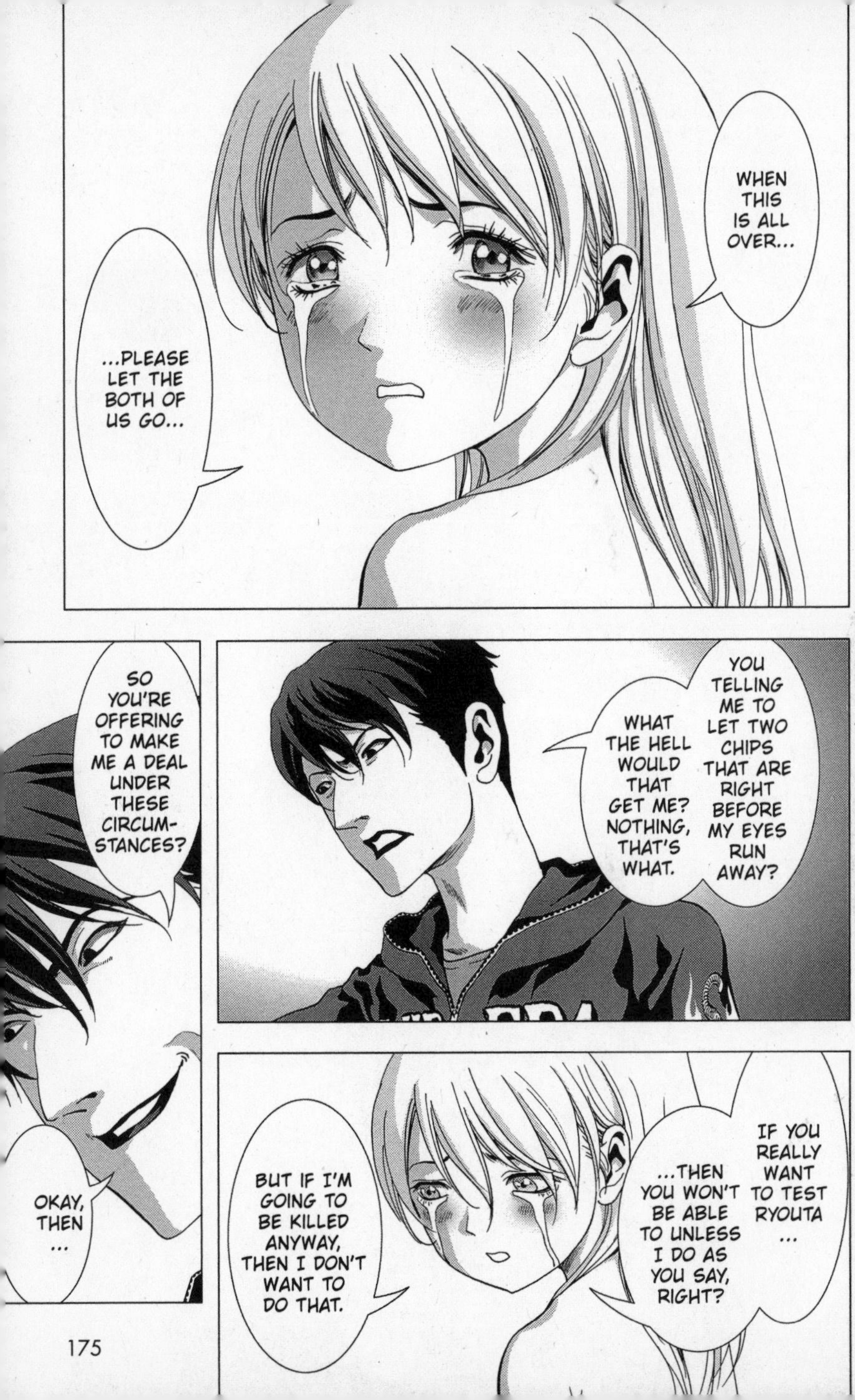
WHEN THIS IS ALL OVER...
...PLEASE LET THE BOTH OF US GO...
YOU TELLING ME TO LET TWO CHIPS THAT ARE RIGHT BEFORE MY EYES RUN AWAY?
WHAT THE HELL WOULD THAT GET ME? NOTHING, THAT'S WHAT.
IF YOU REALLY WANT TO TEST RYOUTA ...
...THEN YOU WON'T BE ABLE TO UNLESS I DO AS YOU SAY, RIGHT?
BUT IF I'M GOING TO BE KILLED ANYWAY, THEN I DON'T WANT TO DO THAT.
SO YOU'RE OFFERING TO MAKE ME A DEAL UNDER THESE CIRCUM-STANCES?
OKAY, THEN ...

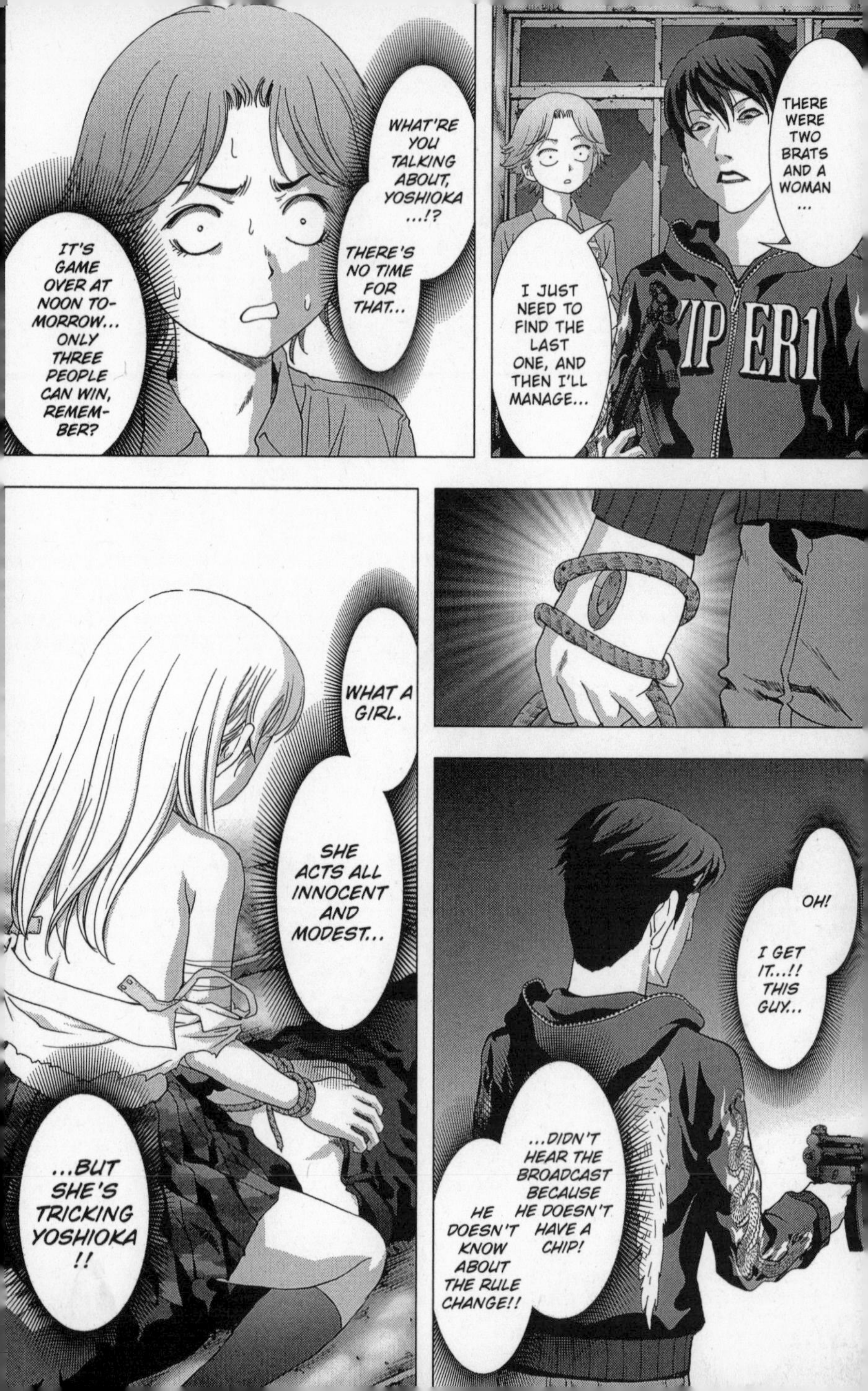
THERE WERE TWO BRATS AND A WOMAN...
I JUST NEED TO FIND THE LAST ONE, AND THEN I'LL MANAGE...
WHAT'RE YOU TALKING ABOUT, YOSHIOKA...!?
THERE'S NO TIME FOR THAT...
IT'S GAME OVER AT NOON TO-MORROW... ONLY THREE PEOPLE CAN WIN, REMEMBER?
OH!
I GET IT...!! THIS GUY...
...DIDN'T HEAR THE BROADCAST BECAUSE HE DOESN'T HAVE A CHIP!
HE DOESN'T KNOW ABOUT THE RULE CHANGE!!
WHAT A GIRL.
SHE ACTS ALL INNOCENT AND MODEST...
...BUT SHE'S TRICKING YOSHIOKA!!

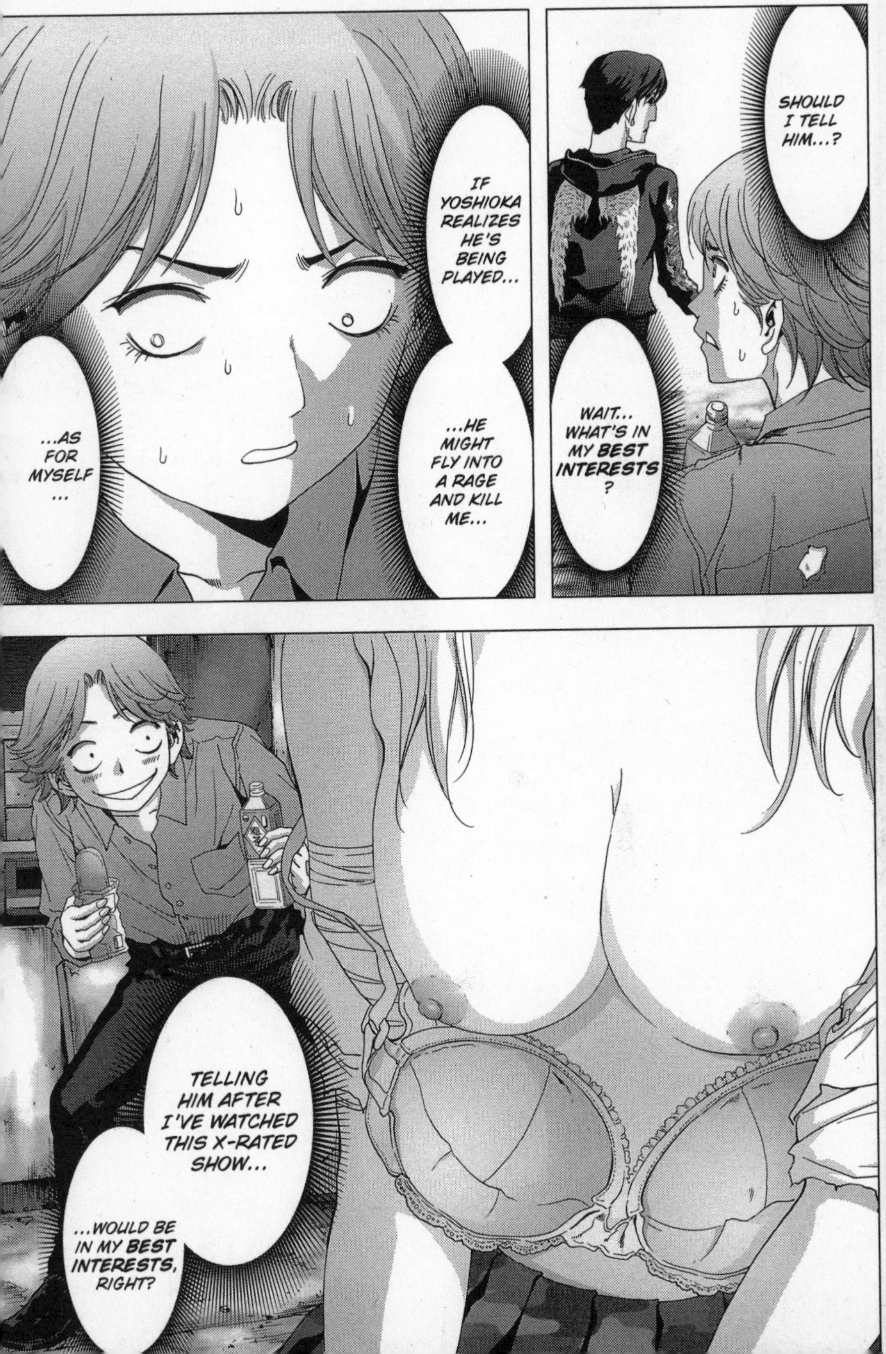
SHOULD I TELL HIM...?
WAIT... WHAT'S IN MY BEST INTERESTS?
IF YOSHIOKA REALIZES HE'S BEING PLAYED...
...HE MIGHT FLY INTO A RAGE AND KILL ME...
...AS FOR MYSELF...
TELLING HIM AFTER I'VE WATCHED THIS X-RATED SHOW...
...WOULD BE IN MY BEST INTERESTS, RIGHT?

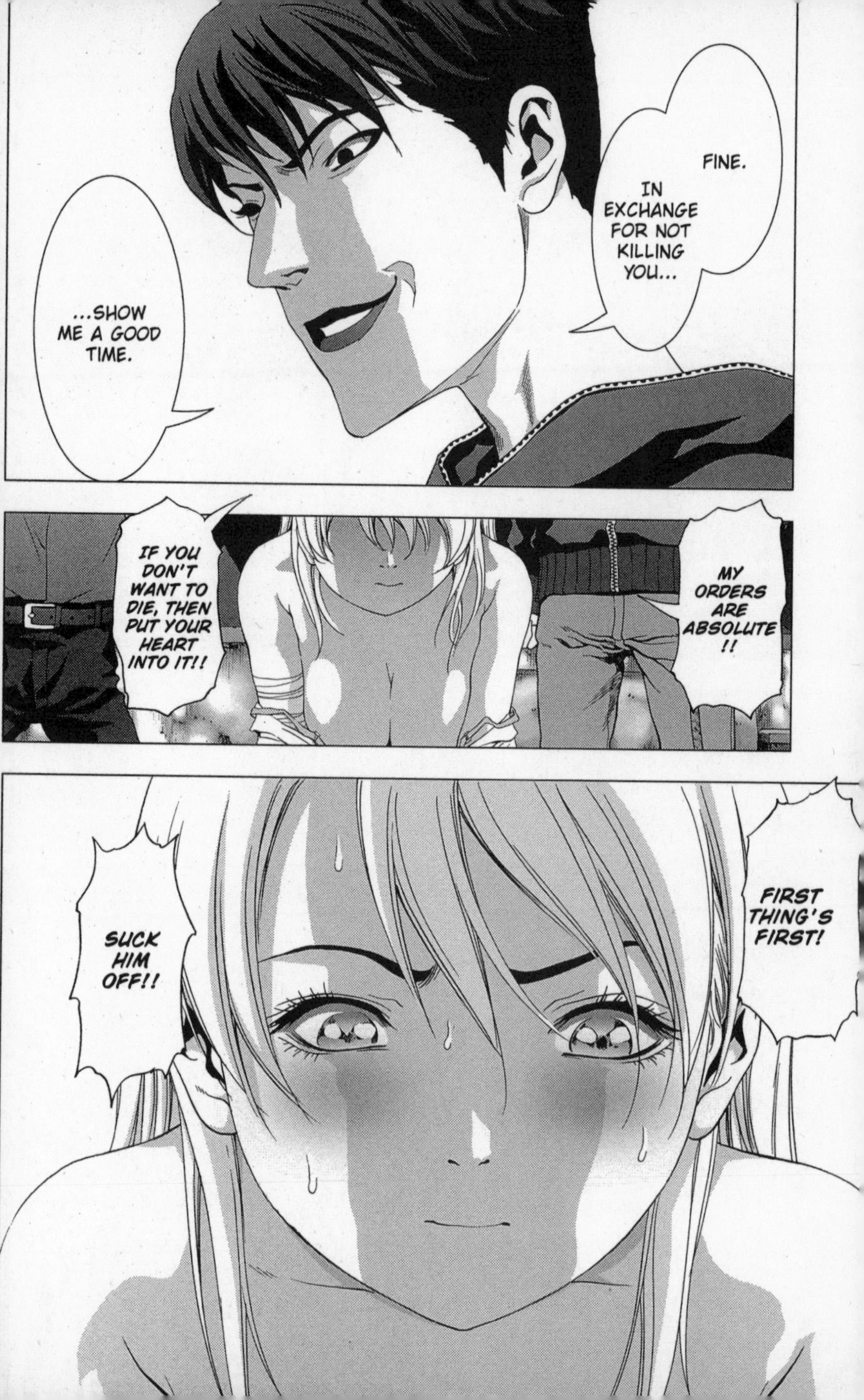
FINE.
IN EXCHANGE FOR NOT KILLING YOU...
...SHOW ME A GOOD TIME.
MY ORDERS ARE ABSOLUTE!!
IF YOU DON'T WANT TO DIE, THEN PUT YOUR HEART INTO IT!!
FIRST THING'S FIRST!
SUCK HIM OFF!!

RYOUTA...

I'M...

...PROTECTING
YOU...

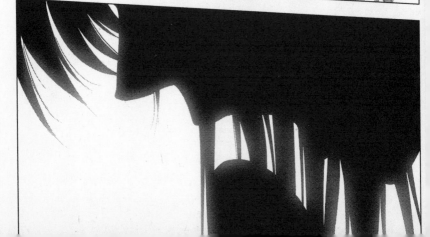

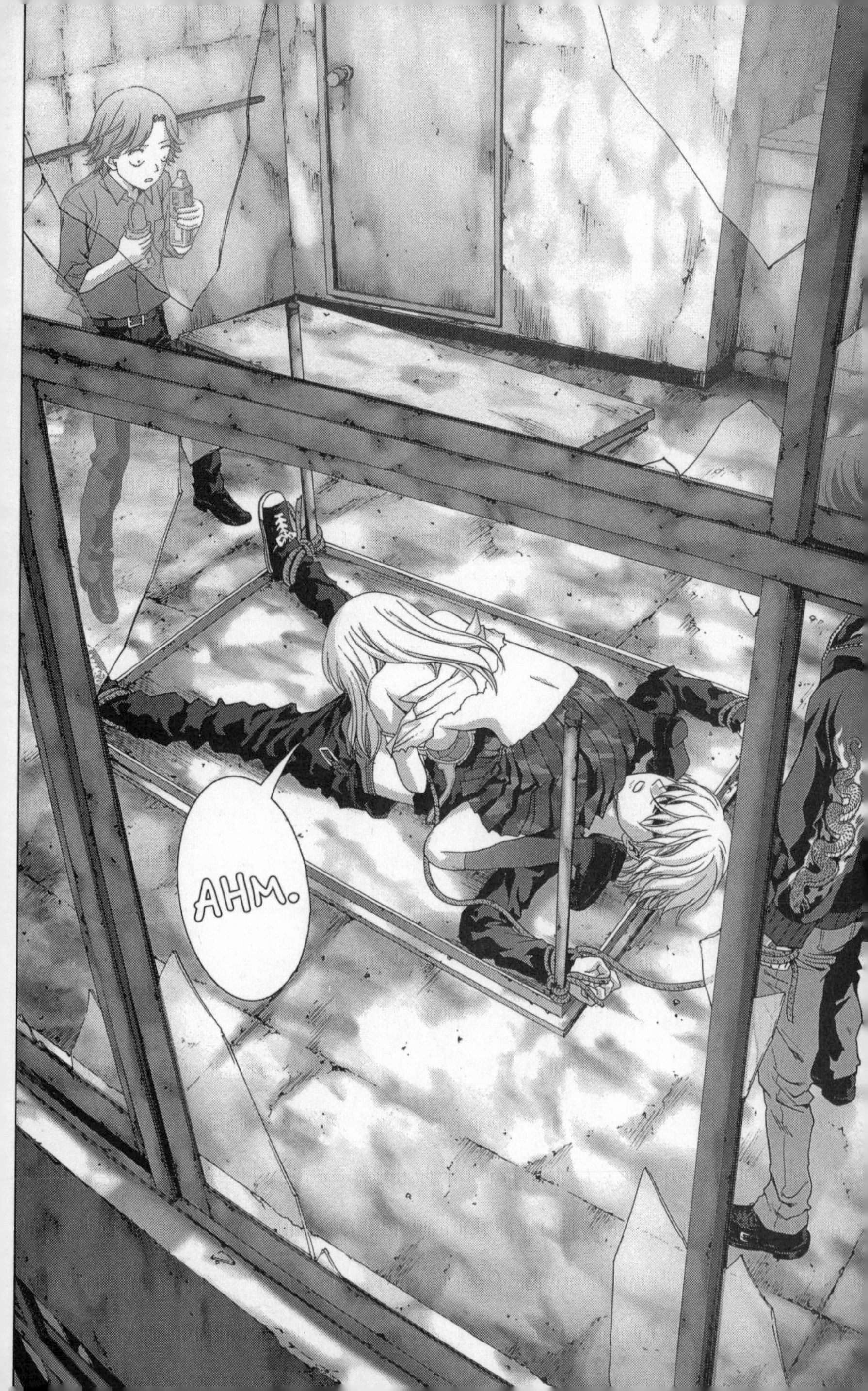
AHM.

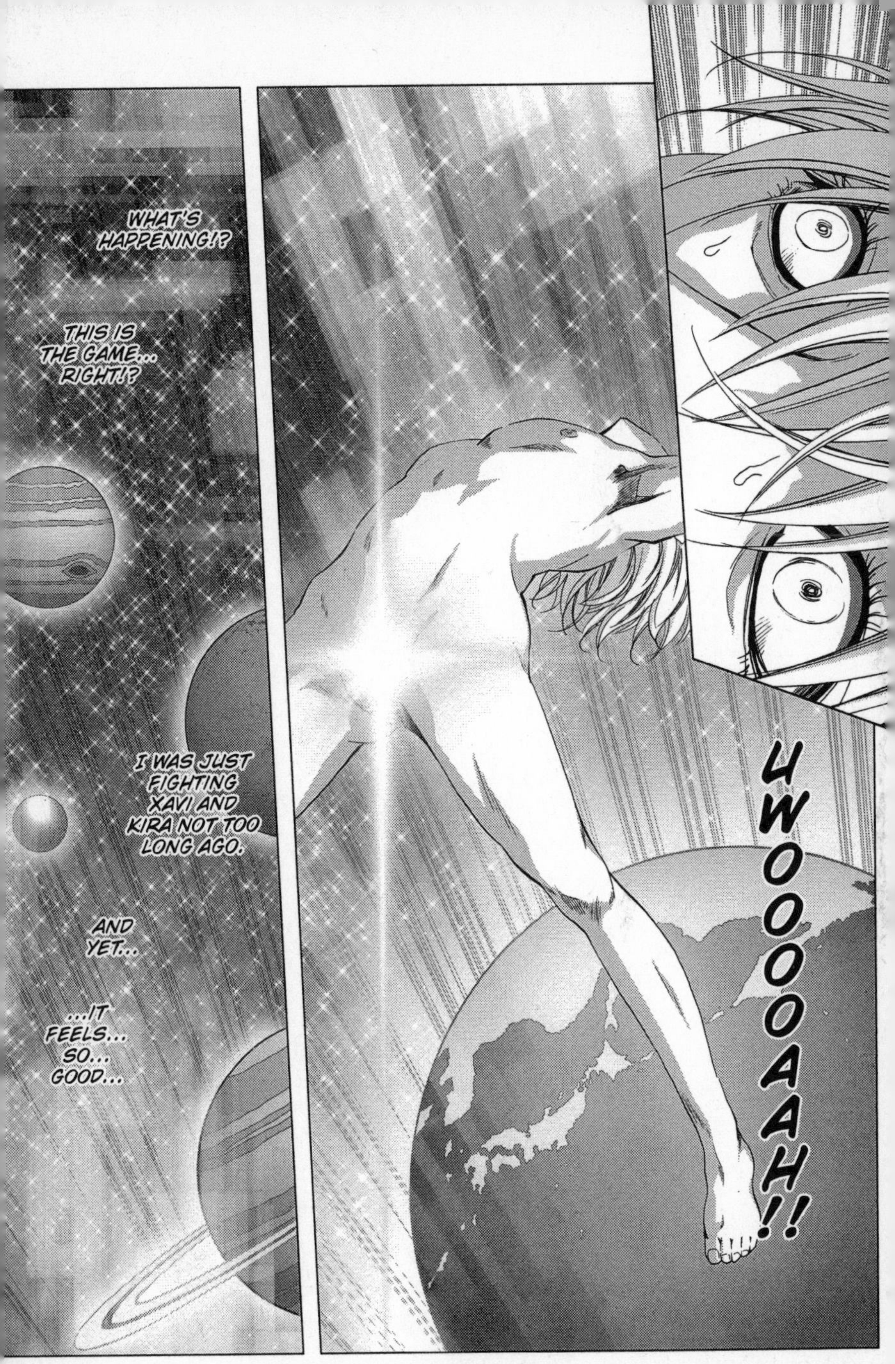
UWOOOOOAAAH!!
WHAT'S HAPPENING!?
THIS IS THE GAME... RIGHT!?
I WAS JUST FIGHTING XAVI AND KIRA NOT TOO LONG AGO.
AND YET...
...IT FEELS... SO... GOOD...

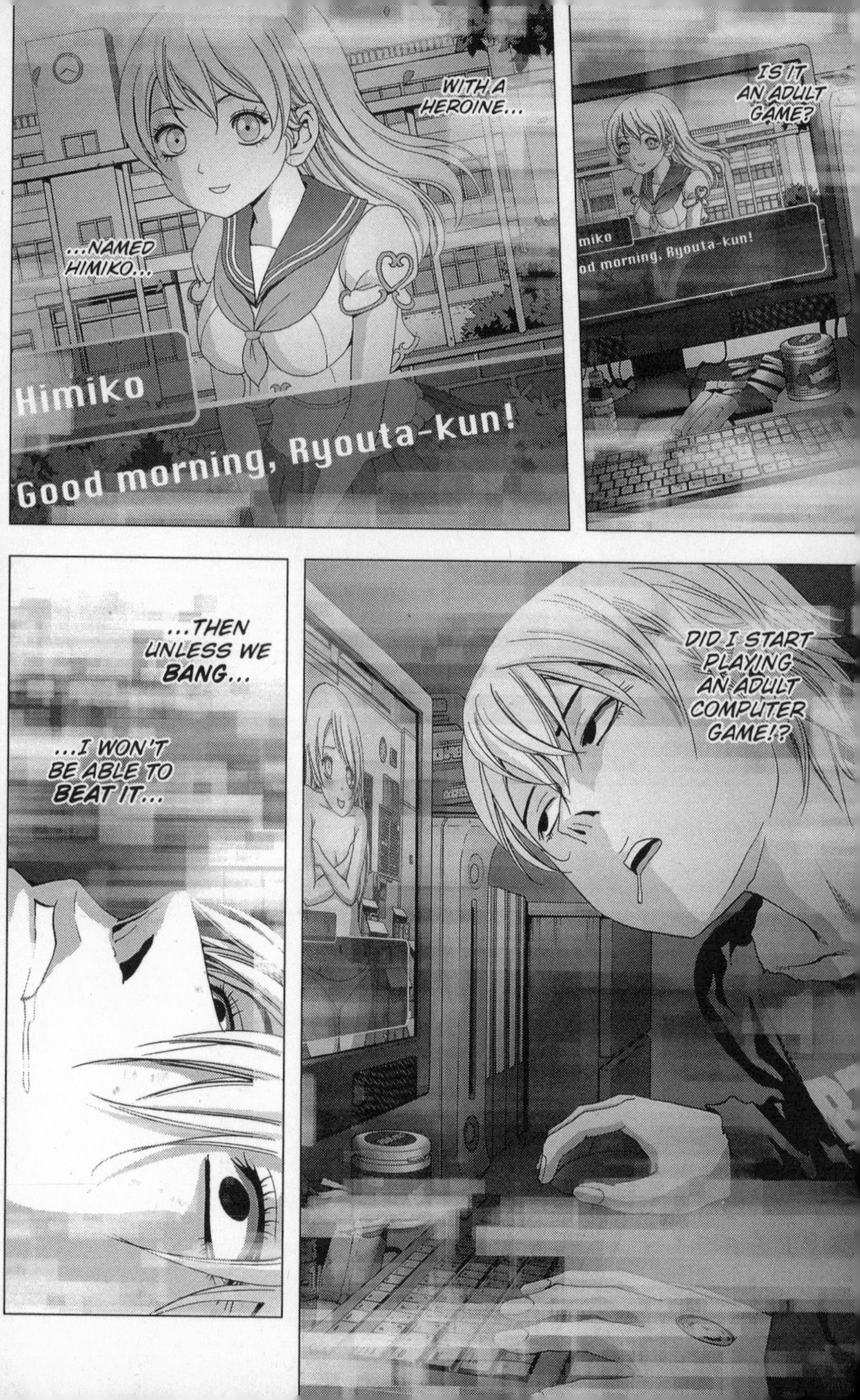
IS IT AN ADULT GAME?
miko
od morning, Ryouta-kun!
WITH A HEROINE...
...NAMED HIMIKO...
Himiko
Good morning, Ryouta-kun!
DID I START PLAYING AN ADULT COMPUTER GAME!?
...THEN UNLESS WE BANG...
...I WON'T BE ABLE TO BEAT IT...

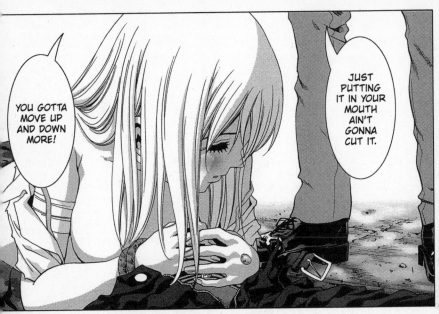

JUST PUTTING IT IN YOUR MOUTH AIN'T GONNA CUT IT.
YOU GOTTA MOVE UP AND DOWN MORE!
AND BE CAREFUL OF YOUR TEETH!
JURU (SUCK)
じゅる
IF YOU HURT HIM, HE'LL GET SOFT.
JURU
じゅる
CHURU (SLURP)
ちゅる
MAKE SURE TO GET IT NICE AND WET WITH YOUR SPIT.
CHUBA (GASP)
THAT'S IT...

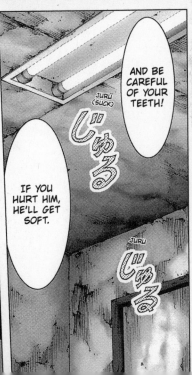

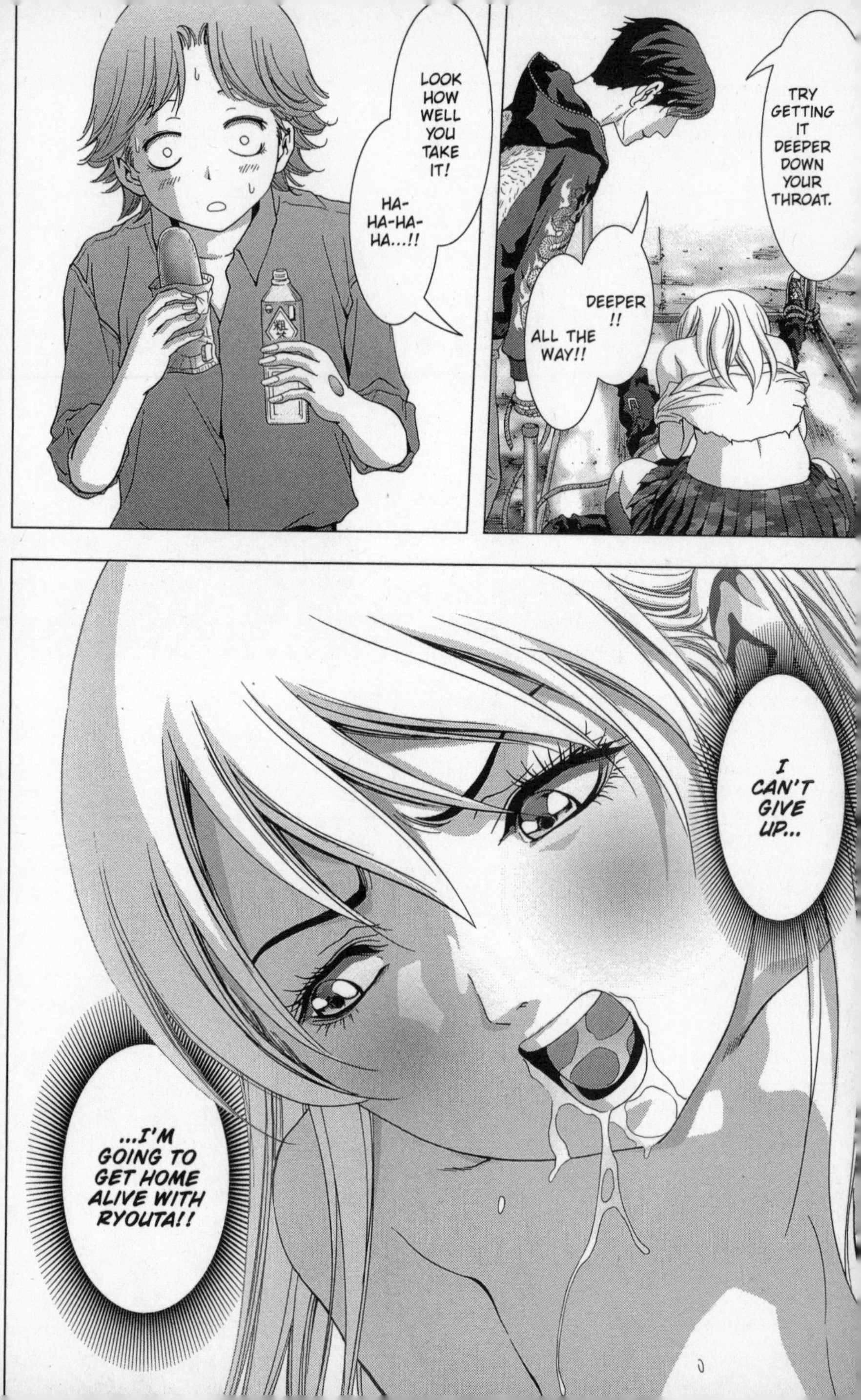
TRY GETTING IT DEEPER DOWN YOUR THROAT.
DEEPER!!
ALL THE WAY!!
LOOK HOW WELL YOU TAKE IT!
HA-HA-HA-HA...!!
I CAN'T GIVE UP...
...I'M GOING TO GET HOME ALIVE WITH RYOUTA!!

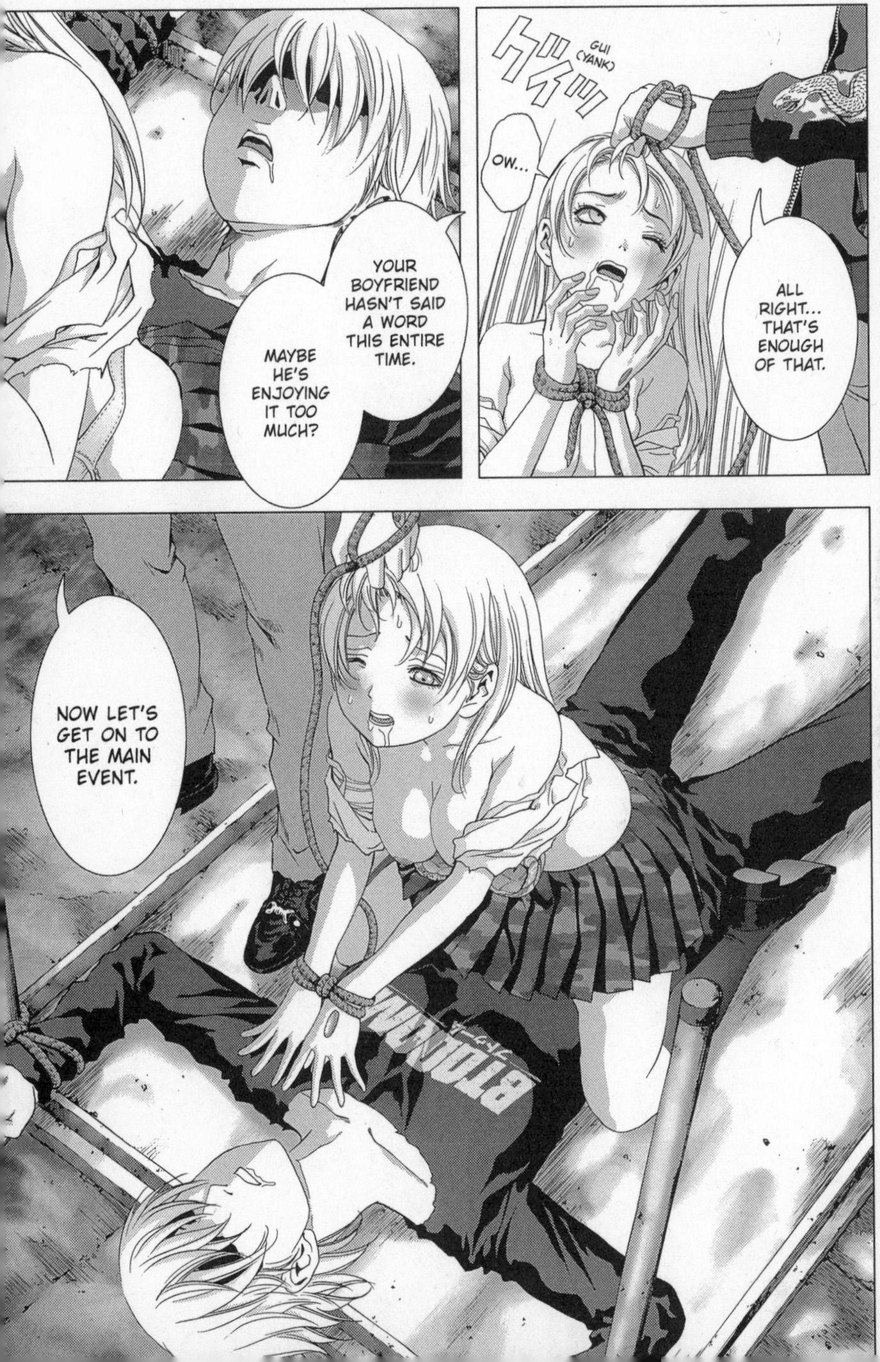
グイッ
GUI (YANK)
OW...
ALL RIGHT... THAT'S ENOUGH OF THAT.
YOUR BOYFRIEND HASN'T SAID A WORD THIS ENTIRE TIME.
MAYBE HE'S ENJOYING IT TOO MUCH?
NOW LET'S GET ON TO THE MAIN EVENT.

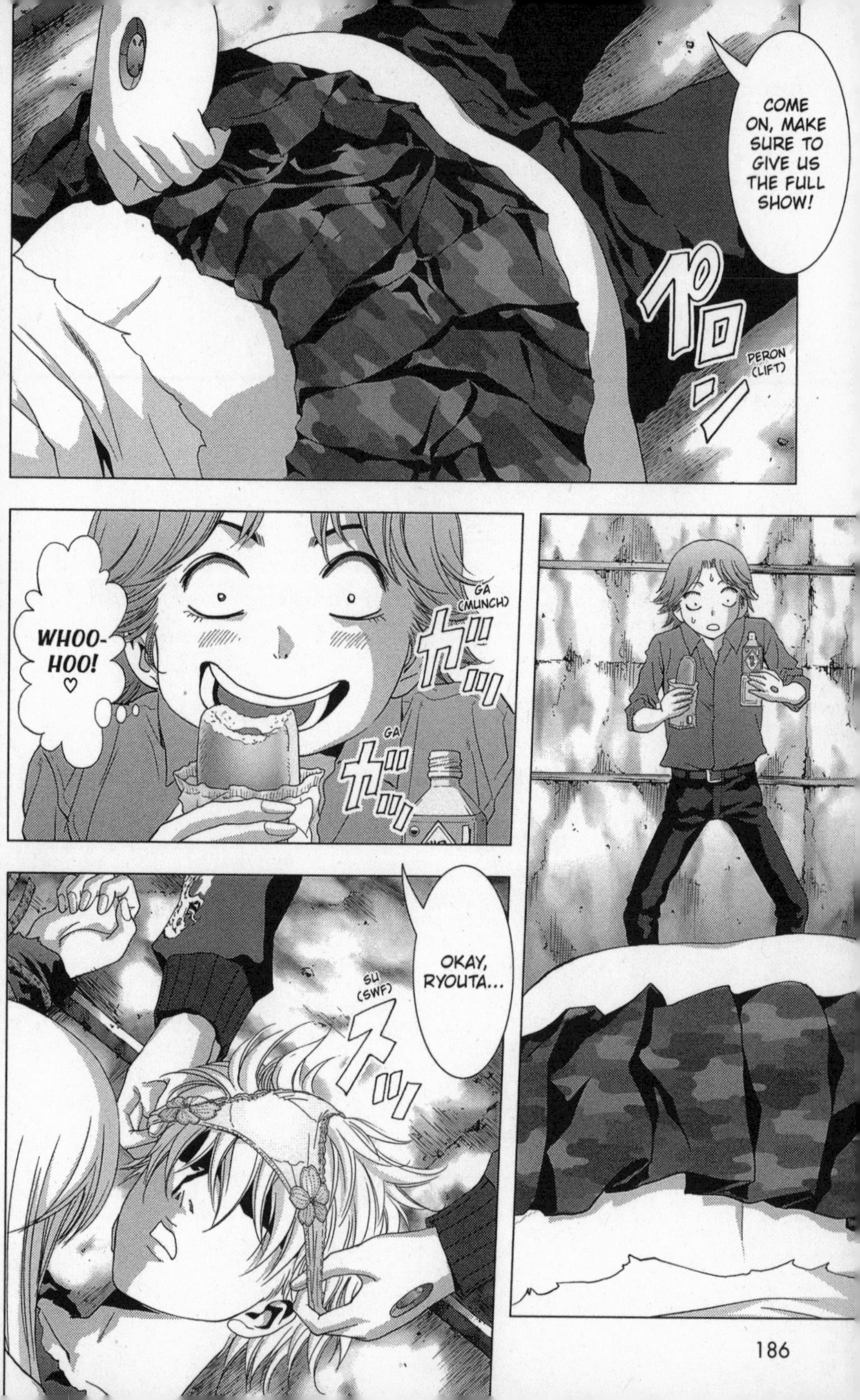
COME ON, MAKE SURE TO GIVE US THE FULL SHOW!
PERON (LIFT)
GA (MUNCH)
GA
WHOO-HOO! ♡
OKAY, RYOUTA...
SU (SWF)

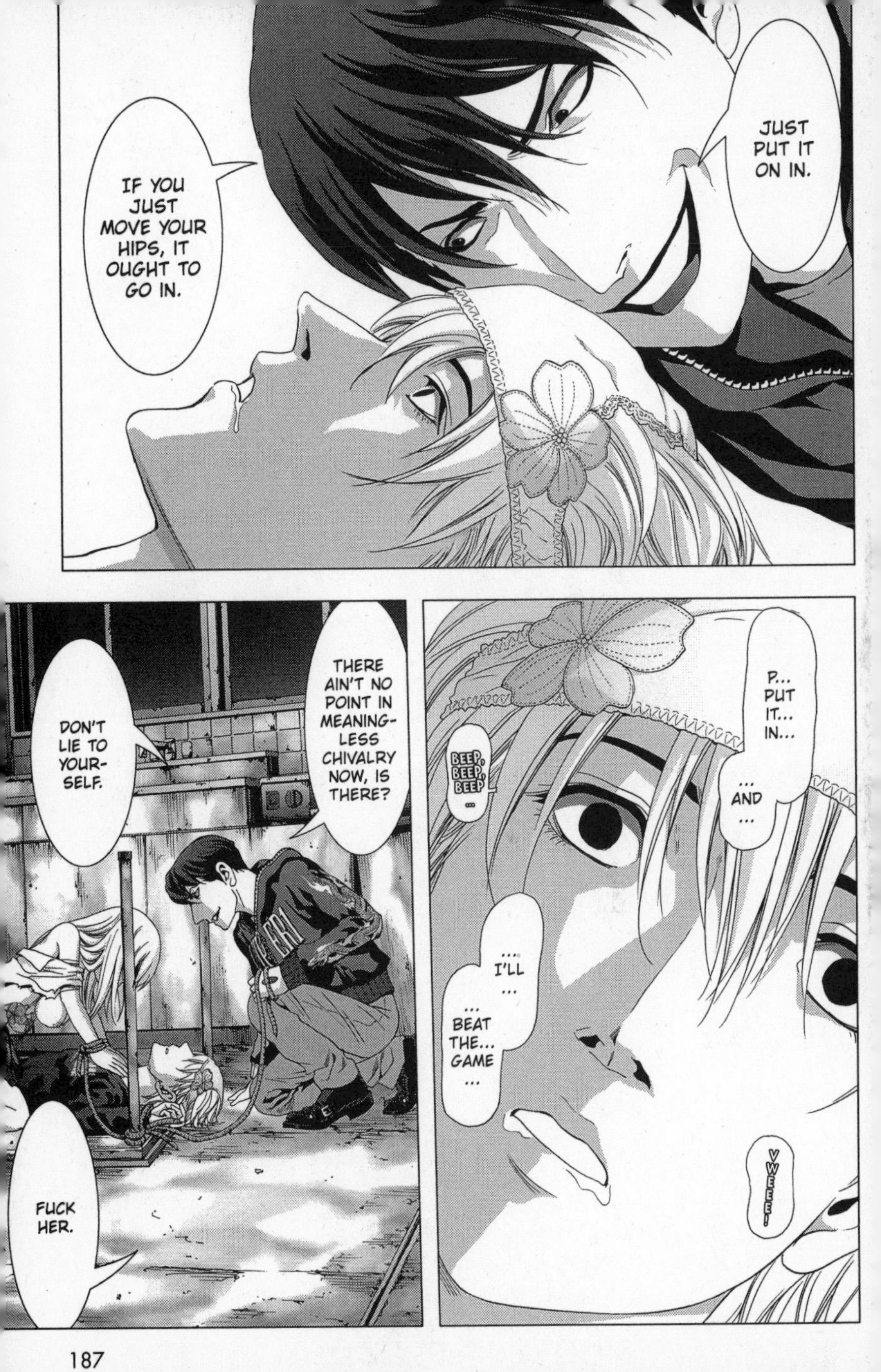
JUST PUT IT ON IN.
IF YOU JUST MOVE YOUR HIPS, IT OUGHT TO GO IN.
P... PUT IT... IN...
... AND ...
BEEP, BEEP, BEEP ...
...I'LL ...
... BEAT THE... GAME ...
VWEEE!
THERE AIN'T NO POINT IN MEANING-LESS CHIVALRY NOW, IS THERE?
DON'T LIE TO YOUR-SELF.
FUCK HER.

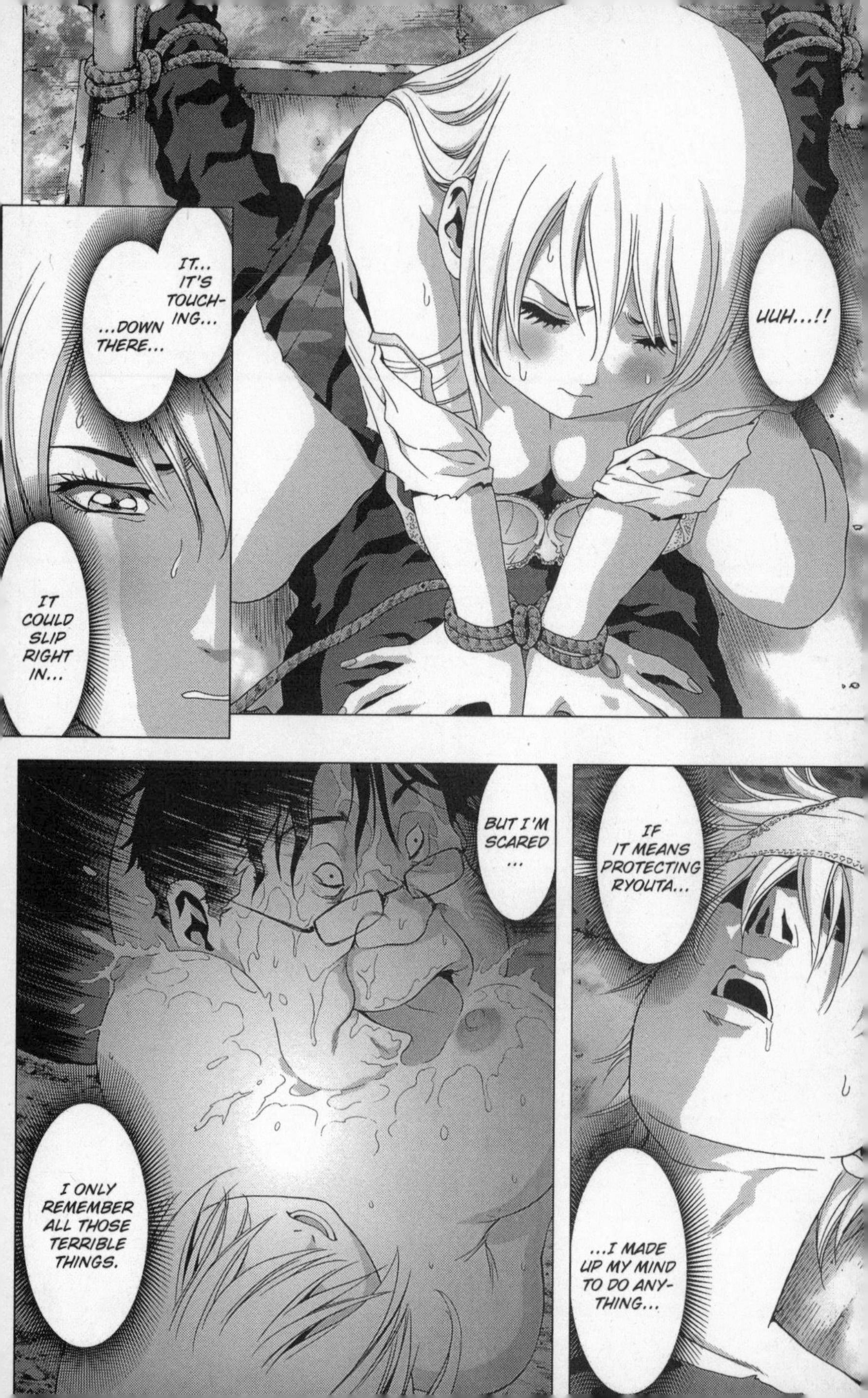
UUH...!!
IT... IT'S TOUCHING... ...DOWN THERE...
IT COULD SLIP RIGHT IN...
IF IT MEANS PROTECTING RYOUTA...
...I MADE UP MY MIND TO DO ANYTHING...
BUT I'M SCARED...
I ONLY REMEMBER ALL THOSE TERRIBLE THINGS.

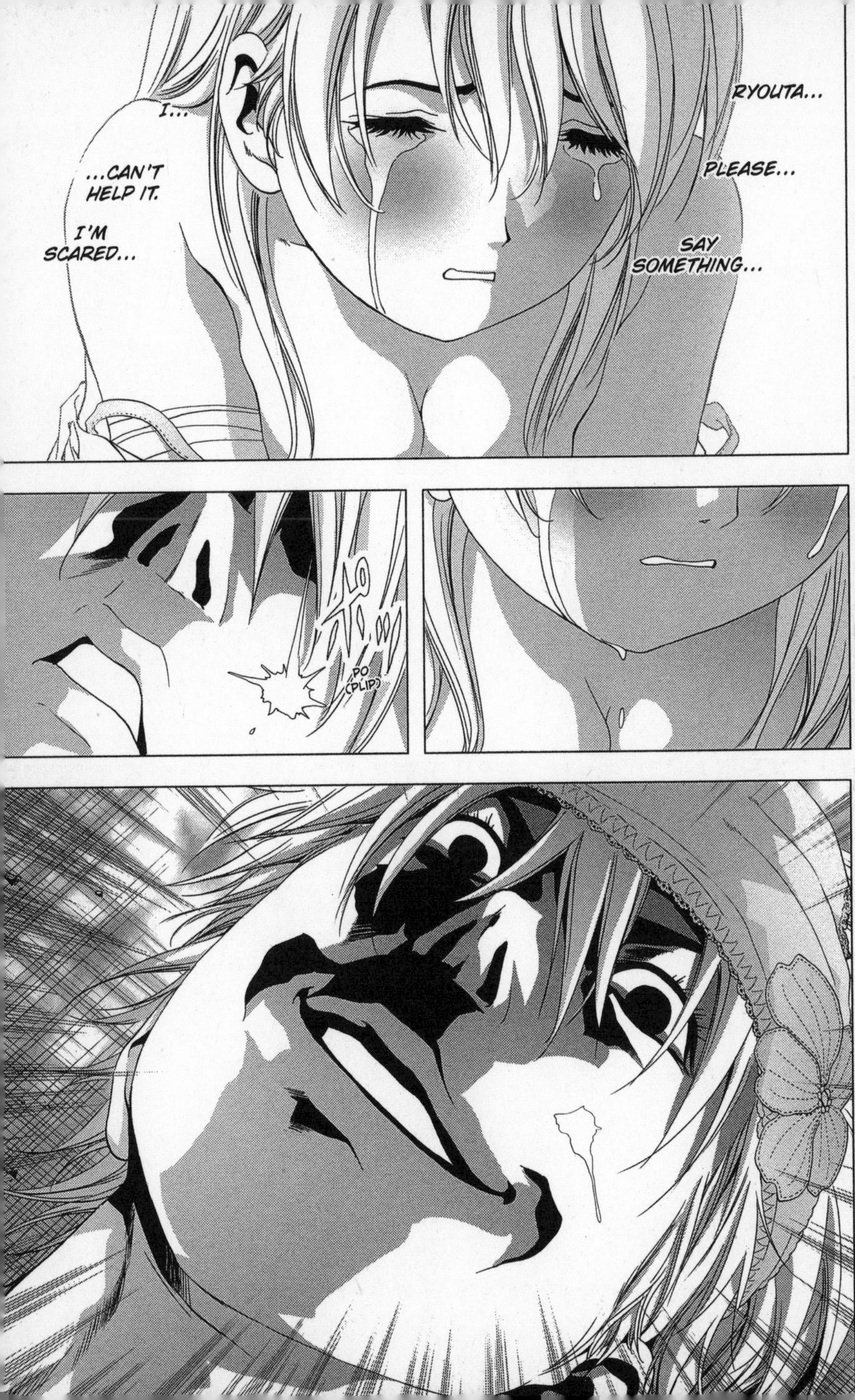
RYOUTA...
PLEASE...
SAY SOMETHING...
I...
...CAN'T HELP IT.
I'M SCARED...
PO (PLIP)

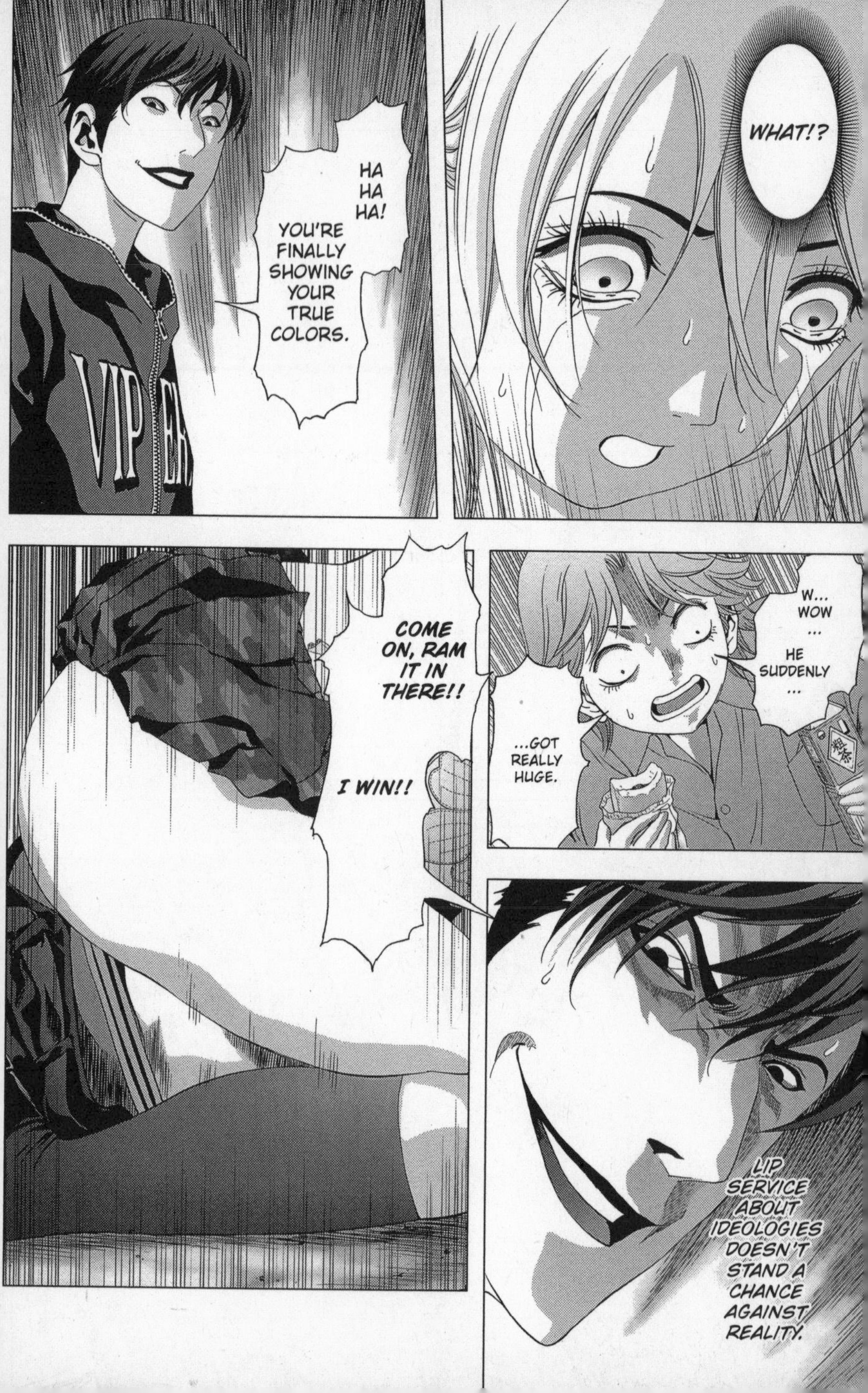
WHAT!?
HA HA HA! YOU'RE FINALLY SHOWING YOUR TRUE COLORS.
W... WOW ... HE SUDDENLY ...
...GOT REALLY HUGE.
LIP SERVICE ABOUT IDEOLOGIES DOESN'T STAND A CHANCE AGAINST REALITY.
COME ON, RAM IT IN THERE!!
I WIN!!

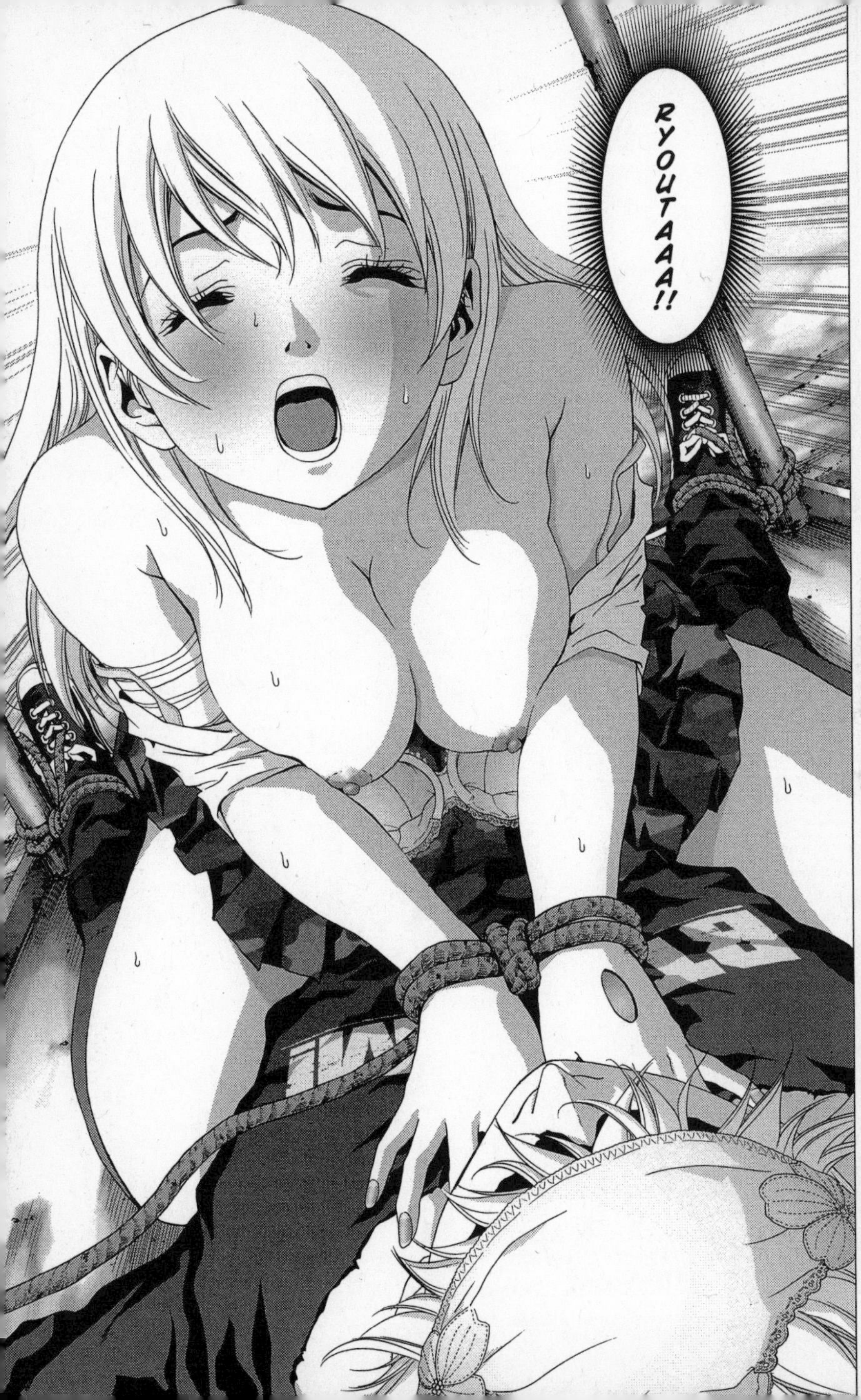
RYOUTAAA!!

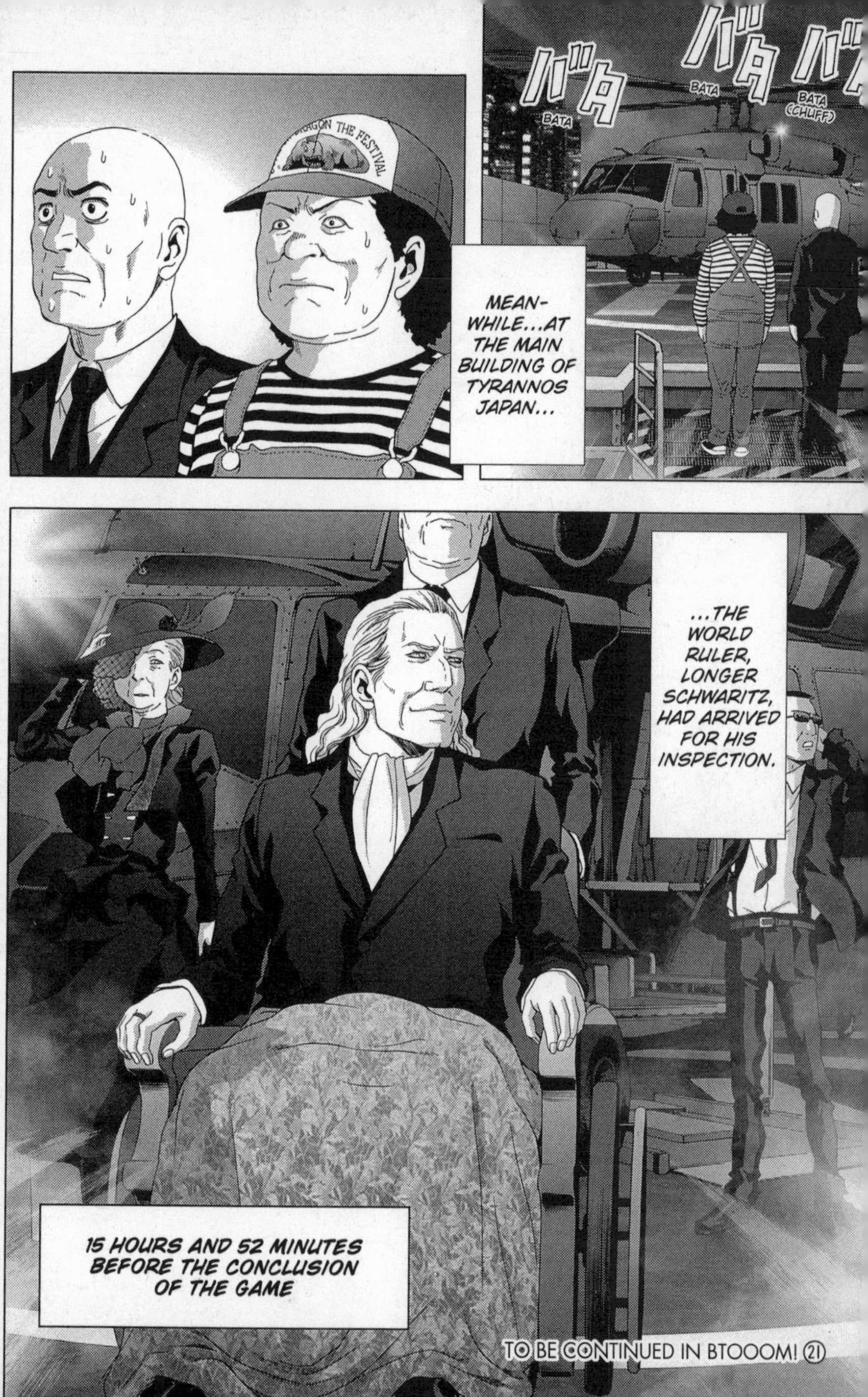
バタ
BATA
バタ
BATA
BATA (CHUFF)
MEAN-WHILE...AT THE MAIN BUILDING OF TYRANNOS JAPAN...
...THE WORLD RULER, LONGER SCHWARITZ, HAD ARRIVED FOR HIS INSPECTION.
15 HOURS AND 52 MINUTES BEFORE THE CONCLUSION OF THE GAME
TO BE CONTINUED IN BTOOOM! 21

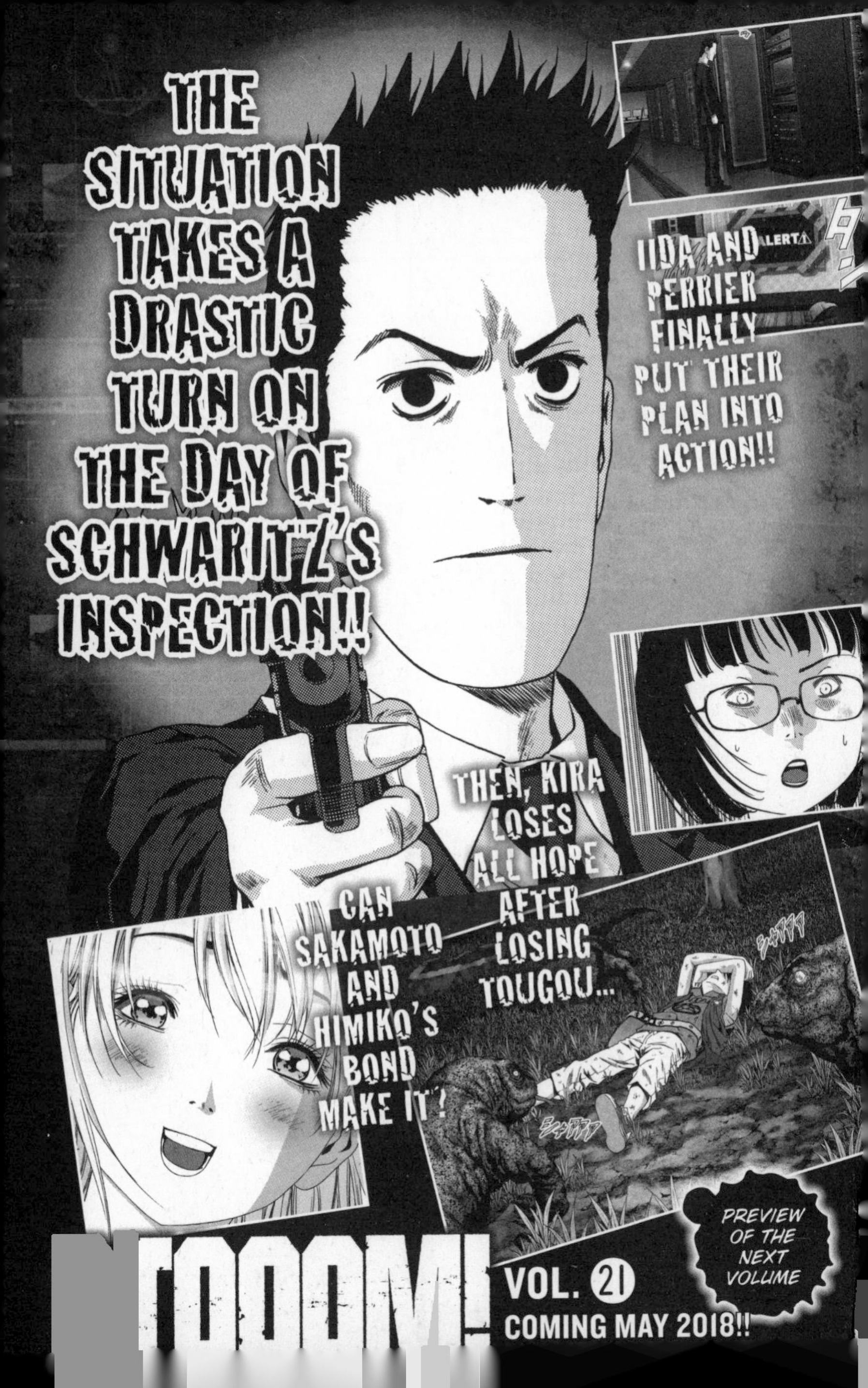
THE SITUATION TAKES A DRASTIC TURN ON THE DAY OF SCHWARITZ'S INSPECTION!!
IIDA AND PERRIER FINALLY PUT THEIR PLAN INTO ACTION!!
THEN, KIRA LOSES ALL HOPE AFTER LOSING TOUGOU...
CAN SAKAMOTO AND HIMIKO'S BOND MAKE IT?
PREVIEW OF THE NEXT VOLUME
VOL. 21
COMING MAY 2018!!

BTOOOM! 20

JUNYA INOUE

Translation: Christine Dashiell

Lettering: Brndn Blakeslee

This book is a work of fiction. Names, characters, places, and incidents are the product of the author's imagination or are used fictitiously. Any resemblance to actual events, locales, or persons, living or dead, is coincidental.

Yen Press
1290 Avenue of the Americas
New York, NY 10104

Visit us at yenpress.com
facebook.com/yenpress
twitter.com/yenpress
yenpress.tumblr.com
instagram.com/yenpress

First Yen Press Edition: February 2018

Yen Press is an imprint of Yen Press, LLC.
The Yen Press name and logo are trademarks of Yen Press, LLC.

The publisher is not responsible for websites (or their content) that are not owned by the publisher.

Library of Congress Control Number: 2013497409

ISBNs: 978-0-316-52058-4 (paperback)
978-0-316-52059-1 (ebook)

10 9 8 7 6 5 4 3 2 1

BVG

Printed in the United States of America